Women's Career Development Throughout the Lifespan

Women's careers have been a topic of research and discussion in many disciplines including sociology, business, industrial, organisational and vocational psychology, and career guidance. Despite the introduction of equal employment legislation in many countries, women's patterns of career development continue to reflect structural labour market disadvantage.

This unique book brings together expert contributions from academic researchers, as well as representing the voices of older women who participated in an international research investigation. Grounded in multidisciplinary empirical studies, the book provides:

- a variety of perspectives on women's careers in the twenty-first century;
- an international exploration of the voice of the older woman;
- an understanding of both the challenges and responses to women as they construct their careers.

Offering a comprehensive understanding of women's career development throughout the lifespan, this book will be of key interest to academics and researchers from the fields of education, psychology, management, geography, labour market economics and sociology, as well as career practitioners, managers, trainers, researchers and policy developers.

Jenny Bimrose is Professor and Deputy Director of the Institute for Employment Research, University of Warwick, UK.

Mary McMahon is Senior Lecturer in the School of Education, The University of Queensland, Australia.

Mark Watson is Distinguished Professor in the Department of Psychology, Nelson Mandela Metropolitan University, South Africa.

Women's Career Development Throughout the Lifespan
An international exploration

Edited by Jenny Bimrose,
Mary McMahon and Mark Watson

LONDON AND NEW YORK

First published 2015
by Routledge
2 Park Square, Milton Park, Abingdon, Oxon OX14 4RN

and by Routledge
711 Third Avenue, New York, NY 10017

Routledge is an imprint of the Taylor & Francis Group, an informa business

© 2015 J. Bimrose, M. McMahon, M. Watson

The right of the editors to be identified as the authors of the editorial material, and of the authors for their individual chapters, has been asserted in accordance with sections 77 and 78 of the Copyright, Designs and Patents Act 1988.

All rights reserved. No part of this book may be reprinted or reproduced or utilised in any form or by any electronic, mechanical, or other means, now known or hereafter invented, including photocopying and recording, or in any information storage or retrieval system, without permission in writing from the publishers.

Trademark notice: Product or corporate names may be trademarks or registered trademarks, and are used only for identification and explanation without intent to infringe.

British Library Cataloguing in Publication Data
A catalogue record for this book is available from the British Library

Library of Congress Cataloging-in-Publication Data
Women's career development throughout the lifespan : an international exploration / edited by Jenny Bimrose, Mary McMahon, Mark Watson.
   pages cm
   1. Women--Vocational guidance. 2. Career development.
   3. Women--Employment. I. Bimrose, Jenny, 1949- II. McMahon,
Mary, 1955- III. Watson, M. B. (Mark Brownlee), 1949-
HF5382.6.W66 2015
331.4--dc23
2014028369

ISBN: 978-0-415-81677-9 (hbk)
ISBN: 978-0-203-58789-8 (ebk)

Typeset in Bembo
by Sunrise Setting Ltd, Paignton, UK

Contents

List of figures and tables viii
List of contributors xi
Foreword by Wendy Patton xiii
Acknowledgements xvi

1 Introduction 1
JENNY BIMROSE, MARY MCMAHON AND MARK WATSON

PART I
The international context: research perspectives 9

2 Geographical perspectives on women's careers: why and how space matters 11
ANNE GREEN

3 Work and older women: interdisciplinary perspectives from India 26
U. VINDHYA

4 Falling between the cracks: older women and employer policymaking 41
CATHERINE EARL, PHILIP TAYLOR, RUTH WILLIAMS AND ELIZABETH BROOKE

5 When good jobs go bad and bad jobs get worse: women's progression opportunities in a polarised labour market 52
DORIS RUTH EIKHOF AND CHRIS WARHURST

6 Organisational perspectives on women's careers: disappointments and opportunities 66
POLLY PARKER AND AMANDA ROAN

PART II
National studies: hearing the voices of older women 77

7 Methodological considerations 79
MARK WATSON, JENNY BIMROSE AND MARY MCMAHON

8 Voices of older women from Argentina 88
PAMELA SUZANNE

9 Voices of older women from Australia 101
MARY MCMAHON

10 Voices of older women from Canada 113
NANCY ARTHUR

11 Voices of older women from China 127
YING KUANG

12 Voices of older women from England 139
JENNY BIMROSE

13 Voices of older women from Germany 152
SIMONE R. HAASLER

14 Voices of older women from Italy 164
MASSIMO TOMASSINI

15 Voices of older women from Portugal 177
FILOMENA PARADA, CAROLINA CORREIA AND ISABEL P. GOMES

16 Voices of older women from South Africa 192
MARK WATSON

17 Life stories: a synthesis of the voices of women 204
MARIA EDUARDA DUARTE

PART III
Looking to the future   217

18 **Implications for career theory**   219
DAVID L. BLUSTEIN

19 **Implications for career research**   231
MARY SUE RICHARDSON, KRISTIN ELIZABETH BLACK
AND YOKO IWAKI

20 **Implications for career policy**   243
KEN ROBERTS

21 **Implications for career practice**   253
MARY MCMAHON, MARK WATSON AND
JENNY BIMROSE

22 **Epilogue**   263
JENNY BIMROSE, MARY MCMAHON AND MARK WATSON

Index   265

Figures and Tables

Figures

2.1	Women aged 15–64 employment rates by region, 2012	13
2.2	Men aged 15–64 employment rates by region, 2012	14
2.3	Dispersion of regional employment rates by gender in the EU27, 1999–2012	15
2.4	Types of work-related geographical mobility	19

Tables

2.1	Regional dispersion in employment rates by gender for selected EU27 countries, 2008 and 2012	16
3.1	Labour participation rates by gender and by age group, 2008	28
3.2	Characteristics of workers in India	33
7.1	Code categories	85
8.1	Argentinian sample	91
9.1	Australian sample	104
10.1	Canadian sample	117
11.1	Chinese sample	130
11.2	The life roles of the participants	135
12.1	English sample	141
13.1	German sample	155
14.1	Italian sample	168
15.1	Portuguese sample	181
16.1	South African sample	196

Contributors

Nancy Arthur is a Professor and Canada Research Chair in Professional Education, Educational Studies in Counselling Psychology at the Werklund School of Education, University of Calgary, Canada. Her teaching and research interests focus on the model of culture-infused counselling, social justice in professional education and practice, career development, and international transitions.

Jenny Bimrose is a Professor and Deputy Director at the Institute for Employment Research, University of Warwick, England. With over thirty years' experience in higher education, researching and teaching at post-graduate level, Jenny has worked extensively in the UK and also internationally. Much recent research has focused on the theory and practice of career guidance counselling and on gender inequality.

Kristin Elizabeth Black is a doctoral candidate in the English Education programme at New York University. She has worked as an English teacher in high schools and community colleges in Chicago and throughout Virginia. Her current research interests include post-secondary literacy, transitions into higher education, and the relationship between vocational and academic identity.

David L. Blustein is a Professor in the Department of Counseling, Developmental, and Educational Psychology at Boston College, USA. He is the author of *The Psychology of Working: A New Perspective for Career Development, Counseling, and Public Policy* (Routledge 2006) and the editor of the *Oxford Handbook of the Psychology of Working* (Oxford University Press 2013). These two books, along with much of his recent work, are devoted to creating a broad and inclusive approach to understanding the role of work in people's lives.

Elizabeth Brooke is an Associate Professor and Director at the Business Work and Ageing Centre (BWA) for Research, Swinburne University of Technology, Australia. She has been researching the effects of the ageing global population on workforce demographics, policies and practices since the late 1990s.

Carolina Correia has a MA in Psychology. Currently, she is a PhD student at the Faculdade de Psicologia e de Ciências da Educação, Universidade do Porto, Portugal. She has extensive experience in the field of adult education and training. She is also involved in several civic associations and movements.

Maria Eduarda Duarte is a Professor at the University of Lisbon, Faculty of Psychology, where she directs the Master Course in Psychology of Human Resources, Work, and Organisations. She is the Research Director of Career Guidance and Development of Human Resources Services.

Catherine Earl is a social anthropologist. She researches social mobility, social welfare and social change in contemporary Vietnam and Australia. Her most recent book is *Vietnam's New Middle Classes: Gender, Career, City* (NIAS Press 2014).

Doris Ruth Eikhof is a Senior Lecturer in Work and Employment at the School of Management, University of Leicester, UK. She researches cultural industries, women's work and work life-boundaries. She has published internationally and is co-editor of *Creating Balance? International Perspectives on the Work-Life Integration of Professionals* (Springer 2011) and *Work Less, Live More? Critical Analyses of the Work-Life Boundary* (Palgrave 2008).

Isabel P. Gomes graduated with a PhD in Psychology in 2011 from the Universidade do Porto (Portugal). She is currently collaborating with the Post-Graduation Office of the Faculdade de Psicologia e de Ciências da Educação, Universidade do Porto. She has an extensive number of publications and other academic work in the domain of adult learning and training.

Anne Green is a Professorial Fellow at the Institute for Employment Research, University of Warwick, UK. A geographer by background, Anne has substantial experience of researching spatial dimensions of employment, non-employment, regional and local labour market issues, skills strategies, migration and commuting, and associated policy issues.

Simone R. Haasler is a Senior Researcher and Lecturer at the University of Bremen, Germany. Her research interests include labour markets and training systems, learning, careers, and identity. Before joining the University of Bremen in 2001 she worked as an Education Specialist for the Human Development Network of the World Bank in Washington, DC (USA).

Yoko Iwaki, PhD is an organisational psychologist and management consultant who works with individuals and organisations to create work with meaning and purpose. Her research focuses on cross-cultural differences in risk perceptions and decision-making. She lives in New York and is studying to become a Licensed Mental Health Counselor at New York University.

Ying Kuang is an Associate Professor and Party Leader at the Institute of Vocational and Adult Education and Deputy Director of the Vocational and Technical Education Centre, East China Normal University, People's Republic of China. With fifteen years' experience in VET researching, and seven years' experience teaching and tutoring at post-graduate level, much of her research has focused on the theory and practice of key skills, career guidance, and apprenticeships.

Mary McMahon is a Senior Lecturer in the School of Education at The University of Queensland, Brisbane, Australia. Mary teaches, researches and publishes in the field of career development. She is interested in how people construct their careers across the lifespan from childhood and through adolescence to later life. Her particular interests are narrative career counselling and qualitative career assessment.

Filomena Parada is a Post-doctoral Fellow at the Instituto de Psicologia Cognitiva, Desenvolvimento Vocacional e Social, Universidade de Coimbra (Portugal). She completed her PhD in 2008 at the Universidade do Porto (Portugal), where she completed her undergraduate training in Psychology. Her main research interests concern career and counselling, contextual action theory, and youth, education, and work-related transitions.

Polly Parker is an Associate Professor in Leadership at The University of Queensland Business School, Australia, who has published in a wide range of international journals. Her research, consulting and advisory work focuses on women's leadership and its development, particularly at the intersection with careers, in academic and industry contexts.

Wendy Patton is a Professor and Executive Dean at the Faculty of Education, Queensland University of Technology, Brisbane, Australia. She has taught and researched in the areas of career development and counselling for more than twenty years. She has co-authored and co-edited a number of books, and is currently Series Editor of the Career Development Series with Sense Publishers. She has published widely with more than 150 refereed journal articles and book chapters. She serves on a number of national and international journal editorial boards.

Mary Sue Richardson is a counseling psychologist and a Professor in the Department of Applied Psychology at New York University, USA, where she teaches in the counselling programmes. Her research focuses on developing holistic approaches to vocational counselling, a dual model of working inclusive of market and unpaid care work, and on integrating vocational and psychotherapy practices.

Amanda Roan is a Senior Lecturer in Human Resource Management, Employment Relations and Organisational Behaviour at the The University of Queensland Business School, Australia. Her research is broadly focused around workforce participation and workplace diversity. She has published in national and international journals, including *Management Learning* and the *Journal of Business Ethics*.

Ken Roberts is a Professor of Sociology at the University of Liverpool, UK. His major research area throughout his career has been youth life stage transitions. His current research is UK based, and focuses on the development of educational and vocational aspirations during secondary education, and the role of higher education in social mobility and class re-formation in Britain.

Pamela Suzanne is a Lecturer at Universidad de San Andrés, Argentina. Her research interests focus on career development, role transitions, women in business, social networks, and identity work. She received her PhD in Employment Research at the University of Warwick, UK. She holds degrees in Organisational Studies (MA) and Business (BA, magna cum laude, UdeSA).

Philip Taylor PhD is a Professor of Human Resource Management at Federation University Australia. He has researched issues of ageing and work for twenty-five years. Interests include individual orientations to work and retirement, employer attitudes and practices towards older workers, and developments in public policies aimed at combating labour market age barriers and prolonging working life.

Massimo Tomassini is a Research Fellow at the Institute for Employment Research, University of Warwick, UK (partner in narrative-based research studies) and a contract Professor at the Faculty of Education Science, University of Roma Tre, Italy (teaching Organisational Learning). He is an independent researcher and trainer in the field of behavioural competencies and a mindfulness trainer (implementing the 'Cultivating Awareness in the Working Life' programme).

U. Vindhya is currently a Professor of Psychology at Tata Institute of Social Sciences, Hyderabad, India. Her research interests are centred on women's mental health, domestic violence, women's political activism, sex trafficking and feminist counselling. She has co-edited the *Handbook of International Feminisms: Perspectives on Psychology, Women, Culture and Rights* (Springer 2011), which won the 2011 Distinguished Publication Award from the Association for Women in Psychology.

Chris Warhurst is the Director of the Institute for Employment Research at the University of Warwick in the UK. He was previously Professor of Work and Organisational Studies at Sydney University Business School in Australia and co-editor of the journal *Work, Employment and Society*. He has been an expert advisor to the UK, Scottish and Australian governments and is currently an International Expert Adviser to the OECD.

Mark Watson is a Distinguished Professor in the Psychology Department of the Nelson Mandela Metropolitan University in South Africa. He is interested in child and adolescent career development, narrative career counselling, qualitative career assessment, and the development of culturally appropriate career counselling approaches. Mark has published in international journals and has contributed chapters to international career texts.

Ruth Williams is a researcher and analyst at the National Seniors Productive Ageing Centre, Australia. Her research focuses on social gerontology, such as the relationship between age and the labour market, decision-making processes around key life transitions, workplace policy affecting mature age workers, and informing public awareness raising campaigns for the over 50s population.

Foreword

This book represents a significant achievement and in many ways is a first in the literature. Its editors and authors are to be congratulated for the book's conceptualisation and its realisation. The book presents an international and multidisciplinary investigation into older women's careers. Its comprehensive content and structure provides an insight into social, political and economic contexts across nine countries, and the voices of older women in relation to their paid and unpaid work decisions and experiences. Part I of the book presents research overviews from a number of disciplines and Part II provides a unique combination of quantitative and qualitative analysis of older women's careers in nine countries. Each part of the book is carefully introduced and synthesised, enabling readers to select chapters for particular countries, or realise its contribution through synthesis. In Part II, documenting the international research study, the quantitative background sets a human backdrop for the actual women's voices. The third and final part of the book presents compelling analyses and reflections on future theorising, research, policy, and practice in relation to this multidisciplinary field of women's careers, or working lives (Patton 2013).

However the book is much more than that – in presenting the socio-political and economic context to the position of women in the workplace it proposes a challenge to theoreticians, to researchers, to practitioners, and to policy makers. As the editors state:

> It is also clear that while the term gender relates to a single social variable, in reality it is often associated with multidimensional disadvantage. Other biological, social and cultural categories, like race/ethnicity, socio-economic status, age and other axes of social identity interact, often simultaneously and at different levels, thus contributing to systematic injustice and social inequality.
>
> (Bimrose *et al.*, Chapter 1)

The book is therefore a powerful political statement, as highlighted by Blustein (Chapter 18), it 'is the next step in this courageous struggle to place women's voices at the forefront of our intention to create a world that offers opportunities for meaning and dignity at work'. The book emphasises that women's voices about the meaning and reality for work in their lives are truly global – voices from women in countries that had experienced major political, social, cultural and economic change all demonstrated a commonality of themes for women's experiences, evident in Western countries as in non-Western and new market economies.

While women's participation in paid work has increased and educational attainments and occupational levels actually exceed those of men in many countries, women continue to experience structural labour market disadvantages in most countries, evidenced by horizontal and vertical gendered segregation in occupations. Wage gaps, although narrowing, continue to be evident, and women continue to be employed in lower paid and lower level positions and in jobs that are often part-time, insecure, and which have fewer prospects for advancement. As Blustein (Chapter 18) commented, 'equal opportunity is the exception rather than the norm'.

The universal challenge of women's role in child care and increasingly in elder care continues, re-emphasising the existence of the double shift referred to by Green (Chapter 2) and Parker and Roan (Chapter 6). Almost all of the women across all countries attempt to develop solutions to these competing demands. Where women contribute financially to the family through their market work roles, they continue to carry family and household responsibilities. Richardson and Schaeffer (2013a, b) and Richardson *et al.* (Chapter 19) have emphasised the need to recognise the value of both market work and care work in both women's and men's lives.

Chapter authors have emphasised that, despite the many advances in developed societies, most societal infrastructure continues to act as an inhibitor for women's occupational participation. The cost, if it does exist, of social and organisational infrastructure for child care, and increasingly elder care, acts to maintain traditional gender roles. Parker and Roan (Chapter 6) note that organisational processes need to be developed such that women do not need to continue the family–work juggle personally. As Duarte (Chapter 17) asserts 'the construction or the designing of a working life is always compromised by the context' – it is evident throughout the book that women develop careers through their own individual pursuits, despite the organisational, social, and infrastructural challenges. As such, their lives demonstrate a multiplicity of career patterns that vary considerably across life stages.

Part III of the book provides chapters which speak to the broad foci of the contribution of the book, and where authors have discussed the challenges for the field. Richardson *et al.* (Chapter 19) emphasise the importance of changing the discourse, as opposed to helping people to adapt to a changing world. Blustein (Chapter 18) emphasises that this volume 'forces a serious reckoning of the fundamental assumptions of existing and emerging theoretical ideas'. Roberts (Chapter 20) acknowledges the importance of policy, and encourages career services and practitioners to listen to the advice provided by the research participants in this book. In the final chapter, McMahon, Watson and Bimrose (Chapter 21) challenge the role of career guidance in women's lives, and suggest major changes to the preparation of career practitioners especially in relation to broadening cultural and global perspectives. Finally, these authors challenge career practitioners to become advocates for social justice and social change, emphasising the need to challenge the systemic underpinning of women's labour market disadvantage.

This book is sure to become a landmark work. It challenges current theorising, it embraces and demonstrates the complexity of multidisciplinary research, and it provides suggestions for policy and practice. More importantly it demonstrates the gendered nature of occupational opportunity, no matter what country and what socio-political and economic stage in a country's development. Fundamentally it is the voices of the women who highlight these challenges, and the editors and authors are to be congratulated for providing the opportunity for them to speak.

Wendy Patton
Queensland University of Technology, Australia

References

Patton, W. (2013) 'Understanding women's working lives', in W. Patton (ed.), *Conceptualising women's working lives: Moving the boundaries of discourse,* Rotterdam: Sense Publishers.

Richardson, M. S., and Schaeffer, C. (2013a) 'From work and family to a dual model of working', in D. L. Blustein (ed.), *Handbook of the psychology of working*, New York: Oxford University Press.

Richardson, M. S., and Schaeffer, C. (2013b) 'Expanding the discourse: A dual model of working for women (and men's) lives', in W. Patton (ed.), *Conceptualising women's working lives: Moving the boundaries of our discourse*, Rotterdam: Sense Publishers.

Acknowledgements

This book represents the culmination of an exciting international project that began in 2010 with a study conducted in three countries, England, Australia and South Africa. Our project sparked the interest of international researchers who then replicated the study in their own countries. We subsequently decided that the whole project might be best represented in a book that contextualised the research and also considered the implications of the nine country studies for theory, research, policy and practice.

We are deeply appreciative of the authors who responded enthusiastically to the concept and so willingly and generously contributed to this important book. We would also like to thank Professor Wendy Patton whose publications testify to a longstanding commitment to women's careers. We were thrilled when she agreed to write a foreword for us.

We would especially like to thank the women from the nine countries who so willingly shared their stories with the researchers and provided the stimulus for this book.

This book tells an international story and will be a valuable resource to career theorists, career researchers, policy makers and career practitioners.

Due thanks is also given to the Belknap Press of Harvard University Press for permission to reproduce text from *CREATING CAPABILITIES: THE HUMAN DEVELOPMENT APPROACH* by Martha C. Nussbaum, pp. 18–19, Cambridge, MA: The Belknap Press of Harvard University Press, Copyright © 2011 by Martha C. Nussbaum in Chapter 18.

1 Introduction

Jenny Bimrose, Mary McMahon and Mark Watson

The Universal Declaration of Human Rights (UDHR), written in the wake of the catastrophically destructive impact of the Second World War (1939–45) states that all human beings are born free and equal in dignity and rights (United Nations UDHR 1948). According to this Declaration, gender equality is a basic human right. Yet the majority of the world's poor are women and their lack of access to financial resources has a profound effect on their overall wellbeing. Gender inequality is deeply entrenched in all societies (United Nations 2010). There is no shortage of data that relate to the persistently unequal and disadvantaged position of women, compared with men, in societies across the world. The Global Gender Gap Index, for example, introduced by the World Economic Forum in 2006, quantifies the magnitude of gender-based disparities, tracking progress across four key areas: economic, political, education and health (World Economic Forum 2013). Similarly, statistical indicators provided by the United Nations in reports, databases and archives similarly testify to continuing gender discrimination, inequality and injustice (United Nations Women's Watch 2014).

These data objectify global gender inequality. Invaluable for understanding the sheer scale, pervasiveness and persistence of the problem, the existence of these data sometimes masks an important subjective dimension. Gender is essentially a social construct. It refers to the membership of a particular social category, masculine or feminine, that aligns more or less to the two sexes. It is different from biological sex, sexual orientation, sexual preference and to other categories or descriptions that relate to various behaviours and identities associated with the sexes (Bimrose 2008, 2012). Gender is defined by reference to those attributes associated with being female and being male (Gilligan 1982). These attributes are fluid, not fixed. They differ between cultures or societies, across different periods in history and change within the same culture or society over time. Such changes are bound up with subtle changes in societal role expectations. Consider, for example, the social expectations and values associated with the role of mothers over the past two or three decades, which have changed dramatically in many societies. In many countries, it is now socially acceptable for women with primary responsibility for young children to be in paid employment in the formal economy, alongside their caring responsibilities, in a way that was not previously the case. In fact, the values and expectations associated with this social role have shifted so dramatically in some societies that dual wage earners (i.e. where both the man and woman in the family earn a wage or salary through formal employment) have become the norm, because of the economic necessity for women in a family to make a financial contribution, alongside men (Paden and Buehler 1995).

Intersections of social disadvantage

The fluidity of these gender role expectations illustrates not only the ways in which gender is constructed and defined by different societies over time. It also highlights how ways in which being male and being female are valued differently – different and not equal. For example, despite women's increased participation in the labour market, little change has occurred in the gendered allocation of domestic duties. Women, on average, continue to take the primary responsibility for domestic and care responsibilities, with studies showing how men's share of domestic labour has actually slowed down or remained the same in some Western countries (Bimrose 2008). The intensification of work, characterised by, for example, long and unpredictable working hours and/or work outside formally contracted hours, has had a particularly negative impact on women shouldering the main responsibility for housework and caring who are consequently forced to develop various coping strategies to help manage the dual demands and stresses of paid employment and domestic duties (Bimrose 2008).

It is also clear that while the term gender relates to a single social variable, in reality it is often associated with multidimensional disadvantage. Other biological, social and cultural categories, like race/ethnicity, socio-economic status, age and other axes of social identity interact, often simultaneously and at different levels, thus contributing to systematic injustice and social inequality. The term intersectionality is useful to our understanding of the complexity of the layers of disadvantage that are often evident in this context (Begum 1994). It refers to the interaction of different types of social oppression and injustice in ways that create multiple manifestations of discrimination (Crenshaw 1991). Despite certain flaws (Davis 2008; Ludvig 2006; Yuval-Davis 2006), intersectionality usefully emphasises the combined impact on an individual of the convergence of factors like gender and age, together with other factors such as race and socio-economic status (Bradley 1996; Moore 2009).

The negative impact on individuals of the interplay of various social factors is being increasingly recognised (Ainsworth 2002; Weller 2007). Where gender and age converge, for example, it has been found that structural factors not only determine the basis on which older women join the labour market (Buchmann et al. 2010; Dex et al. 2008), but they also influence employment destinations (Moore 2009). Additionally, it increases vulnerability to unemployment. In the UK, for example, unemployment 'amongst women aged 50–64 has increased by 41 per cent, compared with one per cent overall' (The Commission on Older Women 2013: 3). Social disadvantage associated with ageing has become a particularly critical issue in countries around the world experiencing increased life expectancy and falling birth rates contiguously through a combination of improved health care and living standards (Del Bono et al. 2007; Roberts 2006; Smeaton and Vegeris 2009). Labour market penalties associated with ageing, like vulnerability to redundancy, forced early retirement and minimum wages (Sussman and Tabi 2004; Taylor and Walker 1997) have been found to interact with gender inequality in a pernicious manner (United Nations 2010). Compared with older men, economic resources are unequally distributed among older women (Del Bono et al. 2007).

Despite the need to extend working lives (Organisation for Economic Co-operation and Development 2006) and with the economic costs associated with the under-utilisation of female labour being a recurrent theme (e.g. International Labour Office 2010), research into how women's career transitions into and through the labour market could be supported effectively is scant (Bimrose 2001). A detailed understanding of the formal career support needs of older people is also lacking (Ford 2005). Age related, gendered labour market discrimination should be a particular concern for those providing formal career guidance and counselling services, since the consistent failure of women to sustain continuous employment can lead to an impoverished old age, which may also be characterised by social exclusion and reduced quality of life (Smeaton and Vegeris 2009). Commentaries relating to the formal support required to facilitate women's career progression (including older women) have tended to reflect traditional and mainly psychological career theories, developed in relatively homogenous Western capitalist contexts that were strongly individualised, masculine, secular, action- and future-focused (Bimrose 2001, 2008). Such theories have largely failed to address the complex contextual and relational nature of women's career development (August 2011; Bimrose 2008), including that of older women, resulting in a paucity of relevant frameworks to inform practice for this particular group.

Gender inequality: multidisciplinary and transnational inquiry

A Commission on older women set up in the UK to investigate the position of older women in society found that:

> Across every generation women are feeling the strain. Women are being hit three times as hard as men by the Government's economic policies, despite earning less and owning less than men, and female unemployment has reached its highest level in 25 years ... They are working hard to hold families together, increasingly relied upon by their sons and daughters for childcare whilst also caring for elderly parents or sick relatives. They make up six in every ten carers and provide over £7 billion in unpaid support to our economy. They are the generation who fought for better rights in the workplace, made the economic arguments for childcare and fought for equal pay, but for whom the workplace has never caught up.
>
> (Commission on Older Women 2013: 5)

It is against this background that a qualitative research inquiry into women's career development across the lifespan was carried out with the specific purpose of investigating the career stories of older women (aged 45 to 65) across different country contexts. A particular motivation for the original three researchers in the study (those who carried out research in England, Australia and South Africa) was their interest in finding out the extent to which the women had been supported in their career transitions across their lifetimes. In-depth interviews were carried out with twelve (in one country thirteen) women in this particular age group in nine countries: Argentina, Australia, Canada, China, England, Germany, Italy, Portugal and South Africa.

A key finding from the research investigation relates to the importance of context. The career development of each of the women in the nine country studies was played out in a particular social, economic and historic context. The impact of these contexts was both profound and unique, as was each woman's story. Each career trajectory reflected the influence of context, mediated by the styles and characteristics of the women. The iterative nature of the dynamic interaction of the individuality of the women in their social contexts is what provides rich and deep insights into the ways in which these women navigated their ways through political and social upheaval (sometimes revolution), economic boom and bust, and their life cycles of production and/or reproduction.

Part I – The international context: research perspectives

The critical importance of social and economic contexts in which women make their way is the common thread running through the first five chapters in Part I of the book. Chapter 2 invites us to consider a much-neglected aspect of career practice – the geography of gendered employment. An examination of one labour market (India) is presented in Chapter 3, with a particular focus on the position of women in that economic context. This broad perspective is narrowed in Chapter 4, which explores through research, employment policies within employing organisations and the ways in which these impact on women, particularly older women. Ways that jobs can be negatively affected when colonised predominantly by one gender are tracked in Chapter 5. The final chapter in Part I, Chapter 6, reverts to a focus on an organisational perspective on gender.

Part II – National studies: hearing the voices of older women

Findings from the research study of women's transitions in nine countries provided the genesis and inspiration for the present book. The research methodology (see Chapter 7) was designed to give the women participants a voice. Although all the women in the study were in the age group 45–65 (the age at which women have difficulty entering or re-entering the labour market), the stories they provided were retrospective and spanned their lifetimes. Powerful insights to the career progression of these women across their entire lifespan were collected and analysed (Chapters 8 to 16). This pivotal section of the book also contains an insightful chapter that synthesises the contents of the section. In this synthesis, Duarte (Chapter 17) reflects on the complex interplay of the multiple dimensions affecting the construction of women's careers, emphasising the importance of the past for an accurate understanding of the present and appreciation of what is possible in the future: 'Listening to the voices of women aged between 45 and 65 years of age, ages during which the past is re-evaluated and during which the future still stretches out ahead, is a challenge that helps to better understand' (p. 214).

Part III – Looking to the future

A key motivation for this book was to scrutinise the career support that older women require in the career transitions that typify their trajectories. The final section of the book, therefore, turns attention to the implications of the findings from this book project for career guidance and counselling. These implications are explored and examined from different angles by thought leaders in their fields. Chapter 18 considers the implications of the international research study and findings for career theory. Chapter 19 takes the same approach for career research. Chapter 20 examines some implications for career policy of the research study. Finally, Chapter 21 reflects on career practice. Each of these chapters is hard hitting, identifying crucial angles and challenging readers to confront uncomfortable questions. For the theory, research, policy and practice of the profession of career guidance and counselling to advance, these are questions with which we must all engage.

Conclusion

Equality and liberty are basic human rights. Despite the formal recognition that the empowerment of women to achieve their full potential not only stimulates economic productivity, but also fuels thriving economies (United Nations 2010), gender inequality continues to exist on a shamefully massive scale worldwide. Its continued existence undermines and challenges the universal truths of equality and liberty. We hope that this book increases understanding of some of the challenges that have been faced by the older women in this study over their lifetimes and contributes to an improvement in the support available to them as they develop their careers across their life courses. There are signs that policy is beginning to espouse this agenda. A key recommendation from The Commission on Older Women (2013: 7) reflects the lack of careers support for older women in the UK: 'The Commission would like to see much better careers service support for older workers.' We hope that the evidence presented in this book can be used to support this aspiration.

References

Ainsworth, S. (2002) 'The "feminine advantage": A discursive analysis of the invisibility of older women workers', *Gender, Work & Organization*, 9: 579–601.
August, R. A. (2011) 'Women's later life career development: Looking through the lens of the Kaleidoscope Career Model', *Journal of Career Development*, 38: 208–36.
Begum, N. (1994) 'Mirror, mirror on the wall', in N. Begum, M. Hill and A. Stevens (eds) *Reflections: The Views of Black Disabled People on their Lives and Community Care*, London: Central Council for Education and Training in Social Work, 17–36.

Bimrose, J. (2001) 'Girls and women: Challenges for careers guidance practice', *British Journal of Guidance and Counselling*, 29: 79–94.

Bimrose, J. (2008) 'Guidance with women', in J. Athanasou J. and R. V. Esbroeck (eds) *International Handbook of Career Guidance* (1st edn), Dordrecht: Springer.

Bimrose, J. (2012) 'Gender', in C. Feltham and I. Horton (eds) *Handbook of Counselling and Psychotherapy* (3rd edn), London: Sage.

Bradley, H. (1996) *Fractured Identities: The Changing Patterns of Inequality*, Cambridge: Polity Books.

Buchmann, M. C., Kriesi, I. and Sacchi, S. (2010) 'Labour market structures and women's employment levels', *Work Employment & Society*, 24: 279–99.

Crenshaw, K. (1991) 'Mapping the margins: Intersectionality, identity politics, and violence against women of color', *Stanford Law Review*, 43: 1241–99.

Davis, K. (2008) 'Intersectionality as buzzword. A sociology of science perspective on what makes a feminist theory successful', *Feminist Theory*, 9: 67–85.

Del Bono, E., Sala, E., Hancock, R., Gunnell, C. and Lavinia, P. (2007) 'Gender, older people and social exclusion. A gendered review and secondary analysis of the data', *ISER Working Paper 2007–13*, Colchester: University of Essex. Available at: www.iser.essex.ac.uk/files/iser_working_papers/2007-13.pdf (accessed 14 August 2011).

Dex, S., Ward, K. and Joshi, H. (2008) 'Gender differences in occupational wage mobility in the 1958 cohort', *Work, Employment & Society*, 22: 263–80.

Ford, G. (2005) *Am I Still Needed? Guidance and Learning for Older Adults*, Derby: CeGS Research Report Series No 5. Derby: Centre for Guidance Studies, University of Derby. Available at: www.jrf.org.uk/sites/files/jrf/guidanceandlearningforolderadults.pdf (accessed 22 June 2014).

Gilligan, C. (1982) *In a Different Voice: Psychological Theory and Women's Development*, Cambridge, MA: Harvard University Press.

International Labour Office (2010) 'Women in labour markets: Measuring progress and identifying challenges'. Available at: www.ilo.org/wcmsp5/groups/public/—ed_emp/—emp_elm/—trends/documents/publication/wcms_123835.pdf (accessed 22 June 2014).

Ludvig, A. (2006) 'Differences between women? Intersecting voices in a female narrative', *European Journal of Women's Studies*, 13: 245–58.

Moore, S. (2009) '"No matter what I did I would still end up in the same position": Age as a factor defining older women's experience of labour market participation', *Work Employment & Society*, 23: 655–71.

Organisation for Economic Co-Operation and Development (2006) *Ageing and Employment Policies. Live Longer, Work Long*, Paris: OECD Publications.

Paden, S. L. and Bueler, C. (1995) 'Coping with the dual-income lifestyle', *Journal of Marriage and the Family*, 57: 101–10.

Roberts, I. (2006) 'Taking age out of the workplace: Putting older workers back in?', *Work Employment & Society* 20(1): 67–86.

Smeaton, D. and Vegeris, S. (2009) *Older People Inside and Outside the Labour Market: A Review*, London: Policy Studies Institute. Available at: www.voced.edu.au/content/ngv51 442 (accessed 22 June 2014).

Sussman, D. and Tabi, M. (2004) *Minimum Wage Workers. Perspectives on Labour and Income*, Ottawa: Statistics Canada, 6.

Taylor, P. and Walker, A. (1997) 'Age discrimination and public policy', *Personnel Review*, 26: 307–18.

The Commission on Older Women (2013) 'Interim report'. Available at: www.yourbritain.org.uk/uploads/editor/files/Commission_on_Older_Women_-_Interim_Report.pdf (accessed 24 June 2014).

United Nations (1948) *The Universal Declaration of Human Rights (UDHR)*. Available at: www.un.org/en/documents/udhr/ (accessed 2 May 2014).

United Nations (2010) *UN Women: Facts And Figures On Women Worldwide*. Available at: www.generoracaetnia.org.br/publicacoes/UNWomen.pdf (accessed 22 June 2014).

United Nations Women's Watch (2014) *Directory of UN Resources on Gender and Women's Issues*. Available at: www.un.org/womenwatch/directory/statistics_and_indicators_60.htm (accessed 2 May, 2014).

Weller, S. (2007) 'Discrimination, labour markets and the labour market prospects of older workers: What can a legal case teach us?' *Work Employment & Society*, 21 (3): 417–37.

World Economic Forum (2013) *The Global Gender Gap Report 2013. Insight Report*. Available at: www3.weforum.org/docs/WEF_GenderGap_Report_2013.pdf (accessed 22 June 2014).

Yuval Davis, N. (2006) 'Intersectionality and feminist politics', *European Journal of Women's Studies*, 13: 193–209.

Part I
The international context
Research perspectives

2 Geographical perspectives on women's careers

Why and how space matters

Anne Green

This chapter focuses on geographical variations in employment and experiences of paid work, with a particular focus on women. Its fundamental premise is that where individuals live is important for the quantity and quality of employment available to them (Green 2009) and so for opportunities for skills utilisation and career development. It outlines quantitative and qualitative dimensions of employment by gender at international and sub-national levels. In particular, at the local level of everyday lives, the chapter uses the concept of gendered localisation to suggest that, due to the so-called double shift of paid and unpaid household work practised by many – albeit not all – women, a geographical perspective is particularly important for understanding the opportunities and constraints faced by women in accessing employment and developing their careers. This is especially so for less-skilled women who are more limited than their more highly-skilled peers in the jobs that they can perform.

It follows that there is considerable heterogeneity in the employment and career development experiences of women, by location, skill level and position in the life course. Those who have the poorest qualifications tend to have a relatively weak position in employment and in the labour and housing markets more generally, and to be more restricted than those with higher skills in the distance that they are able and can afford to travel. They are more likely to be workless (either as unemployed or economically inactive) relative to their more highly-skilled peers. Similarly, those with the least formal work experience and the heaviest caring responsibilities for children and other household/family members are most constrained by geography in their employment opportunities and career development. The quantity and quality of opportunities for education, training and employment available locally is of particular importance to these sub-groups (Green and Owen 2006). By contrast, those who have the highest qualifications, and who have the least burden of non-work responsibilities and/or are best placed to cope with them, are least constrained by geography in opportunities for employment and career development. However, for all women, opportunities and geographical constraints for career development vary by life stage, and the circumstances of other household members.

As the chapter proceeds, the geographical focus of attention shifts successively from the international to the regional and to the local level scale. The next section of this chapter outlines key dimensions of geographical variations in women's economic opportunities internationally. This is followed by a discussion of regional variations in employment rates in Europe. Then the focus shifts to the intra-regional and local level scales of everyday lives, and a consideration of how geographical factors help shape the careers of women in dual career households and of women in weaker labour market positions. The final section synthesises the key findings and looks to the future.

International perspectives

Internationally, there are considerable differences in the economic fortunes of and prospects for women. The Women's Economic Opportunity Index, developed by the Economist Intelligence Unit (2010) and based on international data (from the World Bank, the United Nations, the International Labour Organisation, the World Economic Forum, the OECD and newly created indicators), comprising 26 indicators relating to jobs and the labour market, access to finance, women's legal and social status and the general business environment, captures some of these variations. The geographical pattern of variation indicates that women face fewer economic barriers and have more opportunities in more advanced countries. The ten top-ranked countries on the Index are Sweden, Belgium, Norway, Finland, Germany, Iceland, the Netherlands, New Zealand, Canada and Australia. The next ten countries in the rankings include the United States and countries in Europe. The bottom ten ranked countries are in Africa, the Middle East and South Asia: Sudan, Yemen, Chad, Ivory Coast, Togo, Pakistan, Ethiopia, Syria, Cameroon and Bangladesh.

On the Labour Policy and Practice components of the Women's Economic Opportunity Index (Economist Intelligence Unit 2010), which are derived from measures including legal restrictions on job types, equal pay, non-discrimination, maternity and paternity leave and provision, differential retirement age, de facto discrimination at work, and access to childcare, the countries with the highest scores are Finland, Sweden, Norway and the Netherlands. Hence, it might be in these countries that institutional factors are most conducive to the development of women's careers, holding other factors constant.

Other international data on global employment trends from the International Labour Organisation (2012) indicate that so-called gender gaps in the labour market (defined as the numerical extent to which women are disadvantaged relative to men on any particular labour market indicator) reveal a similar picture of international variation, with the gaps being most pronounced in the Middle East, North Africa and South Asia, and least pronounced in the developed economies and the European Union, East Asia and Sub-Saharan Africa. The data also indicate that convergence in the fortunes of women and men prior to 2008 reversed thereafter. These reversals in fortunes were most pronounced in East Asia, South Asia and Central and Eastern Europe.

Sub-national perspectives

Within countries sub-national variations in economic opportunities and prospects for women's career development would be expected, in accordance with geographical variations in economic circumstances and in the quantity and characteristics (by sector, occupation, hours of work, contract type, etc.) of jobs. Figures 2.1 and 2.2 show

Geographical perspectives 13

variations in employment rates for women and men, respectively, at the regional level scale in Europe. The same class intervals are shown on each, so highlighting the generally higher employment rates for men than for women in (nearly all) regions. Regions in the Nordic countries, in Switzerland, eastern Germany and parts of the UK display amongst the highest employment rates for women. For men, most regions in the Nordic countries, Germany, Austria and the UK have employment rates of 75 per cent or over. These inter-country differences evident in both figures are indicative of the role of institutional factors in shaping employment rates. Within countries, inter-regional differences are apparent also, especially in southern European countries such as Spain, Italy and Greece, which have the lowest employment rates for both women and men.

The trend of dispersion of regional employment rates over the period from 1999 to 2012 in EU27 regions is shown in Figure 2.3. The dispersion of regional employment is zero when employment rates in all regions are identical and rises as differences between regions in employment rates increase. Two key features are apparent here: first, the dispersion in regional employment rates is more pronounced

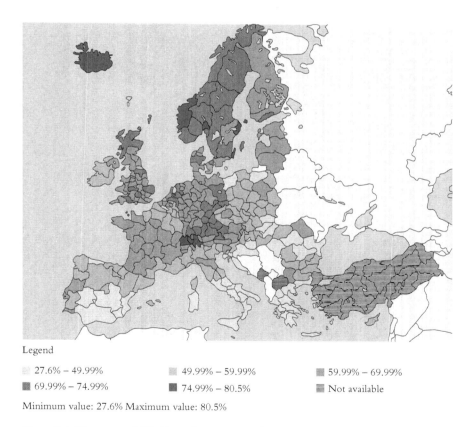

Legend

- 27.6% – 49.99%
- 69.99% – 74.99%
- 49.99% – 59.99%
- 74.99% – 80.5%
- 59.99% – 69.99%
- Not available

Minimum value: 27.6% Maximum value: 80.5%

Figure 2.1 Women aged 15–64 employment rates by region, 2012
Source: EU Labour Force Survey, EUROSTAT.

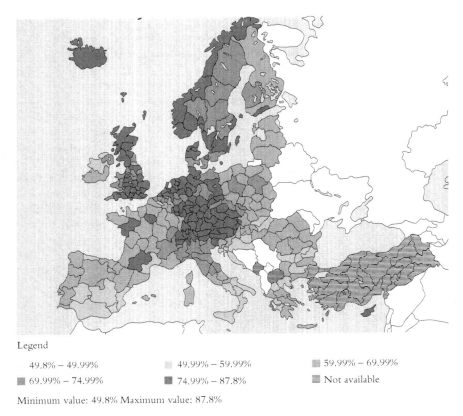

Legend

- 49.8% – 49.99%
- 49.99% – 59.99%
- 59.99% – 69.99%
- 69.99% – 74.99%
- 74.99% – 87.8%
- Not available

Minimum value: 49.8% Maximum value: 87.8%

Figure 2.2 Men aged 15–64 employment rates by region, 2012
Source: EU Labour Force Survey, EUROSTAT.

for women than for men; second, the regional dispersion in regional employment rates was declining prior to the economic crisis, but then tended to become more pronounced thereafter. This might suggest that in favourable economic conditions, regional employment rates tend to converge, while at times of economic crisis regional variations tend to become more pronounced, so highlighting the importance of macroeconomic conditions for geographical differences in employment opportunities and prospects for career development.

These two key trends are apparent when the focus is shifted to inter-regional variations at the country level scale within the EU. Table 2.1 shows the regional dispersion of employment rates for women and men in the larger EU27 member states in 2008 and 2012. Except in the case of Austria, regional dispersion in employment rates was more pronounced for women than for men, albeit in Germany and Finland regional dispersion in employment rates was similar for men and for women. Regional dispersion in employment rates was greatest in Italy (for both women and men). Spain, Slovakia, Romania and Belgium exhibited the next highest dispersion in

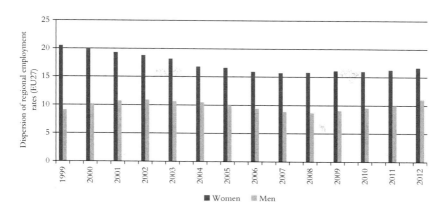

Figure 2.3 Dispersion of regional employment rates by gender in the EU27, 1999–2012
Source: EU Labour Force Survey, EUROSTAT.

regional employment rates for women. In all these instances, inter-regional contrasts were more pronounced for women than men, suggesting that geographical factors have a stronger influence on women's employment, and so for career development, than for men. Contrary to the general trend of reduced regional dispersion in regional employment rates, in Denmark, Germany, the UK, Finland and Hungary, dispersion was less marked in 2012 than in 2008 for both women and men, so indicating the importance of the national scale in shaping patterns of sub-regional variation.

Local perspectives: gendered localisation?

While national and regional statistics can provide useful insights into the scale and nature of jobs available to women (and men) it is not possible to read off directly from them an understanding of women's local employment opportunities and the specific challenges they might encounter in accessing employment and developing their careers (Yeandle 2006). What the statistics discussed above do reveal is that national and sub-national variations are especially important for women. Hence it follows that local variations may be especially important for women also. Indeed, local statistics on travel-to-work patterns suggest that women travel shorter distances to work than men (Coombes and Raybould 2001; Green *et al.* 1986; McQuaid and Chen 2012). Bruegel (2000) used the term gendered localisation to describe the corralling in space of women, leading to greater local dependence than for men. She suggested that this greater restriction to local domains reflected the unequal distribution of domestic work by gender and associated caring responsibilities (which often are associated with part-time paid employment), coupled with unequal access to private transport. She went on to suggest that gendered localisation perpetuated inequalities in paid employment.

16   A. Green

Table 2.1 Regional dispersion in employment rates by gender for selected EU27 countries, 2008 and 2012

Country	Women (%)		Men (%)	
	2008	2012	2008	2012
Belgium	10.5	10.0	6.6	7.3
Bulgaria	8.9	7.7	6.3	7.3
Czech Republic	5.7	5.6	2.9	4.3
Denmark	2.7	1.9	1.1	0.9
Germany	5.2	4.6	5.4	4.1
Spain	12.3	13.5	5.6	9.1
France	8.4	7.6	5.5	5.9
Italy	26.7	30.6	10.4	13.6
Hungary	10.4	9.5	9.9	7.8
Netherlands	2.5	2.8	2.3	2.0
Austria	3.6	3.5	4.1	4.6
Poland	6.6	6.3	4.6	4.8
Portugal	5.2	4.1	3.2	3.8
Romania	6.8	11.2	4.8	4.6
Slovakia	11.5	11.3	5.7	7.3
Finland	4.8	2.9	5.7	2.2
Sweden	3.1	3.4	2.5	2.4
United Kingdom	6.2	5.9	5.5	5.0
EU (27 countries)	15.8	16.7	8.7	11.1

Source: EU Labour Force Survey, EUROSTAT.

The medium-term increase in women in full-time employment and in high level non-manual occupations (Wilson and Homenidou 2012), and the associated growth of dual career households and of multi-car households (Green 1995), has loosened some of the constraints of gendered localisation, at least for some women, suggesting that its importance has diminished. Indeed, analyses of commuting statistics by socio-economic group point to important contrasts in the geographical extent of journeys-to-work according to occupation (Coombes *et al.* 1988), with those in professional and associated occupations travelling longer than average distances to work. Moreover, the trend towards increased professionalisation of employment might be expected to lead to greater residential migration, given the greater propensity for non-local, work-related residential mobility amongst high level, non-manual workers than amongst workers in less skilled occupations. However, it is worth noting when considering geographical perspectives on careers that both commuting and residential migration decisions, but especially the latter, tend to be undertaken with household considerations in mind, not merely on the basis of economic rationality at the individual level.

In this section, geographical perspectives on careers are considered for two contrasting groups of women, both of which may be expected to see relative growth in the context of a professionalising and polarising hourglass economy, with a greater share of jobs concentrated at either end of the occupational spectrum and a relative decline in the number of jobs in the middle (Goos and Manning 2007). The first group of women (aged from their early 30s to late 50s) includes those in managerial, professional and associate professional occupations in dual career households who might be expected to be able to pursue careers free from some of the limits of gendered localisation. The second group of women (encompassing women from all age groups, but with older women being over-represented relative to their share of the female workforce) comprises those in weaker labour market positions for whom such constraints are likely to be stronger.

Women in dual career households

There is no single definition of a dual career household, but in contrast with traditional homemaker/breadwinner households (in which one partner – typically the woman – does not participate in paid work) and middle type dual-earner households in which one partner's career (generally the woman's) is less absorbing than the other (Kiernan, 1992), dual career households may be characterised as egalitarian. Such egalitarian dual career households do not have a place in traditional organisational strategies linking social and spatial mobility (Savage 1988; Whyte 1956), where the trailing spouse (in nearly all cases a trailing wife) would be expected to undertake residential moves as a tied migrant at household level in support of the primary wage earner (nearly always the husband). In such an arrangement the spouse either might not engage in paid work, or might select jobs which fit in around the primary wage earner. Indeed, developments in organisational structures and the operation of internal labour markets, away from bureaucratic models to devolution of decision-making relating to policy design and implementation to lower levels of flatter hierarchies, suggest that there may be either less spatial mobility or different types of spatial mobility associated with career development. Alongside a demise of organisational strategies of social mobility, Savage (1988) also highlighted an increase in the importance of 'occupational strategies', in which social mobility is linked to a reliance on skill-based assets. In geographical terms, this is likely to involve spatial mobility amongst younger people (at the start of their careers – in accordance with kaleidoscope career theory (see Parker and Roan, Chapter 6 of this volume) – but declining spatial mobility thereafter. Likewise, entrepreneurial strategies are linked typically to spatial immobility, because of a reliance on particular place-based resources. In the case of occupational mobility strategies, it is worth noting that for some recent higher education graduates (both women and men), such early career migration is increasingly across international boundaries (especially in the European Union context), leading to a blurring of distinctions between internal and international migration.

So how do dual career households approach location and spatial mobility decisions, given that they are concerned not solely with individual economic gain, but rather with the development of two careers? Should both careers be pursued to the same extent? Whose career should take precedence, and when? What compromises are necessary? And what are the implications of such compromises?

Some insights are available from case study research drawing on work, location and mobility history information derived from 30 in-depth interviews with dual career households (involving both partners working in managerial, professional and associate professional and technical occupations) in which one partner worked for an employer based in the East Midlands region of England (Green 1997). The majority of respondents felt that career progression depended on a willingness to move, but that this might involve moves within (or between) functions in the same location, rather than necessarily involving residential migration to a new location. While the more highly paid or the more locationally constrained partner was often the leader in mobility decisions, one partner was not necessarily the 'leader' for all time and often the follower could exercise a veto against locations deemed particularly difficult or unattractive. Hence women's careers were not necessarily disadvantaged vis-à-vis those of men in these egalitarian households. Rather, the dual career households in the case study invested substantial thought and effort in their location and mobility decisions and traded off individual and household gains and losses.

In geographical terms, most respondents acknowledged that London (in a UK context) offered the largest single quantity and variety of career opportunities (as outlined further below). Accessibility to a range of employment opportunities emerged as being of key significance, along with good schools and appropriate housing. Residential location choices tended to be made in order to maximise (long distance) commuting potential and minimise the need for residential migration.

So for an individual partner in a dual career household, a long journey-to-work might be a price worth paying for career development in order to manage the household balance sheet in location and mobility terms, even though from an employer and an individual worker perspective, job relocation and residential migration may be mutually advantageous. Trends towards increasingly geographically diverse commuting flows, and flexible working and ICT weakening the locational link between residences and workplaces, have led to growing adoption of long distance weekly commuting and dual location households. This involves working away from the main household residence for part of the week and living for that time at a location close to the workplace (Green et al. 1999). The motivation for such working and living arrangements is the pull of the job (variously encompassing prestige, financial benefits and self-fulfilment) in some cases contrasted with push factors (the need to rescue a labour market position) in others.

Given the decreasing importance of organisational careers outlined above, employers might be expected to have less commitment than formerly was the case to the long-term career development of their employees and instead make greater use of short-term assignments and long distance commuting at the expense of relocation. There is increasing policy interest in such short-term assignments (at national and international levels) (Green et al. 2009). Some of these assignments, rather than being part of a long-term linked plan of social and spatial mobility for a primary function of developing an individual's career, might rather be short-term expedient, on a just in place, just in time model, solely to meet operational needs (Green 2004).

These trends suggest that the role of spatial mobility in career development, at least for women and men in dual career households, has shifted from a primary focus on residential migration to other forms of geographical mobility, and especially those falling in the in-between space of Figure 2.4. These other forms of geographical mobility are characterised by greater uncertainty, with individuals taking on more of the onus for their own career development, while at the same time having to take into account the career development of their partners and investment in education (and future careers) of any children.

Yet in this uncertain and more individualised context, location remains important. Empirical analysis using secondary data sources shows that in a British context, dual career households are concentrated disproportionately in towns and cities within the London Metropolitan Region (Green 1995). This is in keeping with the role of South East England as a so-called escalator region (Fielding 1992), in which individuals achieve continuing career advances in a more dynamic labour market, and so-called one-off escalator effects of positive upward movement for careers related to relocation to a more advantaged regional context (see also Champion *et al.* 2013; Findlay *et al.* 2009; Glaeser and Ressenger 2010; Gordon 2012; Newbold and Brown 2012 for further British and international evidence). The agglomeration effects associated with large and thick labour markets proffer individuals and households maximum accessibility, in geographical terms, to a range of employment options in a context of a movement away from predictable and stable careers to more volatile,

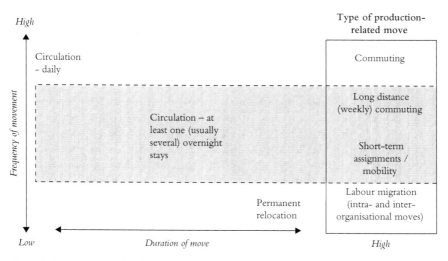

Figure 2.4 Types of work-related geographical mobility
Source: Green *et al.* (2009).

uncertain, complex and ambiguous careers (see Parker and Roan, Chapter 6 of this volume), for further details of such organisational developments). Hence, large cities in economically prosperous regions would seem to be advantageous locations for women in dual career households.

Women in weaker labour market positions

By contrast, women in the weakest labour market positions do not have as many opportunities for employment and career development as those in dual career households. Lack of formal qualifications restricts the volume and range of employment opportunities that they can consider. From a geographical perspective, lack of access to private transport and/or the difficulties posed by the cost and scheduling of public transport – especially where such transport is deregulated (Rivas-Perez, 2013; Tunstall et al. 2012) – along with localist outlooks and a lack of spatial confidence created by limited spatial mobility experiences (Quinn 1986), militate against moving beyond the confines of the immediate local area to pursue employment opportunities, for those individuals who are most disadvantaged in the labour market. Strong place attachment and (largely place-based) social networks based on family and friends – which may act as a 'support' in some instances but a 'brake' in others (Green and White 2007: 37) – highlight how geography plays a role in shaping access to employment and training opportunities.

Strong bonding social networks, while sometimes offering important support in work-related and non-work-related domains (Gore and Hollywood 2009), are also associated with a tendency to look inwards and so to neglect non-local opportunities. While some individuals may be unaware that they are trapped by space in this way, others acknowledge that limited spatial mobility reduces opportunity, but trade this off in favour of proximity to family and friends. Hence subjective opportunity structures may be a subset of objective opportunities, underlining the importance of the perceptions in understanding labour market behaviour. In a context of communal or ethnic division, and associated fear, limited spatial mobility may be part of a mindset of risk and uncertainty, which further constrains opportunities for employment and for training and career development.

Some employment practices that are more prevalent at the bottom end of the labour market than at the top, including unsocial hours of work, temporary positions and zero hours contracts, favour local candidates. Employers may explicitly prefer local people, on the basis of their geographical proximity – which in turn tends to be equated with reliability for such jobs (Nunn et al. 2010; Tunstall et al. 2012). Hence, for women (and men) in such jobs residential location vis-à-vis workplaces, and access to means of travel, can be very important. For part-time, low-paid work there is no economic rationale for travelling far to work.

The changing spatial and temporal nature of employment, particularly at the lower end of the labour market, coupled with increasing computational power of

GIS (geographical information systems) and policy interest from labour market and planning perspectives on economic participation, has led to a resurrection of interest in Time–Space Geography (Hagerstrand 1970). This emphasises spatial and temporal fixity constraints on the actions and movements of individuals in activity spaces or time–space prisms as a framework for individuals' behaviour. Domestic work and caring responsibilities for children and other household members place particular geographical and temporal constraints on employment and career development for women. Given the tendency for women to take on a greater than average share of non-work responsibilities in households, their journeys-to-work are also made more complex by the vagaries of 'trip chaining' (i.e. the incorporation of multiple stops in a single trip – for example, to take an infant to nursery school, a child to school, etc.) and associated temporal fixities (i.e. the need to deliver and collect children at specific times). This suggests that women have to negotiate more spatial and temporal fixity constraints on an everyday basis than do men (Kwan 2000; Schwanen et al. 2008). Geographically, women in densely populated urban areas are likely to be at an advantage relative to their peers in rural areas. Outside such densely populated areas, access to cars to help ameliorate spatial and temporal fixities, is especially important for women.

To remain geographically mobile, albeit to a much more limited spatial extent than is the norm for women in dual career households, women and households with no/low qualifications and/or on low incomes tend to be much more reliant on inter-household exchanges (for caring, offering of lifts, etc.) than their more advantaged counterparts (Grieco 1995). This helps explain the rationale for immobility of some individuals and households in difficult economic circumstances where the foremost emphasis is on getting by rather than getting on, even though in objective terms opportunities for employment and career development may be better elsewhere (Hickman 2010).

Gender and locational context dimensions in shaping and understanding careers are cross-cut by other dimensions, such as age, ethnicity, health, and so on. This is termed intersectionality, with some women facing disadvantage on the basis of their age, their ethnicity and poor health, for example. Precisely how these different dimensions play out in the labour market, and indeed whether or not they are measured, varies between countries in accordance with social norms, institutional structures and data collection instruments (Pries and Pauls 2012). Hence, it is difficult to make generalisations. Older women, especially those with limited work experience in the UK and with poor skills, are at a particular disadvantage here: first, because they have tended to miss out on the medium-term rise in formal qualifications amongst women; second, because pay gaps between men and women increase by age; third, because older women may be subject to discrimination both as women and as older workers (Schuller 2011); and fourth, because of the fixity constraints of caring for parents, grandchildren and others. If they suffer poor health they are likely to be further disadvantaged and, in a UK context, if they are from Pakistani and Bangladeshi ethnic groups they are also likely to be disadvantaged.

Despite the disadvantages faced by some (but not all) older women in the labour market, policies to address worklessness have tended to focus on lone parents and younger returners to the labour market. Furthermore, the reach and likely impact of particular policy measures may be expected to vary according to context. In an international context, the International Labour Organisation (2012) identifies generic policies such as better infrastructure, better care services, rebalancing the gender division of paid and unpaid work, reforms to tax systems and mechanisms to compensate for unequal employment opportunities by gender. Intervention on an individualised basis across policy domains (including training and education, encompassing job-specific and generic skills, health and transport, amongst others), and with local employers, is likely to be particularly important for tackling work-lessness amongst older women.

Conclusion

Variations in women's labour market position by country indicate that institutional factors are important in shaping the experience of employment and career development. At the sub-national level, regional dispersion in employment rates and shorter commutes to work for women than for men, suggest that women face particular geographical constraints in opportunities for employment and career development. Yet the increase in women in full-time employment in professional and associated occupations has weakened, but not eradicated, constraints of gendered localisation; there is considerable heterogeneity in experience amongst women. The relative disadvantage of older women with poor skills has tended to become more pronounced with shifts towards credentialisation. To some extent this represents a cohort effect, such that successive generations, who have more of their skills certified, may be less disadvantaged in this way. Yet it remains the case that given the heterogeneity within age cohorts, some older women remain constrained by gendered localisation (as noted below).

The demise of bureaucratic organisational strategies of social and spatial mobility, in which successive promotions within an organisation were associated with residential migration, has opened up increasingly diverse geographical patterns for career development. In dual career households, where consideration needs to be given to two careers and to the concerns of other household members, long distance and other complex commuting arrangements may be substituted for residential migration. The locational advantages of the agglomeration effects of large metropolitan areas, especially in economically prosperous regions, are clear for individuals in such households.

It remains the case that in comparison with men, women tend to face more spatial and temporal fixity constraints in negotiating paid work and other aspects of their lives, and that those women in the weakest labour market positions are most disadvantaged by lack of access to transport and other financial resources to overcome them. Hence they have geographically restricted activity spaces in which they can pursue career development. Given the circumstances of women in weak economic positions, there is a rationale for spatial immobility.

Looking to the future, information and communications technologies (ICT) related developments such as crowdsourcing (i.e. use of internet-enabled exchanges through which individuals can seek employment and organisations can reach a large pool of workers to outsource tasks which can be undertaken online) have the potential for overcoming geographical constraints by affording the possibility for working from anywhere with non-local others. However, to succeed, most individuals will need to draw on skills and attributes developed in their careers, and to have the foundation of skills and self-efficacy to take charge of their own career development (Green and Barnes 2013). So wherever women are located, the onus for career development is increasingly on the individual.

References

Bruegel, I. (2000) 'Getting explicit: Gender and local economic development', *Local Economy*, 15: 2–8.

Champion, A. G., Coombes, M. and Gordon, I. R. (2013) 'How far do England's second-order cities emulate London as "escalators" of human capital?', *Population, Space and Place*, DOI: 10.1002/psp.1806.

Coombes, M. G., Green, A. E. and Owen, D. W. (1988) 'Substantive issues in the definition of localities: Evidence from sub-group local labour market areas in the West Midlands', *Regional Studies*, 22: 303–18.

Coombes, M. and Raybould, S. (2001) 'Commuting in England and Wales: "People" and "place" factors', *European Research in Regional Science*, 11: 111–33.

Economist Intelligence Unit (2010) 'Women's economic opportunity: A new pilot index and global ranking from the Economist Intelligence Unit – findings and methodology', London: Economist Intelligence Unit. Available at: http://graphics.eiu.com/upload/WEO_report_June_2010.pdf (accessed 28 August 2013).

Fielding, A. J. (1992) 'Migration and social mobility: South East England as an escalator region', *Regional Studies*, 26: 1–15.

Findlay, A., Mason, C., Houston, D., McCollum, D. and Harrison, R. (2009) 'Escalators, elevators and travelators: The occupational mobility of migrants to South-East England', *Journal of Ethnic and Migration Studies*, 35: 861–79.

Glaeser, E. L. and Resseger, M. G. (2010) 'The complementarity between cities and skills', *Journal of Regional Science*, 50: 221–44.

Goos, M. and Manning, A. (2007) 'Lousy jobs and lovely jobs: The rising polarization of work in Britain', *The Review of Economics and Statistics*, 89: 118–33.

Gordon, I. (2012) 'Ambition, capital acquisition and the metropolitan escalator', *Discussion Paper* 107, London: Spatial Economics Research Centre, London School of Economics.

Gore, T. and Hollywood, E. (2009) 'The role of social networks and geographical location in labour market participation in the UK coalfields', *Environment and Planning C*, 27: 1008–21.

Green, A. E. (1995) 'The geography of dual career households: A research agenda and selected evidence from secondary data sources for Britain', *International Journal of Population Geography*, 1: 29–50.

Green, A. E. (1997) 'A question of compromise? Case study evidence on the location and mobility strategies of dual career households', *Regional Studies*, 31: 643–59.

Green, A. E. (2004) 'Is relocation redundant?: Observations on the changing nature and impacts of employment-related geographical mobility', *Regional Studies*, 38: 629–41.

Green, A. E. (2009) 'Geography matters: The importance of sub-national perspectives on employment and skills', *Praxis* 2, UK Commission for Employment and Skills. Available at: www.ukces.org.uk/assets/ukces/docs/publications/praxis-2-geography-matters.pdf (accessed 23 August 2013).

Green, A. E. and Owen, D. W. (2006) *The Geography of Poor Skills and Access to Work*, York: Joseph Rowntree Foundation.

Green, A. E. and White, R. J. (2007) *Attachment To Place: Social Networks, Mobility and Prospects of Young People*, York: Joseph Rowntree Foundation.

Green, A. E. and Barnes, S.-A. (2013) 'Crowdsourcing for paid work: An empirical investigation into the impact of crowdsourcing for paid work on employability', Draft Report to European Commission (IPTS), Coventry: IER, University of Warwick.

Green, A. E., Coombes, M. G. and Owen, D. W. (1986) 'Gender-specific local labour market areas in England and Wales', *Geoforum*, 17: 339–51.

Green, A. E., Hogarth, T. and Shackleton, R. E. (1999) 'Longer distance commuting as a substitute for migration', *International Journal of Population Geography*, 5: 49–67.

Green, A. E., Baldauf, B. and Owen, D. (2009) *Short-term mobility*. Report to the European Commission for 'Study on workers' mobility – Lot 2: Short-term international assignments', Coventry: IER, University of Warwick.

Grieco, M. (1995) 'Time pressures and low-income families: The implications for "social" transport policy in Europe', *Community Development Journal*, 30: 347–63.

Hagerstrand, T. (1970) 'What about people in regional science?', *Papers in Regional Science*, 24: 7–24.

Hickman, P. (2010) 'Understanding residential mobility in challenging neighbourhoods', *Living Through Change in Challenging Neighbourhoods Research Paper* 8, Sheffield: CRESR, Sheffield Hallam University.

International Labour Organisation (2012) *Global Employment Trends for Women 2012*, Geneva: ILO.

Kiernan, K. (1992) 'The roles of men and women in tomorrow's Europe', *Employment Gazette*, 100: 491–99.

Kwan, M.-P. (2000) 'Gender differences in time-space constraints', *Area*, 32: 145–56.

McQuaid, R. W. and Chen, T. (2012) 'Commuting times - the role of gender, children and part time work', *Research in Transport Economics*, 34: 66–73.

Newbold, K. B. and Brown, W. M. (2012) 'Testing and extending the escalator does the pattern of post-migration income gains in Toronto suggeproductivity and/or learning effects?', *Urban Studies*, 49: 3447–65.

Nunn, A., Bickerstaffe, T., Hogarth, T., Bosworth, D., Green, A. and Owen, D. (2010) 'Postcode selection? Employers' use of area- and address-based information shortcuts in recruitment decisions', *Department for Work and Pensions Research Report*, 664, Leeds: Corporate Document Services.

Parker, P. and Roan, A. (in press) 'Organisational perspectives on women's career – disappointments and opportunities', Chapter 6, current volume.

Pries, L. and Pauls, R. (2012) 'Introduction: New dynamics of migration and belonging', in L. Pries (ed.) *Shifting Boundaries of Belonging and New Migration Dynamics in Europe and China*, Basingstoke: Palgrave Macmillan, pp. 1–25.

Quinn, D. J. (1986) 'Accessibility and job search: A study of unemployed school leavers', *Regional Studies*, 20: 163–73.

Rivas-Perez, F. M. (2013) 'The dynamics of access: A study of social inclusion, job opportunities, travel mobilities and developing the Gateshead MetroCentre', Unpublished PhD thesis, University of Leeds.

Savage, M. (1988) 'The missing link? The relationship between spatial mobility and social mobility', *British Journal of Sociology*, 39: 554–77.

Schuller, T. (2011) 'Gender and skills in a changing economy', *UK Commission for Employment and Skills Briefing Paper*, Wath-upon-Dearne and London: UKCES.

Schwanen, T., Kwan, M.-P. and Ren, F. (2008) 'How fixed is fixed? Gendered rigidity of space–time constraints and geographies of everyday activities', *Geoforum* 39: 2109–21.

Tunstall, R., Lupton, R., Green, A. E., Watmough, S. and Bates, K. (2012) *Disadvantaged Young People Looking for Work: A Job in Itself*, York: Joseph Rowntree Foundation.

Wilson, R. and Homenidou, K. (2012) 'Working futures 2010-2020', *Evidence Report*, 41, UK Commission for Employment and Skills, Wath-upon-Dearne and London: UKCES.

Whyte, W. H. (1956). *The Organization Man*, New York: Simon & Schuster.

Yeandle, S. (2006) 'Supporting women's engagement with local labour markets: Introduction', *Local Economy*, 21: 197–9.

3 Work and older women
Interdisciplinary perspectives from India

U. Vindhya

A key feature of scholarship on women and gender in India is the concern with women's participation in paid work and employment. Questions of what constitutes work, the impact of employment on family dynamics and on women's well-being, the segregation of women workers in certain jobs low in occupational hierarchy, payment or status, a concentration of women in the informal sector or in unpaid labour, the gendered economic inequalities reflected through wage differentials and the casualisation of the female labour force, and the construction of identity of women as workers, despite the foregrounding of their domestic/reproductive roles, in colonial and post-colonial India have all been the subject of extensive debates and discussions in social science scholarship in India (Chakravarty and Chakravarty 2010; Raju and Bagchi 1993; Swaminathan 2009). In addition, for over two decades now, the impact of globalisation or the neo-liberal structuring of the economy on women's work patterns has been the focus of research attention, yielding both vast amounts of empirical data and theoretical insights (Mazumdar 2007; Rege 2007; Unni 2002).

Women's work scenario in India is characterised by an overwhelming predominance of informal (largely home-based) over formal workforce participation, the constraints of women's domestic roles and responsibilities and cultural sanctions on work outside the home. The greater representation of women in the informal sector means that older women who have never worked in the formal sector are not likely to start working later in life, and that women in home-based occupations continue to work throughout the life course.

This chapter aims to provide an overview of the women and work scenario in India, with specific emphasis on the cohort of older women. Based on a review of literature published from India in English in the last decade (2000–10), it attempts to highlight themes and issues of work experiences confronting older women in India. The dominant disciplinary prism through which the nature of women's paid workforce participation is analysed is largely through labour economics. Demographers have noted that feminisation of the aging population is an important emerging trend in India, but the literature on the working lives of older women in particular is sparse. Psychological research, in contrast to social science literature, has focused on a narrow segment of women employed in the formal sector – urban, educated, middle-class women – for whom work-related issues, including the impact of work on women's autonomy and identity, are vastly different.

The obvious limitations of the chapter are that, although it draws from a range of interdisciplinary perspectives and literature, spanning the disciplines of psychology, economics and sociology, along with the catch-all of women's studies, no claims are made to an exhaustive review of literature in the field. Another caveat of the chapter is that, for reasons of length, the diversity and intersectionality of women across class, caste, region, and ethnicity have been glossed over, although the presence and differential impact of these factors are acknowledged. There is also a paucity of research on the cohort of older women in India. By and large, women of reproductive age and girl children have been more frequent subjects of research and policy attention, while the two cohorts – adolescent girls and older women – have not received similar attention.

Given these limitations, the chapter makes only a modest attempt to identify some issues of work-related experiences of women, with references wherever available to those of older women in India. After providing a brief overview of some statistical data related to women's work situation, the chapter will focus on the central differences between social science and psychological research in the area of women's work, and on select themes such as women's agency and empowerment in the context of work, state policies and work participation.

Women and work in India: some facts and figures

Women constitute nearly one-third of India's total labour force, with 85 per cent of all women workers concentrated in agriculture and the informal sector. Characterised by a high degree of occupational diversity and employment instability (Balagopal 2009), the nature of work that women perform in this sector is often home-based, subcontracted, or through sources of self-employment. Jobs like domestic help, small trader, artisan, or field labourer on a family farm are some examples in this sector. Most of these jobs are low paid, do not require formal skill training, and do not come with benefits to the worker such as legal rights and clearly defined employer–employee relations, as is the case of workers in the organised sector (Unni and Rani 2003).

Because women's work is often entrenched in domestic activity, a common perception is that these activities do not constitute work. As informal/home-based workers, women's work is often invisible, dependent on informal arrangements and contracts, and on local and domestic markets. Their mobility into new fields is hampered because of factors such as household and care responsibilities, traditional social norms and lack of information and skills (Sudarshan 2009). Underestimation of such work is likely because the boundaries between these activities and other forms of household work done by women are often obscured. Such work is also invisible to national income accounting, since definitions of economic activity are equated with paid or formal work, thereby excluding many types of unpaid or low paying activity, especially home-based, community-based or piece rate work that the majority of women perform. Thus the actual labour force participation rate

28 U. Vindhya

Table 3.1 Labour participation rates by gender and by age group, 2008

Age group	All (%)	Women (%)	Men (%)
15–29	33.4	20.6	45.0
20–24	57.8	29.3	82.3
25–29	68.0	37.7	95.9
30–34	71.1	42.9	97.1
35–39	73.8	47.9	97.7
40–44	72.3	46.3	96.5
45–49	71.9	45.8	96.3
50–54	67.4	39.6	93.4
55–59	60.5	35.4	84.8
60–64	39.9	7.8	72.7
Total 15–64	61.0	35.7	84.6

Source: Klaveren, Tijdens, Hughie-Williams and Martin (2010).

for women is likely to be higher than that which is calculated from available data (Sudarshan and Bhattacharya 2009).

In the formal/organised sector, available data indicate that in 2005 there were around five million women and 21.5 million men in the total population of around one billion people, which amounts to about 8 per cent of the total labour force (Klaveren *et al.* 2010). In the formal sector, it is the service sector in which a majority of women are employed.

A significant feature of women's work in India is that their workforce participation rate is much lower than that of men. What this translates into is that, apart from women's representation in predominantly low-paid employment in the informal sector, a large majority have restricted access to income-generating employment and are consequently compelled to live in conditions of dependency (Balagopal 2009). Table 3.1 shows the labour participation rates (LPR) by gender and 5-year age group for 2008, and reveals that in no cohort were the female LPRs over half the male rates. They were much lower, especially among the 20–24 and the 60–64 age groups. The table also shows the rising LPR of women in successive age groups, beginning with the 15–29 to the 45–49 groups, after which there is a tapering-off. In the 60–64 age group, the LPR for men is 72.7 per cent, while in the corresponding age group in women it is only 7.8 per cent.

Women and work in India: social science and psychological research

Viewing the sphere of women's work in India through the lens of feminist scholarship, two essential features can be gleaned: (1) the invisibility of women's work – the societal undervaluation of women's contribution to the family income and their recognition as supplementary earners even as the incidence of female-headed households increases, and (2) the gendered nature of women's domestic/caring work – such work is time consuming, labour intensive, and socially vital but does not place women in the category of workers. Furthermore, since this work is unpaid, it is also accorded lower status and value (Arya 2008; Swaminathan 2009).

Feminist scholars in the social sciences have drawn attention to the invisibility of women's work in official accounting systems, which do not capture the work women perform and are therefore not categorised as economically productive activity. It was only after the 1991 national census, following vigorous lobbying by women's studies scholars and activists, that the explicit rider 'unpaid work on farm or in family enterprise' was included in the identification of workers to capture women's unpaid family labour to some extent (Krishnaraj 1990: 2663).

Broadly, two descriptive and explanatory themes seem to emerge from this corpus of literature:

1   It is the interaction of socio-cultural prescriptions and practices with economic considerations that plays a determining function in women's participation in the labour force and in characterising their work experiences.
2   Women perform enormous quantities and types of work, often under difficult circumstances, for low returns in wages and valuation by family and society, while being essential to the well-being of their families and communities.

The significant links between culture and economy – the part played by cultural values in influencing work decisions and the nature of women's work, and the role of women in the economy – have been extensively reviewed in feminism-influenced social science scholarship in India (Sudarshan and Bhattacharya 2009; Swaminathan 2009). These themes seem, however, to have missed the research scrutiny of psychological literature. Although the notion of paid employment of women and its impact and linkages with a range of issues has been investigated extensively in psychological research, it almost exclusively has had a narrow focus of research subjects – the small segment of women in the workforce employed in the formal, organised sector. By and large, the preferred topics have been the impact of women's paid employment on children's well-being, on women's own stress and well-being, the quality of marital relations, the spillover of work-stress issues to home and family and vice versa and attitudes towards the woman's employment outside the home (Bharat 2001; Rajadhyaksha and Smita 2004; Vindhya 2007).

A major limiting feature of this research is not only its narrow focus, but the often untenable generalisations from this narrow segment to women in general. The focus of psychological research has been specifically on the linkages between work and family life, and the changing identity of these women – urban, educated and middle class – as agents of modernity and social change (Vindhya 2007). Not only is the class composition and location of these women distinctively different from their counterparts in the informal sector, the nature and conditions of their work and wage patterns are also obviously more protected and secure. This is not to argue that women who work in the organised sector are not to be researched, nor is it to assert that their experiences and issues are not legitimate objects of inquiry. This is only to underscore the point that psychological research in India is characterised by a middle class, urban bias – a bias that leaves a vast majority (of women) unrepresented in research.

Given that social science data indicate that there is a preponderance of poor over non-poor women in the workforce (Jose 2007), the focus of psychological research being confined to middle-class women is indeed a critical lacuna. The number of studies conducted on samples, other than educated middle-class women, and on topics other than work–family balance, is virtually a handful in psychology. Examples of such studies in psychological research, including some from earlier decades, are the issues of work and autonomy among fisher women (Vindhya and Kalpana 1987); the impact of urban slum development programmes on women's work (Vindhya and Kalpana 1988); self-perceptions of municipality sweeper women on their work and their occupational hazards (Ravichandra *et al.* 2007); and the resilience and work of urban slum women (Srivastava 2003). Given, therefore, the pronounced urban and middle-class bias of psychological research on women and work, this chapter largely focuses on issues of work of poor/rural women, who are underrepresented in psychological research.

Even in the formal sector, where decision-making and leadership positions continue to be the mainstay of men, while the large bottom rung of the pyramid is clustered by women, who are relatively recently recruited, the impact and precise nature of these power differentials have not been the subject of research attention. For instance, in the higher education sector, wherein relatively greater numbers of women are making their entry in recent decades, not even 10 per cent of women occupy top decision-making positions, such as Vice-Chancellors (Kaushik 2008). However, at the entry level of Lecturers/Assistant Professors, women form a sizeable proportion of around 40 per cent, signalling the need to document the consequences of the changing patterns of recruitment and possible feminisation of this sector and its undervaluation as a result of increasing numbers of women entering this kind of work. The issue of power imbalances and their gendered impact, with its feminist overtones, has in fact been scarcely touched on by psychological research (Vindhya 2010).

While the major point of departure of psychological research from social science scholarship seems to be the choice of class location of research samples, with its varying implications, and addressing issues such as power, both have not paid much attention to age-disaggregated data and specific issues confronting older women. The bulk of psychological research on older women has been on health concerns, and elder care policies and practices (Jamuna 1994; Jamuna and Kalavar 2009; Prakash 1993; 1996; Ramamurthy and Jamuna 2009). Conversely, social science research on older women has highlighted the situation of widowed women, a group that is clearly disadvantaged by social, economic and cultural constraints and sanctions ranging from ritual inauspiciousness to deprivation of property rights (Chen 1998). To draw a distinction once again between psychological and social science research, the focus of the latter has been mainly on manifestations of gender inequalities and examining the impact of power structures, while psychological research on the other hand chooses not to utilise or apply the power and control thesis that feminism espouses. However, as the vast social science literature on questions of gender shows, any discussion on women and gender has to contend, necessarily, with changes in social and power relations and redefinitions of notions of power and powerlessness.

Empowerment, employment and identity

Empowerment, defined in its broadest sense as the 'expansion of freedom of choice and action' (Narayan 2002: xviii), is the current buzz expression in the development literature in Asian countries and is the shorthand employed for the distinctly psychological processes and outcomes of autonomy, self-direction and self-worth. It has also become near synonymous with the state policies and strategies addressing poverty reduction and gender (Narayan 2005). Does paid work empower women? Does it enable the construction of identities beyond the familial? Research does suggest that the participation of women in economic activities outside the home is often a significant enabling factor in the economic and social empowerment of women (Kishor and Gupta 2004). Not only is paid work said to lead to economic independence but, more crucially, it is held to enhance a sense of self-worth, and, by exposing women to the outside world, it leads to the development of support systems other than kinship-based ones. The role of women's work participation for their empowerment is complex, however, as borne out by several studies. While paid work is seen as allowing women to negotiate for expanded economic and social spaces, marriage and reproductive responsibilities appear to take precedence over work for women whenever necessary (Banerjee and Raju 2009).

Furthermore, women's paid work is mediated by several additional factors, such as the economic position of the family. Beginning with the observations and insights of Boserup (1970), feminist scholars in India have maintained that women's work is a double-edged sword. If the family is poor, the woman is driven to work but the opportunities available to women of low-income groups who lack formal education and skills, and negotiating capabilities, are in the informal, unregulated sector that renders them more vulnerable to exploitative, insecure work conditions. Empowerment for such women then remains rather questionable. Conversely, if the family income improves, women are withdrawn from the public domain, which could be translated to conditions where choices and decision-making are curtailed and susceptibility to violence increased. The following paradoxes and cultural constraints influencing women's work have been emphasised in the literature:

- Women are regarded as a flexible resource of the household, the implication being that they often lack the autonomy to make decisions about work.
- Whether or not women work after marriage will depend not on the individual decision and choice of the woman, but primarily on the external environment and ideology of the marital household.
- In both rural and urban India, it is poverty status that drives women to greater workforce participation, not subjective decisions.

- In recent years, economic opportunities created by liberalisation policies have thrown up several inequalities. While those who are better endowed with access to resources, skills and markets – the women in the organised sector and at the upper income end – are able to derive benefits from the new opportunities, studies show that for the majority of women, workers largely in the informal sector, the quality of employment is poor – with scarcely any opportunities for skill development and for moving up the ladder – with low income returns (Bannerjee 1998; Chagar 2006; Jhabvala and Sinha 2002; Mazumdar 2007).

Changes in the urban industrial economy in recent years, and emerging work spaces such as the information technology (IT) sector and related avenues of work, have led to transformations of critical dimensions of urban and educated women's lives. Essentially, new definitions of womanhood are sought to be created (Rajadhyaksha and Smita 2004). Even in the case of this new class of urban, educated middle-class women, the rider is that, while they are expected to embody modern India, and to negotiate the contradictions of tradition and modernity, they are called upon to do so without jeopardising their traditional roles as 'good wives and mothers' (Puri 1999:16).

The participation of urban employed women in the production process often impinges on the presence of substitutes for the domestic and caring work they traditionally and routinely are expected to do. For instance, when middle-class women enter the work-force, the household responsibilities that they are traditionally expected to perform are still their responsibility and must be done, regardless of their employment status. If the working woman's household and caring work has to be substituted, it is more often via the unpaid labour of another female family member, either girl children and/or older women in the household; or through the service market for women who have the resources, which means hiring the services of generally poorer women for domestic and household work (Chakravarty and Chakravarty 2010). The emergence of nuclear families and the increased participation of educated women in activities outside homes have, among other factors, resulted in the demand for women-centred services such as domestic help, childcare giver and full-time, home-based caretakers (Pillai 2008). The replacement of what is termed women's socially reproductive work (Ozler, cited in Arya 2008) is thus by women once again, either from within family networks or by poorer women seeking work. The absence of the notion of woman as co-provider serves to reinforce women's domestic role as the primary role and is the main impediment for women to take on roles and responsibilities in the public domain (Rajadhyaksha and Smita 2004).

Therefore, even though the term empowerment is conceived essentially as the expansion of (individual) capabilities and freedom to make choices, a key aspect of women's empowerment in countries like India is the impact of community culture. What is of crucial importance is that women's empowerment is not impacted by individualistic characteristics such as access to resources of education and income alone, but more significantly by 'a shared cultural consensus about who has the right to power and resources' (Narayan 2005: 27).

This shared cultural consensus stems from sources ranging from the micro institution of the family and the household or the domestic unit as one of the prime manifestations or determiners of gender inequality, to the broader social and economic structures of religion and the market. At all these levels, apportioning of resources to individuals is embedded within the shared understanding of rights, needs and duties. The cultural ideal of the male as breadwinner and of the female as reproducer has had a momentous influence on how women's work within the household and outside, and the contribution of their work to the national and domestic economy, is understood.

Sustained engagement of women's studies scholars over the past few decades with socio-cultural institutions such as the family shows that gender discrimination within the family results in women being allocated a smaller share of resources but a larger share of work (Deshmukh-Ranadive 2006). The family continues to mediate micro-level decisions regarding education, health or employment, and the dominant conceptions of masculinity and femininity privilege the male working subject and female domesticity (Eapen and Kodoth 2002). For women, household and interfamilial relations constitute a key feature of their disempowerment in ways that are not manifested in other socially and economically disadvantaged groups (Deshmukh-Ranadive 2006). Table 3.2 gives an idea of how entrenched domestic activities are for the majority of women in India.

In addition to the family, caste ideology is a strong determinant affecting whether women will work outside the home, the nature of the work they will perform and the distance from home such work entails and is allowed to them (Harris-White 2003). It is this layered hierarchical social order, beginning with the family and the household and extending beyond to other structures such as caste and religion, that provides the overarching context for women and work in India, ranging from the decision whether to work or not, to what kind of work, the wages they receive, the conditions of their work and the identity they acquire because of work.

Women's agency, work participation and state policies

The impact of traditional norms impeding women's work participation in India is likely to give a picture of singular docility – of women submitting passively to tradition. However, a component of empowerment that has been noted by feminist scholars is also agency – the ability to 'formulate strategic choices and to control

Table 3.2 Characteristics of workers in India

Indicator, NCEUS, 2007	Male	Female
% of workers in agriculture and allied activities	49	73
% of unorganised non-agricultural workers working from own home	16	55
Time spent on care and household maintenance per week	4 hours	35 hours

Source: National Commission for Enterprises in the Unorganized Sector (NCEUS) (2007).

resources and decisions that affect important life outcomes' (Malhotra and Schuler 2005: 73). In other words, agency refers to the capacity of women themselves to be significant actors in the process of change. Agency, as the essence of women's empowerment, does not imply that all improvements in the position of women must be brought about through the actions of women alone, or that it is the responsibility of individual women alone to empower themselves. State policies that aim to strengthen gender equality through various means and mount interventions that give women and other socially excluded groups greater access and control over resources, have the capacity to facilitate agency.

In recent years there has been a burgeoning literature on women's empowerment that provides us with several insights about poor and marginalised women's identity, self-worth and assertiveness. This literature identifies economic security as a key facilitator for empowerment to take place, but it also has to be accompanied by processes of social mobilisation and collective agency (Rajan and James 2004; Sudarshan 2009). The participation of women in economic activities outside the home is posited as a crucial enabling dynamic in the economic and social empowerment of women with paid work opening new doors, new ways of being, creating new sources of self-worth and developing support systems other than familial, all of which in turn impact on how women perceive themselves and others (Rajan and James 2004). What is of significance here is to what extent the ability to work outside the home enables women to recognise, challenge or confront structures of hierarchy and to what extent women perceive the possibilities of transformation in identities and perceptions through employment. It is here that state policies that enforce and protect women's rights to work play a significant role.

Current policy initiatives on the empowerment of women (e.g. the National Empowerment of Women Programme 2001) emphasise a reinterpretation and redefinition of work to reflect women's contribution as producers and workers. The role of work participation in women's empowerment in reality is seen to be complex and multifarious. Reference is made here to only two national policies – the Development of Women and Children in Rural Areas (DWCRA) – launched in 1982 – and the National Rural Employment Guarantee Scheme (NREGS) – introduced in 2006. Both are social protection policies with gender-sensitive content; they signal the state's role in enforcing and protecting women's rights to work (Sudarshan 2011). DWCRA aims to help poor rural women to organise themselves and engage in economically viable activities. Of the evaluation studies conducted on its impact, several refer to the significant presence of middle-aged and older women, who not only demonstrated greater awareness about the objectives and activities of the programme, but also showed higher levels of involvement. This is attributed to the relative freedom from domestic and childcare responsibilities that older women have (see, for example, Bishnoi and Singh 2007).

The other example is the National Rural Employment Guarantee Scheme (NREGS), a national policy aimed at providing 100 days of guaranteed employment at the statutory minimum wage in public works for every poor, rural household (Khera and Nayak 2009). As one of the largest programmes of its kind in the world, currently benefiting around 44 million people across the country, the

Scheme contains special provisions to ensure the full participation of women and stipulates that at least one-third of participants must be women. Studies document that, typically, workers on NREGS sites are women aged 33–45 years (Sudarshan 2009). Reducing the distance between work site and home, providing crèche facilities, paying a ratio of food and cash (given that women would have greater control over the use of grain) and equal wages are core programme features that have a marked impact on women's participation in public works (Sudarshan 2011).

Field surveys on the impact of this scheme have shown the benefits for women – availability of work at the statutory minimum wage (thereby allowing workers to remain in their villages and avoiding the several hazardous consequences of hunger migration), repayment of debts, ensuring children's schooling, autonomy over decisions of how to spend the money and, most significantly, the work provided under the NREGS has 'opened up a new opportunity for them' (Khera and Nayak 2009: 51), and the state scheme is 'helping women to take charge of their lives in little (and not so little) ways' (ibid.: 53). Studies have shown that women have found a new identity and economic empowerment – taking wages directly through their own accounts and increasing their spending on fodder, consumer goods, the education of children as well as offsetting debts (Sharma 2010). Significant benefits for single women, and for widows in particular, have been demonstrated. They were able to overcome the additional social constraints of single woman status through the 'dignity associated with doing government work' (Khera and Nayak 2009: 54) and the opportunity that such work provided to avoid possible sexual exploitation and coercion from private employers such as contractors and landlords.

Work, gender and generation

National data indicate that female workers tend to be younger than males. According to the 2001 census, the average age of all female workers was 33.6 years compared to the male average of 36.5 years. Although these data may not be entirely accurate, one would expect that as cultural impediments to work decrease (due to forces of modernisation), younger women would be the ones entering the workforce; older women who have never worked in the formal sector are not likely to start working later in life. This means that work opportunities in the formal sector remain more or less closed to older women, who have to restrict themselves either to unpaid domestic work or engage in the unregulated informal sector with its attendant uncertainties.

In 2006, the median age for women at first marriage was 17.8 years (although the minimum legal age of marriage is 18 years for women) and 42 per cent of all Indian women aged 20–24 had given birth before age 20. This means that a majority of women in India assume marital, child-rearing, and domestic responsibilities at an early age, setting off a chain of disempowering factors including the curtailment of educational and formal work opportunities as well as compromising their health. Again, this combination of early marriage, restricted opportunities and poverty status drives these women to greater labour force participation (in the unorganised sector), with poverty – interlaced with social and cultural dimensions – assuming an important role in women's work participation.

Regardless of their social location and participation in the productive process however, middle age, for women, signals a significant shift. This phase in a woman's life cycle has been studied and commented on in the literature – from psycho-analytic writings (Kakar 2005) to sociological and economic studies (Dube and Palriwala 1990; Patel 1999; 2005; Sen 1997) reflecting the interplay of multiple social hierarchies – of gender and generation. Middle age for women in India marks their entry into positions of familial–social power that were hitherto not open to them. Within the hierarchical structure of the patriarchal household, all women are not in identical positions in the hierarchy. Power and control are deployed by older women and, in patriarchal fashion, this flows from the woman's status as mother of the son rather than from her seniority status in terms of age and experience alone. This power and control is again asserted over other younger women, notably daughters-in-law. The popular conception of the oppressing mother-in-law reflects the power that older women in the family wield over young daughters-in-law in extended households. The relative position of older women within the hierarchy is based on their ability to recruit and channel the labour and sexuality of younger women so as to reproduce patriarchal domination. Thus, the power of the older woman could range from control over sexuality of the daughter-in-law in the interests of reproducing the patriarchal hierarchy over the allocation of food grains, and to decisions about whether the younger women should go out to work, and the nature of this work (Sen 1997). While for the younger women, the resentment directed against the mother-in-law is a channelling of their anger against socially-imposed roles and restrictions, for the older women their position as mother-in-law is often the only source of power they have ever had in their lifetime, resulting in a reluctance to let go of this power (Kakar 2005).

In recent decades, in the post-neo-liberal reform period in India, state-sponsored efforts for women's empowerment have been characterised by the twin processes of social mobilisation and collective agency. These efforts, while seeking to make women participants in the development process, have focused on enhancing consciousness and supporting women's collective action projects, known as self-help groups (SHGs) (Singhal 2003; Visvanathan 1997). Empirical evidence from one of the states, Andhra Pradesh in south India, in which SHGs have by now well-established roots – 30 per cent of total SHGs in India are found in this state alone – points to the increasingly assertive roles played by older women in these groups. In addition to goals of poverty reduction and access to resources like credit, the SHG programme has a well-articulated gender intervention and sensitisation agenda. The gender sensitisation training that the women are said to receive through this programme has been claimed to lead to significant changes in intra-family relations like: reduction in domestic violence; household decision-making, including the prevention of child marriage, and control over assets; and women's ability to act in the public sphere in order to effectively protect and promote women's rights (Jamuna personal communication 2010; Ramalakshmi 2003; Reddy 2008). Because of their relatively fewer domestic responsibilities, older women have assumed leadership positions, playing key roles in ensuring beneficial changes for other women, and in questioning traditional hierarchical power structures that undermine women's autonomy and well-being. This observation is a telling pointer to the constraining role played by domestic, child-bearing/rearing, and care giving responsibilities in women's participation in the public productive process, and it illustrates how freedom from these constraints because of older age facilitates women's visibility and assertiveness in the public domain.

Conclusion

Women's work in India is characterised by an overwhelming predominance of informal (largely home-based) over formal workforce participation, the constraints of women's domestic/caring roles and responsibilities, and cultural sanctions on work outside the home. This chapter aimed to provide an overview of the women and work situation in India, with specific emphasis on the cohort of older women. Two major explanatory and descriptive themes can be identified in the interdisciplinary literature – (1) a layered combination of economic considerations along with socio-cultural prescriptions and practices playing a determining role in women's entry into work and in defining their work experiences; and (2) older women assuming familial power as mothers of sons, while in the public domain recent evidence indicates their increasing assertiveness and decision-making positions in state-sponsored women's empowerment programmes. The emergent picture is therefore one of complexity and contradiction, of exploitation and of empowerment, and of challenging singular notions of docility and passivity.

References

Arya, S. (2008) 'Gender and public policy in India: Invisibilizing socially reproductive labour', *The Indian Historical Review*, XXXV: 49–76.

Balagopal, G. (2009) 'Access to health care among poor elderly women in India: How far do policies respond to women's realities?' *Gender & Development*, 17: 481–91.

Banerjee, A. and Raju, S. (2009) 'Gendered mobility: Women migrants and work in urban India', *Economic and Political Weekly*, XLIV: 115–23.

Bannerjee, N. (1998) 'Household dynamics and women in a changing economy', in M. Krishnaraj, R. Sudarshan and A. Shariff (ed.) *Gender, Population and Development*, New Delhi: Oxford University Press.

Bharat, S. (2001) 'On the periphery: Psychology of gender', in J. Pandey (ed.) *Psychology in India Revisited – Developments in the Discipline, Vol. 2: Personality and Health Psychology*, New Delhi: Sage.

Bishnoi, B. and Singh, A. (2007) *Effectiveness of Women Self Help Groups in the Promotion of Micro Enterprises in Rajasthan and Tamil Nadu*, New Delhi: National Commission for Women.

Boserup, E. (1970) *Women's Role in Economic Development*, London: George Allen and Unwin.

Chagar, R. (2006) 'Protection or obstruction? Women and precarious work in India', paper presented at the Annual Meeting of the Canadian Political Science Association, Toronto, Ontario, June.

Chakravarty, D. and Chakravarty, I. (2010) '"Bed and board" in lieu of salary: Women and girl children domestics in post partition Calcutta (1951–1981)', *Working Paper no. 84*. Hyderabad: Centre for Economic and Social Studies.

Chen, M. A. (ed.) (1998) *Widows in India*, New Delhi: Sage.

Deshmukh-Ranadive, J. (2006) 'Gender, power and empowerment: An analysis of household and family dynamics' in D. Narayan (ed.) *Measuring Empowerment: Cross-disciplinary Perspectives*, Washington, DC: The World Bank and New Delhi: Oxford University Press.

Dube, L. and Palriwala, R. (1990) *Structures and Strategies: Women, Work and Family in Asia*, New Delhi: Sage.

Eapen, M. and Kodoth, P. (2002) 'Family structure, women's education and work: Re-examining the high status of women in Kerala', *Working Paper Series 341*. Thirunvananthapuram: Centre for Development Studies.

Harris-White, B. (2003) *India Working: Essays on Society and Economy, Contemporary South Asia*, Cambridge: Cambridge University Press.

Jamuna, D. (1994) 'The psychological and social correlates of successful aging among elderly Indian women', *Indian Journal of Gerontology*, 8: 18–23.

Jamuna, D. and Kalavar, J. (2009) 'Life experiences of elderly living in senior residential care homes', paper presented in the symposium Positive Approaches to Coping with the Challenges of Ageing in Diverse Cultures, 8th Biennial Conference of the Asian Association of Social Psychology, New Delhi, December.

Jhabvala, R. and Sinha, S. (2002) 'Liberalization and the woman worker', *Economic and Political Weekly*, XXXVII: 198–209.

Jose, S. (2007) 'Women, paid work and empowerment in India: A review of evidence and issues', *Occasional Paper, 48*. New Delhi: Centre for Women's Development Studies.

Kakar, S. (2005) *Culture and Psyche: Selected Essays*, New Delhi: Oxford University Press (2nd ed.).

Kaushik, S. (2008) *Women's Studies Perspectives*, New Delhi: University Grants Commission.

Khera, R. and Nayak, N. (2009) 'Women workers and perceptions of the National Rural Employment Guarantee Act', *Economic and Political Weekly*, XLIV: 49–57.

Kishor, S. and Gupta, K. (2004) 'Women's empowerment in India and its states: Evidence from the NFHS', *Economic and Political Weekly*, 39: 694–712.

Klaveren, M., Tijdens, K., Hughie-Williams, M. and Martin, N. R. (2010) *An Overview of Women's Work and Employment in India*, Amsterdam: University of Amsterdam and Amsterdam Institute for Advanced Labour Studies.

Krishnaraj, M. (1990) 'Women's work in Indian census: Beginnings of change', *Economic and Political Weekly*, 25: 2663–72.

Malhotra, A. and Schuler, S. R. (2005) 'Women's empowerment as a variable in international development', in D. Narayan (ed.) *Measuring Empowerment: Cross-disciplinary Perspectives*, Washington, DC: The World Bank, pp. 71–88.

Mazumdar, I. (2007) *Women Workers and Globalization: Emergent Contradictions in India*, Kolkata: Stree.

Narayan, D. (ed.) (2002) *Empowerment and Poverty Reduction: A Source Book*, Washington, DC: World Bank.

Narayan, D. (2005) 'Conceptual framework and methodological challenges', in D. Narayan, (ed.) *Measuring Empowerment: Cross-disciplinary Perspectives*, Washington, DC: The World Bank and New Delhi: Oxford University Press.

National Commission for Enterprises in the Unorganized Sector (NCEUS) (2007) *Conditions of Work and Promotion of Livelihood in the Unorganized Sector*, New Delhi: NCEUS.

Patel, T. (1999) 'Women's agency, household progressions, and fertility in a Rajasthan village', *Journal of Comparative Family Studies*, 30: 429–51.

Patel, T. (ed.) (2005) *The Family in India: Structure and Practice*, New Delhi: Sage.

Pillai, N. (2008) 'Female employment in the service sector: Trends and patterns', paper presented in the seminar on Making Growth Inclusive with Reference to Employment Generation, 28–29 June, Shimla: CESP-JNU and IIAS.

Prakash, I. (1993) 'Gender aging: Psycho-social issues', *Indian Journal of Gerontology*, 7: 24–9.

Prakash, I. (1996) 'Aging women: A liability or an asset?' *Research and Development Journal*, 2: 28–32.

Puri, J. (1999) *Woman, Body, Desire in Post-colonial India: Narratives of Gender and Sexuality*, New York: Routledge.

Rajadhyaksha, U. and Smita, S. (2004) 'Tracing a timeline for work and family research in India', *Economic and Political Weekly*, 39: 1674–80.

Rajan, I. and James, K. S. (eds) (2004) *Demographic Change, Health Inequality and Human Development in India*, Hyderabad: Centre for Economic and Social Studies and New Delhi: Manohar Publishers and Distributors.

Raju, S. and Bagchi, D. (eds) (1993) *Women and Work in South Asia: Regional Patterns and Perspectives*, London: Routledge.

Ramalakshmi, C. S. (2003) 'Women empowerment through self help groups', *Economic and Political Weekly*, XXXVIII 12 and 13: 489–93.

Ramamurthy, P. V. and Jamuna, D. (2009) 'Gero psychology in India', in G. Misra (ed.) *Psychology in India: Advances in Research, Vol. I*, New Delhi: Pearson.

Ravichandra, K., Beena, C. and Regani, R. (2007) *Psychological Well-being: Correlational and Intervention Studies*, New Delhi: Global Vision Publishing House.

Reddy, A. R. (2008) 'Self-help groups in India - a catalyst for women economic empowerment and poverty eradication', paper presented at the 33rd Global Conference of ICSW, Tours, France, June–July.

Rege, S. (2007) 'More than just tacking women on to the macro-picture: Feminist contributions to globalization discourses', in R. Ghadially (ed.) *Urban Women in Contemporary India*, New Delhi: Sage.

Sen, G. (1997) 'Subordination and sexual control: A comparative view of the control of women', in N. Visvanathan, L. Duggan, L. Nisonoff and N. Wiegersma (eds) *The Women, Gender and Development Reader*, New Delhi: Zubaan.

Sharma, A. (2010) 'Mahatama Gandhi National Rural Employment Guarantee Act, 2005: A rights based law for inclusive growth', Presentation at Ministry of Rural Development, New Delhi.

Singhal, R. (2003) 'Women, gender and development: The evolution of theories and practice, *Psychology and Developing Societies*, 15: 165–85.

Srivastava, A. (2003) 'Resilience of low income working couples', in U. Vindhya (ed.) *Psychology in India: Intersecting Crossroads*, New Delhi: Concept Publishing Company.

Sudarshan, R. (2009) 'Examining India's National Regional Employment Guarantee Act: Its impact and women's participation', *SPA Working Paper*.

Sudarshan, R. (2011) *India's National Rural Employment Guarantee Act: Women's Participation and Impacts in Himachal Pradesh, Kerala, and Rajasthan: CSP Research Report 06*. New Delhi: Institute of Development Studies and Centre for Social Protection.

Sudarshan, R. and Bhattacharya, S. (2009) 'Through the magnifying glass: Women's work', *Economic and Political Weekly*, 44 (48): 59–66.

Swaminathan, P. (2009) 'Outside the realm of protective labour legislation: Saga of unpaid labour in India', *Economic and Political Weekly*, XLIV: 80–7.

Unni, J. (2002) 'Globalization and securing worker rights for women in developing countries', *Working Paper 132*. Ahmedabad: Gujarat Institute of Development Research.

Unni, J. and Rani, U. (2003) 'Social protection for informal workers in India: Insecurities, instruments and institutional mechanisms', *Development and Change*, 34: 127–61.

Vindhya, U. (2007) 'Quality of women's lives in India: Some findings from two decades of psychological research on gender', *Feminism and Psychology*, 17: 337–56.

Vindhya, U. (2010) 'Issues of gender in psychology: Traversing from sex differences to quality of women's lives', in G. Misra (ed.) *Psychology in India: Theoretical and Methodological Developments, Vol. IV*, New Delhi: Pearson.

Vindhya, U. and Kalpana, V. (1987) 'Relatively autonomous: *Jalari* fisherwomen of Andhra Pradesh', *Manushi*, 42–3: 35–42.

Vindhya, U. and Kalpana, V. (1988) 'Women victims of slum resettlement', *Manushi*, 49: 27–36.

Visvanathan, N. (1997) 'Introduction' in N. Visvanathan, L. Duggan, L. Nisonoff, and N. Wiegersma (eds) *The Women, Gender and Development Reader*, New Delhi: Zubaan.

4 Falling between the cracks
Older women and employer policymaking

Catherine Earl, Philip Taylor, Ruth Williams and Elizabeth Brooke

Until recently early retirement was the norm in many industrialised nations, but of late a new consensus has emerged around the need to extend working lives. This has occurred against a background of population ageing and dire warnings about the sustainability of social welfare systems and problems of declining labour supply, made more acute by current global economic uncertainty. In this context, influential bodies such as the Organisation for Economic Co-operation and Development (OECD) (see Keese 2006) are calling for greater efforts from industrialised nations to prolong working lives, with new public policies emerging which aim to combat age barriers and extend careers (Taylor 2008). Demographic and economic changes have resulted in a new retirement landscape. Individuals in the industrialised world are becoming healthier and living longer and the traditional life course is changing, with an 'Emphasis on a more blended lifecycle [which] can allow for integration and continuation rather than demarcation between phases of life' (Curl and Hokenstad 2006: 87). Furthermore, at the corporate level and beyond the global economic downturn significant labour shortages are anticipated due to demographic change, with employers needing to do more to attract and retain older workers (Szinovacz 2011).

Older women form an increasingly significant segment of the paid workforce (Vickerstaff 2010), but an understanding of their place in organisational policymaking and specifically the effects of domestic roles – in particular caring – in constraining employment opportunities is lacking (Loretto 2013). In the context of an ageing workforce, as a critical mass of workers reaches retirement, it becomes increasingly important to understand the factors that affect choices to extend careers, continue working, reduce working hours, or retire. For women, labour force participation is often interconnected with the availability of social welfare provisions and flexible working options, particularly concerning caregiving and family responsibilities (OECD 2011; Taskforce on Care Costs 2007).

While previous research has investigated issues for the workforce participation of younger women in particular, recent research has considered a range of issues affecting older women workers. On the one hand, important interactions between work, age and gender have been identified for older women in terms of: their financial security before and after retirement (e.g. Olsberg 2006); influences of education, health and marital status on their retirement decisions (e.g. Warren 2006);

their responsibilities for unpaid family caregiving (e.g. Fine 2007); challenges they face in maintaining a work–life balance, including their access to secure part-time work (e.g. Pocock 2003; Warner-Smith et al. 2006); and inequality and discrimination stemming from occupational and sectoral segregation of the labour market (Moore 2009). On the other hand, there is limited evidence on older women's labour market trajectories and experiences and how these may influence later life transitions and roles. While there have been notable recent exceptions in the Australian context (e.g. Everingham et al. 2007; Warner-Smith, et al. 2006; Warner-Smith et al. 2008) and the UK context (e.g. Loretto 2013; Loretto and Vickerstaff 2013; Moore 2009; Vickerstaff 2010), as noted by Russell (2007: 100), the 'problem of old age' has historically been applied primarily to men because it was involved with stopping work and losing identity, whereas women were expected to continue in the domestic role. However, increasing female labour force participation rates have been identified as generating potentially significant economic benefits (Access Economics 2006) and there is evidence that working may provide potential health benefits for older women, along with supplementing superannuation funds, which are generally much less than those held by men (Warner-Smith et al. 2008). There is, therefore, good reason for further consideration of the labour market status of older women workers.

The ageing workforce is increasingly female, presenting employers with challenges as 'women may have employment goals, career patterns, and work styles different from their male counterparts' (Hansson et al. 1997: 221). In choosing to extend their working lives, older women take into account their work and non-work roles, particularly their caregiving roles, and structural and economic constraints that diminish their earnings (Post et al. 2013). These experiences, which may include caring for younger generation family members, such as children and grandchildren, while simultaneously caring for elderly family members, such as ageing parents and spouses, differentiate older women workers not only from older men but from younger women also. In dealing with an ageing workforce, employers will need to consider older women's career development needs, the likelihood that they will have caring responsibilities, and that they may have different orientations to work and retirement. While there have been recent international developments in public policies aimed at combating age barriers in the labour market, and extending working life, there has been little consideration of older women's needs in terms of employer policymaking (Taylor 2006). That older women's needs were not being met led Itzin and Phillipson (1995: 84) to coin the term 'gendered ageism' to describe the double jeopardy of sexism and ageism, but the state of knowledge has not moved very far beyond this initial spadework.

This chapter considers the intersection of age and female gender in organisational policymaking within three Australian industry sectors. We draw on the concept of intersectionality to consider multiple, interlocking identity statuses. Rather than treating age or gender as a mathematical model that is dichotomous and oppositional, we deal with age and gender through an integrative approach that aims to develop awareness of both individual choices and social structural constraints in older women's workforce participation. In dealing with this intersection of age equality and gender, we attempt to move beyond one-dimensional or additive approaches, although also acknowledging the lack of synthesised best practice resources for intersectional policymaking (Hankivsky and Cormier 2011). What intersectionality promises, however, is not without limitations. Some inequalities can draw more attention than others, resulting in differential rankings between inequalities (Lombardo and Verloo 2009). Further, age equality presents a challenging case as every person can potentially become part of this grouping. Moreover, older people might be treated as a homogenous grouping (Chaney 2013). Through this lens we consider relationships between age and the female gender in the workplace from the perspective of the employer, drawing on the findings from empirical work carried out in 2011. At this time the Australian labour market was buoyant and skills shortages remained a frustration for business activity as levels of unemployment remained low and projections suggested that employment growth would be solid and labour market activity strong (Reserve Bank of Australia 2010).

To investigate the intersection of age and gender in employer policymaking for older women in the workforce, the research targeted three industry sectors in Australia. The university education, financial services, and state and emergency services sectors offered large workforces with significant proportions of older women workers as well as evidence of efforts to address the needs of women workers. Interviews were conducted with 56 human resource (HR) managers across these sectors. The respondents comprised 19 HR directors, managers and team leaders across a variety of business units in the finance sector, 17 HR directors and managers from varied industries across the state and emergency services sector, and 20 HR directors and managers from universities across Australia. These managers took part in a half-hour, semi-structured telephone interview which asked about workplace policies relating to older women workers, including: flexible work options, work–life balance initiatives, professional development schemes, opportunities for advancement, managing a culture of age diversity, transition to retirement, succession planning and knowledge retention programmes.

Findings

Interviews revealed a significant disjunction between the specific needs of older women employees and current HR policy and practice. Respondents across all sectors found it difficult to identify policies that met the specific needs and aspirations of older women workers. Many HR managers stressed that flexible work options, such as part-time and flexi-work, were available to all employees, although they were more likely to be applied to younger women, and were particularly associated with childrearing. Consequently, older women employees were not targeted as an equity group and their specific needs were not differentiated from other employee groups, such as older men or younger women. In the words of one respondent:

> Our flexibility option is open to everyone regardless whether they're retiring or whether they have family responsibilities … I guess for women going on maternity leave there's more. I mean we've been quite successful culturally

in terms of getting managers to really consider the application for flexible work arrangements. But it's not something that's really pushed for mature aged workers. They have the same option as, say, myself if I wanted to take a break to study part time. So it's not something that's really pushed.

(Interview 17, financial services)

This approach that treated all employees equally actually affected older women negatively. HR managers recognised a detrimental impact on the career development and pre-retirement planning of women whose needs were often not acknowledged in masculine models of career progression that assumed the availability of domestic 'backup'. As one respondent explained:

I think it's more challenging in trying to assist women to reach some sort of balance as they move into senior positions. Senior positions across all of Australia still sit in a culture where they were held by middle-aged men who had a backup in their own domestic division of labour. There's still that model there. Even when your Vice-Chancellor's a female, it's the same model. It's a huge cultural shift, I think, for Australia, and certainly for our sector.

(Interview 23, university education)

Organisations had strongly articulated policies concerning women on maternity leave and had developed highly effective approaches to retaining them, with the consequence that most of the respondents reported around 90 per cent retention of women returning from parental leave. In the words of one respondent:

We have a big thing about keeping in touch with employees that are on parental leave ... In my team I've got five people off on parental leave. I know we do make sure that we keep in touch with them. They regularly send us photos of the children to share with the rest of the team and I keep in touch with them on a social level. Just very quick updates of what's going on so that they still feel engagement with work.

(Interview 6, financial services)

In outlining efforts to maintain contact with employees on long-term leave, most respondents referred to maternity leave. In this regard, other forms of long-term leave, such as providing disability care or palliative care for a parent or spouse, were not considered, illustrating a bias against older women carers in the workforce.

The needs of older women employees

It was generally perceived by HR managers, and reinforced through policy, that younger staff were a sounder organisational investment. In particular, where concerted structural efforts were made to focus on furthering career development opportunities, staff in early- to mid-career stages were the beneficiaries. HR practice centred on the career development of younger women who were returning from parental leave and moving into flexible work options. Much attention was directed to the needs of younger women and women in the early stages of their careers. Few HR managers recognised that women might require access to flexible work options and career development opportunities not only after returning from parental leave, but throughout their careers. Offering flexible options throughout women's working lives could increase the retention of older women in the workforce and enable them to build their careers. As one respondent outlined:

> I think from a pure recruitment point of view we're cutting off our nose to spite our face. We've got an ageing demographic, we've got skill shortages and then we're reducing our candidate pool ... Women do require career breaks through their lives so that [they have] good return to work, good development opportunities and there is consistency and continuity in their careers which means that they can genuinely compete at later stages in life.
>
> (Interview 38, university)

Offering flexible options and career development opportunities to women throughout their careers are among the practices it was argued might be successful in achieving the retention of female employees. Further, the specific needs of individual female employees, particularly those working reduced hours, need to be taken into account. As one HR manager in the financial services sector explained, skills acquired rather than time invested should be the focus of individual career progression:

> We're absolutely champions of flexible working practices and diversity and flexibility and so on ... It's really trying to empower the women, and still concentrate on their tie in to their development planning and their career progression, to show that you can absolutely reach a senior position on three days a week. It's not about your work pattern, so we absolutely treat each individual, whether you're working two days a week or five days a week, on a fair and equitable basis. We try to focus in on where they want to go next in their career, what they need in terms of what are the gaps and where can we work with them to be able to progress them.
>
> (Interview 18, financial services)

We found that the particular needs of older women employees were not on the minds of HR managers. While there was some awareness of gender equality, their awareness centred on avoiding gender discrimination, particularly concerning maternity leave. Older workers, in general, were treated as a homogenous group and were treated no differently from other employees despite their differing needs. In the words of one respondent:

> I don't know that we need to manage [age diversity] to be honest. There's no adverse reaction to older people here providing they are still performing. Of course, along with everybody else, they have to go through the performance

management systems every year ... It's more that they're treated exactly the same as everybody else and if they start to show lack of performance then often we'll reduce their fraction or offer them a pre-retirement contract or one of those things. In the last three or four years that type of treatment has certainly increased.

(Interview 31, university education)

Notably, older women workers had less access to long-term carer's leave than younger women. Where it was available, the provision of leave for carers of older people (such as mature women caring for elderly parents or a spouse) seemed to be more *ad hoc* and less well developed than support for those involved in childrearing. Moreover, the majority of the carers' leave taken by older women seems to have been either sick leave or unpaid leave. Nevertheless, there was evidence of an increasing awareness among HR managers of the care responsibilities placed on older workers and, generally, older carers were assumed to be women. Respondents from each of the three sectors were cognisant of this issue. Two respondents highlighted the gap between policy and practice for older women carers seeking leave, as follows:

I couldn't tell you for definite, but I'm certainly aware anecdotally that there are increasing numbers of people – not necessarily just women – who are seeking leave or needing to take leave, to act as care givers to elderly parents.

(Interview 49, state and emergency services)

There's certainly a formal policy for academics – if they need to have extended time to care for other people, they can. On the general staff side it would probably be unpaid leave if they've run out of accumulated leave. I mean I can even tell of cases in the last couple of years when we've allowed people to take extensive leave unpaid to care for partners or parents ... Certainly in my experience here, when we've had people who have issues like that, we've worked with them to make their time more flexible here. I mean I really can't imagine any case where we've not to be honest. It's just something that we do.

(Interview 31, university education)

Another respondent specified how a genuine need among employees led to the development of a policy for older carers:

We also have a grandparental policy – for grandparents looking after their grandchildren. They can take time if they're going to be the primary carer for their grandchildren ... They're allowed to take any of their leave balances that they have and then the rest of it is non-paid leave but they're entitled to be able to take that and then they have a job to come back to.

(Interview 6, financial services)

Caring for grandchildren was one aspect that clearly differentiated the needs of older women employees from older men. In the words of one respondent (in an organisation without a grandparental policy):

> I think there's certainly more pressure from older women themselves and from society and from family for older women to make themselves available for their children and their grandchildren. I think there's definitely an expectation that [older] men will be working – people will be likely to say, 'Isn't that great that they're still engaged and interested.' But I think it's a little bit more blurred with older women if they're still working and they've got grandchildren: 'Gosh, why aren't they helping their struggling children to look after their kids?' – that sort of thing. So I do think there are different pressures on older women in the workplace.
>
> (Interview 39, university education)

Another lacuna in HR policy and practice that impacted more on older women employees than men was pre-retirement planning. Several HR managers indicated their awareness of this issue, although they also recognised that it was not being addressed effectively in policy. One respondent, in particular, articulated a stark gender difference in pre-retirement contract negotiations concerning salary, conditions and perks:

> In the last six months, the only pre-retirement contracts I've written have been for men. This is men knowing they're going to retire and [seeking] a transition process. They say what they want, when they'll stop being an employee, and ... it all gets written into a document. It's all very sound. I go over all of them, and look at what we can do and we can't do. But I don't get women lined up at my door, saying, 'Look, I think I'm going to retire in another 12 months, and this is what I think I want to do.' ... I don't think they know some of this stuff is okay to ask for.
>
> (Interview 23, university education)

This respondent elaborated further, connecting the gender division she observed in pre-retirement negotiations to senior staff contract negotiations:

> It's a bit like when I do senior staff contracts – the male contracts take up to a fortnight. The female contracts I can do in an hour. I've even got to drop hints to some of those women: 'Do you think you might want to ask about blah-de-blah?' I don't need to do that with the men. In fact, over the last 10 years, I've kept data on it because it horrifies me. In my last institute, when I finished there, I presented a paper to the Vice-Chancellor saying to her, over these last eight years, as I've written senior staff contracts, the men have negotiated on 58 different sets of things. I jotted them down for her. I said, 'The women we've recruited have negotiated on their base salary, and maybe a car.' Two things. I said to her, 'Some of us have got to open up these conversations a little bit better'.
>
> (Interview 23, university education)

Further, there was recognition among HR managers of an unconscious bias against employees using flexible options. HR managers reported a perception among managers and employees that when an employee is not physically present in the workplace, there is a sense that she is not serious about her career or not committed to getting ahead. This perception negatively impacts on women, since they are the most likely to engage in flexible work options, as one respondent implied:

> Our culture is such that we don't necessarily actively promote that sort of work/life balance. We do things such as make sure you take your annual leave, but in terms of a daily basis, I don't know that we necessarily do enough to actually role model work/life balance. We talk about work/life balance but it's definitely harder to achieve in reality. Because our culture is one where you start early, you finish late, particularly if you want to get ahead or be promoted. That need to be seen is quite culturally ingrained.
>
> (Interview 9, financial services)

Good practice in employer policies

While policy generally did not cater to the specific needs of older women, there were limited examples of good practice in the areas of carers' leave, career development and superannuation. For instance, one HR manager identified elderly care as a reason to request long-term leave and outlined her organisation's policy response. In her words:

> Our reversible part-time appointment policy refers to anyone who needs to take on a carer responsibility. So it applies for people having young children, but it is equally – or it is increasingly – being used for people who have to, for a period of time, take on a major caring role for sick, ailing, dying parents, partners ... We don't make the distinction. It's just for carer responsibilities ... It can be anything from six months to five years. So that really takes in – enables – somebody who's got a parent who's terminally ill and needs to work part time, they've got that capacity to do that for a short period of time.
>
> (Interview 28, university education)

Another HR manager recognised that the efficacy of practices for career development of employees returning from long-term leave rests with the competence of line management. In this manager's words:

> For every person returning from leave – and I'm thinking specifically of maternity leave or people returning from other long-term leave – the policy says you must sit down with your manager and complete this professional development assessment – a PDA. If a manager is doing that well, contained within that is a discussion around personal development and what might be some needs that that individual has.
>
> (Interview 46, state and emergency services)

Finally, within the financial services sector, a notable policy achievement has acknowledged the potential for a significant shortfall in the funding of women's pensions. One bank decided to step in, as one of its HR managers explained:

> In my experience, I've identified that while in our operations area, we had men who had been there for 30 years, some of our women had only been there for 10 years ... We were finding ... women who typically take time off to care for children were retiring with less super[annuation] because they'd taken that time off work. Women who were taking a year or two off were also retiring with less super because they were taking those periods as unpaid leave ... So the [bank] introduced superannuation for the unpaid period of parental leave ... to try and combat the gap that women and men have when it comes to their super when they retire.
>
> (Interview 10, financial services)

Conclusions

The HR manager respondents in our study were generally unable to articulate how different equity agendas could be combined. Although there was awareness of issues facing older women employees, age and gender were treated as two operationally distinct categories and seldom integrated in their application. While purporting to treat all employees equally, HR policy overlooked the specific needs of older women. In general, intersectionality of policy remains an underdeveloped concept within policy discourses (see Hankivsky and Cormier 2011). In particular, in our study HR manager rhetoric was largely absent at the intersection of age and gender. Drawing on evidence from three industry sectors in Australia, this research has confirmed that there is an absence of organisational policies that reflects the needs and aspirations of older women in the workplace, often leaving them to fall between the cracks of current HR policy and practice.

This absence suggests that there is a role for public policymakers, advocacy groups, employer organisations and trade unions in sensitising employers to the specific workplace needs of older women and in assisting and encouraging them to devise solutions. An illustration of such an approach comes from the UK-located and employer-led Employers Network for Equality and Inclusion (ENEI),[1] which supports employers in such areas as: preparing a convincing business case for diversity; understanding the nature of social categorisation, stereotyping, prejudice and organisational bias; recruiting from a diverse talent pool; and talent development and retention. Cohesive approaches of this kind may address issues raised by intersectional analysis of inequalities and encourage employers to develop boundary-spanning policies that address the needs of workers with a diverse range of attributes, experiences and needs.

Note

1 See www.enei.org.uk (accessed 8 August 2014).

References

Access Economics (2006) 'Meeting Australia's ageing challenge: The importance of women's workforce participation, Canberra: Report for the House of Representatives Standing Committee on Family and Human Services'. Available at: www.mskills.com.au/DownloadManager/Downloads/Meeting%20Australia's%20Ageing%20Challenge.pdf (accessed 27 May 2013).

Chaney, P. (2013) 'Mainstreaming intersectional equality for older people? Exploring the impact of quasi-federalism in the UK', *Public Policy and Administration*, 28: 21–42.

Curl, A. L. and Hokenstad, M. C. (2006) 'Reshaping retirement policies in post-industrial nations: The need for flexibility', *Journal of Sociology and Social Welfare*, 33: 85–106.

Everingham, C., Warner-Smith, P. and Byles, J. (2007) 'Transforming retirement: Re-thinking models of retirement to accommodate the experiences of women', *Women's Studies International Forum*, 30: 512–22.

Fine, M. D. (2007) *A Caring Society? Care and the Dilemmas of Human Service in the 21st Century*, New York: Palgrave Macmillan.

Hankivsky, O. and Cormier, R. (2011) 'Intersectionality and public policy: Some lessons from existing models', *Political Research Quarterly*, 64: 217–29.

Hansson, R. O., DeKoekkoek, P. D., Neece, W. M. and Patterson, D. W. (1997) 'Successful aging at work: Annual review, 1992–1996: The older worker and transitions to retirement', *Journal of Vocational Behavior*, 51: 202–33.

Itzin, C. and Phillipson, C. (1995) 'Gendered ageism: A double jeopardy for women in organizations', in C. Itzin and C. Phillipson (eds) *Gender, Culture and Organizational Change Putting Theory into Practice*, Routledge: London.

Keese, M. (2006) *Ageing and Employment Policies: Life Longer, Work Longer*, Paris: OECD. Online. Available at: www.globalaging.org/pension/world/2006/ocde.senemp.pdf (accessed 27 May 2013).

Lombardo, E. and Verloo, M. (2009) 'Institutionalizing intersectionality in the European Union?', *International Feminist Journal of Politics*, 11: 478–95.

Loretto, W. (2013) 'Not seen or heard? Older women in the workplace', in S.-M. Bamford, and J. Watson, *A Compendium of Essays: Has the Sisterhood Forgotten Older Women?*, London: International Longevity Centre.

Loretto, W. and Vickerstaff, S. (2013) 'The domestic and gendered context for retirement', *Human Relations*, 66: 65–86.

Moore, S. (2009) '"No matter what I did I would still end up in the same position": Age as a factor defining older women's experience of labour market participation', *Work, Employment and Society*, 23: 655–71.

OECD (2011) 'Help wanted? Providing and paying for long-term care'. Available at: www.oecd.org/health/health-systems/helpwantedprovidingandpayingforlong-termcare.htm (accessed 27 May 2013).

Olsberg, D. (2006) 'Major changes in Australia's superannuation system, but women are still Ms…ing out', *Australian Accounting Review*, 16: 47–52.

Pocock, B. (2003) *The Work/Life Collision: What Work is Doing to Australians and What to Do About It*, Annandale, NSW: Federation Press.

Post, C., Schneer, J. A., Reitman, F. and Ogilvie, D. T. (2013) 'Pathways to retirement: A career stage analysis of retirement age expectations', *Human Relations*, 66: 87–112.

Reserve Bank of Australia. (2010) 'Minutes of the monetary policy meeting of the Reserve Bank Board, September'. Available at: www.rba.gov.au/monetary-minutes/2010/07092010.html (accessed 27 May 2013).

Russell, C. (2007) 'What do older women and men want?: Gender differences in the "lived experience" of ageing', *Current Sociology*, 55: 173–92.

Szinovacz, M. (2011) 'Introduction: The aging workforce: Challenges for societies, employers, and older workers', *Journal of Aging & Social Policy*, 23: 95–100.

Taskforce on Care Costs (2007) 'The hidden face of care: Combining work and caring responsibilities for the aged and people with a disability'. Available at: www.families-australia.org.au/publications/pubs/TOCCreportNov2007.pdf (accessed 27 May 2013).

Taylor, P. (2006) *Employment Initiatives for an Ageing Workforce in the EU-15*, Luxembourg: Office for Official Publications of the European Communities.

Taylor, P. (2008) *Ageing Labour Forces: Promises and Prospects*, Cheltenham, UK: Edward Elgar.

Vickerstaff, S. (2010) 'Older workers: The "unavoidable obligation" of extending our working lives?', *Sociology Compass*, 4: 869–79.

Warner-Smith, P., Everingham, C. and Ford, J. (2006) 'Mid-age women's experiences of work and expectations of retirement', *Just Policy*, 40: 45–53.

Warner-Smith, P., Powers, J. and Hampson, A. (2008) *Women's Experiences of Paid Work and Planning for Retirement*, Canberra: Office of Women, Department of Families, Community Services and Indigenous Affairs. Available at: www.fahcsia.gov.au/sites/default/files/documents/05_2012/womens_experiences_of_paid_work_final_report_survey.pdf (accessed 27 May 2013).

Warren, D. (2006) *Aspects of Retirement for Older Women*, Canberra: Office for Women, Department of Families, Community Services and Indigenous Affairs. Available at: www.fahcsia.gov.au/sites/default/files/documents/05_2012/aspect_of_retirement__report_final.pdf (accessed 27 May 2013).

5 When good jobs go bad and bad jobs get worse

Women's progression opportunities in a polarised labour market

Doris Ruth Eikhof and Chris Warhurst

On the basis of projections to 2020, the UK labour market is forecast to keep its hourglass economy shape. At the top end the number of services jobs that are highly paid and highly skilled is expected to increase; likewise the number of low-wage, lower skills services jobs at the bottom. In the middle, the number of workers employed in manufacturing will decrease (Wilson and Homenidou 2011). With the hollowing out of the middle and the expansion in the number of jobs at the top and bottom, what appears to be emerging is not just an hourglass but a polarised labour market of good and bad jobs, or what Goos and Manning (2007) call lovely and lousy jobs. Such polarisation trends are not confined to the UK, but exist across the EU countries (Hurley *et al.* 2011) as well as the US (Kalleberg 2011). As such, the points that we make about women's progression opportunities in the UK may resonate more internationally, as we indicate in the chapter.

Whilst many service jobs at both ends of the hourglass could, in principle, be offshored to the emerging economies, national and regional governments in the developed countries strive to attract and retain a share of them as part of socio-economic development strategies. Even before the current economic downturn, the creative and retail industries featured heavily in such strategies. For the creative industries, policy-driven definitions typically include architecture and design; film, television, video, radio and publishing; fine arts; music and the performing arts; software and computer gaming; advertising and crafts (e.g. Department for Culture, Media and Sport 2001; United Nations Conference on Trade and Development (UNCTAD) (2010). Retail is a similarly heterogeneous industry, ranging from the sale of white goods, to food and fashion for example (Grugulis and Bozkurt 2011). This chapter discusses jobs in the creative and retail industries in general but uses examples from specific sub-sectors to illustrate particular points.

In urban regeneration strategies for so-called de-industrialised cities these creative and retail industries were, and continue to be, promoted as capable of creating vibrant regional service hubs (e.g. Florida 2004 and King Sturge 2006 respectively). In particular, the creative and retail industries are hailed as engines of job growth and generators of economic recovery for the UK (Clifton *et al.* 2009 and O'Connor 2013 respectively). Both industries are significant employers of women. However, whilst both industries are regarded as important in providing job growth, academics as well as policy-makers have recognised differences in the job quality they offer.

On the basis of advancement prospects, the creative industries are positioned as offering good jobs, even jobs emblematic of the kind desired by government, not just in the UK but worldwide (European Commission 2012; UNCTAD 2010). The retail industry is regarded as indicative of bad jobs – though it is useful perhaps, government hopes, in offering entry-level jobs leading to something better in the future (see Dutton et al. 2005).

This chapter focuses on the career prospects for female workers in these two industries in the UK, but makes occasional reference to debates and developments in other countries. Drawing on secondary material, the chapter reveals how putatively good jobs in the creative industries can go bad for women and how jobs already acknowledged to be bad in retail can get worse for women. As a consequence, career opportunities diminish in both cases. In presenting this evidence and attendant arguments, the chapter highlights important discrepancies between the political ambitions and empirical realities of women's workforce participation and advancement and thus of key foundations of women's career development in the twenty-first century. In order, the following two sections first outline women's participation and advancement in the creative and then retail industries. The concluding section raises a number of implications from our observations about the apparent limitations to this participation and advancement in the UK and how other countries might not be immune from the problems that we identify in these industries.

The creative industries: when good jobs go bad

From the early 2000s onwards, the creative industries emerged as a key focus of economic policy across the developed countries (e.g. Clifton et al. 2009; European Commission 2012; UNCTAD 2010). Policy-makers believe that these industries combine high skill/high wage employment with high economic growth prospects. In addition, the presence of a creative class working in coffee shops and spending high wages in stylish bars, lifestyle shops and on personal services, allegedly facilitates the development of vibrant and inclusive communities (Florida 2004). Re-branding itself as Cool Britannia (Oakley 2004) the UK was an early adaptor in converting these assumptions into economic policy. Despite criticisms about the actual contribution to job growth (Warhurst 2010) and the potential for creating a socio-economic dystopia (Peck 2005), the creative industries continue to be promoted as offering good jobs (e.g. Florida 2004; Leadbeater and Oakley 1999); interestingly, high skill work undertaken in hip or cool environments and rewarded by high wages and intrinsic satisfaction. Government interest has further been fuelled by Richard Florida's prominent claim that the creative industries would not only facilitate socio-economic development but would, at the individual level, provide 'new avenues of advancement' and 'full opportunity and unfettered social mobility for all' (Florida 2004: 79 and 321).

With respect to gender, these allegedly equal career opportunities are seen to rest on three foundations (see also Eikhof et al. 2013). First, creative work requires intellect and creativity rather than physical strength, which removes the gender-bias inherent in heavily physical labour. Moreover, as Henry (2009) claims, because communication and interpersonal relationships are particularly important, creative work requires intellectual skills that women tend to be more likely to possess than men. Second, the circumstances under which creative work is undertaken appear to match well the inclinations and needs of female workers. Generally, women are more likely to run the smaller, customer-oriented and human capital-intensive businesses (Marlow and McAdam 2013; Small Business Service 2003), and such enterprises are typical for the creative industries (Henry 2009). The creative industries also feature a high share of part-time and flexible employment (Eikhof 2013; Skillset 2010). Work that can be undertaken flexibly, particularly from home, can allow women to combine professional commitments with caring responsibilities and might thus be conducive to their careers (Eikhof 2012). Third, creative workers allegedly value diversity and, despise old social divides, including those premised on gender (e.g. Florida 2004; Henry 2009). Given the focus on individual intellectual resources, the prevalence of small businesses and flexible employment, and an allegedly diversity-friendly culture, creative work has been discussed as women's natural career choice (Banks and Milestone 2011; Gill 2002). Skillset's (2010) Creative Media Workforce Survey suggests that young women certainly see these industries as offering attractive career prospects: in entry-level jobs, female creative workers outnumber male creative workers.

With women artists and entertainers such as Hillary Mantel or Adele beating their male counterparts to one accolade after the other, and Sheryl Sandberg and Marissa Mayer leading Silicon Valley multi-nationals, the creative industries do indeed have a distinctly more feminine public appearance than, for instance, the banking or oil industry. However, a closer look at women's workforce participation and advancement shows that women's careers in the creative industries are less likely to progress as well as those of men.

Reliable employment data for the creative industries is difficult to come by. For the UK, Skillset's[1] series of Workforce Surveys constitutes the most comprehensive source, covering the creative media industries, i.e. television, film, radio, interactive media, animation, computer games, facilities, photo imaging and publishing (Skillset, 2010 and previous editions). For women's workforce participation and pay, these data show clear patterns. With respect to workforce participation, women are under-represented in the audio-visual industries overall (38 per cent compared to 46 per cent UK as a whole). More importantly, women are over-represented in the younger age bands to 34 years (51 per cent of all women, but only 34 per cent of all men, in the industry are 34 years or younger) and under-represented in older age bands (only 16 per cent of women in the industry are aged 50 or older, compared to 25 per cent of men; all figures Skillset 2010). Women are thus not only less likely to work in the creative industries than men, they are also much less likely to sustain careers in these industries and to advance into senior, i.e. more powerful and better paid, positions. Instead, women drop out of the labour force in their mid-30s to mid-40s.

With respect to pay, women's overall annual earnings are lower than those of their male counterparts (Skillset 2010, see Christopherson 2008 for similar findings from the US film industry). These differences are partly consequences of occupational segregation and of female workers leaving the creative industries before they advance to better paid positions. Women are over-represented in lower paid occupations in the sector, such as make-up, hairdressing and costumes, and under-represented at career stages with higher earnings. However, previous analyses by Skillset (2005) showed that the gender pay gap remained when age and occupation were controlled for, indicating the existence of genuine gendered pay discrimination. As in other industries, women's (creative) contributions are valued less than men's (Henry 2009; Hughes 2011). Notwithstanding the Mantels, Adeles, Sandbergs and Mayers, on average women fail to achieve the same recognition of their creative prowess as their male colleagues (e.g. Dowd *et al.* 2005 for popular music; Ekelund and Börjesson 2002 for publishing).

While occupational segregation, under-representation in older age bands and under-valuation are important obstacles to gender equality in the creative industries, they are common in other areas of the economy as well. However, we argue that the creative industries' production system and the resulting circumstances of work and employment pose additional challenges that are specific to the creative industries and which compound gender inequalities. Production in the creative industries is focused on projects, for instance a film, a theatre show, an advertising campaign or a new media service. Project-based production has a number of impacts on work and employment practices (for a detailed exposition see Eikhof 2013; Eikhof and Warhurst 2013). First, employment is often temporary and undertaken on the basis of freelance contracts. Workers compete for participation in projects in overcrowded labour markets, facing tough rivalry for jobs as well as substantial income insecurity. Second, careers in the creative industries typically – and increasingly – require working in low or unpaid entry-level positions. Training takes place through 'learning by watching' (DeFillippi and Arthur 1998: 132), with industry entrants working as runners, assistants and interns. Third, project work tends to feature long and unsocial working hours and requires considerable geographical mobility. Fourth, recruitment onto projects is typically through personal networks and informal connections. These work and employment practices make careers in the creative industries precarious: low or unpaid entry-level jobs lead into highly competitive labour markets, in which employment depends heavily on personal networks, offers little income security and requires long and unsocial hours as well as geographical flexibility.

Precarious work and employment practices have gendered consequences. First, recruitment through personal networks disadvantages women. The crucial social capital is built up in informal gatherings such as launches, gallery openings or premiere celebrations, where women are perceived primarily in terms of embodied femininity and their professional skills are at best recognised as a secondary feature (Gill 2002). In addition, while self-promotion and informally exerting influence are socially accepted practices in men, the same behaviour is viewed negatively in women (Banyard 2010; Eagle and Carli 2007). Gendered stereotypes about women's physical attractiveness and appropriate behaviour thus result in female creative workers being perceived and assessed according to different and professionally less favourable criteria than their male counterparts (Eikhof and Warhurst 2013; Gill 2002).

Second, the creative industries' typical work and employment practices constitute significant career obstacles for workers with caring responsibilities (Randle et al. 2007; Skillset 2008b), and those workers still tend to be predominantly female. To buffer unstable income from project-based employment, workers have to rely either on financial help from a partner or parents (e.g. Dex et al. 2000; Jarvis and Pratt 2006) or on additional work from outside the respective industry. Women are more likely than men to have teaching jobs outside their creative industry (Gill 2002), which then curtails the time and effort that they can devote to their creative career. The intensity of project-based working, with its long and unsocial hours and demands on geographical mobility, constitutes further obstacles to combining careers and caring (Randle et al. 2007; Skillset 2008a, 2009). Clashes between careers and caring are, of course, the prime cause of gender inequalities in other industries as well (Eikhof 2012; England 2005). However, while in other industries maternity leave, job sharing schemes or on-site crèches, for instance, help facilitate women's careers (Appelbaum et al. 2006), the creative industries typically lack the stable employment relationships within medium or large-sized employers that provide these work-life balance policies. Even when there is more stable employment, highly competitive labour markets mean that employers have little incentive to implement work-life balance policies in order to retain staff (e.g. Skillset 2008a). In addition, the dominant view within the industry is that creative work requires total dedication and that the creative industries' project-focused, high intensity model of production is irreconcilable with family-friendly working hours (Skillset 2008a).

In sum, precarious work and employment practices in the creative industries pose challenges that women, both without children and as (potential) mothers, are less likely to successfully address. An additional challenge arises from these industries' emphasis on aestheticised labour and youth-oriented bohemian lifestyles. Where workers' corporeality is part of the creative output, for instance in the performing arts, film or TV, pressures to maintain a youthful, sexy appearance are particularly high (e.g. Eikhof et al. 2013). But across the creative industries generally, workers have to comply with specific habitus and lifestyle expectations. Advertising workers, for instance, have to appear 'free, independent and a bit lawless' (Alvesson 1994: 549) and new media workers 'artistic, young and "cool"' (Gill 2002: 70). As signs of ageing are perceived to diminish women's attractiveness more than men's, female creative workers are much less able to keep up the appearances required for career success in these industries. Both physical ageing processes and lifestyle changes relating to parenthood dent their usefulness and credibility as creative workers (Eikhof et al. 2013).

Given the obstacles arising from precarious work and employment conditions and expectations regarding appearance and lifestyle, many women either leave the creative industries in their mid-30s to mid-40s or scale back their work (Skillset 2010). Both alternatives prevent women from advancing to more influential and better paid positions. At the collective level, gender inequalities result. At the individual level, what looks to be a good job with good career development that could (be made to) fit women's professional and personal aspirations, turns bad. The full opportunities and new avenues of advancement claimed by Florida (2004) have failed to materialise. Thus if the overall socio-economic impact of the creative industries remains unclear, the image of the creative industries as particularly women-friendly is proving to be a mirage.

Retail: when bad jobs get worse

If one urban renewal strategy has centred on the creative industries, another has involved retail. Over the last 20 years or so, retail has gained an important role in economic development and regional positioning. A former ship-building city, by the 1990s Glasgow was undergoing a process of urban regeneration, with shopping replacing shipping, and malls replacing the mills. The smart designer retail stores were matched by a plethora of boutique hotels and style bars, restaurants and cafes. Glasgow was branded as Scotland with style. It became an exemplar of services-driven economic regeneration for other de-industrialised cities in the UK such as Manchester, Newcastle, Sheffield and Leeds. By the mid-2000s around three million workers, or 11 per cent of all UK workers, were employed in retail. Indeed retail is an industry with relatively high labour intensity (Mason and Osborne 2008).

The retail industry's heterogeneity impacts employment and the type of worker employed, what they do at work, what skills they need, the quality of their jobs and how those jobs are perceived socially. Men are more likely to sell electrical goods, women to work in supermarkets and middle-class youth to work in boutique fashion for example. Overall though, most sales assistants in the UK are female (73 per cent) and are employed part-time, working fewer than 30 hours per week (64 per cent), with 46 per cent of workers aged 16–24 years (Mason and Osborne 2008).

However, there is some consistency: employment in retail constitutes what might be termed a 'bad job' (Williams and Connell 2010). As Carré et al. (2010) demonstrate, most jobs in retail are routine and low skilled, with low entry requirements in terms of qualifications needed. Retail is the largest employer of non-graduate labour in the UK. Fifty-nine per cent of the retail workforce has no or low qualifications. It is for this reason that governments often target retail to provide entry-level jobs for the unemployed and female labour market returners such as lone parents (e.g. Dutton et al. 2005). Typical annual pay is below the national average, and can start at half that average, making retail one of the main low-wage industries in the UK (Shaheen et al. 2012). Indeed over a quarter (26 per cent) of all low-wage employees in the UK work in retail. The key factors related to this low pay in this industry are being female, aged 16–24 or 50-plus, being part-time and having low qualifications (Mason et al. 2008).

As with their male colleagues, female retail employees regard personal 'internal' drivers such as the acquisition of new skills and qualifications along with hard work as the key to career development within the industry (Broadbridge 2007). However, despite the EU Part-time Workers Directive, part-time workers, who are predominantly female, are often denied the training opportunities of full-time workers that might lever this career development (Tomlinson 2006). Moreover, in reality, Broadbridge (2007) notes, it is external barriers that restrict female employees' career development – a male-orientated organisational culture and a lack of organisational accommodation of women's care responsibilities. Significantly, according to Tomlinson, it is increasingly local or line managers who determine workplace employment practice within the organisational policies of their companies, and do so informally.

This bad job is getting worse, however, as retail companies seek to aestheticise their workforce, placing greater emphasis on employee corporeality in order to attract customers. Fashion retailer Abercrombie and Fitch, is a good illustration of this practice: it overtly hires young, good-looking workers with a 'preppy look' as customer-facing staff, who it subsequently refers to as 'models' (e.g. Smith 2013). In recent years there has been growing interest in the concept of 'aesthetic labour' to explain current business strategies in retail work and employment, amongst other routine interactive services. Aesthetic labour is the supply of embodied capacities and attributes possessed by workers at the point of entry into employment. Employers then mobilise, develop and commodify these capacities and attributes through processes of recruitment, selection, training and regulation, transforming them into competencies or 'skills', which are then aesthetically geared towards producing a style of service encounter. Employees are, for example, hired because of the way they look and talk; once employed, they are instructed how to stand whilst working, what to wear and how to wear it. This encounter involves face-to-face or voice-to-voice interaction in which employees' corporeality is managed to deliberately appeal to the senses of customers or clients and thereby, companies expect, boost competiveness in a crowded marketplace.

The concept was developed from analysis of higher value added interactive services in retail and hospitality in the 'new' Glasgow – the emerging designer boutique stores and style bars, cafes and restaurants noted above (Warhurst *et al.* 2000). Demonstration effects are now apparent in other retail sub-sectors, with Williams and Connell (2010) claiming that all retail now involves some workforce aestheticisation. Nevertheless this aestheticisation is most salient in the upmarket niche (Pettinger 2004). Three developments have emerged as a consequence of this aestheticisation strategy by employers.

First, it is clear that some workers are being excluded from these jobs and so denied access to a key job growth sector and one that might provide an important first step into the labour market. Whilst all retail jobs now involve some level of worker aestheticisation, its intensity can vary depending upon the market niche and marketing strategy of companies (Hall and van den Broek 2010). It is the upmarket, style-driven niche in which employers most explicitly attempt to match labour markets and product markets, with only those applicants who have the right habitus – more specifically 'middle classness' – likely to be hired. As one manager of a fashion retail store told Crang and Martin (1991: 106) in Cambridge, he avoided hiring workers from the working class:

> [saying] to us, the residential origins of his employees is an important consideration: none came from the large council estates … as they were not the 'right type of people' he was looking for. They lacked the 'cultural capital' … to display and sell the middle-class clothes in the store.

Middle-class youth, particularly students, are the employer preference. As a consequence, the middle class displaces working-class women from working-class jobs. These middle-class workers are attracted to what are, formally, working-class jobs by the allure of working for cool company brands, the opportunity to model stock and the availability of significant product discounts that enable them to wear these cool companies' products. Some companies deliberately employ customers, with walk-in casual hires not uncommon (Warhurst and Nickson 2007). It is a twist on consumer fetishism, Williams and Connell note, in which companies' consumers become its workers, attracted by the glamour and status associated by representing a cool brand. These workers are hired – and work – 'driven by their consumer desires not by their labour interests' (ibid.: 360). To ensure that these types of workers are the ones hired, employers often have prolonged hiring processes that act to filter out workers with immediate monetary needs.

The second development is the emphasising of the importance of age to employability. As Ainsworth and Cutcher (2008) note, age has yet to be explicitly explored in the research of aesthetic labour. However it needs to be, as there are indications that the combination of age and aesthetic labour impacts on career opportunities in retail. For example, in focus groups that one of us conducted in Glasgow with retail managers, there was an articulated acceptance that the industry's workforce is segmented by age, with particular sub-sectors employing younger or older staff. Aestheticised labour tends to be younger. As one female manager explained: 'department stores where it's really trendy – jewellery, cosmetics – they're looking for the younger, the younger body', continuing 'I mean you look through applications and this person might have absolutely fabulous experience but they might, say, be forty-five, forty [years old] and that's it. You're not even going to bring them in [for an interview].' Age discrimination is therefore a feature of aesthetic labour. Access to jobs in the style labour market can be limited to younger workers. However because their employment is predicated on their youth, these workers have, literally, a limited shelf-life, after which they are no longer deemed employable. There is thus an absence of internal labour markets by which these workers can progress. This absence is an outcome of organisational strategy and local management choice in which, again, labour and product markets are matched by employer.

The third development arises from the first and second: the type of worker being employed in these 'style labour market' jobs has little interest in improving what, despite the ascription of being cool, are still objectively bad jobs. That these workers consume the products of these companies means that the product discounts offered to employees, some of which can be considerable, are attractive. Discounts can be 10–30 per cent and even higher for new starts. Importantly, from middle-class backgrounds and often still living at home, these workers can use their wages to buy these products because they do not need their wages to survive. They are, Williams and Connell (2010) claim, 'paradigmatic "decommodified" workers', able to maintain their lifestyles without relying on their jobs' (ibid.: 350).

While aesthetic labour shapes who is employed and what they do in work, a key issue is its effect on jobs. Skill equilibrium theory posits that companies' product and labour strategies align: high-value added products need high skilled workers who receive high pay; low-value added products require workers with low skills who receive low pay. If skill equilibrium theory holds, it might be expected that these high-value added retailers would offer relatively better jobs in a bad jobs industry (for a discussion, see Lloyd et al. 2013). In fact, emerging evidence suggests otherwise: these jobs remain bad and the prospects for improvement are undermined.

Despite being in high-value added product market segments, jobs in these boutique and upmarket retail stores remain low-paid, very routine, highly monitored and, in the case of the US at least, staffed through just-in-time scheduling that results in highly variable working hours and thus income (Williams and Connell 2010). Likewise in her analysis of sales workers in fashion retail, Belisle (2006) notes that her work was minimum wage and assurances of future pay raises and promotion never materialised. This experience is one that resonates broadly across retail, as Tomlinson cited above has noted: part-time workers, who are predominantly female still, are often denied opportunities that might lever promotion.

This reality soon impacts workers' job experience. Being so highly monitored and unable to express their middle-class sensibilities makes for an unpleasant job for these workers. The realities of the job come as an unpleasant surprise for them, clashing with their feelings of class entitlement to something better, and their consumerist fantasies are quickly dispelled (Williams and Connell 2010). However rather than voice their demands for better jobs, they quit. One of Williams and Connell's interviewees claimed that only one in four new starts lasted in the job beyond their first day. This turnover appears not to be a problem: given the allure of cool, new recruitment is not difficult for employers. Certainly, lacking interest in the usual demands of labour – decent working conditions, pay, and prospects – these workers do not agitate for change. These middle-class workers do not regard retail as offering a career, nor do they push for change in company practice and policy that might create career opportunities. Moreover, despite their work experience resonating with other retail workers more generally, these aesthetic labourers do not identify with other retail workers for whom these jobs are a key source of income, despite being low-paid jobs. Aesthetic labourers do not see themselves as retail workers, but rather as knowledgeable consumers. This disinterest, Williams and Connell (2010) believe, disables worker solidarity and prevents efforts to improve jobs in the retail industry. As a consequence, bad jobs have become worse, compounding labour market exclusion, limiting progression opportunities for those workers who make it into work and making the likelihood of job amelioration more distant, all of which disproportionately affect the career prospects for women workers in retail.

Conclusion

With an hourglass economy, the UK and other labour markets are polarising into good and bad jobs. In this chapter we have examined jobs in the creative and retail industries as illustrations of good and bad jobs respectively. Both industries have become targets of economic policy, eulogised as providing important job growth and socio-economic development. Significantly, both industries claim to offer workforce participation and advancement opportunities for female workers. By examining secondary data and debates about developments within these industries, this chapter has shown that such claims need to be tempered.

Polarised by good jobs and bad jobs, as female workers are encouraged into both industries, it might be expected that women's workforce participation and advancement would reflect this polarisation. The reality is less simple. As we have shown, putatively good jobs in the creative industries can go bad for women workers and already bad jobs in retail might get worse for women workers.

There are strong indications that jobs in both industries do not offer prospects for advancement for female workers, and that participation may also be limited. In the creative industries a putatively good job is good for male workers but can go bad for female workers. Precarious work and employment practices pose obstacles that women, in particular mothers, find disproportionately more difficult to address, and expectations about appearance and lifestyle diminish employment opportunities in particular for older women and mothers. These influences compound gender discrimination, resulting from an under-valuation of women's creative achievements. Consequently, a considerable share of women leave the creative industries before they advance to better-paid and more influential positions. Jobs in retail are already regarded as bad. Features that make these jobs bad, for example part-time working and low entry skill requirements, mean that women, particularly those with care responsibilities, are encouraged into retail as a first step back into the labour market, and women are disproportionately employed in retail. Once employed, however, those same features result in fewer training opportunities, which in turn diminish opportunity for advancement. Moreover, the recent turn by employers to the use of aesthetic labour, and the employment of more middle-class workers, both displaces working-class workers from these jobs and undermines the capacity for job amelioration. Already bad, these jobs are thereby becoming worse.

The chapter has drawn on mainly, though not exclusively, UK data to support its points. However, we noted at the start of the chapter that not only is this polarisation of jobs evident in the US and elsewhere in Europe, the creative and retail industries are offered as an economic panacea by a number of governments, not just by that of the UK. The points that we make are likely to have resonance beyond the UK therefore. Indeed, we have already highlighted the use of aesthetic labour in the US and contributions to a 2012 special issue of the *Journal of Economic and Industrial Democracy*[2] revealed aesthetic labour as a strategy of retail and other employers in countries as diverse economically as Australia and Sweden. The creative industries have been a cornerstone of economic policy internationally for over a decade now. Hartley's (2005) edited collection, for instance, comprises research accounts of such policies from Hollywood to Delhi and St Petersburg to Hong Kong (for a critical account of international creative industries policy, see Banks and O'Connor 2009). The United Nation's Creative Economy Programme (UNCTAD 2010) extends such policy to the developing world and has recently published reports on developing the creative industries in Mozambique and Zambia (UNCTAD 2011a, 2011b). In parallel to these developments in international policy, critical voices about gender discrimination in the creative industries are emerging as well (e.g. Eikhof *et al.* 2013), although often confined to individual industries such as new media in

Germany (Henninger and Gottschall 2007), craft in the UK (Hughes 2011) or arts in Sweden (Flisbäck 2013).

Both empirical evidence and emerging critical voices from academics and practitioners thus suggest a need to look beneath headline statistics about job number growth within the hourglass economy and aggregated accounts of job quality within labour market polarisation. Such lumpy accounts need to be made sensitive to workers' variable career experiences, particularly those of women. To this end, a more nuanced understanding of companies' business strategies and industry production models within the hourglass economy is needed. As we have shown, both business strategies and production models influence the utilisation of female labour and thus, at the individual level, women's career workforce participation and advancement. If women's workforce participation and advancement are to be improved, economic policy needs to target not only job growth, but develop industrial policies that lessen the gender discriminating impacts of business strategies and production models. Without this better understanding and interventionist industrial policy, women workers will continue to fair badly in a polarised labour market.

Notes

1 Skillset (from 2012 Creative Skillset) is one of the UK government's sector skills councils. These bodies are organised around specific industries and work with employers to define skills needs and skills standards in their particular industry.
2 *Economic and Industrial Democracy* vol. 33, no.1 2012.

References

Ainsworth, S. and Cutcher, L. (2008) 'Staging value and older women workers: When "something more" is too much', *International Journal of Work Organisation and Emotion*, 2 (4): 344–57.
Alvesson, M. (1994) 'Talking in organizations: Managing identity and impressions in an advertising agency', *Organization Studies*, 15(4): 535–63.
Appelbaum, E., Bailey, T., Berg, P. and Kalleberg, A. (2006) 'Organizations and the intersection of work and family: a comparative perspective' in S. Ackroyd, R. Batt, P. Thompson and P. S. Tolbert (eds) *The Oxford Handbook of Work and Organization*, Oxford: Oxford University Press.
Banks, M. and O'Connor, J. (2009) 'After the creative industries', *International Journal of Cultural Policy*, 15(4): 365–73.
Banks, M. and Milestone, K. (2011) 'Individualization, gender and cultural work', *Gender, Work and Organization*, 18(1): 73–89.
Banyard, K. (2010) *The Equality Illusion: The Truth about Women and Men Today*, London: Faber and Faber.
Belisle, D. (2006) 'A labour force for the consumer century: Commodification in Canada's Largest department stores, 1890 to 1940', *Labour/Le Travail*, 58: 107–44.
Broadbridge, A. (2007) 'Dominated by women: Managed by men? The career development process of retail managers', *International Journal of Retail & Distribution Management*, 35(12): 956–74.

Carré, F., Tilly, C., van Klaveren, M. and Voss-Dahm, D. (2010) 'Retail jobs in comparative perspective', in J. Gautié and J. Schmitt (eds) *Low Wage Work in a Wealthy World*, New York: Russell Sage Foundation.

Christopherson, S. (2008) 'Beyond the self-expressive creative worker: An industry perspective on entertainment media', *Theory, Culture and Society*, 25: 73–95.

Clifton, J., Dolphin, T. and Reeves, R. (2009), *Building A Better Balanced UK Economy*, London: Ippr.

Crang, P. and Martin, R. L. (1991) 'Mrs Thatcher's vision of the "new Britain" and other sides of the "Cambridge Phenomenon" ', *Environment and Planning D: Society and Space*, 9: 91–116.

DeFillippi, R. J. and Arthur, M. B. (1998) 'Paradox in project-based enterprise', *California Management Review*, 40(2): 125–39.

Department for Culture, Media and Sport (DCMS) (2001) *Creative Industries Mapping Document*, London: DCMS.

Dex, S., Willis, J., Paterson, R. and Sheppard, E. (2000) 'Freelance workers and contract uncertainty: The effects of contractual changes in the television industry', *Work, Employment and Society*, 14: 283–305.

Dowd, T., Liddle, K. and Blyler, M. (2005) 'Charting gender: The success of female acts in the US mainstream recording market, 1940–1990', *Research in the Sociology of Organizations*, 23: 81–123.

Dutton, E., Warhurst, C., Nickson, D. and Lockyer, C. (2005) 'Lone parents, the new deal and the opportunities and barriers to retail employment', *Policy Studies*, 26(1): 85–101.

Eagle, A. and Carli, L. (2007) 'Women and the labyrinth of leadership', *Harvard Business Review*, 85: 63–71.

Eikhof, D. R. (2012) 'A double-edged sword: 21st century workplace trends and gender equality', *Gender in Management*, 27(1): 7–22.

Eikhof, D. R. (2013) 'Making a living from creativity: Careers, employment and work in the creative industries', in J. Chan and K. Thomas (eds) *Handbook of Research on Creativity*, London: Edward Elgar.

Eikhof, D. R. and Warhurst, C. (2013) 'The promised land? Why social inequalities are systemic to the creative industries', *Employee Relations*, 35(5): 495–508.

Eikhof, D. R., Haunschild, A., Schößler, F. and Warhurst, C. (2013) 'Gender inequalities in the creative industries: A tale of two halves', unpublished mimeo, Universities of Stirling, Hannover, Trier and Warwick.

Ekelund, B. G. and Börjesson, M. (2002) 'The shape of the literary career: An analysis of publishing trajectories', *Poetics*, 30: 241–364.

England, P. (2005) 'Gender inequality in labor markets: The role of motherhood and segregation', *Social Politics*, 12: 264–88.

European Commission (EC) (2012) *Digital Agenda for Europe (Europe 2020 Flagship Initiative)*. Available at: http://ec.europa.eu/information_society/digital-agenda/index_en.htm (accessed 6 August 2012).

Flisbäck, M. (2013) 'Creating a life: The role of symbolic and economic structures in the gender dynamics of Swedish artists', *International Journal of Cultural Policy*, 19(4): 462–80.

Florida, R. (2004) *The Rise of the Creative Class*, New York: Basic Books.

Gill, R. (2002) 'Cool, creative and egalitarian? Exploring gender in project-based new media work in Europe', *Information, Communication and Society*, 5: 70–89.

Goos, M. and Manning, A. (2007) 'Lousy and lovely jobs: The rising polarization of work in Britain', *Review of Economics and Statistics*, 89: 118–33.

Grugulis, I. and Bozkurt, Ö. (eds) (2011) *Retail Work*, London: Palgrave.

Hall, R. and van den Broek, D. (2010) 'Aestheticising retail workers: Orientations of aesthetic labour in Australian fashion retail', *Economic and Industrial Democracy*, 33(1): 85–102.

Hartley, J. (ed.) (2005) *Creative Industries*, London: Routledge.

Henninger, A. and Gottschall, K. (2007) 'Freelancers in Germany's old and new media industry: Beyond standard patterns of work and life?', *Critical Sociology*, 33(1–2): 43–71.

Henry, C. (2009) 'Women and the creative industries: Exploring the popular appeal', *Creative Industries Journal*, 2(2): 143–60.

Hughes, C. (2011) 'Gender, craft labour and the creative sector', *International Journal of Cultural Policy*, 16(3): 305–21.

Hurley, J., Storrie, D. and Jungblut, J.-M. (2011) *Shifts in the Job Structure in Europe During the Great Recession*, Dublin: Eurofound.

Jarvis, H. and Pratt, A. (2006) 'Bringing it all back home: The extensification and "overflowing" of work. The case of San Francisco new media households', *Geoforum*, 37: 331–9.

Kalleberg, A. (2011) *Good Job, Bad Jobs: The Rise of Polarised and Precarious Employment Systems in the United States, 1970s to 2000s*, New York: Russell Sage Foundation.

King Sturge (2006) *The Contribution of the Retail Sector to the Economy, Employment and Regeneration*, London: King Sturge.

Leadbeater, C. and Oakley, K. (1999) *The Independents. Britain's New Cultural Entrepreneurs*, London: Demos.

Lloyd, C., Warhurst, C. and Dutton, E. (2013) 'The weakest link? Product market strategies, skill and pay in the hotel industry', *Work, Employment and Society*, 27(2): 254–71.

Marlow, S. and McAdam, M. (2013) 'Gender and entrepreneurship: Advancing debate and challenging myths. Exploring the mystery of the under-performing female entrepreneur', *International Journal of Entrepreneurial Behaviour and Research*, 19(1): 114–24.

Mason, G. and Osborne, M. (2008) 'Business strategies, work organisation, and low pay in United Kingdom retailing', in C. Lloyd, G. Mason and K. Mayhew (eds) *Low Wage Work in the UK*, New York: Russell Sage Foundation.

Mason, G., Mayhew, K., Osborne, M. and Stevens, P. (2008) 'Low pay, labor market institutions, and job quality in the United Kingdom', in C. Lloyd, G. Mason and K. Mayhew (eds) *Low Wage Work in the UK*, New York: Russell Sage Foundation.

Oakley, K. (2004) 'Not so cool Britannia: The role of the creative industries in economic development', *International Journal of Cultural Studies*, 7(1): 67–77.

O'Connor, S. (2013) 'Shoppers and services predicted to drive future growth', *The Financial Times*, 31 May, p. 2.

Peck, J. (2005) 'Struggling with the creative class', *International Journal of Urban and Regional Research*, 29(4): 740–70.

Pettinger, L. (2004) 'Brand culture and branded workers: Service work and aesthetic labour in fashion retail', *Consumption, Markets and Culture*, 7(2): 165–84.

Randle, K., Leung, W. F. and Kurian, J. (2007) 'Creating difference', Creative Industries Research and Consultancy Unit, University of Hertfordshire.

Shaheen, F., Seaford, C. and Chapman, J. (2012) *Good Jobs for Non-graduates*, London: New Economics Foundation.

Skillset (2005) *Survey of the Audio Visual Industries' Workforce 2005*, London: Skillset.

Skillset (2008a) *Feature Film Production. Workforce Survey Report 2008*, London: Skillset.

Skillset (2008b) *Balancing Children and Work in the Audio Visual Industries*, London: Skillset.

Skillset (2009) *Why her? Factors That Have Influenced the Careers of Successful Women in Film and Television*, London: Skillset.

Skillset (2010) *2010 Creative Media Workforce Survey*, London: Skillset.

Small Business Service (2003) *A Strategic Framework for Women's Enterprise*, London: DTI Small Business.

Smith, M. (2013) 'Abercrombie & Fitch under fire again for cool kids comment', *The Guardian Express*. Available at: http://guardianlv.com, 10 May (accessed 2 September 2014).

Tomlinson, J. (2006) 'Part-time occupational mobility in the service industries: Regulation, work commitment and occupational closure', *The Sociological Review*, 54(1): 66–86.

United Nations Conference on Trade and Development (2010) *Creative Economy Report 2008*, New York: UNDP.

United Nations Conference on Trade and Development (2011a) *Strengthening the Creative Industries for Development in Mozambique*, New York and Geneva: United Nations.

United Nations Conference on Trade and Development (2011b) *Strengthening the Creative Industries for Development in Zambia*, New York and Geneva: United Nations.

Warhurst, C. (2010) 'The missing middle: Management in the creative industries', in B. Townley and N. Beech (eds) *The Discipline of Organising Creativity*, Cambridge: Cambridge University Press.

Warhurst, C. and Nickson, D. (2007) 'Employee experience of aesthetic labour in retail and hospitality', *Work, Employment and Society*, 21(1): 103–20.

Warhurst, C., Nickson, D., Witz, A. and Cullen, A.-M. (2000) 'Aesthetic labour in interactive service work: Some case study evidence from the "New" Glasgow', *Service Industries Journal*, 20(3): 1–18.

Williams, C. and Connell, C. (2010) '"Looking good and sounding right": Aesthetic labor and social inequality in the retail industry', *Work and Occupations*, 37(3): 349–77.

Wilson, R. A. and Homenidou, K. (2011) *Working Futures 2010–2020: Main Report*, Wath-upon-Dearne: UKCES.

6 Organisational perspectives on women's careers

Disappointments and opportunities

Polly Parker and Amanda Roan

Career is an overarching concept that comprises an individual's work-related experiences over time, and links individuals and society. Long considered a moving perspective (Hughes 1958), the career concept continues to evolve despite a marked lack of unity among career scholars about exact definitions (Arthur 2008). Traditional notions of career stem from the dominance of organisations in the twentieth century, giving rise to the normative context for career and its development. A stable predictable environment made it easy for people working within organisations to organise work to achieve specific goals and simultaneously enable career advancement to more senior positions through promotions and in an upward linear trajectory (Etzioni 1964).

The organisation man, so named in the seminal work by Whyte (1956), was associated with traditional careers and reliant on traditional socialised gender roles of male breadwinner and female homemaker (Moen and Roehling 2005). Norms of complete availability (Burke 1998) and devotion to work accentuated the boundary between life domains, meaning that women's careers were not widely accepted until the second half of the twentieth century. Previously, in advanced Western countries, women who had jobs were confined to a limited number of industries and occupations (Probert 1998), which they occupied for only a short time until their marriage, after which children and domestic responsibilities occupied their time. As women's presence in the labour force increased in the 1980s, dual career couples became more common and women gained entry into previously male domains (Blau *et al.* 2002).

The stability underpinning traditional models of career was interrupted in the 1980s, due to a range of factors including improved technology, global mobility, shifting demographics in the workplace, and altered expectations of the work–family interface. Unprecedented change followed. Career progression was predicated on continuous learning rather than one-off credentialing (Hall 2002). The career dynamic and the psychological contract, that is the individuals' beliefs about their terms and conditions of employment that are shaped by the organisation, were irrevocably changed; loyalty was less valued than in previous times, as the focus shifted to competence and performance (Rousseau 1995). Subsequently, a broader range of career choices emerged as career paths were neither clearly defined nor based on organisational longevity.

The broader range of options seemed important for women to afford different career decisions, and to be judged less on traditional models of success. However, women's careers today continue to reveal distinct career patterns reflecting unequal processes and outcomes compared with men (Duberley and Cohen 2009; Tharenou 2001). These patterns indicate that 'male defined constructions of work and career success continue to dominate organisational research and practice' (O'Neil et al. 2008: 734). The lack of women in senior positions in organisations indicates ongoing disadvantage (O'Neil et al. 2008; Reitman and Schneer 2008; Shapiro et al. 2008).

In this chapter we discuss women's careers in organisations. While we note that this context covers organisations of a variety of forms and sizes, we concentrate first on traditional organisations rather than the self-employed or contractors. We discuss factors that have supported and constrained women's career development. Our focus on women moving into senior positions reflects a measure of career equity in organisations. We discuss two key approaches used to explain women's career disadvantage within organisations before discussing new career forms and the impact they have had on women. We conclude with issues that affect the reality of women's career patterns.

Women's careers within an organisational context

Women's careers reflect the co-existence of both meaningful work and family in their lives (O'Neil et al. 2008). Difficulties from combining paid work and unpaid domestic labour have been described as a 'double shift' (Bratbert et al. 2002: 246), which obstructs progression and results in variable career patterns. Accommodating competing demands has led to more heterogeneous career patterns than those of men, marked by discontinuity and zigzags as women 'compose a life' (Bateson 1990:1). The deviation from conventional models suggests women's career experiences have been undervalued (Clarke 2010). Organisations require a separation of work and family domains, resulting in career decisions in which women are judged to lack ambition (Hofstede 2001) as they opt out of career tracks (Siegel 2000), take scenic routes, i.e. non-linear pathways (Ragins 2011) or lack commitment (Storey and Shrimpton 1991).

Human Resource management systems predominantly organise for, and reward, traditional career paths (O'Neil et al. 2008). The negative language associated with the choices that shun a primary emphasis on paid work highlights the liabilities for women's organisational careers (Shapiro et al. 2008). Research continues to focus on identifying impediments and barriers, such as lack of mentors, hostile organisational cultures, societal expectations and the needs of family to inform policy measures to effect change (Ismail and Ibrahim 2008; Rosser 2004; Williams et al. 2012).

Women's minority status and the presence of the male norm in corporations was recognised in Kanter's (1977) seminal work on women in management. Kanter's study highlighted the significance of organisational cultures, dominated by masculine norms and power structures, which allow informal structures such as the existence of men's clubs to exclude women from positions of power. Locker room culture, such as conversations dominated by sport or sexual innuendo, reinforce predominantly white male values and confirm positions of power (Maddock and Parkin cited in Simpson 1997: 122). The deeply embedded masculine norm in organisational processes and structures, coupled with the indivisibility of gendered practices, perpetuates acceptance of the male worker and the norm of their preferred career path (Acker 1990; Britton and Logan 2008; Williams et al. 2012).

Internationally, from the 1990s, the lack of upward mobility for women in organisations was attributed to a seemingly invisible barrier called the glass ceiling (Davidson and Cooper 1992; Durbin and Tomlinson 2010). Recently more appropriate metaphors such as the labyrinth or kaleidoscope invoke more accurate depictions of discrimination and lack of equal access to opportunity at all levels of advancement rather than a ceiling that prevents women from reaching senior positions. The labyrinth metaphor explicitly acknowledges 'the complexity and variety of challenges that women face' (Eagly and Carli 2007: 64), and the multiple, subtle and evasive career barriers, twists and turns women face in their personal career journey. Unequal career outcomes for women matter to individuals, and also to organisations wanting to recruit and select from a full talent pool (Baruch and Bozionelos 2010).

There are two key categories of approaches that address women's disadvantage, specifically, ensuring that women remain in the internal talent pool represented through the pipeline metaphor (Bennett 2011), and increasing the critical mass of women in organisations. The underlying assumption of the pipeline metaphor is that increasing the number of qualified women pushes them through the pipeline to longer and more successful careers. The model was first recognised in the careers of women in non-traditional industries. In a 1983 report, Berryman noted that the pipeline, including the entire trajectory of training and employment, narrowed for women (Bennett 2011). The metaphor has been further characterised as leaky to explain why women fall out at various points of career progression (Blickenstaff 2005; Emerick and Larsen 2011; Etzkowitz and Kemelgor 2001; Helfat et al. 2010).

The critical mass approach was 'borrowed from nuclear physics where it refers to the quantity needed to start a chain reaction, an irreversible turning point, a takeoff into a new situation or process' (Dahlerup 2006: 215). Obtaining a critical mass of women in masculine-dominated occupations or organisational contexts has fostered affirmative action campaigns and associated targets and quotas for women's participation. Both pipeline and critical mass approaches can be supported by numerous development initiatives such as mentoring, and personal and occupational development activities (Elstad and Ladegard 2012; Konrad et al. 2008).

Overall, improvement has been disappointingly slow. Women's lack of progression from entry level through the organisational ranks to senior management positions has not changed significantly in the last decade in most advanced Western economies. There has been a negligible increase in Australia – over the last decade – of females in executive ranks of the Australian Stock Exchange top 500 companies and, in 2012, women held only 9.2 per cent of board directorships (Equal Opportunity for Women in the Workplace Agency (EOWA 2012)). Similarly in the United Kingdom (UK), women represented only 16.7 per cent of its top listed (FTSE)

100 companies (Centre for Women and Democracy (CWD) 2013: 7). Despite being better educated than ever before

> These women step on the career ladder and work hard, with a position at the top firmly in sight ... However, several years down the track a different picture emerges – one where many have disappeared from the paid workforce or remain trapped in the *'marzipan layer'* [emphasis in the original] below senior management, leaving the higher ranks to be dominated by men.
> (Equality and Human Rights Commission 2011: 1)

The picture is similar worldwide, with some variation. In Europe there are higher levels of proportional representation at board level in countries such as Norway and France, where legally binding quotas for women have been set, or countries such as Sweden, where policies actively encourage women's boardroom participation (McKinsey & Co. 2012). In 2011, Sweden reported that 25 per cent of board membership was female, Norway 35 per cent and France 20 per cent (McKinsey & Co. 2012). Deloitte (2013) reported that in 2012 in the USA, the representation of women on boards was 16.6 per cent, while in China it was approximately 8 per cent and it was 7 per cent of listed companies in Brazil.

Not all women and men who enter the corporate world aspire to top management positions nor are these positions achievable for all. The current emphasis on the under-representation of women in senior positions by CEOs, equal rights campaigners, policy makers and career scholars, stems from the widespread agreement that the problem does not lie in women's abilities or commitment to the organisation (Carli and Eagly 2011). Indeed, it is an issue of access to talent and senior women are needed to influence change and create career opportunities (Meyerson and Fletcher 2000). However, women's numerical representation in levels and positions in organisations and linear pipelines tends to relate to traditional organisational forms. Organisations must respond to external environmental changes that affect career patterns, which we outline below.

The changing career landscape: the context for new forms of career

The external environment in which organisations operate changed from being predictable and stable to one known to be volatile, uncertain, complex and ambiguous (VUCA) (Johansen 2012). Globalisation enabled international competition and collaboration, and drove changes in technology allowing work to be out-sourced and off-shored. Organisations responded to the VUCA environment by downsizing, changing reporting lines and integrating and differentiating functions.

A new reality affected all workers and organisations of all sizes. Alternate forms of career emerged, less dependent on traditional organisational hierarchies and organisational boundaries, and more on the external environment (such as marketability of expertise), external networks and information, (Arthur and Rousseau 1996). Workers needed to identify opportunities for advancement both inside and outside their firms

(Williams et al. 2012: 551). Career security now meant being employable rather than employed, and the responsibility for that shifted to the employees (Fugate et al. 2004). New forms include boundaryless, protean and intelligent careers.

Boundaryless careers emerged when career patterns extended beyond the traditional organisational boundaries (Arthur and Rousseau 1996). Six forms of boundary conditions were suggested. Specifically identified were separate employers, marketability beyond organisations (as in academia), careers sustained through networks (such as in Real Estate), and when a person rejected a career opportunity for personal or family reasons. However the boundary separating work and home was omitted, despite the permeability of which might be expected to support women the most. Boundaryless careers suffer from a noted lack of empirical support for the concept despite theoretical acceptance of its predominance (Crozier 1999; Lazarova and Taylor 2009). The concept is usually narrowly interpreted, despite the broad conceptual idea (Sullivan and Arthur 2006). The agency associated with the boundaryless careers created stress, anxiety and insecurity for male and female workers but particularly for women (Williams et al. 2012).

The new career paradigm carried the expectation that people could integrate personal and professional lives (Fletcher and Bailyn 1996), and therefore advance women's career success (Fondas 1996). However, numerous studies found that this has not been the case for many women and men (Campbell et al. 2009; Durbin and Tomlinson 2010; Williams et al. 2012). Women had to choose between their careers and family relationships (Valcoeur and Talbot 2003); their careers were secondary, with many working part time (Reitman and Schneer 2008), and they were more likely than men to show extra-organisational mobility by moving employers, leading to different effects on objective and subjective career success (Ng et al. 2005). The shift from using objective measures of success – traditional markers such as status, titles and salaries (Heslin 2005) – to subjective measures including personal values, beliefs and aspirations, (Khapova et al. 2007) is another feature of the new career environment.

Focus on psychological measures of success led to the identification of the protean career (Hall 1976, 2004), driven by the individual, underpinned by individual values rather than organisational goals and predicated on continuously learning. Achievement through personal growth became more important than an upward trajectory or job titles (Hall 2002). Subjective criteria allowed women to explicitly include work and family priorities in their plans, allow for periods of interruption and reflect their personal values (Valcoeur and Talbot 2003). They were more likely to reach their career-related goals. Furthermore, the achievement of such goals can in turn feed into objective outcome measures (Hall and Chandler 2005). Women on protean paths were as successful in terms of income, management level and career satisfaction as those on traditional paths (Reitman and Schneer 2003). Thus career success for women, measured against subjective criteria, does not reflect the disadvantage evident from objective measures (Ng et al. 2005).

The intelligent career model (Arthur et al. 1995; DeFillippi and Arthur 1994) elicits the subjective career through three ways of knowing: individuals' knowing-why (motivation and identity), knowing-how (skills and expertise) and knowing-whom (relationships and reputation). The three ways of knowing enable individuals to respond directly to organisations' areas of competitive advantage (their culture, know-how and networks), thus providing a direct link between an organisation's operations and the career strengths of employees working within them.

Knowing-why highlights a person's motivation to work, personal values and beliefs, identity and individual interpretations that take into account the different amounts of energy and time that may change across life and work domains at different life stages, a factor that affects women in particular (Powell and Mainiero 1992). Knowing-why includes the sacrifices of non-work activities taken to attain organisational goals (Bateman and Crant 1993), and has strong correlations with subjective career success (Eby *et al.* 2003). Knowing-how focuses on work-related knowledge and expertise that accumulates human capital to benefit individuals and organisations. Human capital factors are considered the most important for men and women (Lortie-Lussier and Rinfret 2005), yet are critical in women's careers (O'Neil *et al.* 2008). Knowing-whom encompasses relationships that provide support, access to information and transmission of reputation, thus drawing attention to the relational strength of women. The emphasis and centrality of relationships in women's lives provides connection, support, attachment and influence, a primary differentiator between male and female careers (Hall 1996).

A relational perspective was proposed to explain differences between men and women's growth and development, using language and concepts from women's experience (Belenky *et al.* 1986; Fletcher and Ragins 2007; Mossholder *et al.* 2011). A relational context 'allows for a different understanding of career choice, career development stages, multiple life roles, decision making, and career success' (Crozier 1999: 244). Women incorporate relationships into their career decisions from an earlier age than men, who typically come to value relationships later in life (Mainiero and Sullivan 2006). For instance, the cross-over point about mid-life, when women move into the realm of work and men embrace the home life more fully, has long been recognised (Giele 1980). A large body of literature suggests that women's attention to their careers changes at different life stages (O'Neil and Bilimoria 2005). Indeed, O'Neil and Bilimoria (2005: 170) argue that women find a renewed sense of purpose and energy for work pursuits, citing Margaret Mead's concept of 'post-menopausal zest'. Regardless, 'women encounter numerous double-binds as they drive their careers' (Shapiro *et al.* 2008: 311). Many of the double binds are due to the demands of personal and family relationships at the various life stages. McMahon *et al.* (2012) demonstrated that career adaptability remains important for older women and is embedded within the networks and the broader social systems in which they live.

Women's changing focus is well explained by Manierio and Sullivan's (2006) kaleidoscope career theory, which describes three key foci that women face in their career crafting: authenticity, balance, and challenge. Challenge, which dominates early career, is replaced by a search for greater balance in mid-career, and a focus on authenticity in late career. The kaleidoscope metaphor reflects the way women embed career within a larger life context and its changing demands at different stages. Personal adjustments are made to harmonise with other circumstances, so that the career does not overtake their lives (Mainiero and Sullivan 2006).

New career patterns: problems and possibilities

The emerging career patterns discussed above are highly attractive to women and allow them to retain family as central in their lives. Promoted by new career theories, Shapiro et al. (2008) proffered a self-employed model of career in which women act as career-self agents. They explain that women's decisions are not necessarily driven by choice, but because of life circumstances such as the birth of children or elderly care and other life commitments, they cannot meet the temporal and other demands of work as a primary model of career (Shapiro et al. 2008: 310). Women, as career self-agents, may be able to craft careers based on personal values and subjective career success, yet this individually focused perspective is only one aspect of the dynamic interplay with the organisation.

Women still face many problems in the way they are viewed by organisations, their families and society (McKinsey & Co., 2012; Shapiro et al. 2008). New forms of career have not changed the cultural aspects within organisations, so women continue to face discrimination and disadvantage when their career paths are not aligned with traditional structures. Although many overt barriers have been largely addressed through equal employment opportunity legislation and flexible work options, as previously discussed, organisations are still not represented by women in equal numbers at senior levels across the globe (Carli and Eagly 2011; Catalyst Census 2012; Equality and Human Rights Commission 2011; McKinsey & Co. 2012). However, studies of individual career patterns do not account for the disadvantage of not choosing to take the options which are seen to be 'generally incompatible with ascending to the ranks of senior management positions' (O'Neil et al. 2008: 731). Furthermore, Shacklock et al. (2007: 163) showed 'a gendered effect in the desire to work in retirement', and suggested that to meet labour shortages organisations need to create environments and offer flexible work options to attract older women to stay in or return to the workforce.

We note two key issues for women's career progress in organisations. First, it is not clear how the presence of a critical mass of women in an environment of career self-agency supports progress within organisations until organisational cultures change so that masculine models of work stop resulting in advantages for men. One factor would be for men to embrace change and support and sponsor women for more senior roles. A mass of self-managed career agents may provide the human resources needed by organisations, yet the position for women may still be precarious. An example, and well documented already, is women's over-representation in part-time and casual work (Baxter et al. 2008) and the persistence of a gender pay gap, particularly across life-long earnings (Campbell et al. 2009; Jenkins, 2006). Further, earning power is exacerbated when women are mostly employed in feminised industries (e.g. teaching, nursing, etc.) which draw lower salaries (Perales 2013).

The second issue is how to extend the current approaches to women's careers, such as blocking the leaky pipeline (Blickenstaff 2005), to recognise new career forms. The policies and practices within organisations must recognise how women develop human and social capital in a variety of career patterns. Awareness of these critical activities is less clear in the absence of organisational structures. Equal outcomes are possible for women despite their career patterns if organisations commit to developing cultures that interrupt the masculine norms and truly support those patterns. Only then can women remain in the pipeline to senior positions so that at the most senior levels, selection is from the full range of talent available.

In conclusion, we agree with Shapiro *et al.* (2008: 328) that 'today's discourse as it is currently configured lets organisations off the hook'. Much of the current dialogue focuses on women and their individual choices rather than looking at organisational processes and practices as contributors to the challenges women face when juggling work and family commitments.

References

Acker, J. (1990) 'Hierarchies, jobs, bodies: A theory of gendered organizations', *Gender and Society*, 4: 139–58.

Arthur, M. B. (2008) 'Examining contemporary careers: A call for interdisciplinary inquiry', *Human Relations*, 61: 163–86.

Arthur, M. B. and Rousseau, D. M. (eds) (1996) *The Boundaryless Career. A New Employment Principle for a New Organizational Era*, New York: Oxford University Press.

Arthur, M. B., Claman, P. H. and DeFillippi, R. J. (1995) 'Intelligent enterprise, intelligent career', *Academy of Management Executive*, 9: 7–20.

Baruch, Y. and Bozionelos, N. (2010) 'Career Issues', in S. Zedeck (ed.) *APA Handbook of Industrial and Organizational Psychology*, Washington, DC: American Psychological Association.

Bateman, T. S. and Crant, J. M. (1993) 'The proactive component of organizational behavior', *Journal of Organizational Behavior*, 14: 103–18.

Bateson, M. C. (1990) *Composing A Life*, New York: Plume Printing.

Baxter, J., Hewitt, B. and Haynes, M. (2008) 'Life course transitions and housework: Marriage, parenthood and time on housework', *Journal of Marriage and Family*, 70: 259–72.

Belenky, M., Clichy, B., Goldberger, N. and Tarule, J. (1986) *Women's Ways of Knowing: The Development of Self, Voice and Mind*, New York: Basic Books.

Bennett, C. (2011) 'Beyond the leaky pipeline: Consolidating understanding and incorporating new research about women's scientific careers', in *The UK Brussels Economic Review*, 54: 149–76.

Blau, F. D., Ferber, M. A. and Winkler, A. E. (2002) *The Economics of Women, Men and Work*, Upper Saddle River, NJ: Prentice Hall.

Blickenstaff, J. C. (2005) 'Women and science careers: Leaky pipeline or genders filter?' *Gender and Education*, 17: 369–86.

Bratbert, E., Dahl, S.-A. and Risa, A. E. (2002) 'The double burden: Do combinations of career and family obligations increase sickness absence among women?' *European Sociological Review*, 18: 233–49.

Britton, D. M. and Logan, L. (2008) 'Gendered organizations: Progress and prospects', *Sociology Compass*, 2: 107–21.

Burke, R. J. (1998) 'Dual career couples: Are men still advantaged?' *Psychological Reports*, 82: 209–10.

Campbell, I., Whitehouse, G. and Baxter, J. H. (2009) 'Australia: Casual employment, part-time employment and the resilience of the male-breadwinner model', in L. Vosko, M. Macdonald. and I. Campbell (eds) *Gender and the Contours of Precarious Employment*, London: Routledge.

Carli, L. L. and Eagly, A. H. (2011) 'Gender and leadership', in A. Bryman, D. Collinson, K. Grint, B. Jackson and M. Uhl-Bien (eds) *The Sage Handbook of Leadership*, London: Sage.

Catalyst census (2012) *Catalyst Census: Fortune 500 Women Board Directors*, New York: Catalyst.

Centre for Women and Democracy (CWD) (2013) *Sex and Power – Who Runs Britain?* Leeds: Centre for Women and Democracy.

Clarke, M. (2010) 'Advancing women's careers through leadership development programs', *Employee Relations*, 33: 498–515.

Crozier, S. D. (1999) 'Women's career development in a "relational" context', *International Journal for the Advancement of Counselling*, 21: 231–47.

Dahlerup, D. (2006) 'The story of the theory of critical mass', *Politics and Gender*, 2: 511–22.

Davidson, M. J. and Cooper, C. (1992) *Shattering the Glass Ceiling: The Woman Manager*, London: Paul Chapman Publishing.

Defillippi, R. J. and Arthur, M. B. (1994) 'The boundaryless career: A competency-based perspective', *Journal of Organizational Behavior*, 15: 307–24.

Deloitte (2013) *Women in the Board Room A Global Perspective*, UK: Deloitte Global.

Duberley, J. and Cohen, L. (2009) 'Gendering career capital: An investigation of scientific careers', *Journal of Vocational Behavior*, 76: 187–97.

Durbin, S. and Tomlinson, J. (2010) 'Female part-time managers: Networks and career mobility', *Work, Employment and Society*, 24: 621–40.

Eagly, A. H. and Carli, L. L. (2007) 'Women and the labyrinth of leadership', *Harvard Business Review*, September: 62–71.

Eby, L. T., Butts, M. and Lockwood, A. (2003) 'Predictors of success in the era of the boundaryless career', *Journal of Organizational Behavior*, 24: 689–708.

Elstad, B. and Ladegard, G. (2012) 'Women on corporate boards: Key influencers or tokens?', *Journal of Management and Governance*, 16: 595–615.

Emerick, R. and Larsen, B. O. (2011) 'The first steps into a "leaky pipeline". A longitudinal study of the pipeline within a Danish university', *Brussels Economic Review*, 54: 213–36.

Equal opportunity for women in the workplace agency (EOWA) (2012) *Australian Census of Women in Leadership*, Canberra: EOWA.

Equality and human rights commission (2011) *Sex and Power – Who Runs Britain?* London: EHRC.

Etzioni, A. (1964) *Modern Organizations*, Englewood Cliffs, NJ: Prentice Hall.

Etzkowitz, H. and Kemelgor, C. (2001) 'Gender inequality in science: A universal condition?' *Minerva*, 39: 239–57.

Fletcher, J. and Ragins, B. (2007) 'Stone Center relational cultural theory', in B. Ragins and K. E. Kram (eds) *The Handbook of Mentoring at Work. Theory, Research and Practice*, Thousand Oaks, CA: Sage.

Fletcher, J. K. and Bailyn, L. (1996) 'Challenging the last boundary: Reconnecting work and family', in M. B. Arthur and D. M. Rousseau (eds) *The boundaryless Career A New Employment Principle For a new Organizational Era*, New York: Oxford University Press.

Fondas, N. (1996) 'Feminization at work: Career implications', in M. B. Arthur and D. M. Rousseau (eds) *The Boundaryless Career: A New Employment Principle For a New Organizational Era*, New York: Oxford University Press.

Fugate, M., Kinicki, A. J. and Ashforth, B. E. (2004) 'Employability: A psycho-social construct, its dimensions, and applications', *Journal of Vocational Behavior*, 65: 14–38.

Giele, J. (1980) 'Crossovers: New themes in adult roles and life cycle', in D. McGuigan (ed.) *Women's Lives: New Theory, Research and Policy*, Ann Arbor: Center for Continuing Education of Women, University of Michigan.

Hall, D.T. (1976) *Careers in Organizations*, Pacific Palisades, CA: Goodyear.
Hall, D.T. (1996) 'Long live the career!', in D.T. Hall and Associates (eds), *The Career is Dead. Long Live the Career*, San Francisco, CA: Jossey Bass.
Hall, D.T. (2002) *Careers In and Out of Organizations*, Thousand Oaks, CA: Sage.
Hall, D. T. (2004) 'The protean career: A quarter-century journey', *Journal of Vocational Behavior*, 65: 1–13.
Hall, D.T. and Chandler, D.A. (2005) 'Psychological success: When career is a calling', *Journal of Organizational Behavior*, 26: 155–76.
Helfat, C. E., Dubois, C. L. Z. and Fox-Cardamore, L. (2010) 'The pipeline to the top: Women and men in the top executive ranks of US corporations', *Academy of Management Perspectives*, 20: 42–64.
Heslin, P. (2005) 'Conceptualizing and evaluating career success', *Journal of Organizational Behavior*, 26: 113–36.
Hofstede, G. (2001) *Culture's Consequences: Comparing Values, Behaviors, Institutions and Organizations Across Nations*, Thousand Oaks, CA: Sage.
Hughes, E. (1958) *Men and Their Work*, Glencoe, IL: Free Press.
Ismail, M. and Ibrahim, M. (2008) 'Barriers to career progression faced by women: Evidence from a Malaysian multinational oil company', *Gender in Management: An International Journal*, 23: 1754–2413.
Jenkins, A. (2006) 'Women, lifelong learning and transitions into employment', *Work Employment & Society*, 20: 309–28.
Johansen, B. (2012) *Leaders Make the Future*, San Francisco: Berrett-Koehler.
Kanter, R. M. (1977) *Women and Men of the Corporation*, New York: Basic Books.
Khapova, S., Arthur, M. B. and Wilderom, C. P. M. (2007) 'The subjective career in the knowledge economy', in H. Gunz and M.A. Peiperl (eds), *Handbook of Career Studies*, New York: Sage.
Konrad, A., Kramer, V. and Erkut, S. (2008) 'Critical mass: The impact of three or more women on corporate boards', *Organizational Dynamics*, 37: 145–64.
Lazarova, M. and Taylor, S. (2009) 'Boundaryless careers, social capital, and knowledge management: Implications for organizational performance', *Journal of Organizational Behavior*, 30: 119–39.
Lortie-Lussier, M. and Rinfret, N. (2005) 'Determinants of objective and subjective success of men and women', *International Review of Administrative Sciences*, 71: 607–24.
Mainiero, L. A. and Sullivan, S. E. (2006) *The Opt-out Revolution: Why People are Leaving Companies to Create Kaleidoscope Careers*, Mountain View, CA: Davies-Black.
McKinsey & Co. (2012) *Making the Breakthrough*. Paris. Available at: www.mckinsey.com/features/women_matter (accessed 21 April 2014).
McMahon, M., Watson, M. and Bimrose, J. (2012) 'Career adaptability: A qualitative understanding from the stories of older women, *Journal of Vocational Behavior*, 80: 762–8.
Meyerson, D. E. and Fletcher, J. K. (2000) 'A modest manifesto for shattering the glass ceiling', *Harvard Business Review*, 78: 126–36.
Moen, P. and Roehling, P. (2005) *Carer Mystique: Cracks in the American Dream*, Lanham, MD: Rowland and Littlefield.
Mossholder, K. W., Richardson, H. A. and Settoon, R. P. (2011) 'Human resource systems and helping in organizations: A relational perspective', *Academy of Management Review*, 36: 33–52.
Ng, T.W. H., Eby, L.T., Sorensen, K. L. and Feldman, D. C. (2005) 'Predictors of objective and subjective career success. A meta-analysis', *Personnel Psychology*, 58: 367–408.

O'Neil, D. A. and Bilimoria, D. (2005) 'Women's career development phases: Idealism, Endurance and Reinvention', *Career Development International*, 10(3): 168–89.

O'Neil, D. A., Hopkins, M. M. and Bilimoria, D. (2008) 'Women's careers at the start of the 21st century: Patterns and paradoxes', *Journal of Business Ethics*, 80: 727–43.

Perales, F. (2013) 'Occupational sex-segregation, specialized human capital and wages: Evidence from Britain', *Work Employment & Society*, 27: 600–20.

Powell, G. N. and Mainiero, L. A. (1992) 'Cross-currents in the river of time: Conceptualizing the complexities of women's careers', *Journal of Management*, 18: 215–37.

Probert, B. (1998) *Working life: Arguments About Work in Australian Society*, Ringwood, Australia: Penguin.

Ragins, B. R. (2011) 'Relational mentoring: A positive approach to mentoring at work', in K. S. Cameron, and G. M. Spreitzer (eds) *The Oxford Handbook of Positive Organizational Scholarship*, New York and Oxford: Oxford University Press.

Reitman, F. and Schneer, J. A. (2003) 'The promised path: A longitudinal study of managerial careers', *Journal of Managerial Psychology*, 18: 60–75.

Reitman, F. and Schneer, J. A. (2008) 'Enabling the new careers of the 21st century', *Organization Management Journal*, 5: 17–28.

Rosser, S.V. (2004) *Science and the Glass Ceiling – Academic Women Scientists and the Struggle for Success*, New York: Routledge.

Rousseau, D. M. (1995) *Psychological Contracts in Organizations*, Thousand Oaks, CA: Sage.

Shacklock, K., Fulop, L. and Hort, L. (2007) 'Managing older worker exit and re-entry practices: A "revolving" door?', *Asia Pacific Journal of Human Resources*, 45: 151–67.

Shapiro, M., Ingols, C. and Blake-Beard, S. (2008) 'Confronting career double binds: Implications for women, organizations and career practitioners', *Journal of Career Development*, 34: 309–33.

Siegel, P. H. (2000) 'Using peer mentors during periods of uncertainty, *Leadership and Organization*', 21: 243–53.

Simpson, R. (1997) 'Have times changed? Career barriers and the token woman manager', *British Journal of Management*, 8: 121–30.

Storey, K. and Shrimpton, M. (1991) '"Fly-in" mining: Pluses and minuses of long distance commuting', *Mining Review*, 15: 27–35.

Sullivan, S. E. and Arthur, M. B. (2006) 'The evolution of the boundaryless career: Examining physical and psychological passages', *Journal of Vocational Behavior*, 69: 19–29.

Tharenou, P. (2001) 'Going up? Do traits and informal social processes predict advancing in management?', *Academy of Management Journal*, 44: 1005–17.

Valcoeur, M. and Talbot, P. S. (2003) 'Gender, family and career in the era of boundarylessness: Determinants and effects of intra- and inter-organizational mobility', *International Journal of Human Resource Management*, 14: 768–87.

Whyte, W. H. (1956) *The Organization Man*, New York: Simon & Schuster.

Williams, C. L., Muller, C. and Kilanski, K. (2012) 'Gendered organizations in the new economy', *Gender & Society*, 26: 549–73.

Part II
National studies
Hearing the voices of older women

7 Methodological considerations

Mark Watson, Jenny Bimrose and Mary McMahon

This chapter describes the methodology followed in the research on older women's career trajectories that was conducted by an international, multidisciplinary team from nine countries and representative of the disciplines of psychology, sociology, business, management and education. While the detail of individual country sample demographics and results are provided in subsequent chapters of this section of the book, the present chapter describes the methodological parameters within which all nine countries were required to conduct their research. The research methodology has been previously, albeit briefly, described in the literature (Bimrose *et al.* 2013, 2014; McMahon *et al.* 2013). The present chapter collates and expands on these earlier descriptions.

The aim of the research into older women's work and learning trajectories was to consider the potential recursiveness between their career stories and career theory, policy, research and practice. More specifically, it considered how the women's career stories could guide the development of career policy and practice and how the latter could support the career development of older women. There has been increasing concern that understanding individual career development needs to go beyond the scientific paradigms that have informed most career theories to date (O'Neil *et al.* 2008; Patton and McMahon 2006; Young and Valach 2000). Thus a qualitative, interpretative research approach, based on grounded theory, was considered the most appropriate methodology for the research.

Qualitative research allows for an in-depth exploration that can 'unpack and ultimately [to] transform the intertwined contextual and individual factors that shape our working lives' (Blustein *et al.* 2005: 367). In addition, qualitative research considers the real life contexts of individuals and attempts to describe such life experiences in everyday language (Polkinghorne 2005). Adopting a qualitative research approach is considered particularly appropriate when it focuses on more neglected, under-researched populations, where less is known and where existing theory is regarded as questionable (Blustein *et al.* 2005). Qualitative research investigates real life in context and concerns itself with vivid, dense and full descriptions of the phenomena studied in natural language. However, researchers need to be flexible with this type of research and ensure that they do not prejudge the issues that they seek to explore and describe. The present research aims to contribute to career theory, policy, research and practice that is internationally applicable to women and that explores how age and gender can interactively influence older women's career development.

Within qualitative research, grounded theory is recognised as an established paradigm and this approach was adopted for the present international project. Grounded theory researches a chosen issue with the major goal of constructing a theory, grounded in research data, that will help us better understand the researched issue (Charmaz 2007). In this way, theory is developed that reflects the realities of the population studied (Fassinger 2005; Glaser and Strauss 1967; Lapour and Heppner 2009). In addition, the grounded theory method guides data collection and analysis through a systematic process while, at the same time, allowing for an interpretivist concern for subjectivity and meaning (King and Horrocks 2010).

Qualitative research reflects context and takes an holistic approach to investigation. Quantitative research, on the other hand, has been criticised for decontextualising individuals' career development and failing to provide a more holistic perspective of influences that impact on career development. The use of qualitative research in women's career development is endorsed by O'Neil et al. (2008), who stress both a narrative and a grounded theory approach in calling for research to provide a 'voice to women's own career and life experiences with the intent of building integrated theory about these experiences' (ibid.: 737).

The following subsections of the chapter describe the methodological considerations of this international research project. While these considerations are discussed separately, it is important to note that in grounded theory sampling, research design, data coding, data collection and data analysis are interrelated. Such a methodological approach thus provides flexibility in that it accommodates changes in research focus as well as the ongoing generation of hypotheses and key concepts (Bryman and Burgess 1994; Charmaz 2007).

Sampling

The sampling procedure reflected the grounded theory approach of the research. Blustein et al. (2005) state that purposive sampling is appropriate when data need to be generated that consider new conceptual frameworks or categories. Adult women participants were recruited across the nine nations in ways that were appropriate to the researchers' contexts. For example, participants were drawn from previous on-line survey research in England, where those willing to participate and who fitted the sampling criteria were contacted by email. Another form of sampling was to send out an invitation to participate through an employer website (e.g. in South Africa). Alternatively, information about the research project was distributed to career counsellors (e.g. in Australia), who then made the information and the researcher's contact details available to women in the specified age group. Common to all purposive sampling procedures across the nine countries were several criteria that needed to be met. These included informed consent, anonymity and voluntary participation. In addition, pseudonyms have been used throughout the research to protect the confidentiality of participants. Ethical clearance was secured where required.

Twelve women (with the exception of Canada, where there were 13 women) were interviewed in depth from each of nine countries: Australia, Argentina, Canada, China, England, Germany, Italy, Portugal and South Africa. The research was initiated in 2009 in Australia, England and South Africa and grew over a four-year period to 2012. Importantly, the spread of countries has included both developed and developing countries as well as contrasting national economic contexts. The research findings over the following nine chapters are based on 109 interviews of older women's career stories of their work and learning pathways. The lower and upper brackets for defining older women were determined in terms of the literature. The lower age bracket was set at 45 years, as this is considered the benchmark for describing mature age workers. It is also an age after which it becomes difficult for women to re-enter the workforce once they have left (Commonwealth of Australia 2001). In terms of the participating countries at the time of the data collection, the older age bracket of 65 years was commonly the age beyond which women's labour market participation dramatically reduced.

While the sample demographics are described per country over the following nine chapters, an overview of the total sample of 109 women is provided here. The following was the age range of the sample in five-year categories: 45 to 50 ($N = 48$); 51 to 55 ($N = 32$); 56 to 60 ($N = 2$); and 61 to 65 ($N = 17$). In terms of marital status, 68 participants were married or in a long-term relationship, 18 were single, 19 were divorced or separated and 4 were widowed. The participants' educational levels ranged from no formal education ($N = 1$), primary ($N = 4$) and secondary ($N = 14$) education through to tertiary level (sub-degree) ($N = 15$), degree ($N = 38$), postgraduate diploma ($N = 6$), honours ($N = 4$), masters ($N = 21$) and doctorate ($N = 6$). In terms of the employment status of participants there were 67 full time, 16 part time, 7 self-employed, 7 unemployed, 7 retired, 1 in a vocation (this is the participant's wording for a religious minister), 3 students, and 1 voluntary worker.

Data collection

A frequently-used method for gathering data in qualitative research is interviewing. Use was made of semi-structured interviews of approximately one hour in duration. Semi-structured interviews seek to describe the realities of interviewees' lives in order to interpret the meaning of their description (King and Horrocks 2010). In the context of the present research, semi-structured interviews were considered particularly appropriate as they allowed for the immediate recording of in-depth contextual descriptions of the older women participants' learning and career development and their career changes and transitions. A number of different procedures, determined by the research contexts, were followed in conducting the semi-structured interviews, varying from telephonic interviews to face-to-face interviews or a combination of these methods. All 109 semi-structured interviews were recorded and transcribed verbatim.

The interview protocol focused on the domains of: (1) demographic information; (2) present, past and future work and learning experiences; (3) previous work and learning transitions; (4) learning from previous transitions; and (5) moving forward. The interview thus encouraged the women participants to reflect on connections between their work and learning experiences, the contextual influences on those experiences, and their feelings about and reactions to those experiences. The interview protocol was co-developed by the researchers through several iterations. It provided in-depth contextual accounts of the women's career and learning trajectories and, consistent with grounded theory method, it allowed for the focus to shift marginally in order to reflect insights gained as the women's stories unfolded.

As much as quantitative research, qualitative research requires that issues such as validity are addressed. Thus there is a need to ensure that the data described in qualitative research are trustworthy. In the present research, four criteria of trustworthiness (Lincoln and Guba, 1985) were considered in order to validate the findings. These criteria have previously been reported on in relation to the present research (Bimrose *et al.* 2014; Bimrose *et al.* 2013) but are summated here. The first criterion is credibility, which is defined as allowing others to recognise the experiences contained within the interpretation of participants' stories. In the present research this involved a number of strategies such as spending sufficient time with participants, examining the interview techniques used, ensuring the use of participants' words and a process of peer validation in which the researchers read transcripts other than those of their national sample (Thomas and Magilvy 2011). The second criterion involves the issue of the transferability of findings to other contexts and other participants. This was demonstrated in the present research by describing the research population in depth, and providing both demographic and geographic information. Dependability has been described as the third validity criterion in qualitative research, and it requires that other researchers should be able to follow the decision trail used by the researchers (Thomas and Magilvy 2011). This was addressed in the present research through a detailed description of the methodology underpinning the research. Finally, the fourth validity criterion of confirmability is evident in the present research because credibility, transferability and dependability were established.

Data analysis and coding

A grounded theory approach within qualitative research suggests systematic and rigorous procedures for interpreting and analysing rich qualitative data (Charmaz 2007; King and Horrocks 2010). A grounded theory approach is generally based on the reading of participant transcripts, the subsequent identification of variables (for example, themes) and the possible interrelationship of these themes (Blustein *et al.* 2005). This coding process in qualitative research involves both the differentiation and combination of transcribed data, and a process of reflection on the coded data (Miles and Huberman 1994).

In the present research, the data analysis and coding initially involved a three-stage, ten-phase thematic analysis across three countries (Australia, England and South Africa) (McMahon *et al.* 2012). While the thematic analysis involved regular meetings, the international nature of the present research called for the frequent use of remote methods such as Skype and email, as well as face-to face meetings, when possible. The first stage of the analysis involved five phases of code category development, using one transcript from each country that resulted in a set of nine major code categories and 19 subcodes. The five phases of the data analysis in Stage 1 are described in greater detail below.

Phase 1 (data familiarisation) involved each researcher independently reading the transcript of one of their own interviews and identifying key codes. Thus this phase involved independent scrutiny of three interview transcripts, each originating from one of the three participating countries. Criteria used to select the first transcript reflected researcher preference. For example, two researchers simply selected the transcript of the first interview undertaken for the investigation and the third researcher selected the sixth interview completed. An initial reading of these transcripts resulted in the development of 13 Phase 1 codes (transition, work, role balance, role identify, self, time, finance, support, planning, role salience, learning, role impact and decision-making), and 14 subcodes.

Phase 2 (independent analysis) involved researchers scrutinising and validating each other's transcripts, with each researcher taking the transcripts of the other two researchers and reviewing their assignation of broad codes. A few minor queries were resolved by discussion, which continued until the resolution of each query was reached. On completion of this phase, three sets of researcher codes had emerged, each aligned to one country transcript.

Phase 3 (emergence of master codes) involved the three researchers developing common codes. Initially, two researchers analysed each other's transcript according to their own set of Phase 1 codes. Thus each transcript had two sets of codes, which the researchers discussed in order to resolve discrepancies. This resulted in a rationalisation of the two sets of codes and the emergence of an initial set of master codes. In Phase 4 (initial validation of master codes), the Phase 3 codes were compared with the codes developed by the third researcher in Phase 1. The correspondence of both sets of codes was examined and their possible convergence considered. Subsequent discussion amongst all three researchers resulted in the refinement of the Phase 3 codes and ultimately the development of Phase 4 codes.

Phase 5 (trustworthiness of codes) involved intense scrutiny and discussion of the Phase 4 codes in comparison with the previous codes from Stage 1 to ensure both the comprehensiveness and trustworthiness of the master codes. This resulted in the 13 original codes being rationalised into 11 master codes and 19 subcodes.

The second stage consisted of a further four phases of refinement of the codes identified in the first stage on a further transcript from each of the three countries involved in the initial stage of the research. The first phase of refinement in Stage 2 was Phase 6 (defining and applying the master codes), and this involved the random selection of a fourth transcript from the remaining 33 transcripts from the three countries. Each researcher independently analysed this transcript using the master codes, noting questions and points of clarification on the transcript. This was followed by a comparison of codes across researchers and a discussion of discrepancies until agreement was reached. Refinement of the definitions followed, together with a second iteration of the master codes that merged some codes. By the end of this process, there had been a rationalisation of master codes from 11 to 8 and subcodes from 19 to 18.

In Phase 7 (refinement of the master codes) a fifth transcript was randomly selected from the remaining 32 transcripts from the three countries. This was, fortuitously, from a different country to that of the transcript analysed in Phase 6. Each researcher independently analysed the fifth transcript using the master codes, noting questions and points of clarification on the transcript. This was followed by a comparison of codes across researchers and a discussion of any discrepancies until full agreement was reached. Agreement across the three researchers was reached on the analysis of the fifth transcript, with the addition of one code and one subcode, to make nine master codes and 19 subcodes.

An independent coder was introduced to the research team and trained in the codes for Phase 8 (verification by an independent coder). This independent coder analysed the fifth transcript. The research team then compared the codes of the independent coder with the codes agreed on during Phase 7. Subsequent discussion between the research team and the independent coder resolved any remaining discrepancies and resulted in a minor refinement of code descriptions and definitions, but no additional codes.

In the final phase of Stage 2, Phase 9 (saturation of codes), a sixth transcript was randomly selected from the remaining transcripts of the third country. The independent coder analysed this transcript using the refined master codes from Phase 8. The research team then examined the codes and confirmed agreement. Nine master codes, together with 19 subcodes, emerged as the final version.

A subsequent third stage and Phase 10 (application of codes) of the initial data coding and analysis comprised the deductive application of the developed framework to the remaining interview scripts. Analysis of the interview scripts was undertaken using the software package, QSR NVivo 9, the main function of which is to allow for the coding and retrieval of data. To create a meaningful and coherent understanding of 'what was going on in the interview' and to address the criticism that using a software package can only signpost data as it breaks up the text, care was taken to analyse sections of the text. Where sentences could be categorised using more than one code, the most meaningful code was used to ensure an accurate representation of the interview process and its various elements. To ensure a 'closeness' to the data needed in qualitative research, the interview transcripts were initially analysed on paper.

From the thematic analysis nine major codes emerged: learning across the lifespan; transitions and responses; intrapersonal influences; work influences; financial influences; social influences; relocation; advice to others; and future planning. These codes as well as the 19 subcodes are presented in Table 7.1.

The thematic analysis and resultant codes and subcodes met three criteria identified by grounded theory for this process in that codes and subcodes were repeated across two or more interviews, were distinct from each other and, thirdly, that researchers made decisions about what to include and how to interpret the participants' comments (King and Horrocks 2010).

Table 7.1 Code categories

Master codes	Subcodes
1 Learning across the lifespan	1(a) Formal and informal 1(b) Response to/reflection on learning
2 Transitions and responses	2(a) Unexpected/unanticipated chance events 2(b) Response to circumstances/chance events 2(c) Adaptability
3 Intrapersonal influences	3(a) Self 3(b) Values 3(c) Personality traits 3(d) Age-related 3(e) Role satisfaction (i) past (ii) present
4 Work influences	4(a) Employment description (past and present) 4(b) Workplace dynamic (past and present) 4(c) Unpaid activities outside the home 4(d) Work–life balance/tension between roles
5 Financial influences	5(a) Current financial situation 5(b) Future financial situation
6 Social influences	6(a) Support networks 6(b) Role models 6(c) Life roles
7 Relocation	
8 Advice to others	
9 Future planning	

The application of the codes to the transcripts of the six countries that joined after the initial data analysis and coding across Australia, England and South Africa involved a researcher from one of those three countries coding a minimum of two scripts from each of the six countries independently until saturation (i.e. 100 per cent agreement) was reached on the established codes. Some researchers also identified codes specific to their particular country contexts. For example, a code 6(d), 'Administrative/systemic influences', referring to procedures and rules constraining individual development, was identified by the German context, and a code 10, 'Formal support systems', was identified from the Canadian context. This coding step provided validation of the coding system across country contexts.

Conclusion

This chapter has reported on the methodology that was followed by the authors of the nine chapters in this section of the book. In choosing a qualitative, grounded theory approach to researching the work and learning transitions of older women across nine countries, the research focuses on the voices of these women rather than on the voice of prescribed theory and the more statistical voice of quantitative research. Given the present methodology chapter, the chapters that follow do not describe methodological issues. Instead these international authors are able to focus on the context within which their national sample of older women live and the stories they have to tell about their work and learning transitions and changes. Stead *et al.* (2012) state that 'qualitative research methodologies open avenues for new understandings of the world of work' (ibid.: 107). It is the hope of the following chapters that the stories told and themed across nine countries will help to achieve a better and more nuanced understanding of the work and learning experiences of older women.

References

Bimrose, J., Watson, M. and McMahon, M. (2013) 'Career trajectories of older women: Implications for career guidance, *British Journal of Guidance and Counselling*, 41: 587–601.

Bimrose, J., McMahon, M. and Watson, M. (2014) 'Older women's retrospective narratives of their work and learning pathways', in G. Arulmani, A. Bakshi, F. Leong and T. Watts (eds), *Handbook of Career Development: International Perspectives*, New York: Springer.

Bimrose, J., Watson, M., McMahon, M., Haasler, S., Tomassini, M. and Suzanne, P. (2014) 'The problem with women?: Challenges posed by gender for career guidance practice', *International Journal for Educational and Vocational Guidance*, 14: 77–88.

Blustein, D., Kenna, A., Murphy, K., DeVoy, J. and DeWine, D. (2005) 'Qualitative research in career development: Exploring the center and margins of discourse about careers and working', *Journal of Career Assessment*, 13: 351–70.

Bryman, A. and Burgess, R. G. (1994) 'Reflections on qualitative data analysis', in A. Bryman and R. G. Burgess (ed.), *Analyzing Qualitative Data*, London: Routledge.

Charmaz, K. (2007) *Grounded Theory: A Practical Guide Through Qualitative Analysis*, London: Sage.

Commonwealth of Australia (2001) 'National strategy for an ageing Australia: An older Australia, challenges and opportunities for all'. Available at: www.health.gov.au/internet/wcms/publishing.nsf/content/ageing-ofoa-agepolicy-nsaa-nsaa.htm/$file/nsaabook.pdf (accessed 10 May 2008).

Fassinger, R. E. (2005) 'Paradigms, praxis, problems, and promise: Grounded theory in counseling psychology research', *Journal of Counseling Psychology*, 52(2): 156–66.

Glaser, B. G. and Strauss, A. L. (1967) *The Discovery of Grounded Theory: Strategies for Qualitative Research*, Chicago, IL: Aldine.

King, N. and Horrocks, C. (2010) *Interviews in Qualitative Research*, London: Sage.

Lapour, A. S. and Heppner, M. J. (2009) 'Social class privilege and adolescent women's perceived career options', *Journal of Counseling Psychology*, 56(4): 477–94.

Lincoln, Y. S. and Guba, E. G. (1985) *Naturalistic Inquiry*, Newbury Park, CA: Sage.

McMahon, M., Watson, M. and Bimrose, J. (2012) 'Career adaptability: A qualitative understanding from the stories of older women', *Journal of Vocational Behavior*, 80: 762–8.

McMahon, M., Watson, M. and Bimrose, J. (2013) 'Older women's careers: Systemic perspectives', in W. Patton (ed.), *Conceptualising Women's Working Lives: Moving the Boundaries of our Discourse*, Rotterdam, The Netherlands: Sense.

Miles, M. B. and Huberman, A. M. (1994) *Qualitative Data Analysis*, Thousand Oaks, CA: Sage (2nd ed.).

O'Neil, D. A., Hopkins, M. M. and Bilimoria, D. (2008) 'Women's careers at the start of the 21st century: Patterns and paradoxes', *Journal of Business Ethics*, 80(4): 727–43.

Patton, W. and McMahon, M. (2006) *Career Development and Systems Theory: Connecting Theory and Practice*, Rotterdam, The Netherlands: Sense (2nd ed.).

Polkinghorne, D. E. (2005) 'Language and meaning: Data collection in qualitative research and practice in adult literacy', *Journal of Counseling Psychology*, 52(2): 137–45.

Stead, G. B., Perry, J. C., Munka, L. M., Bonnett, H. R., Shiban, A. P. and Care, E. (2012) 'Qualitative research in career development: Content analysis from 1990 to 2009', *International Journal for Educational and Vocational Guidance*, 12: 105–22.

Thomas, E. and Magilvy, J. K. (2011) 'Qualitative rigor or research validity in qualitative research', *Journal for Specialists in Pediatric Nursing*, 16: 151–5.

Young, R. A. and Valach, L. (2000) 'Reconceptualising career theory and research: An action-theoretical perspective', in A. Collin and R. A. Young (eds), *The Future of Career*, Cambridge: Cambridge University Press, pp. 181–96.

8 Voices of older women from Argentina

Pamela Suzanne

The context in which women and men experience their career development is affected by the socio-political factors of their countries (McMahon, Bimrose and Watson 2010). In Argentina, women who are 45 to 65 years old have experienced profound political changes during their careers. Following years of alternating between military governments and weak civil governments, in 1976 a violent military dictatorship started which is remembered for the disappearance and assassination of 30,000 men and women, torture, ideological persecution, and mandatory exile (Barrancos 2010). For many of the women participants in this study, this terrorist phase of Argentinian history coincided with their university years, impinging upon their studies. In 1983, democracy returned and stabilised the country (Suriano 2005).

In terms of the Argentinian labour market, women increased their participation from the 1970s to 1990s, after which it stabilised. Between 1970 and 1980, women's participation in the labour market in the country grew from 29 per cent to 33 per cent. The group of women who entered the labour market in greater numbers in this decade was 25–55 years old, married, well educated, and belonging to the middle and high socio-economic sectors. Between 1980 and 1997, in the metropolitan area of Buenos Aires, women increased their participation in the labour market from 28 per cent to 53 per cent (Wainerman 2000). During these years, increased participation was associated with the need to compensate for their partners' reduced salaries as a consequence of the economic crisis (Barrancos 2010; Wainerman 2000). In 2010, the labour market activity rate for women in the metropolitan area of Buenos Aires had slightly decreased to 51 per cent, while it was 49 per cent for the country as a whole (CEMyT 2011). Employment rates differ greatly depending on education levels; for instance, the activity rate for women with incomplete secondary school education was 34 percent in 2010, 56 per cent for women with complete secondary school education, and 80 per cent for women holding a university degree (CEMyT 2011).

Related to this, during recent decades, women have also achieved higher education levels. While the general completion average (including men and women) is 79 per cent, 82 per cent of women complete secondary school. Women are also attending university in greater numbers. For example, by 2007 women comprised 52 per cent of university students (Wainerman 2007). At the same time, there has been an increase in the number of women students undertaking degrees that used to be exclusive to men, such as engineering, veterinary and economic sciences, to the point where there are few degrees where women are not a majority (Wainerman 2007).

However, women remain concentrated in certain occupations. In 1970, 91 per cent of all pre-school and primary school teachers were women and 60 per cent of secondary school teachers were women, yet only 20 per cent of educators at university level were women. In the same year, a substantial majority (86 per cent) of nurses, obstetricians, and social assistants were women, and most (67 per cent) of opticians, dieticians, and technicians in the human and animal health sector were women. However, only a quarter of doctors, dentists, and surgeons were women (Wainerman 1996). In the 1980s, women were the majority in a small number of service occupations, with 98 per cent of those in domestic service, 90 per cent in primary school teaching and 83 per cent in nursing (Wainerman 1996). In 2010 these percentages had not changed much, with still only 26 per cent of women working in industry (CEMyT 2011).

Research shows that besides horizontal segregation, there has also been vertical segregation (Barrancos 2010). For example, in 1977 in the national public sector, the number of men was three times greater than the number of women in management, advice, and supervision positions, while women equalled or exceeded them at the operational level (Garcia de Fanelli et al. 1990). This inequity has persisted, despite women's education achievements being higher at all levels. In 1985, although more women joined the workforce, male dominance in higher positions persisted. Discrimination was also observed in the health and education sectors (Tiramonti 1995; Wainerman and Geldstein 1990). At universities, the number of women professors was low at the more prestigious levels. For example, in 1990, 47 per cent of the teaching staff of eight faculties were women, while only 26 per cent of the higher ranked professors were women (Tiramonti 1995). In terms of salaries, university-educated women currently earn on average 29 per cent less than men in comparable jobs, while the gap increases to 44 per cent for women who have not finished secondary school (CEMyT 2011).

Despite horizontal and vertical segregation, female employment has grown in the low, middle and high socio-economic classes. This has had consequences for families. Between 1980 and 2001, in households with partners between 20 and 60 age of age and with children, the model of a male provider (i.e. economically active husband, inactive wife) decreased from 74 to 54 per cent, while the two-provider model increased from 25 to 46 per cent (Wainerman 2002; Wainerman and Cerrutti 2001). In this context, a discourse has developed among Argentinian men and women related to the need for more equality between men and women's opportunities and rights to individual development. However, changes in behaviour are slow (Wainerman 2000). Research undertaken in Buenos Aires in 2002, in which members of 200 families were interviewed, suggests that, although women are entering the labour market in greater numbers, they still work 50 per cent fewer hours outside the house than men, work closer to their homes, and work in occupations that give them greater flexibility to attend to family emergencies (Wainerman 2007). In fact, in 2010 almost half of working women worked less than 35 hours per week, while this rate was 21 per cent for men (CEMyT 2011). At the same time, women carry greater responsibility for the house and children than their husbands do. Although they delegate some activities to maids and older children, they remain ultimately responsible (Wainerman 2007).

Listening to the older women

The following section of the chapter is based on the stories of 12 Argentinian women. The purposive sample included women who represent diverse occupations and formal qualifications (see Table 8.1). They all live in the city of Buenos Aires and its suburbs.

Learning across the lifespan

Most of the women interviewed had undertaken further studies after secondary school. Choice of subject was influenced by parents, work prospects, and (limited) knowledge of available degrees. For example, Valeria chose to become an accountant because of her parents' advice on the economic value of degrees and a career suitable for women: 'I chose an economic science as a major, a bit influenced by my parents. [...] I wanted to study medicine. And my dad told me: "but medicine is going to be pretty difficult for a woman".'

Marcela recognised that another degree would probably have been interesting, but that she was not aware of its existence at the time:

> The degree did not exist, or it didn't occur to me. It may have been because of the socioeconomic level, like not having access... the truth is that I don't know why. Afterwards I got to know that it did exist.

Some women studied for a degree with no clear calling or work prospects since the idea was 'just to marry'. Later, they realised that other degrees would have been more interesting or have had greater labour market value, as in the case of Lorena:

> I didn't really know what I wanted to do, and perhaps at that time vocational aptitude tests didn't really exist, and my parents weren't really the investigating type either, they believed that the four girls had to marry and so on. It was another way of seeing things.

Undertaking formal studies involved meeting many challenges. First, learning opportunities were concentrated in the city of Buenos Aires, so women living in the suburbs had to commute every day to attend classes. At the same time the university years of this age group coincided with times of intolerance, when the military forces had taken over the State. This created further barriers which had to

Table 8.1 Argentinian sample

Pseudonym	Age	Marital status	Employment status	Dependants	Highest qualification	Current employment
Liliana	61	Married	Full-time	0	Degree (technical)	School librarian
Laura	52	Informally married after divorce	Full-time	2	Degree (masters)	Executive education director
Rosa	49	Divorced	Full-time	3	Degree (technical)	Managing partner at family business
Alicia	47	Married	Full time (two part-time jobs)	3	Degree (technical)	Administrative employee
Ana	61	Divorced	Full-time	0	Degree (masters)	Coordinator of education materials at public sector (plus other self-employed jobs)
Carmela	53	Single	Full-time	0	Primary School	Secretary
Marcela	52	Married	Retired and self-employed	3	Degree (university)	Beauty consultant
Leticia	59	Married	Full-time	0	Secondary school	Manager at family business
Valeria	65	Married	Volunteer worker	1	Degree (university)	Down syndrome foundation director
Lorena	52	Divorced	Full-time	3	Degree (university)	Secretary
Juana	53	Married	Self-employed	0	Degree (university)	Translator and english language teacher
Cristina	47	Married	Part-time	4	Degree (university)	Kindergarten headmistress

be negotiated, like undertaking risks to attend classes, or having to study both at university and at the homes of professors who had resigned or had been dismissed following a policy of ideological cleansing because they did not share the political beliefs of the military government (van der Kooy 1996). Leticia remembers the risks associated with attending classes:

> I had to go to class on a first floor, get on the scaffolding, walk for ... pass three rooms through the scaffolding and come back into the gallery ... No, one of those things that ... 'I was crazy'. Yes, going to university implied being exposed [to risks] and it [that] wasn't justified in any way.

Ana remembers the effort of studying both formally and informally while working:

> So we were studying twice, with a professor in university and another one at home [...] You must keep in mind that I studied my whole degree whilst working... I come from a middle class family. So the fact that we were studying twice, although it can be considered very enriching because of what the professor that had resigned taught you, it implies that you must make double the effort.

Some women managed to complete their degrees despite all the difficulties. Others, like Leticia, withdrew because there were just too many risks as well as family commitments: 'It required some serious thinking to say "no, no more, I don't want this for me, I need to keep living; I have a little son, no more."'

Besides political reasons, other women also ended their university studies because of family issues, such as getting married or having a child. However, women studying for prestigious degrees in the city, or new degrees that were uncommon, felt that it was worth persevering. They have benefited, since they have found jobs easily throughout their careers. This is true for Marcela, who has a university degree, works as a professor in economics and lives in a small town: 'I have always been privileged in my town since no one had my degree, so I always got to choose.'

Later in their careers, some women undertook further university studies. The reasons given were that through work experience, they realised they needed further learning or studied just for pleasure. Rosa, who experienced a traumatic divorce, decided to begin studying when she was 41 years old; she wanted to do something she liked. Unintentionally this stimulated a career change:

> I get to the university and I love the environment ... I love the people, I love the young people, I love the professors, the knowledge, you know? [...] like in that moment there was nothing that I liked ... with what I'd feel comfortable doing then, just separated and working with my ex in the business, came this studying thing. [...] Likewise, although I liked it a lot, just as of, let's say, a year ago it's that I can think of it as a profession. At no time had I thought that I could work as a psychologist. Never. [...] Like it opened a lot of possibilities

that I felt I didn't have, and it showed me that I could do a lot of things besides what I do here.

Women also undertook a great deal of informal learning, both for professional advancement and for hobbies they enjoyed. Most felt that they had been learning throughout their whole careers. They valued it greatly, even more than formal learning, as in the case of Laura: 'Working with intelligent people. It teaches me much more. The challenge from someone I respect.'

Similarly, Ana mentioned that being a member of the panel for an award in her area of specialisation provoked more learning than the master's programme she had undertaken.

> And, well, you have access there to the best of children's literature from 70 countries ... I learnt a lot there, and it's probably an even more fruitful experience than the masters, you know? Although you don't get a certificate, besides from the thank you card ... I mean they don't give you any kind of proof, but it's a very important learning occasion.

Informal learning took place mostly through working with others, both with colleagues inside and outside the workplace. For example, Marcela developed relationships that supported informal learning throughout her career:

> First I have learnt quite a lot with an excellent principal the first five years of my career and with generous colleagues that shared a lot. Then, I made up nice working groups with young colleagues and friends, and we developed quite innovative projects for that time. I have kept in touch with people with much more experience than me in other areas in which they also taught.

Transitions

Women participants experienced unexpected events that affected their careers, both personal events and work-related events such as workplace closure and changes in management.

In terms of personal situations, unexpected family events encouraged women to make changes in their work, prioritising their families and health. For example, Laura gave up her career in international consulting work and accepted a job at a university's business education centre for a year in order to have more time and energy to take care of her ill mother:

> ... when I'm offered a post as a Consultant to the business education centre for a year I say "well, university, an organisation this size wasn't very difficult". I favoured being able to be near my mother during this whole process and the truth is that I was; and I am proud of having done that.

Women who disapproved of unexpected events related to employment, such as changes in management, refused to continue working in that environment. Laura explained:

> So, personal issues got combined with a management change that I disapproved of. [...] So, these people, with whom I was no longer interested in working with, added to this feeling of a people-eating work dynamic and where, really, the style was – you're useful now, or you are not useful at all. [...] And that's when I said, well, I decided to leave, but not knowing where to go.

Intrapersonal influences

Most of the women were confident about themselves and their work skills, so were not afraid of undertaking transitions. Cristina, for example, said:

> There was a moment when I said "I'm leaving", I'm not going to be unemployed, I can get another job, it doesn't matter if it's not a kindergarten headmistress position, whatever, I know I am going to work hard and do well because that's the way I like doing things.

The core value of most of these women related to making a difference to people with whom they worked and, in turn, being valued for their contributions. For example, in teaching roles, they valued students' and parents' feedback. Marcela commented: 'the most rewarding thing is the recognition from students'.

In workplaces where people were not valued, women participants felt very uncomfortable. Liliana talked about a high-status job, which was very well paid and which she left, partly because helping others was not valued:

> ... helping others wasn't important, what was important was to sell and sell and sell and create a bigger need in the other. Because the job was to create the need in a woman to buy everything, and the saleswoman was to offer everything and buy everything. So, it's very interesting but ... it wasn't right, it wasn't for me.

Many women made spontaneous comments regarding their age and how it affected them. For example, Marcela enjoyed sewing and her children encouraged her to develop this activity when she retired, but her sight was deteriorating: 'My children tell me I should do something now, but my sight is not good enough to sew at the moment.'

The women in the study also felt that as age passed, they changed how they performed their work roles: at some point, maturity impacted and they got better at what they did, and some years later, they began feeling tired. Marcela experienced this:

> I think when maturity comes along, right? When you have more than forty years you give classes more calmly, you go to the essentials; you spot the special

capacities in your students and try to develop them. [...] You feel that you are in an age when you are not very patient. In my last job I did not have as much patience as before and you start to assume that, right? And the students deserve more dedication, perhaps I didn't want to go every day, and in a specific schedule, right? Tiredness.

Age discrimination also featured in the womens' stories. Among many others, this happened to Carmela:

> The truth is that at my age it's difficult to get a job. Because jobs always go to the younger people. Which is fine, I'm not saying otherwise, but it is hard on us older people who have to work.

Work influences

Most of the women participants were still working in a variety of jobs when interviewed. Additionally, some have undertaken and currently perform unpaid activities outside the house, such as the coordination of religious classes, working in a literature foundation, providing accounting services for non-governmental organisations (NGOs), and helping in foundations that assign scholarships. With the passing years, they have tried to decrease this involvement as they think it is good for the younger generation to take charge and it is increasingly difficult for them to continue with these activities, plus work. For example, Leticia quit for health reasons: 'I coordinated the catechism of my parish... The catechists' group for moms, until two years ago, but ... for health issues I had to quit, because it demanded a lot of hours, quite a lot of physical effort.'

All women in the study experienced tension between their work and other life domains at some point. This was especially the case when taking care of young children. Many of them left jobs they enjoyed as a consequence. This was the case for Leticia:

> I quit work because of a serious issue with my son, he wasn't speaking. My son was 3 years old and didn't speak. [...] And the paediatrician only said "quit working, quit working", "Stay with this kid, stay with this kid". Ok, that's settled. The kid is a very intelligent boy, normal, absolutely normal, and what he wanted was mom at home. He was taken care of very well by my mother-in-law.... but he didn't speak. I went to stay at home and he started speaking right away.

Others switched to part-time work to be able to enjoy their children more:

> I was working full time at school, morning and afternoon and it was taking up too much energy, too much time and I had no energy left, because I really give my all at work so I hadn't any left for my family, which is a priority ... the children ... and so all I wanted was for them to go to sleep, I was nervous ...

For some women, these career changes were positive in the long run as they could develop in a new job they liked and enjoy caring for their children at the same time. This was the case for Valeria:

> ... when I got my degree I preferred working for a multinational company. And since I got pregnant soon after I got my degree I quit the job. [...] I prioritised the fact that I was pregnant and having my baby and so, with a lot of sacrifice, I set up an accounting office. At first, it was very small, but I only wanted clients from the area, so that I could take care of my baby. And well, that office is still operating with my husband and my son in it, so I did not do so badly.

For others, like Lorena, it involved sacrifices within her career:

> I prioritised having children and so on so, well, I always focused everything I do to be able to accompany... [...] And I never could go back to dedicating myself to designing or what I liked the most, then I got divorced and well, there, goodbye, you know?

Financial influences

Although it was not the only factor, women did make career decisions based on money. For example, Lorena explained: 'I was tired of the routine, and the wage wasn't "wow" for me and I saw that with the children being older I was going to need more money and well, I started searching.'

The career decisions of the married women were affected by their own salaries and those of their partners. For example, to be able to make risky career decisions it was useful to have the support of their husband's salary. This was the case for Valeria: 'Support from my husband, for example, it was economic, right? Because if there isn't any income it's a lot harder to have your accounting office where you can't support yourself for the first few years.'

In contrast, Laura, who was considering becoming an entrepreneur, decided against this option because she had recently divorced, did not have a partner's salary, and so could not afford the risk: 'I would say that I didn't think about it too much because the first barrier, in that sense, was that I was recently divorced, I needed a stable income, right?'

Social influences

All the women had support from their families. To be able to work, many of the women's children were taken care of by their mothers or mothers-in-law. At the same time, they would employ a woman as a house cleaner. In the case of Lorena, she even moved in with her parents when she got divorced, and her mother helped with the children:

> I went to live with my parents, because I worked and let's say, needed to keep on working. [...] While the children were little, mom couldn't really keep up with all three by herself, right? So I had a maid, who stayed with me a long time.

Husbands were also an important part of the support network for many women. For example, they helped take care of the children when the women undertook further studies. This was the case of Laura, who was able to study for a very demanding master's programme when her children were six and 12 years old because her husband took care of them.

For many women, their therapists were an important part of their support networks. In Argentina, people attend therapy sessions regularly to discuss personal matters; in fact, Argentina has 145 psychologists per 100,000 residents – far more compared with Denmark, which is in second place with 85 psychologists per 100,000 residents (Moffett 2009). Important life decisions were made with their therapists, and from them the women also received the support they needed to carry through those decisions. For example, Cristina decided to start working part time as she was very tired, but this required her husband to generate more income. She took this decision during therapy sessions and her therapist gave her the strength to implement it: 'And then when we realised that the situation was complicated we had some discussions where I just blocked everything out and then I would go to the next therapy session to refuel with the strength I needed.'

Women also received support from friends and acquaintances, specifically in finding new jobs. They counted on work colleagues to enable them to reduce work hours both for taking care of personal matters or studying. Laura, who was a manager and undertook a very demanding MBA programme, counted on her work team for support:

> And because I had managed to build a work team that also put up with it. I would say that the work team I had, was a work team that helped me, covered for me a lot, helped me a lot, covered me a lot, backed me up, loved me a lot ... took care of me a lot; they never exposed me, on the contrary; whilst if at any time something happened, I was the first to ... they came to my house on Saturdays to solve the issue, you know?

Relocation

A few women moved within the city and the Buenos Aires Province due to personal reasons. For example, when she got divorced, Lorena moved in with her parents and commuted long hours to her work:

> It was before the highway was widened so I left at 7 in the morning, left the eldest child at school, went to the city, got there at 10, finished working at 7

and got home around 9:30–10, so I didn't see the baby because when I left in the morning he was asleep and when I arrived at night too.

Advice to others

Most advice related to feeling passionate about one's work. An example is given by Marcela: 'That you have to like your job. She has to like the job and has to feel passionate about it. I think that you can stand up to anything if you have passion for what you do.'

Regarding education and employment transitions, the advice of women participants related to:

- Accepting change: 'And then, well, you shall approach change because life is a change. If you are going through a change, you have to deconstruct the head, so that you can see it as something positive.' (Marcela)
- Persevering: 'No matter the amount of time that passes, keep the same perseverance, always, consistency is key … keep on, on, and on and on … without anxiety, right? Because you'll get it, you'll get it.' (Lorena)
- Being certain of the reason for change: 'Understanding a bit about what is the ultimate motivation behind the change, or the desire behind the change. Because changes are not easy and transitions are not easy.' (Laura)

Participants expressed different opinions regarding whether young women should stay at home taking care of the children or devote themselves to their professional careers. Although most of them made career sacrifices for their children and were proud of having raised them, these older women respected both options. For example, Leticia commented about someone working for her: 'And as a mom with two kids I find it more logical for her to stay at home. But she thinks differently and I'm ok with it.'

Valeria, however, had a different perspective: 'You have to work hard outside; women's lives have changed a lot, for the better. One must not disregard one's family either, or your kids will be bad and you'll say, "well, but I devoted myself to my profession."'

Future

For the future, the women were considering further learning, making career changes, maintaining the current situation, relocating, travelling, and devoting time to hobbies. Learning was an important issue for many women who were waiting to retire, or for their children to grow older, to have more time. Some women were planning career changes. For example, Laura was considering whether to undertake a PhD and to build an international career: 'If I can turn into an academic consultant or a consultant with academic credentials, it'll be a very interesting source of work and of development for the next 20–30 years.'

A few women who had made an important change recently were not expecting further imminent changes. Valeria, who left an accounting office to set up a foundation, explained: 'For the future, at the moment, to keep doing this, I have a lot of stuff.'

Finally, some women living in the suburbs were considering relocating to the city once their children started university there.

Reflections

The learning and working pathways of these women were influenced both by their society's and their own gendered scripts. For example, some of them studied degrees that were not their calling, following parental advice on what a woman should do, or they just chose any subject as they did not think they would actually work, because they just wanted to marry. Many of them also sacrificed jobs they liked to take care of their families. Although not regretting anything, their advice to younger women does relate to being passionate about their work and choosing occupations they love.

These stories portray how families presented not only barriers to, but also support for, women's career development. For example, although parental advice had been conservative in their early years, in many cases mothers provided the assistance that allowed women to keep working. Some husbands were also supporters of their wives' careers, through taking care of children so that the women could study and through backing their career decisions psychologically and financially. The micro social environment that emerged as critical gave these strong women the resources to deal with their learning and work transitions. In addition, formal and informal learning occasions emerged as positive influences on these women's lives by enhancing their careers, giving them joy during difficult situations, and opening new career directions.

References

Barrancos, D. (2010) *Mujeres en la sociedad argentina*, Buenos Aires: Sudamericana.
CEMyT (2011) *Informe n°3: Situación laboral de las mujeres período 2009-2010*. Available at: www.wim-network.org/2011/10/argentina-la-situacion-laboral-de-las-mujeres-2009-2010 (accessed 4 February 2014).
García de Fanelli, A. M., Gogna, M. and Jelin, E. (1990) *El empleo femenino en el sector público nacional*, Buenos Aires: CEDES.
McMahon, M., Bimrose, J. and Watson, M. (2010) 'Older women's career development and social inclusion', *Australian Journal of Career Development*, 19(1): 63–70.
Moffett, M. (2009) 'Its GDP is depressed, but Argentina leads world in shrinks per capita'. Available at: http://online.wsj.com/article/SB125563769653488249.html (accessed 12 June 2012).
Suriano, J. (2005) 'Introducción: Una Argentina diferente', in J. Suriano (ed.) *Dictadura y democracia: 1976-2001*, Buenos Aires: Sudamericana.
Tiramonti, G. (1995) 'Incorporación y promoción de las mujeres en el circuito formal de educación nacional', *Desarrollo económico*, 35: 255–74.
Van der Kooy, E. (1996) 'Los archivos de la represión cultural'. Available at: http://edant.clarin.com/diario/96/03/24/claridad.html (accessed 26 July 2013).

Wainerman, C. (1996) '¿Segregación o discriminación? El mito de la igualdad de oportunidades', *Boletín Informativo Techint*, 285: 59–75.
Wainerman, C. (2000) 'División del trabajo en familias de dos proveedores: relato desde ambos géneros y dos generaciones', *Estudios demográficos y urbanos*, 15: 149–84.
Wainerman, C. (2002) *Familia y trabajo. Prácticas y representaciones*, Buenos Aires: CENEP, Cuadernos del CENEP N° 53.
Wainerman, C. (2007), 'Conyugalidad y paternidad: ¿Una revolución estancada?', in M. A. Gutiérrez (ed.) *Género, familias y trabajo: rupturas y continuidades*, Buenos Aires: CLACSO.
Wainerman, C. and Cerrutti, M. (2001) 'Dual earner couples in Buenos Aires. Structural adjustment and the female and male labour force', paper presented at XXIV IUSSP General Conference, Salvador, Brasil.
Wainerman, C. H. and Geldstein, R. N. (1990) *Condiciones de vida y de trabajo de las enfermeras en la Argentina*, Buenos Aires: CENEP, Serie Cuadernos del CENEP N° 44.

9 Voices of older women from Australia

Mary McMahon

Australia is an island continent with a population of slightly more than 23 million people of whom just over half are women. Because much of Australia is arid or semi-arid, the population is concentrated in coastal strips in the east, south-east and south-west of the continent. Aboriginal and Torres Strait Islander people comprise approximately 2.5 per cent of the population (Australian Bureau of Statistics [ABS] 2013b). Australia's population growth has been stimulated by international immigration. In 2010, approximately 27 per cent of the population was born overseas. The United Kingdom is the largest source of immigrants, followed by New Zealand. Reflecting its place in the Asia Pacific region, many people immigrate to Australia from Asian countries, primarily China, India, Vietnam, Philippines and Malaysia (ABS 2013b). Similar to many other countries, Australia is confronting labour market and social issues related to an ageing population. Older women comprise 17 per cent of the Australian labour market (Tilly *et al.* 2013). Described as a 'critical underutilised talent pool' (ibid.: 6), older women have lower labour force participation rates and higher underutilisation rates than their male counterparts, resulting in Australia lagging behind other comparable countries.

While Australia takes pride in the ideal of giving people a 'fair go', progress on gender equity has been slow despite the introduction of the Equal Opportunity for Women in the Workplace Act in 1999 (Commonwealth of Australia 1999). Even though equal opportunity for women has not been achieved, the Act was renamed the Workplace Gender Equality Act in 2012 (WGE Act) (Australian Government WGEA 2012a). The agency that focused specifically on achieving equal opportunity for women in the workplace (the Equal Opportunity for Women in the Workplace Agency) has been renamed the Workplace Gender Equality Agency (WGEA). Thus Australian women's unequal place in the Australian labour market is no longer the specific focus of either the Act or the Agency, but part of a broader focus on gender equity. The objectives of the Act include promoting and improving gender equality, promoting the elimination of gender discrimination and supporting employers to 'remove barriers to the full and equal participation of women in the workforce, in recognition of the disadvantaged position of women in relation to employment matters' (Australian Government WGEA 2012b: 1), and they reflect an ongoing commitment to improving Australian women's labour market position.

Between 1961 and 2011, women's labour force participation increased from 34 per cent to 59 per cent (ABS 2011). Between 2010 and 2011, males aged 20–74 years had a higher labour force participation rate (80 per cent) than females in the same age group (65 per cent). For males, the labour force participation rate remained steady between 2001–2 and 2010–11, while it increased by five percentage points for females during this period, with most of the increase achieved in the older age groups.

A gender pay gap persists (Gilfillan and Andrews 2010), which results in women being at a considerable disadvantage as they age. Comparatively, the gender pay gap is 1.3 percentage points wider now than it was in 1994 (Australian Government WGEA 2013b). In professional employment, where women comprise 51.2 per cent of the total workforce (Gilfillan and Andrews 2010), the gender pay gap between male and female mean weekly earnings is 21.1 per cent for full-time workers and 12 per cent for part-time workers (Australian Government WGEA 2013a). For full-time workers in female dominated occupations, the gender pay gap is highest (i.e. sales workers (27.6 per cent); community and personal service workers (26.5 per cent); and clerical and administrative workers (25.8 per cent) (Australian Government WGEA 2013b). On average, women who work part-time earn 17.6 per cent less than men who work part-time (Australian Government WGEA 2013c). Salaries of female graduates are 90.9 per cent that of male graduates. Implications of the gender pay gap are that for women, average superannuation payments are 43.1 per cent less than for men and that women comprise 56.5 per cent of people aged over 65 years receiving the aged pension (ibid.). Between the ages of 45 and 49, men working part-time earn 26.7 per cent more than women who work part-time. Women comprise almost three-quarters of Australian part-time workers (ABS 2011) and those who leave the workforce to take parental leave are not likely to regain their earning capacity (Australian Government WGEA 2013a).

Women comprise more than half of the workforce in six industries, namely education and training, the retail trade, accommodation and food services, financial and insurance services, administrative and support services, and healthcare and social assistance, where over three-quarters of the workforce is female (Australian Government WGEA 2013d). In three of these industries (healthcare and social assistance, retail trade, and accommodation and food services), at least one-third of the workforce comprises women who work part-time.

Australian women are less likely than men to be found in leadership positions (ABS 2013a). In public and private sector senior leadership positions women are outnumbered by men (ibid.). Australia has fallen behind other countries in relation to women in corporate leadership positions and in national parliaments. Although women represent slightly more than half of Australia's population, less than one-third of federal and state parliamentarians are female (ibid.). Women remain underrepresented at the most senior corporate positions of the top 200 companies listed on the Australian Stock Exchange, although there was an increase in female representation at board director level from 8.4 per cent in 2010 to 12.3 per cent in 2012 (ibid.). In the Australian Public Service, women remain underrepresented at 39 per cent of the Senior Executive Service, an increase from 28 per cent in 2002 (ibid.).

At middle management level, almost half (47 per cent) of managers are women, an increase from 36 per cent in 2002.

More women are employed part-time in all industries except transport, postal and warehousing, and construction (Australian Government WGEA 2013d). In older age groups, women comprise a higher percentage of part-time workers than men (e.g. 42 per cent in the 45 to 54 age group compared with 10 per cent of men) and this percentage rises with age (Gilfillan and Andrews 2010). More older Australian women are in the labour force and their contribution to the total hours worked by people of working age has increased from 6 per cent in 1979 to 15 per cent in 2009 (ibid.). Older women now account for 39 per cent of the total working hours worked by women of working age, an increase from 21 per cent in 1979.

The proportion of older women in the Australian workforce is less than that of older Australian men or women in similar OECD countries (ibid.). Interestingly, 'most mature aged women who are not in the labour force appear to prefer not to work' and 'around 7 per cent of mature aged women could potentially be induced to enter the labour force; however, the barriers or obstacles to participation of many in this group are significant and difficult to address' (ibid.: xiv). Encouraging Australian organisations to 'better harness the skills and talents of Australia's older female workforce' (Tilly et al. 2013: 6) is the focus of a joint initiative between Diversity Council Australia (DCA) and the Australian Human Rights Commission (AHRC). Significantly, 10.0 per cent of Australian women are underemployed, which is almost double that of the rate for men (Australian Government WGEA 2013d). Women spend almost twice as much time as men on caring and nurturing responsibilities. Since 1997, the time spent by men on caring for children in families has remained the same whereas the time spent by women has increased by almost an hour (ABS 2013b).

It is against this background of a long history of an unequal labour market that we listen to the voices of older Australian women.

Listening to the older women

The women ranged from 45 to 63 years of age, with an average age of 53.6 years. All could be regarded as middle class. Table 9.1 provides an overview of the sample. The voices of the women provide nuanced insight into their experiences of navigating the Australian labour market for over two decades.

Learning across the lifespan

All of the women valued learning. For some, learning had been a seamless progression of formal learning from secondary schooling to further education to entry into the workforce. Sophia entered teacher training after secondary school, was subsequently employed as a teacher, was 'happy as a bird' and remained teaching until her retirement. By contrast, Janice had a technical qualification that enabled her to have high paid work, which she totally enjoyed until she left to have children in her mid-thirties. Re-engaging in formal study enabled Vera to successfully change her

Table 9.1 Australian sample

Pseudonym	Age	Marital status	Employment status	Income per annum	Dependants	Highest qualification	Current employment
Sandra	45	Long-term partner	Student (part-time) Volunteer retired	$20,000 desired	No	Degree	Retired/unemployed
Kay	62	Divorced	Permanent part-time	$60–70,000	No	PhD	Human service work
Sophia	63	Single	Retired	$20–30,000	No	Diploma	Retired teacher
Clare	56	Married	Part-time	$67,000	2	Degree	Teacher
Lorraine	51	Married	Student (part-time)	No regular income	1 (partly)	Diploma degree (current study)	Student
Denise	63	Divorced	Part-time	$60–70,000	No	Degree	Business owner
Patricia	62	Married	Part-time	$50–60,000	No	Degree (honours)	Consultant (own business)
Fleur	61	Married	Retired	No regular income	1	Trade certificate	Retired; volunteer work
Megan	53	Single/widow	Part-time (30 hours per week)	$50,000	No	Graduate certificate Masters (current study)	Human service worker
Janice	62	Married	Permanent part-time	$45,000	No	Certificate	Laboratory manager
Vera	62	Single	2 permanent part-time jobs equivalent to 5 days a week	$40,000	No	Post-graduate diploma	Historian
Kate	59	Divorced	Full-time	$80,000	No	Degree	Teacher

career: 'I knew I had gone in the right direction because both those things I was enjoying an awful lot.'

For others, engaging in formal learning later in life opened up opportunities not previously available to them. Megan explained how, 'I grew up in a very abusive house and I was kicked out the day I turned 15 so I never finished high school. I went back to study in my thirties and did my undergraduate.' Megan continued to study, had a postgraduate certificate and was completing a master's degree. Prior to re-engaging with formal learning, Megan, who was widowed at a young age, had been employed in many low-skilled jobs to support her child. Subsequent to obtaining a professional qualification, she found employment she loved and had lived and worked overseas.

Some women advanced their employment opportunities through informal learning. Returning to work after having her children, Janice developed skills and knowledge for her new position through informal self-initiated learning, a situation which did not change, as her employer did not provide opportunities for her to upgrade her knowledge and skills. She explained:

> I went back to work ... I had to sort of, as I said learn again. Yeah that was hard work because you really taught yourself. I mean you watched ... the head who'd been doing it for a while ... it's just learning new equipment and then as the years progressed, the equipment got very sophisticated ... even till now to this day is constantly learning again but teaching yourself or going to somewhere like I went yesterday, I went to the uni to do a little short course.

Some employers provided professional development, which was not always a positive experience, as related by Sophia who said 'some of them were really, really valuable and very good, and some of them were just rubbish'.

In reflecting on their learning, the women stressed their love of learning and how they had kept learning in various ways throughout their lives. This is exemplified by Sandra who emphasised:

> I love learning. I love the challenge of it. I love getting into something that I've got absolutely no idea about and finding out how it all works. It really inspires me and I guess that's why I keep going back, keep going back.

Learning in its various forms was present in the lives of all of the women and was frequently associated with career transition, as it provided new opportunities.

Transitions

Transition was pervasive in the women's lives and included changes brought about by relocation, family circumstances, employment and unexpected circumstances. A recursive relationship seemed to exist between life circumstances and the women's work, best summed up by Kay as 'they're more life transitions'. Following a transfer to another setting, Clare explained how 'I felt very lonely, very lonely. It wasn't pleasant. I felt very much under scrutiny and that there was a lot to prove and I did.'

Some transitions were a result of poor workplace practices. The women's responses varied and for many were intensely emotional. Clare described her shock of being unexpectedly transferred to a different location: 'I didn't know that I was being sent ... I didn't have time to think about it, I didn't even know that's where I was going to go.'

The experience of transition to retirement varied. Sandra described her transition to retirement as 'the longest relationship I've ever had so it was very hard to say goodbye'. Sophia explained 'I was burnt out, I really think I was burnt out' and was frustrated by changes in her field:

> I just was very unhappy and uncomfortable with what was going on ... I just thought I don't want to do it anymore. So I took 12 months off ... I thought, I don't want to go back ... I was happy enough to fade away from the scene, which I did ... it was the right decision ... I just had to do it. So I was happy.

The women demonstrated career adaptability in their responses to retirement. Sandra described recursiveness between her feelings and employment changes: 'it's an intuition thing. If I'm not moving in the right direction, I don't feel confident. If I am moving in the right direction, it's a sense of it's going to be alright and it's just trusting that intuition'.

After working in many jobs which had not been fulfilling, Lorraine began a university degree in her late-forties. She had 'always enthusiastically taken on the transitions. I've always got my mind into a place that – you know, I can do this'. Denise explained how her transitions became very pervasive in her life for some time prior to making a decision:

> No decision I make is made suddenly ... I will be sitting in front of the television and realise that I am thinking ... it is just in the background. In the car I will be thinking ... Then from there it was rather quick. The actual putting into place is much, much shorter than the finding what is going to happen ... I knew that I had thought it through extremely well ... I always have an escape plan.

Intrapersonal influences

The women's sense of self, values, personalities, and age were all influential factors. While Janice perceived herself as 'a quite confident person' and having 'good self-esteem', other participants struggled; Emily explained:

> Not being naturally very confident and outgoing I did find it pretty hard ... I can never understand people who are able to go from job to job and from one adventure to another. It always seemed rather scary to me.

Similarly, Lorraine reflected that, 'I've never been happy with what I was doing ... Unconsciously I knew that I had capabilities of doing far more than what I was actually doing.' She went on to explain how, since she had begun to study at university, she felt 'good enough ... and that nothing was too hard ... I wasn't having any more difficulty than anyone else ... I'm as good as them ... my motivation has come from within more than without'.

Values were important to all of the women. Sandra had realised that: 'these people who were earning a lot of money at work were miserable and that maybe there was another option of how to live your life and so I just changed the way I started to approach things'. The women had various opinions on what they valued most in their careers. For Patricia, it was 'working with a range of different disciplines, people with different skills' and learning, whereas for Fleur it was 'dealing with people'. Emily, by contrast, felt 'besotted with ... anything that I can connect with my ideal of beauty'.

Of the women, ten had children. Some described parenting as their most valued role. Janice believed that 'I'm really pleased that we did have two children. It would have been a very selfish life without them ... parenting has been very satisfying.' Similarly, Clare valued most 'being a mother. That's my most important role in my life above all else.'

Personality traits influenced the careers of a number of the women. Janice was 'a very positive person' who likes to 'get out there and be proactive'. Denise was 'fairly strong' and said 'I don't need a lot of support from people around me', because she sometimes spent years thinking through decisions. Contrasting Denise's long term cognitive decision making process, Kate explained that 'I just tended to go with the heart.'

Age was a consideration for most of the women. Janice was anticipating retiring and explained to her employer how, 'I don't want to go past my use by date.' She believed that:

> you get to a stage, where you think ... maybe I am a bit past it ... it's a very physical job and I'm up and down stairs all day, walking from one end of the (organisation) to the other and I do get very tired and I think well maybe that's my body telling me. I mean the brain's good but maybe just the body's telling me, hey you can't keep doing this for much longer.

Kay experienced the disappointment of seeing funding cuts on at least two occasions and a reduction in the services she could provide. She concluded that: 'I guess I'm too old to just fight it any more ... I could work smarter, influence people ... but I think I'm too tired ... I can't be bothered doing it.'

Work influences

The workplace influenced some women. Several had experienced discrimination. As a young adult, Kay who had a disability, was denied employment even though she was qualified and had to re-train in another field. Subsequently she applied again to the same employer and explained 'But this time I wasn't 17, I was 30, and I fought it, and I won.' Some of the women had to resign when they married. Kay recounted how she had been unable to get a job at a time of over-supply in her profession because, 'they were only giving it to breadwinners, which were mainly men'.

Clare explained inequities in her work and how her manager had been given modern resources and she hadn't. While recognising unfairness and potential disadvantage, she simply explained, 'I don't need to take that on and I don't fight the things I can't do.' By contrast, Megan explained that in her workplace, 'I can be totally open and honest about where I'm at and not feel I'm going to be sacrificed or burnt … it's such a professional supportive place to work.' Patricia also felt valued in her present work and said, 'The most satisfying is having my knowledge and my opinion valued by people.'

Janice remained in a job where, 'the atmosphere was very unpleasant' and she was 'very stressed' and 'really, really had a difficult time' for nine-and-a-half years because it suited her parenting need to have a job near her children's school. The changeable nature of workplaces was evident in Denise's story about her workplace going from a place where 'the dynamics was just fabulous. I loved it. My co-workers were great' to where, after a management change, she 'found myself in a position where I couldn't support (the manager) on anything'. Megan described a difficult occasion when she witnessed workplace bullying, which she found 'such a complex issue'. In another situation where she was a whistle blower, she believed that the organisation:

> dealt with it incredibly badly. I didn't lose my job or anything but he went back to work there and nothing changed. They actually didn't even understand their own whistle blowing policy … They didn't follow the guidelines, they didn't do it well and nothing changed, which is really scary.

All of the women who had children spoke about the tension between parenting and employment. Lorraine described the sacrifice and difficulty of balancing her role as a parent with that of a paid worker:

> I had just agreed to take on that position of being at home with the children … my job was second place, that I was just supplementing the income and so if I never really attained what I really wanted it was not that detrimental … I had the sense that probably I didn't have the right to make those sorts of demands. It was – you just worked for the family.

Janice explained how she didn't return to paid employment for ten years after the birth of her children and how she would have loved to have stayed in her previous highly paid position. Instead she took a part-time job that enabled her to 'be there when they came home' and felt that 'the children were not suffering because I was at work because I could take them to school and I could pick them up after school and I could do all the extra things with them'. This job that she remained in for the rest of her working life was 'just very poorly paid' and consequently 'a supplementary income', and that 'very, very few men do it for that reason'. She did not have family support where she lived and stressed how hard it had been to juggle her competing roles. Emily described the stress of returning to paid employment when her children were young and worrying about what her children were doing after school.

Financial influences

The women's current and future financial situations influenced their career decisions. Sandra explained: 'I'm lucky enough that I've got enough of a monetary base that I can pick and choose. I don't have to go somewhere and do stuff that I don't want to do simply because I need money'. Emily, who had retired from work due to ill-health, also felt a lack of financial pressure:

> we're lucky enough not to have a mortgage now. Although we have no savings at least the children are more or less independent. My husband has a job and I'm hoping … while I'm at home I might be able to qualify for some sort of allowance or pension. That will enable us to just live quietly and that's all I want to do … The house isn't finished … that's the sort of thing that can wait until I'm well enough to go back to work and earn a little bit more.

Sandra wanted to earn a small wage 'that would be enough with my little nest egg … to be nice and comfortable'. Kate also wanted financial security in her retirement and 'to also keep working because financially I was sort of comfortable but since the financial crash … my superannuation has improved, it's still not what it … It wouldn't have been like luxury, but it was just comfort'.

Social influences

All of the women spoke of their support networks. Janice explained how when she lived overseas she was a member of 'a wonderful expat network' and joined a similar network when she returned to an Australian city where she had no family: 'I ended up with a similar sort of group who were women who didn't have family … and we all helped each other.' Sophia appreciated high levels of family support throughout her life. Fleur, who had immigrated to Australia, spoke of her isolation and lack of support living in a remote part of Australia 'on a cattle property where my closest neighbour was about 100 miles away, and the closest place for us to get groceries or anything was five hours' drive'. Remote Australia is served by the Royal Flying Doctor Service and Fleur described how much she looked forward to contact with other people on their monthly visit. A nurse who visited was 'absolutely brilliant' and her 'lifeline' and:

> I don't know how I would have coped without her. I used to … pour my heart out to her and she listened and often didn't really give a lot of advice but just helped me to understand where I was.

Relocation

All of the women had experienced relocation during their lives as a result of work or study opportunities or the relocation of a partner. Kate reflected how she moved to a mining town because of her husband's work and had to get a new job, which she found 'very difficult'. They subsequently moved back to a city and began a family. Kate's story is reflective of the stop and start career patterns of many of the women.

Several of the women had lived and worked overseas. For Kay, relocation because of her husband's work involved moving to other countries where she had limited opportunities to work even though she had an Australian professional qualification. On their return to Australia, she also relocated twice more because of her husband's work and once because of her work. By contrast, Megan's relocation related to seeking a better life in a different state and beginning to study. She also described moving overseas to find work when her children were adults as being 'really significant for me. … for the first time I didn't have to care for anybody … I was 44 when I moved over there'.

Advice to others

All of the women gave a 'just do it' response as advice they would give to other women. Some had more detailed advice to offer, as reflected by Kay:

> Identify your network, … you've got to do a lot of it on your own. Having confidence to do it on your own. And knowing that you're not always going to be supported. Don't close your eyes to the full range of opportunities. Don't be too narrow in what you think you might want to do … There could be all sorts of interesting things that you could do. I think building on the skills you have is good.

Sandra and Kate also offered strong advice to other women with Sandra urging: 'Do something that makes you feel good … just have patience, a bit of patience that it's going to take a while especially as you get older'. Similarly, Kate advised 'you shouldn't look at what other people think of you. Yeah, I think go with your heart. Don't be influenced by other's opinions because if it's from your heart, I think it's got to be true, true to you'. In essence, the women's words of encouragement to other women were tempered with messages related to self-belief and self-reliance.

Future planning

The women had begun to consider what they would do when they were no longer in paid employment. Some were considering voluntary work, which emphasised women's traditional caring role. Janice was considering volunteer work with Food Bank, Meals on Wheels and a hospital. Kay saw volunteer work as her ideal, but wondered 'whether I've got the energy to actually make it happen'. Both Kay and Denise had considered travelling, with Denise expressing a reservation about,

'Whether that comes to fruition I don't know, because who knows at my age.' Thus, similarly to Kay, she did not have complete confidence that her plans would be fulfilled.

Reflections

Overall, the stories of the older women's careers reflect the situation portrayed by Australian labour market data (e.g. Australian Government WGEA 2013). Unlike the quantifiable data, the stories provide a more nuanced understanding of women's lived experience in the labour market. The stories reveal the individual nature of the women's careers and the recursive relationship between their objective experiences and their subjective experiences. Moreover, the stories reveal the intersectionality of a range of influences (e.g. age and gender), which recursively weave through the women's lives.

A considerable portion of the careers of these women occurred prior to the introduction of the Equal Opportunity for Women in the Workplace Act in 1999 (Commonwealth of Australia). Disappointingly since the Act's introduction, equality of opportunity has not been achieved. It is likely that these women may witness young women, including their daughters and granddaughters, facing many of the same challenges and inequalities faced by them. Moreover, older women wanting to remain in employment in the Australian labour market are facing a new set of labour market challenges, where employers are not recognising and underutilising their experience and talent (Tilly *et al.* 2013). Thus it seems that the ideal of a 'fair go' for women, including older women, in the Australian labour market remains elusive.

References

Australian Bureau of Statistics (2011) 'Fifty years of labour force: Now and then'. Available at: www.abs.gov.au/ausstats/abs@.nsf/Lookup/6105.0Feature+Article1Oct%202011 (accessed 25 June 2013).

Australian Bureau of Statistics (2013a) 'Women in leadership'. Available at: www.abs.gov.au/AUSSTATS/abs@.nsf/Lookup/4102.0Main+Features30Dec+2012 (accessed 25 June 2013).

Australian Bureau of Statistics (2013b) *1301.0 Year Book Australia, 2012*. Available at: www.abs.gov.au/ausstats/abs@.nsf/Lookup/by%20Subject/1301.0~2012~Main%20Features~Aboriginal%20and%20Torres%20Strait%20Islander%20population~50 (accessed 25 June 2013).

Australian Government Workplace Gender Equality Agency (2012a) 'WGE Act at a glance'. Available at: www.wgea.gov.au/sites/default/files/Branded_act_at_a_glance_wgea.pdf (accessed 25 June 2013).

Australian Government Workplace Gender Equality Agency (2012b) 'What's changing? Comparison of key aspects of the old and new legislation'. Available at: www.wgea.gov.au/sites/default/files/Branded_WGEA_whats_changing.pdf (accessed 25 June 2013).

Australian Government Workplace Gender Equality Agency (2013a) 'Gender pay gap: Fact or fiction'. Available at: www.wgea.gov.au/sites/default/files/gender_pay_gap_fact_fiction.pdf (accessed 25 June 2013).

Australian Government Workplace Gender Equality Agency (2013b) 'Gender pay gap statistics'. Available at: www.wgea.gov.au/sites/default/files/2013-02-Gender%20pay%20 gap%20statistics.pdf (accessed 25 June 2013).

Australian Government Workplace Gender Equality Agency (2013c) 'Gender workplace statistics at a glance'. Available at: www.wgea.gov.au/sites/default/files/2013-04%20-%20 Stats%20at%20a%20glance_0.pdf (accessed 25 June 2013).

Australian Government Workplace Gender Equality Agency (2013d) 'Women in the workforce: By Industry'. Available at: www.wgea.gov.au/sites/default/files/2012-12-13%20-%20Women%20in%20the%20workforce%20by%20industry%5B1%5D.pdf (accessed 25 June 2013).

Commonwealth of Australia (1999) 'Equal Opportunity for Women in the Workplace Act 1999'. Available at: www.comlaw.gov.au/Details/C2004A00572/Download (accessed 25 June 2013).

Gilfillan, G. and Andrews, L. (2010) 'Labour force participation of women over 45', *Productivity Commission Staff Working Paper*, Canberra, Australia: Australian Government Productivity Commission. Available at: www.pc.gov.au/research/staff-working/women-over-45 (accessed 25 June 2013).

Tilly, J., O'Leary, J. and Russell, G. (2013) *Older Women Matter: Harnessing the Talent of Australia's Older Female Workforce*, Sydney, Australia: Diversity Council of Australia. Available at: www.dca.org.au/files/file/DCA%20Older%20Women%20Matter%20Exec%20 Summary%20online.pdf (accessed 25 June 2013).

10 Voices of older women from Canada

Nancy Arthur

Contemporary theory and practices in career development need to account for the intersections of cultural identities (Arthur and Collins 2011; Arthur and McMahon 2005; Leong *et al.* 2010; Pope 2011). Culture is most often defined by shared clusters of worldview, beliefs and values; rituals, practices, customs, or norms; social, religious, or spiritual traditions; language, history, ties to geographic locations; and/or adherence to social, economic, or political structures (Arthur and Collins 2010). Culture is not a static, essential characteristic of individuals; individuals and groups may hold multiple, complex, and sometimes conflicting cultural identities that shift over time as they navigate diverse social structures and interactions.

The career development literature on women has tended to homogenise their experiences, using binary comparisons with men, with few perspectives considering the impact of important cultural and systemic influences (Bimrose 2008; Bimrose and McNair 2011). Researchers and practitioners need to move beyond a general understanding of women's career development to considering how dimensions of culture, such as age, ethnicity, ability, social class, religion, ability, and/or sexual orientation intersect with gender in relevant ways for understanding women's life stories (Collins 2010; Cook *et al.* 2005; Fouad and Bingham 1995). Cultural identities are formed through social interactions and social reactions to prescribed cultural identities and position some members of society as less powerful and non-dominant (Arthur and Collins 2010). Such interactions are relevant for understanding the experiences of women in a hierarchical world that stratifies people according to their perceived social value. The importance of cultural identities for career development rests not only with the salient aspects identified by women, but also with the social perceptions and actions shown towards women across their life contexts.

The focus of this chapter will be on women's career development in the context of immigration. Immigrant women face a multitude of career-related issues associated with setting up life in a new country. However, similar to the literature on women's career development, it is important to consider that the transition experiences of immigrants are not uniform. The discussion in this chapter describes the experiences of older immigrant women aged between 45 and 65, and the influences on their integration into the Canadian labour market. The chapter begins with providing contextual information about immigration trends, and recent statistics about immigrant women in Canada. Next, the participants are introduced. Results are discussed according to nine themes to illustrate their career journeys of living, learning, and working in Canada. The concluding section of the chapter contains reflections about the stories told by immigrant professional women.

Beyond the diversity found within indigenous populations, immigration has been a major force towards increasing diversity in the Canadian population. Canada's immigration policy incorporates categories under which individuals may apply for immigration (Citizenship and Immigration Canada 2005). The economic category includes policy directives to assess the viability of immigrants to be successful in the labour market, and includes highly educated and/or skilled labour. Family class immigrants have family reunification with relatives who are already established in Canada. The refugee category refers to persons who require protection or relief, and who most often have fled their countries involuntarily. Since 2006, Canada has sustained an annual average of about a quarter of a million immigrants to Canada, welcoming 248,660 permanent residents in 2011, including 156,077 economic immigrants and 56,419 family class immigrants (Citizenship and Immigration Canada 2012). Although there are distinctions between the general categories of immigrant versus refugee, these are often arbitrary categories. There is a spectrum of pre-migration conditions between and within source countries, and there are often individual differences between family members regarding the motives for immigration (Arthur 2012).

Changes in the source countries of immigrants have introduced wide variations in the customs and cultural norms practiced in the Canadian context. During the early part of the twentieth century, most immigrants came to Canada from European and North American source countries, but recent immigration involves Asian, Middle Eastern, Caribbean, Central American, and African countries (Statistics Canada 2007). Within the next decade, it is estimated that one in five Canadians will be a member of a visible minority group (Statistics Canada 2007).

Immigration is inextricably linked to Canada's economic policies and the demand for skilled labour and population growth (Arthur and Flynn 2011; Chen 2008). Yet policies to attract new immigrants do not always translate to equity for entering educational and employment systems. Securing gainful employment is pivotal for social and economic integration. Yet many immigrants, even those accepted under the economic class, experience oppression, discrimination, and inequitable access to education and employment (Chen 2008; Schellenberg and Maheux 2007). Consequently, many immigrants live on the margins of Canadian society, due to challenges of language, recognition of international education and credentials, and employer practices for hiring people with local Canadian experience (Ngo and Este 2006). Many well-educated and skilled women who are recent migrants remain unemployed or underemployed, in comparison to women who are Canadian-born and in comparison to women who have immigrated for a longer period of time, primarily due to a lack of recognition of their international qualifications (Chui 2011; International Organization for Migration 2012). Attitudes towards immigrants also shift during times of economic downturn. Perceptions that immigrants take jobs from people who have lived longer in Canada, e.g. racist attitudes about which individuals are real Canadians, are expressed as hostilities within companies and in local communities (Palmer 1996).

Statistics collected by Status of Women Canada (2013) provide a portrait of immigrant women based on population numbers, education, employment, and earnings. Approximately half the immigrants accepted to Canada each year are female. About 20 per cent of the total female population is comprised of immigrants and half of the immigrant female population arrived in Canada prior to 1991. It is noteworthy that immigrant women are more likely to be university graduates than Canadian-born women, but women between the ages of 25 and 54 are less likely to be university-educated than immigrant men. It appears to take immigrant women time to integrate into the labour market as employment rates for more established immigrants, defined as women who have lived in Canada from five to ten years or longer, are over 50 per cent.

Based on statistics collected in the 2006 national census, immigrant women accounted for 21 per cent of the female labour force population, which totalled 8.1 million. Canada's total female labour force population showed increases of almost 10 per cent, while the rate of increase for immigrant women was almost double that of Canadian-born women; this represented approximately 1.7 million women immigrants in the labour force (Chui 2011). However, the employment sectors where women work, whether immigrant or Canadian born, continue to show clustering in traditional female sectors, such as retail sales and services as well as in business, finance, and administrative fields. In general, immigrant women have lower employment rates than immigrant men, when comparing length of time living in Canada. It has also been suggested that the labour market downturn in the last five years has had a greater impact on unemployment rates for immigrant women than for Canadian-born women (Status of Women Canada 2013). Longitudinal research needs to account for a fuller picture of integration, over time, to determine whether or not immigrant women achieve equitable vertical employment integration in comparison to male immigrants, and in comparison to Canadian-born women, based on a fuller analysis of occupational sectors (Tastsoglou and Preston 2005). Research also needs to account for the experiences of racialised Canadians, who continue to experience levels of unemployment and earnings that are lower than non-racialised Canadians (Block and Galabuzi 2011). Racialised women immigrants are at-risk of labour participation in jobs that are low-paying, temporary, and insecure.

Although available statistics provide information regarding the status of immigrant women on selected indicators, they do not fully account for the diversity found within Canada's immigrant female population. Statistics obscure the fact that not all immigrant women will have the same experiences in trying to gain entry into the labour market upon arriving in Canada, and that both individual and structural forces can have profound influences on women immigrants' experiences

(Koert *et al.* 2011; McCoy and Masuch 2007). The research reported in this chapter focused on older immigrant women, ages 45 to 65, and their experiences of navigating entry into the labour market. Further, as the literature on immigrants, in general, tends to focus on the problems of adjustment and barriers to employment success (Chen 2008), the current study sought to better understand facilitating factors for older immigrant professional women to make the transition to living, learning, and working in a Canadian context.

Listening to the women's stories

Participants for the study were recruited through one immigrant-serving settlement agency in an urban centre in Western Canada. The coordinator of Employment Services at the agency made the initial contact and provided the researcher with e-mail addresses and/or phone numbers of volunteer participants. Criteria for participation were immigrant women aged 45 to 65, who had been living in Canada during the previous two to five years, who had the minimum of an undergraduate degree, and who had obtained prior work experience in their chosen professional field prior to immigration. Participants were paid an honorarium of 50 Canadian dollars. Consent for participation was obtained either through writing or through audio recording. Semi-structured individual interviews were conducted by a doctoral-level graduate student who had prior training in multicultural counselling and qualitative interview skills. Interviews were conducted at the location of each participant's choice, including office, home, or coffee shops. The interview questions for this study are outlined in Chapter 7, along with other details of the methodology.

Demographic information regarding the Canadian participants is presented in Table 10.1. Due to issues of confidentiality, the countries of origin for each woman are reported separately, including Bangladesh ($N = 2$), China, Iraq, Jordan, Malaysia, Philippines ($N = 2$), Pakistan, Romania, Russia, and Togo. Each participant selected a pseudonym, which was used to illustrate examples of the themes.

Learning across the lifespan

Formal learning provided the foundation of the women's educational experiences in their home countries and their pursuit of professional careers. Participants also described their formal learning in light of how it positioned them for the employment market in the Canadian work context. They became aware of how well, or not, their credentials transferred across countries and, in some cases, discovered that education in their home countries did not hold the same currency for seeking employment in Canada. For example, Carmen noted that her MBA from the Philippines was regarded as an undergraduate degree in Canada. Ellen encountered challenges in transferring her education, as her formal education was for a specialist position in an industry that had few local opportunities where she was living in Canada.

Table 10.1 Canadian sample

Pseudonym	Age	Marital status	Employment status	Income per annum	Dependents	Years living in Canada	Highest qualification	Current employment
Sammy	45	Married	Full-time	$50,000–70,000	2 children	3	Bachelor (1990)	Supervisor, senior support programs
Sally	51	Single	Full-time	$20,000–30,000	none	3	Bachelor (1983)	Cashier
Carmen	47	Married	Full-time	$30,00–50,000	2 children	5	Master's (1998)	Client services assistant
Katie	45	Married	Full-time	<$20,000	4 children	1	Bachelor (1988)	Self-employed
Ellen	50	Married	Full-time	$30,000–50,000	1 child	2	PhD (1995)	Accountant
Vivian	46	Separated	Full-time	$30,000–50,000	1 child and mother	4	Bachelor (2002)	Fast food server
Shereen	52	Single	Part-time	<$20,000	None	1	Master's (1991)	Cook
Mala	47	Married	Full-time	<$20,000	1 child	6	Master's (1991)	Grocery store clerk
Maria	45	Married	Full-time	$30,000–50,000	1 child	4	Bachelor (1992)	Assistant program coordinator
Pako	51	Married	Full-time	$30,000–50,000	3 children	4	Bachelor (1998)	Teacher assistant
Mari	48	Married	Full-time	>$100,000	1 child	5	Bachelor (1987)	Self-employed contractor
Madhuri	49	Married	Full-time	$30,000–50,000	1 child	5	Master's (1986)	Accountant
Mimidek	54	Single	Full-time	$20,000–30,000	4 children and 6 extended family members	3	Bachelor (1984)	Security officer

Beyond formal education in their home countries, participants accessed formal education as part of their commitment to upgrade their eligibility for employment in Canada. Participants, like Ellen, emphasised the informal learning in the workplace, trying to figure out new systems, and upgrade their skills:

> I think about informal learning, I'm always in this process, because I try to learn new things, new things. And especially in this job I learned a lot because I used my experience, my professional experience, from my native country … And some things is connected with the professional field and some things are connected with some … only specific for this company … But for me it was completely new. And I know that it's not connected with education and professional knowledge. It's only some specific details for this company … So learning, learning, learning every time.

Learning in the new cultural context appeared to be an intervention for the women that were interviewed, as they could actively pursue new understandings and ways of working in the Canadian context.

Transitions

All of the participants were experiencing an immigration transition, and still coming to terms with the meaning of their new lives in Canada. This is an important point, because immigration transitions do not end with the physical movement between countries. Rather, transition is an ongoing process of learning about themselves, relationships, and the world around them (Schlossberg 2011). The participants in this study were mentally prepared for many of the changes between cultural contexts, but there were some unexpected and unanticipated events that proved to be emotionally taxing. For example, Madhuri's husband experienced a serious illness after coming to Canada. Mala's husband lost his professional job after employment for 18 months, due to the downturn in the economy. The participants' experiences of transition were often complicated by daily demands for new adjustments. The women interviewed openly talked about the strong emotional toll that was triggered by their immigration transition, naming emotions such as frustration, anxiety, stress, and depression, like Sally:

> When I … when I first took the train … I saw all the people, and then I said they … they look all the same … Yeah. And the first time I took the train I said, 'How I'm going to … going to differentiate those people from one another, because they all look the same.'

Or Vivian:

> It's like why I change my life, like, roll over … It's totally different way. I never ever expected before I came here, but life changed dramatically … I feel like

overwhelmed and almost like stressed out or depression ... But fortunately I overcome ... and I still survive and I hope ... I'm doing better than before.

The vast differences between their home cultures and conditions in Canada required major learning and adjustment. Participants in the study compared their circumstances between home and host countries and initially felt overwhelmed. Shareen felt depressed when she realised that social and economic circumstances in Canada were less than what she had in her home country. Carmen noted the frustration of leaving a good life and starting over, with no family support. When asked about how they managed to cope through the transitions, participants detailed their stories about adaptability. This did not happen by chance, rather the women described their active strategies to overcome adversity and learn new ways of living in the Canadian context. They actively engaged in problem-solving and were open to learning and trying new ways of approaching workplace and social interactions.

Intrapersonal influences

The intrapersonal characteristics that were mentioned included confidence, embracing a sense of challenge, and resilience. Madhuri mentioned that at times she felt that she should be able to do things at the workplace on her own, and that having to ask people for help was viewed as a personal weakness. Pako was able to reframe her experiences as challenges and stay motivated. Sally's openness to accepting what came her way was described as personal resiliency:

> I guess I'm very resilient. And so whatever life has offered me ... or whatever decisions I've made ... I'm more accepting of things ... Whatever changes that comes I ... like I live in the present, whatever present that ... I'm willing to work it out ... Yeah, constant thing that whatever comes my way, whether it be failure or success ... I ... I'm open to the things.

There were mixed experiences among the participants in terms of how they viewed their age and the impact of this on their transition experiences. For example, Carmen felt the toll of her age, after moving to Canada, on physical, mental, and emotional levels. Mala found that her age impacted her performance in jobs. Mimidek was able to reframe her age in terms of continued possibilities for learning:

> I feel sometimes frustrated every ... sometimes, but I say, Wow, I learn a lot. I can cut meat, I can work in deli, I can work as cashier, I can work as security officer. So I'm still learning and, like I say, fighting for me, you know. It's like I'm still young, I'm still at school ... I'm still learning and ... Yeah. That's why I don't feel that I'm getting old.

There were connections made between participants' perceptions of their personal qualities and their capacity to impact the environment around them. Evaluating their progress, seeing positive changes, and finding opportunities for continued learning, was internalised as increased confidence and commitment for integrating into Canadian society.

Work influences

The participants in the study compared the types of jobs that they held in their home countries with their current employment situation. Although several of the participants were able to find employment in their professional field, the majority reported being underemployed for their professional qualifications. They compared workplace dynamics, such as the status they enjoyed in their employment, the status of women in the workplace, and the quality of workplace relationships and support. Three of the participants noted how important volunteer experience was for helping them gain local experience. Volunteering provided them with more than experience; it was an avenue that enabled them to discover and affirm capabilities and a passion for work. Sally noted the similarity between her work in the Philippines with street children and her volunteer work in the local parish. Maria found that her volunteer work in the resource centre of an immigration agency gave her a sense of purpose and supported her love of books. Carmen noted some tensions between the suggestion to obtain volunteer experience as a form of Canadian experience, and the need for new immigrants to earn an income. Her experience uncovers some of the overt and covert discrimination against immigrants who lack local experience, as preferred by employers:

> The thing is because you are an immigrant, you don't have Canadian experience so they will tell you, Oh, you have to do…to do volunteering first so you can have Canadian experience, right. But for how long will you be taking voluntary work just so you can have Canadian experience…You need to earn immediately…So that's why now you will take whatever job that lands in your lap, right. And that's why there's a lot of…most immigrants won't get in… won't get into their mind of professional education until they have, like, 4 or 5 years' experience already…Canada will say there was no discrimination, but there is…the government of Canada who allows people to like…to immigrate here has no hold on employers, right…It's still the employer's choice who they'll hire.

Other participants noted the pressure they felt to secure employment as a source of income, despite their professional education. However, this led to a vicious cycle of underemployment, in which it was hard to leave the source of income to pursue employment in their professional field.

Some participants mentioned that they felt pressured by employment counsellors to take any job offer, described as 'survival jobs'. Carmen noted how important it was for her to try to find a job in her field. Even though she was underemployed, she felt that a job in her professional field of the banking industry was much better than taking a survival job.

Financial influences

Financial influences for the participants involved comparisons of income, terms of sponsorship, and standard of living in the Canadian context. Both Sally and Sammy had relatives who offered financial support to them when they arrived in Canada. Pako and Katie noted the decrease in their financial situation, compared to income earned in their home countries. Shareen and Mimidek noted the hardship they experienced upon first arriving in Canada, when trying to support themselves and family members on meagre government support or money saved prior to coming to Canada. Differences in the cost of living and the expenses involved in starting over in a new country were financial stressors for the majority of participants. In contrast, Ellen was able to connect to the workforce soon after arriving in Canada and she earned more salary than expected in her occupational field.

Social influences

Family and community support were viewed as key resources. The immigration transition was often pursued as a way to secure a better future for their children. Ellen noted her personal conviction, 'to give our children the best we can give'. In turn, several of the women noted the support that they received from their family members. Madhuri described the support and encouragement she felt from her husband and children to pursue her studies. Maria noted that her husband immigrated first and 'he prepared everything for us; for my son and myself'. Pako told a story of when she was particularly discouraged about her employment situation: 'And my sons, they support me a lot. Sometimes I feel so sad and they say, "Oh don't worry mommy, you will be fine. You are a brave mommy".'

The participants were grateful for new support systems and the people in Canada who showed interest in their wellbeing and helped them to feel a sense of belonging. Carmen stated that initially she and her husband had 'no relatives, friends. So we have only one old lady that's not even a friend, just an acquaintance, she took us in'. Mari appreciated the social support that a friend offered to help find a job. Mimidek developed peer support with other newcomers who were living in the same residence upon arrival in Canada: 'People are new like me, so we make friends between us. I still call them, we call each other, so we still are like friends or family'. The support and encouragement to manage the immigration transition came from family, staff at the immigrant settlement agency, new friends, and former teachers. Participants also noted the importance of having role models, particularly other immigrants who had been successful and could provide advice and direction.

Relocation

The stories of participants centred on their transition experiences, but immigration to Canada was not a uniform process. Some participants who immigrated to Canada for family reunification came to a supportive environment with family members to guide their initial settlement process. Other participants dealt with long delays in processing their immigration application, for example, Katie waited six years for the paperwork to be processed in her home country. Shereen faced the reality that her credentials as a dentist would not be recognised in Canada, and was refused positions requiring lower qualifications.

Carmen noted how hurtful it was to experience discrimination and misinformation about immigrants, and how public perceptions often did not match many immigrants' experiences:

> Sometimes it pains me when I read all those comments … talking about the immigrants and how we are sucking up the system, something like that … And I said, Oh, okay. As an independent immigrant you have to have a university degree … And you have to have the money that you really need to take … to bring here. You have to have the money just to process all your papers, right. It did not come to us free … We waited 5 years for it – right. And then when we came here we started looking for jobs. It doesn't matter what kind of jobs … We looked at whatever jobs it is. So I don't think that will … that we can call that sucking up the system.

Maria's experience illustrates how newcomers compare lifestyles between home and host cultures in evaluating their experience of relocation through immigration:

> So when you see yourself in a different country … like, different culture, the responsibilities, of course, family and not knowing the language … and looking around you and say, Okay, and now what? What am I doing here? Why did I come? So, looking back I left something … I – I left a good position … a good life to come to … to Canada because I do believe that Canada offers many opportunities and a good life. When I say 'good life,' I'm not … I don't only mean financially … Just … now, I don't know, I mean much freedom; freedom of … less pressure … It's a change for the better.

Relocation to Canada inevitably involved a combination of losses and gains, relative to the financial, social, and political situations found in the country of origin in comparison to perceptions about the quality of life in Canada.

Advice to others

Participants in this study had lived through the initial settlement stage of immigration and were attached to the labour market. They benefitted from the experience and advice of family members, staff of settlement agencies, and immigrants who were role models to them; in turn, their experiences offer insightful suggestions for new immigrants. A key message repeated was the importance of embracing learning opportunities for self-improvement. Ellen emphasised that, despite adversity, it is important to stay positive, confident, and to seek information. Maria also emphasised how information is the key to success. She emphasised being confident as a strategy to cope and as a way to maintain motivation when faced with the hard work of managing a new job, of upgrading language, and when volunteering. Sally noted the importance of remaining clear about goals and to be prepared to face the challenges that surface along the way. Shereen's comments emphasised the importance of having a good social network to find information, to know where to go to seek help, and to access resources.

Sammy offered insights about giving the transition process more time and sustaining a commitment to pursue personal goals. Sammy noted the importance of being careful about what compromises are made: 'I refused to compromise on the industry. I will compromise on where you start, but I would not compromise on this way unless, of course it comes to a mouth that needs to be fed at home.' Her advice to 'stick to it' was in regard to meeting career goals that might be initially very challenging but will pay off in the longer term.

Future planning

The reflections of participants were primarily directed at what had helped them to successfully manage the transition to living, learning, and working in Canada. Carmen was pursuing more course work so that she could gain licensure for a change of occupations within her professional field. Madhuri also linked her future planning to continuing learning to improve her English language skills and her professional knowledge. Katie and Mala shared their dream of opening up their own businesses. Katie planned to combine her skill set with her husband's expertise to open up their own business. Mala recognised an opportunity to open a home-based business that would allow her to have more time at home while serving a community need. Mimidek's future plans also emphasised the connections between continued learning, personal growth, and pursuing her professional interests.

Reflections

The career development literature on immigrants has often obscured important cultural and systemic influences on career development such as age, gender, ethnicity, socioeconomic circumstances, and the availability of employment in the new country. Consistent with previous research (Koert *et al.* 2011; McCoy and Masuch 2007), both internal/personal and external factors were identified as influential for the employment transition experiences of older professional immigrant women. The influence of gender for employment and occupational mobility is not a single story: rather the experience is nuanced by the intersections of cultural identity, including the ways in which the age of immigrant women may be a factor in the pursuit of gainful employment. It is presumptuous to assume that younger immigrant women, who are at the early stage of career, immigrant women at mid-career, or older immigrant women will share the same experiences of employment and social integration. Future research is needed to determine what might be in common across women immigrants' experiences, but also how their experiences may vary due to the intersections of age, social class, and ethnicity. Immigrant women are a diverse group, according to country and cultures, by educational background, work experience, available family support, and stage of life. Future research needs to account for the diversity of experiences to inform theories and models of career development and career counselling.

The women interviewed in this study represent a group of volunteers who were recruited from one immigrant-serving agency in Western Canada. It should be noted that there are wide disparities in the economic conditions between regions within Canada and the resources allocated to various sectors of the labour market. Correspondingly, there are variations in the resources allocated by federal and provincial governments to support agencies whose mandates involve the employment and job placement of newcomers. This study focused on older immigrant women who self-defined themselves as professional and who had accessed the employment market. It is conceivable that the stories of other older immigrant women who were not working may reveal more insights regarding the barriers involved in their experiences.

The results of this study suggest that the journey of immigrant professional women is one marked by learning as a formal and informal intervention, by embracing the motivation to build a better life for family, and through personal commitment to overcome perceived barriers and keep working towards a preferred future. The older immigrant women in this study offered many insights and much advice about how to overcome structural barriers such as the recognition of credentials, getting hired in their chosen professional fields, and the steps that they were taking to successfully integrate into the labour market. They focused on what is possible, and what it takes to make personal connections, to remain inspired, and to see the fruition of their efforts. Their stories are connected to their lives in their home countries, their experiences of navigating a new cultural context, and of finding ways that they could continue improving themselves and build towards a better future.

References

Arthur, N. (2012) 'Career development and international transitions', in M. McMahon and M. Watson (eds) *Career Development: Global Issues and Challenges*, Hauppauge, NY: Nova Science.

Arthur, N. and Collins, S. (2010) 'Introduction to culture-infused counselling', in N. Arthur and S. Collins (eds) *Culture-infused Counselling*, Calgary, AB: Counselling Concepts (2nd ed.).

Arthur, N. and Collins, S. (2011) 'Infusing culture in career counselling', *Journal of Employment Counseling*, 48: 47–9.

Arthur, N. and Flynn, S. (2011) 'Career development influences of international students who pursue permanent immigration to Canada', *International Journal of Education and Vocational Guidance*, 11: 221–37.

Arthur, N. and McMahon, M. (2005) 'A Systems Theory Framework for multicultural career counseling', *The Career Development Quarterly*, 53: 208–22.

Bimrose, J. (2008) 'Guidance for girls and women', in J. Athanasou and R. Van Esbroeck (eds) *International Handbook of Career Guidance*, New York: Springer.

Bimrose, J. and McNair, S. (2011) 'Career support for migrants: Transformation or adaptation', *Journal of Vocational Behavior*, 78: 321–92.

Block, S. and Galabuzi, G. (2011) *Canada's Colour Coded Labour Market: The Gap for Racialized Workers*, Ottawa, ON: Canadian Centre for Policy Alternatives. Available at: www.policyalternatives.ca/sites/default/files/uploads/publications/National%20Office/2011/03/Colour%20Coded%20Labour%20Market.pdf (accessed 29 October 2013).

Chen, C. (2008) 'Career guidance with immigrants', in J. Athanasou and R. Van Esbroeck (eds) *International Handbook of Career Guidance*, New York: Springer.

Chui, T. (2011) *Immigrant Women*, Ottawa, Canada: Statistics Canada (July). Available at: www.statcan.gc.ca/pub/89-503-x/2010001/article/11528-eng.htm (accessed 29 October 2013).

Citizenship and Immigration Canada (2005) 'Annual report to Parliament on immigration, 2005'. Available at: www.cic.gc.ca/ENGLISH/RESOURCES/PUBLICATIONS/multi-report2008/part1.asp (accessed 24 January 2009).

Citizenship and Immigration Canada (2012) 'News release – Canada continued to welcome a high number of immigrants in 2011', Ottawa, ON: Government of Canada. Available at: www.cic.gc.ca/english/department/media/releases/2012/2012-03-02a.asp (accessed 29 May 2013).

Collins, S. (2010) 'The complexity of identity: Appreciating multiplicity and intersectionality', in N. Arthur and S. Collins (eds) *Culture-infused Counselling*, Calgary, AB: Counselling Concepts (2nd ed.).

Cook, E. P., Heppner, M. J. and O'Brien, K. M. (2005) 'Multicultural and gender influences in women's career development: An ecological perspective', *Journal of Multicultural Counseling and Development*, 33: 165–79.

Fouad, N. A. and Bingham, R. P. (1995) 'Career counselling with racial and ethnic minorities', in W. B. Walsh and S. H. Osipow (eds) *Handbook of Vocational Psychology: Theory, Research, and Practice*, Mahwah, NJ: Lawrence Erlbaum (2nd ed.).

International Organization for Migration (2012) *Crushed Hopes: Underemployment and Deskilling Among Skilled Migrant Women*, Geneva, Switzerland. Available at: http://publications.iom.int/bookstore/free/Crushed_Hopes_3Jan2013.pdf (Accessed 6 November 2013).

Koert, E., Borgen, W. and Amundson, N. (2011) 'Educated immigrant women workers doing well with change: Helping and hindering factors', *Career Development Quarterly*, 59: 194–207.

Leong, F. T. L., Hardin, E. and Gupta, A. (2010) 'A cultural formulation approach to career assessment and career counselling with Asian American clients', *Journal of Career Development*, 37: 465–86.

McCoy, L. and Masuch, C. (2007) 'Beyond "entry-level" jobs: Immigrant women and non-regulated professional occupations', *International Migration and Integration*, 8: 185–206.

Ngo, H. and Este, D. (2006) 'Professional re-entry for foreign-trained immigrants', *Journal of International Migration and Integration*, 7: 27–50.

Palmer, D. (1996) 'Determinants of Canadian attitudes towards immigration: More than just racism', *Canadian Journal of Behavioral Science*, 28: 180–92.

Pope, M. (2011) 'The career counseling with underserved populations model', *Journal of Employment Counseling*, 48: 153–5.

Schellenberg, G. and Maheux, H. (2007) 'Immigrants' perspectives on their first four years in Canada: Highlights from three waves of the Longitudinal Survey of Immigrants to Canada'. Available at: www5.statcan.gc.ca/bsolc/olc-cel/olc-cel?catno=11-008-X20070009627 (accessed 29 May 2013).

Schlossberg, N. K. (2011) 'The challenge of change: The transition model and its applications', *Journal of Employment Counseling*, 48(4): 159–62.

Statistics Canada (2007) 'Ethnic diversity and immigration'. Available at: www41.statcan.ca/2007/30000/ceb30000_000_e.htm (accessed 15 June 2009).

Status of Women Canada (2013) 'Women in Canada at a glance: Statistical highlights'. Available at: www.swc-cfc.gc.ca/rc-cr/stat/wic-fac-2012/sec7-eng.html (accessed 29 May 2013).

Tastsoglou, E. and Preston, V. (2005) 'Gender, immigration and labour market integration: Where we are and what we still need to know', *Atlantis*, 30: 46–59.

11 Voices of older women from China

Ying Kuang

The establishment of the new China in 1949 liberated millions of Chinese women, who were able to enjoy equal employment rights and opportunities for the first time alongside men. The redistribution of jobs effected by the government through the employment management system entitled almost every woman of employable age to a job in the planned economy (Zhou 1995). The women in this study were born just before or just after the establishment of the new China, with most of them employed for the first time in the period between 1960 and 1980. Thus they were at the forefront of this particular set of social and economic transformations, experiencing first-hand China's dramatic transition from a traditional planned economy to a socialist market economy, with commensurate changes to their employment experiences and labour market transitions.

During the early years (1956–1979) of the planned economy, urban women who reached the age of employment (16 years old) and who were able to work were assigned to a job that was needed by the nation (Chen 2004). Women living in rural areas continued with their work either planting or farming. Jobs were both a right and an obligation, without any possibility of choice being exercised by the individual. As well as being allocated a job, the education and/or training required for the assigned job was also planned and arranged by the nation (Jiang 2000). Despite these constraints, the women in this study complied with the nation's employment requirements, alongside men, even if they disliked or hated the job that had been allocated.

However, since the implementation of further major economic reforms as part of the introduction of the socialist market economic system in 1992, the position of women in the labour market has deteriorated markedly. Because women's physical stamina is regarded as less than men's, they began to be regarded as less valuable in the labour market (Sun 1989). Additionally, entrepreneurs increasingly concluded that employing women was not profitable, since they also had to pay for maternity insurance (Yu 2011). The inferior position of women in the labour market was exacerbated by the restructuring of state-owned organisations, which attracted large numbers of female employees. When state-owned organisations began to cut their costs by downsizing, many female employees were laid off. Of the ten million workers who were laid off nationally in the early 1990s, females comprised 62.8 per cent. In some provinces, the proportion of females laid-off was between 70 and 80 per cent. Of these, many middle-aged female employees suffered discrimination as they were forced into lower-income jobs, or they simply left the labour market altogether and went back to their families (Li and Li 2008). Most of the urban middle-age women in this study were laid-off during the period of reform dating from 1992.

In China, there are two distinct categories of unemployment, each with different implications for financial support. One category relates to individuals who lose their jobs as a result of bankruptcy, cancellation (that is, cancellation of a labour contract) or organisational restructuring. Once unemployed, these individuals severed all links with their employers and were eligible to receive social assistance from the relevant government department. The other type of unemployment relates to being laid-off from state-run enterprises. With the introduction of a market economy, these employers cut their costs by downsizing. Those who were laid-off were jobless. However, these particular individuals were able to retain a link with their original employers, benefitting from a financial allowance, pension and medical insurance, together with other welfare benefits. Despite these advantages, those who were laid off from state-run organisations suffered a loss of social and family status, becoming socially marginalised (Jiang and Dang 2008). This group of women had previously enjoyed considerable privileges, including superior social status, a high degree of social respect, political participation, material advantages and other social rights (such as state-subsidised housing, reimbursement for medical bills and so on). Nevertheless, they became an increasingly vulnerable group with a loss of social status and occupational identity who, when re-employed, were mostly engaged in low-paid work.

The psychological pressures caused by loss of status and income from the loss of employment were compounded by these women having to share a greater economic burden of responsibility for their family. In China, it is a traditional and well-established social norm that men are oriented beyond their families towards the wider society, while women are more family-oriented. This role differentiation defines two distinct kinds of activities and responsibilities for men compared with women. Being home-based, women are expected to focus attention on taking good care of their husbands and children (Zhao 2006). In economic terms, gender relations are clearly apparent in the gendered divisions reflected across the labour market and the different values placed on different types of jobs, with women's employment status remaining subordinate to men's. Indeed, it is generally recognised that men are engaged mainly in production, while women are engaged in reproduction, with men enjoying the social status and higher pay linked with their work. There is a gender gap in Chinese society that cannot be underestimated. Neither women's labour nor their reproductive capacity has been valued, remaining largely ignored both by society and history. Men enjoy a much higher employment rate, while the occupations and industries in which women are employed typically relate to their traditional roles, with consequent lower status and pay (Zhao 2003).

Even though it is true that the Chinese women who have participated in this study have technically enjoyed social liberation for decades, deeply embedded traditional beliefs and norms, reflected in colloquialisms like 'women are inferior to men', and 'men are in the marketplace and women are in the home', prevent them from achieving their true potential. Constrained by these beliefs, it is much more difficult for women to get promotion in the labour market, with the so-called glass ceiling making it difficult to progress beyond a certain level (Zhao and Wang 2006). Perhaps unsurprisingly, therefore, and especially for women aged 45–65, being promoted at work is typically not their most important career goal. Rather, it is more usual for them, from the age of 50 or 55 years, to enjoy their retirement by taking care of their grandchildren at home. Indeed, few of these women re-enter the labour market after retirement (Zhao 2003). Chinese women in the 45–65 years age group are typically either about to enjoy, or have already begun to enjoy, a less pressurised period of their lives. According to Regulations on Retirement issued by the State Council, once a worker has retired, a state pension will be provided until his/her death. In addition, this regulation specifies that a woman can retire at the age of 50 if she has been working continually for ten years (Labour Act, dated 5 July 1994). This discourages older women in China from changing their jobs.

Listening to the women

Demographic details of the 12 Chinese women who participated in this study can be found in Table 11.1.

A semi-structured interview protocol was used mainly through face-to-face interviews, telephone interviews, email, and QQ (QQ is similar to the Skype software and commonly used in mainland China). One participant was interviewed several times; because of the particular complexities of her work and learning transitions, it was thought necessary to follow up the first interview further. The research team comprised nine individuals, a professor and her postgraduate students, all of whom were from mainland China. Each researcher recruited between 1 and 3 participants and conducted the interviews. The researchers worked closely together to guarantee the reliability and richness of the data collected from the participants. Selected findings from the study are presented below.

Learning across the lifespan

Eleven of the 12 participants had benefitted from formal education. Three of the participants had remained in education to senior high school education level, five held a diploma, one had a Masters degree, and two participants received less than senior high school education. Only one had not received any type of formal education. The women who had participated in further education had mainly done this to meet the requirements of their jobs. Four had engaged in education in their spare time in order to obtain their degrees. Only two women had a Junior College Diploma before they were employed for the first time, but this number increased to six, through on-the-job training. Additionally, two women gained qualifications through self-learning and training to obtain promotion.

Table 11.1 Chinese Sample

Pseudonym	Age	Marital status	Employment status	Income per annum (RMB)	Dependents	Highest qualification	Employment status
Rong	51	Married	Full-time	24,000	4	Junior high school	Self-employment, runs a repair shop
Ping	45	Divorced	Full-time	36,000	2	Junior college	Self-employment, runs a motel
Feng	49	Married	Full-time	12,000	2	Primary school	Self-employment selling potatoes
Hua	48	Married	Full-time	33,600	5	Junior college	Primary school teacher
Su	57	Married	Full-time	36,000	4	Senior high school	Self-employment
Fang	45	Married	Full-time	120,000	3	Part-time masters degree	Vocational school teacher
Wei	45	Married	Full-time	120,000	3	Junior college	Professional teacher on marketing in the secondary vocational school
Liu	55	Married	Full-time	24,000	3	Senior high school	Full time employment
Ling	52	Married	Full-time	19,200	4	Junior college	Farmer
Ying	56	Married	Part-time	More than 600,000	4	Junior college	Self-employment, part-time job
Yang	47	Married	Full-time	More than 14,400RMB/M	4	Without formal education	A worker in a garment factory
Sun	45	Married	Full-time	More than 21,600RMB/M	3	Senior high school	A chief accountant

All 12 participants had engaged in workplace learning, which helped enrich their knowledge in different ways. This had proved to be very important. One participant explained how she had taken every opportunity to participate in training in her spare time. Hua, currently working as a primary school teacher, said: 'But I didn't have any formal teaching education and training. What I could do was only to rely on my self-study'. She also reflected on her self-learning:

> Working in the kindergarten also gave me a chance to learn a lot of professional preschool education knowledge and it made me suddenly realise the duty of parents, I thought it gave me great help in how to educate and take care of my children after my marriage.

Another participant, Ping, who was self-employed and ran a motel, explained how she acquired the skills she needed by studying in her own time: 'I had to spend one month on computer training to study typing after work.' Opportunities for more formal learning were sometimes offered by employers. For example, Sun, a chief accountant in a travel agency, was sent away to a city to be trained for about three days by her company. Informal learning on the job from experienced workmates, leaders and friends was also in evidence from the participants' stories, and this played an important role in the women's lives.

Transitions

Filial piety is one of Chinese women's traditional family values. It is so deeply immersed in their life and soul that family roles come first among all other social roles. Consequently, the main motivation identified by participants for their employment transitions was to meet the needs of the family. Seven of the participants changed jobs for this reason. For example, Rong changed her job from planting vegetables to carrying wood to earn more money to help support the family, even though carrying wood was very tiring and dangerous:

> That (planting vegetables) involved very long hours and the salary was very low. I am the oldest one in my family; I had to help my parents to keep our big family. There were eight people in our family, three younger sisters and two younger brothers. I had stayed there [carrying wood] for one year.

One other illustration of this core filial value is provided by Ping, who said:

> I am a Chinese, and one returns to one's roots. My mother wanted me to stay in my hometown. I thought that I could look after my mother if I stayed in my hometown. I chose to stay. So I started my own business.

In total, the 12 women participants in this study reported 50 job changes. Those caused by unexpected or unanticipated events accounted for exactly half. These included bankruptcy or the merger of employing organisations ($N = 6$). Ying, working part-time, explained how: 'Two years later, I was promoted to be a chief accountant. Due to amalgamation of companies, I was assigned to a new company.' Job changes because of the impact of economic crisis and/or scientific and technological progress was reported in four cases. Family reasons, such as the sudden sickness of the husband, also led to job changes. Rong described how 'in 2001, my husband fell ill, and my daughter wanted to go to school. I was anxious about how to earn money'.

A range of responses to circumstances and changes during these transitions was recorded, including some negative emotional responses. Ling described how badly she had felt when being transferred away from her home against her will because of her job:

> Several years ago I also felt pity and regret and even imagined what would happen if I kept doing business in (name of) province. I complained about the destination and it felt unfair ... (name of) province is very far away from my hometown. Knowing few people, we were strangers there.

The research illustrates some of the barriers, obstacles and difficult circumstances that the participants faced when making labour market transitions. These included a lack of relevant experience or knowledge. For example, Feng talked about a business failure because she did not have basic knowledge about how to operate profitably: 'Lack of business experience, we lost it [her business] and made no profit, although our potatoes grew well.' Another example is Fang. When a teacher in her early career, she did not understand the characteristics of the students in the vocational school where she was employed. This created considerable difficulties when dealing with their psychological problems. Physical exhaustion was another difficult factor. Hua commented: 'Our school opened at 8 a.m. and closed at 6 p.m., officially. But in practice I had to work longer than 10 hours, especially in the summer.' Lack of fit between personality and the job had also created problems. For example, when working in a clothes business, Ping explained:

> We had to talk with the customers all the time to persuade them to buy our clothes and make them believe that the clothes fit them well. It was a little difficult for me and my husband was not good at talking either.

Being homesick and feeling lonely also caused difficulties. Rong used to be the cook for workers on different mountain locations. She said 'I was feeling alone and homesick so used to cry after I finished my work. However, I could not go home.'

Overall, the 12 older women participants had experienced multiple and complex job transitions. Despite such barriers and difficulties, these women were sufficiently resilient to survive and move on.

Intrapersonal influences

Nine of the 12 participants revealed their understanding of 'self' in their stories. For example, Feng reflected on her lack of education and training, which resulted in her having to take unskilled jobs: 'I didn't have enough knowledge to get a good job. So I had to do work involving hard labour.' Sometimes they had derived no satisfaction from their jobs, but to earn money to survive, they had persevered. For example, Rong talked about one of her jobs, which had caused her considerable physical suffering, yet she remained in this same job for more than three years.

> Carrying wood, which was really hard work, made my shoulder swell badly. Sometimes I could hardly put wood on my shoulder. My mother told me not to work there anymore. I was too tired to do this job.

Only two of the 12 older women participants demonstrated a clear level of self-confidence during their stories. The best example is Ying (aged 56): 'I always feel that as long as I want to do something, I can always do it successfully. I am always very confident.' Although some of the 12 participants suffered in their early years in the labour market, their beliefs kept them going. Examples include Ling who believed: 'So work hard, and man proposes, god disposes.' One other example is provided by Rong: 'Nothing is impossible to a willing heart.'

Work influences

Six participants mentioned the influence of economic policies on their working lives, linked to three distinct periods. During the period 1956–1991, the jobs of these women were determined by the Employment Distribution Policy, characteristic of the planned economic system, and the Educated Youth to the Countryside Policy. Then the period 1992–2002 brought the restructuring of enterprises, which led to the bankruptcy of many state-run companies, with the consequent laying-off of many women (examples of women participants who were laid off for this reason are Ling and Liu). The next period (from 2002 to the present day) has been typified by encouraging self-employment. For example, Ling, who used to run a clothes shop, said: 'We didn't need to pay the tax in the first year and it was rather cheap to rent the shop.'

According to the official declaratory average wage for each province, the incomes of six participants in this study were below the average wage. Perhaps because of the precarious nature of older women's employment in China, five of the 12 participants (42 per cent) were self-employed. This level of self-employment reflects fundamental changes at the macro level that resulted from the 1990s reforms to China's economic system and the government's encouragement of entrepreneurship. For the women participants, this change was important since it meant that they could start their own businesses. They realised that, for the first time, they had the opportunity to improve their life status. For example, Rong, explained: 'In 2001, I had an idea: opening my own restaurant.' Entrepreneurship also provided the women with the opportunity to support their families and raise their children independently. This was important for Rong, who said: 'I am proud that I have supported my two daughters through university, through self-employment. If I had chosen to work in a factory, my daughters would not have had enough money to complete their studies.'

Four of the 12 participants had been continuously employed, but the other eight had experienced periods of unemployment. One woman lost her job because of breaking the One-child Policy (in China, every family could only have one child, according to the population regulations) (Feng et al. 2012), though this seems set to change. One other gave up her job to take better care of her mother. More than half of the participants had changed jobs more than three times ($N = 7$), with Sun reporting eight changes (curator; primary school teaching; urban management; insurance; accountancy (hotel); accountancy (retail); accountancy (wholesale); accountancy (travel)). Just over half of the participants ($N = 7$) were teachers at some stage. The large number of participants who had been employed in teaching is first, because it is regarded as suitable for women, and second, because the entry requirements for teachers were easy to meet in some areas, especially in the countryside in the 1980s.

Many factors led to the participants' dissatisfaction with their jobs, like heavy workloads ($N = 3$), poor interpersonal relationships in the workplace ($N = 1$) and poor work environments ($N = 4$). One participant, Ying, reported how she had suffered from workplace discrimination with her colleagues despising her because she originated from a small place. Despite the discrimination suffered, she had not changed her job.

Financial influences

Six participants reported the importance of financial factors associated with various job changes. For example, Hua changed her job once for financial reasons:

> The income of teaching in the kindergarten was very little and didn't have a good reputation. Teaching in the primary school is very stable and I could earn much more than in the kindergarten. It made me feel confident, because with my hard work I could improve our standard of living.

For Sun, two of her eight job changes were motivated by financial reasons. She described one of her experiences when she was working in the transportation business: 'the wages provided were only 70 per cent of what they should have been, and then this was reduced even further. My husband told her: "You simply quit" '. So she left her first job. Her second job also presented financial challenges. She reported how she was on a low wage and her efforts to secure the money she was owed by her employer resulted in her dismissal:

> It was low-wage, only 460 yuan a month. The (mentions name) company moved and the distribution of money was controlled by the government. One person could get 5000-6000 yuan. So I contacted, with dozens of workmates, the (mentions name) company with determination every day in order to get the money. When I got the money, I also lost my job.

Social influences

Interpersonal relationships are an important factor in regulating social relationships in China, particularly in rural regions. Everyone has their own social network, consisting of both close and distant relationships. People in these networks take care of each other and treat people outside the network differently (Qian 2009). Since there was no formal career support available, when the women participants changed their jobs they often received various help and support from their own social support networks. Some used social networks for job recommendations, especially families, friends and teachers and other people or organisations. Three had benefitted from job recommendations from their families (sister, husband and father); the friends of four participants had provided this type of support; and three participants had been provided with job recommendations by a teacher, a resident's committee and a villagers' committee.

Being older women, the participants had many life roles, often simultaneously (see Table 11.2).

Overall, of the 82 per cent of successful job transitions, 58 per cent were accomplished through the help of personal relationships. Among these transitions, four of the participants were advised when they were to change job by their families. Sometimes they were advised to consider the needs of their families more; for example Rong explained how: 'My father-in-law hoped that the whole family would live together.' Sometimes their social networks influenced the type of work

Table 11.2 The life roles of the participants

Name	Children	Life roles mentioned in the interview
Fenghua Fan	3 daughters, 1 son	daughter, wife, mother, employee
Qiufang Shen	1 daughter	mother, employee
Ying Wei	1 daughter	mother, employer
Shufeng Yu	1 son	daughter, wife, mother, employer, curator, housewife
Shurong Yu	2 daughters	daughter, wife, mother, sponsor, employee, curator, housewife
Shuping Yu	1 daughter	daughter, wife, mother, curator, housewife, employee
Ying Wang	2 sons	mother, employee
Yuying Su	1 son, 1 daughter	daughter, mother, curator, housewife, employee
Yang	1 son, 1 daughter	mother, curator, housewife, employee
Xiaoping Liu	1 daughter	mother, employee
Ying Sun	1 son	wife, mother, curator, housewife, employee
Huiling He	1 son, 1 daughter	daughter, mother, employee

they should undertake. Again Rong described how her brother-in-law influenced her employment direction: 'My husband's brother stopped my idea (to run a restaurant), and advised me to run a repair shop.' Other participants reported how they had received help from families, leaders and friends with material support, advice, or understanding of their difficulties and solutions.

The importance of the support offered by families and the wider community is evident in the stories of the women's transitions. In particular, the importance of personal relationships, especially family members (for example, brother, husband, niece, parents) and work colleagues (for example, manager, team member) featured strongly. However, the negative influence of family members emerged from five of the participants' stories. Three women identified husbands as having had a negative impact and two talked about the negative influence of their parents. For example, Ping explained how, when she wanted to return home from a different part of the country: 'my daughter's grandmother asked me not to return (from abroad) because she was ill'.

Relocation

Two participants changed their jobs because of relocation. Ying's husband worked in a different place to her and helped her find a job in his location, so she had to leave her job to join him. The other participant was Sun, who left her job to look after her son when he relocated in order to study.

Advice to others

Advice that the Chinese women participants identified as relevant for others included: maintain job stability by minimising transitions ($N = 2$); persevere with study ($N = 2$); develop a positive working attitude ($N = 4$), like being honest, persevering, being generous, and having a passion for the job. They also emphasised the importance of clear career planning and seizing opportunities when they arose. The married women in the sample suggested that more effort should be made to spend time with family.

Future planning

The ages of these older women played an important role in their future planning. For example, Liu was planning to retire. It would have been very difficult for her to be promoted because of her age, so she did not wish to invest the effort that would have been required. She just wanted to retire on time and help her daughter take care of her grandson. Her situation is typical of women of her age.

Reflections

The employment transitions of the 12 women participants who are the focus of this chapter provide vivid illustrations of the career trajectories of older women in China and how these are closely related to the cultural historical and political contexts of China. In turn, these have impacted on their life experiences, social status and social roles. Their stories illustrate how their career trajectories are deeply embedded in the social context. For example, marriage and child rearing frequently prompted career change. Relocation and family illness were also key triggers for change. The women's stories demonstrate the importance of workplace learning to successful accommodation, especially after job changes. They adapted and improved themselves mainly by self-learning in the workplace or learning from their colleagues and managers or community leaders. However, it became evident during the study that the levels of self-awareness of these older Chinese women are extremely restricted, perhaps because of the Chinese collectivist culture. Many became subsidiary to the men in their family and can be regarded as powerless victims of the family.

Two distinct orientations can be identified from the women's career transitions: survival and developmental. Nine of the 12 cases illustrate a survival orientation, with only three cases developmentally-oriented. For those exemplifying a survival orientation, employment transitions were constrained – determined by the location of their homes and the need for financial survival. There is no indication of the extent to which their jobs suited their abilities, aspirations or aptitudes, because the goal of the employment transition was to survive or live better. Only the three women participants demonstrating a developmental orientation took the initiative to pursue career exploration. They thought about jobs that would be more suitable for them and which would be more conducive to their own career development.

The participants of this study were women aged 45–65 who grew up in a special period of China's social transformation. They went through many social transformations, such as the Cultural Revolution, the Educated Youth to the Countryside movement, reform and opening up of the economy and the reform of state-owned enterprises (which led to a surge in lay-offs). These social shifts and policy changes required them to tolerate hard work and develop perseverance. Despite the low status of many of the jobs occupied, the women took any kind of employment for the benefit of their family. They accepted poor working conditions and low wages in order to survive. The hard work and sacrifices of these older women have contributed significantly to the period of economic development that China is currently enjoying. The career progression of these older women is truly distinctive. From an historical perspective, significant differences are set to emerge between their career concepts and trajectories and those of the women who have come after them.

References

Chen, Y. (2004) 'Why China selected the planned economy in the 1950s', *Research in Chinese Economic History*, 13: 48–55.

Feng, W., Cai, Y. and Gu, B. (2012) 'Population, policy, and politics: How will history judge China's one-child policy?', *Population and Development Review* 38 (Supplement): 115–29. Available at: www.popcouncil.org/pdfs/PDRSupplements/Vol38_PopPublicPolicy/Wang_pp115-129.pdf (Accessed 25 July 2013).

Labour Act (Dated 5 July 1994), *China Daily*, 6 July 1994, p. 2. Available at: www.ilo.org/dyn/natlex/docs/WEBTEXT/37357/64926/E94CHN01.htm (Accessed 27 July 2013).

Li, C. and Li, S. (2008) 'Rising gender income gap and its dynamics in China: Market competition or sex discrimination?', *Sociological Studies*, 2: 94–117.

Jiang, Mh. and Dang, M. (2008) 'The difficulty of laid-off women's re-employment and their involvement in social work', *Journal of Women's Academy at Shandong*, 79: 20–4.

Jiang, Y. (2000) 'Review of 50 years of Chinese urban women's employment', *Human Resources and Social Security in China*, 3: 29–30.

Qian, Jp. (2009) 'On the conflict and value change of traditional interpersonal relations and modern public ', *Journal of Jiangsu Administration Institute*, 6: 27–32.

Sun, Cc. (1989) 'Looking at the crisis of women employment from the perspective of value conflict theory', *Journal of China Women's University*, 6: 31–4.

Yu, Y. (2011) 'Employment of women in China: Economics perspective', *Guizhou Social Sciences*, 259: 86–90.

Zhao, H. (2006) 'Analysis of the factors that hinder women's career development', *Research on Economics and Management*, 2: 26–9.

Zhao, Y. (2003) 'Re-employment pathway and its influencing factors – survey results of laid-off workers in Wuhan', *Journal of Social Sciences*, 1: 73–8.

Zhao, Hj. and Wang, D. (2006) 'A discussion on the realization of glass ceiling of Chinese career women and its effects', *Human Resource Development of China*, 5: 97–9.

Zhou, Y. (1995) 'Transformation of Chinese society, anomie and female employment', *Socialism Studies*, 5: 48–51.

12 Voices of older women from England

Jenny Bimrose

An island off the northwest coast of Europe, England has had significant cultural, economic, historic and social impacts on the wider world, with hundreds of millions of people speaking the English language in many countries. At the most recent census in 2011, England's population stood at approximately 53 million (Office for National Statistics 2012a). This represents 84 per cent of the total population of the UK, which currently stands at 63.2 million (Office for National Statistics 2012b). England is both part of Great Britain (GB) and the United Kingdom (UK). While Great Britain comprises the two kingdoms of Scotland and England, together with the principality of Wales, the UK also includes Northern Ireland (though it should be noted that the push for Scottish independence is gaining ground). In the UK, women (32.2 million) marginally outnumber men (31 million) (Office for National Statistics 2012c). In common with many other countries in the European Union, the UK has an ageing population, with more women than men in older age groups, reflecting the higher life expectancy of females (82 years for women compared with 76 for men in 2008) (Advisory Committee on Equal Opportunities for Women and Men 2012).

In the UK, the health and well-being of the working age population has become a particular focus of concern for employment policy (Dolan *et al.*, 2011). Paid employment provides significant psychological and social benefits to individuals, as well as having intrinsic economic value, whilst unemployment can have a lasting negative impact on well-being (Robertson 2013). However, recent labour market changes in the UK have had a disproportionate and negative effect on women, primarily because a large proportion were employed in the public sector, which has been hardest hit by austerity measures introduced by the government in response to the effects of global economic recession resulting in cuts to public spending (Fawcett Society 2013). These changes include: a growth in the size of the labour force as the population has increased; a reduction in the size of the manufacturing sector, as a consequence of a series of economic recessions in the 1970s, 1980s, 1990s and from 2008; and an increase in the proportion of women in the labour market, both for women with and without dependent children (Spence 2011). Women continue to dominate in part-time work, which tends to be low paid, with few promotional prospects and limited training opportunities (Fawcett Society 2013; Trade Union Congress 2012).

A persistent feature of the UK labour market is occupational segregation. Women are concentrated in a much narrower range of jobs than men (horizontal segregation). For example, 77 per cent of administrative and secretarial posts are filled by women, as are 83 per cent of personal services posts (these are commercial services such as catering and cleaning that supply the personal needs of customers) and 65 per cent of sales posts (Equality and Human Rights Commission 2010). Vertical as well as horizontal segregation is also still very much in evidence. A study into the representation of women in politics and public decision-making in Britain found not only that 'Britain is a country run largely by men', but also that progress is painfully slow: 'And at the current rate of progress, a child born today will be drawing her pension before she has any chance of being equally represented in the Parliament of her country' (Centre for Women and Democracy 2013: 5). Five per cent of women are editors of national newspapers; 22.3 per cent are Members of Parliament; 16.7 per cent are directors of the top performing 100 Companies; 13.6 per cent are senior judiciary (high court judge and above); and only 14.2 per cent are university vice chancellors (Centre for Women and Democracy 2013).

The measured gender pay gap increased in 2011 from 8.3 per cent to 9.6 per cent (Low Pay Commission 2013) with part-time women suffering a significant pay penalty in both private and public sectors, though this is lower in the public sector (Trade Union Congress 2012). Age has a significant effect on pay. Women in their 50s earn nearly a fifth less than men of the same age – the widest gender pay gap of any age group (Trade Union Congress 2013a). These low pay rates are of particular concern because of the consequent inability of older women to provide for their own retirement:

> Women of all ages continue to battle against low and unequal pay and women aged over 50 are no exception. It is striking that the generation of women who fought for equal pay in the 60s and 70s have not themselves reaped the rewards.
> (Trade Union Congress 2013b: 2)

The number of older women (over 50 years) in work has increased by 1.5 million since 1992, which is the most dramatic shift in the labour market of any age group. A strong link exists between caring responsibilities and economic activity in women between the ages of 50 and 60. For women in that age group who are economically inactive, one in five has caring responsibilities (Trade Union Congress 2013b).

There is no shortage of labour market statistics about gender and age in the UK. However, it is only individual stories that can provide insights to the individual experiences that lie beneath these statistics. It is against this shifting demographic and labour market profile that the education and employment trajectories of older women in England were examined.

Listening to the older women

The research methodology is detailed in Chapter 7, so will not be repeated here. Details of the sample can be found in Table 12.1. Experiences of the 12 English

Table 12.1 English sample

Pseudonym	Age	Marital status	Employment status	Income per annum	Dependents	Highest qualification	Current employment
Sue	52	Married	Self-employed	£50,000 +	2	Masters	Unemployed
Jennie	59	Widowed	Full-time	£5 – 10,000	No	Degree	Alternative
Debbie	60	Married	Full-time	£40-50,000	2	Masters	Therapy tutor (higher education)
Alice	46	Married	Full-time	£40-50,000	3	Masters	Clinical midwife specialist
Sam	47	Married	Part-time	£40-50,000	3	Degree	Health informatics
Louise	63	Married	Retired	None	2	BTEC diploma	Retired
Isabel	53	Married	Full-time	£50,000 +	No	Masters	Management
Paula	46	Married	Full-time	£50,000 +	1	Masters	(Health) workforce
Mary	51	Divorced	Self-employed	£50,000 +	No	Doctorate	Planning management consultant
Laura	52	Divorced	Full-time	£30-40,000	No	Masters	Data manager (health)
Rosalie	54	Divorced	Full time	£20-30,000	3	PG diploma	Careers adviser
Stella	64	Married	Vocation	None	No	Degree	Religious minister

women reflected trends in the UK labour market. They were all employed in occupational sectors that are traditionally female, with five in health-related occupations. One participant, who was self-employed and part-time, earned significantly less than others in the sample. Most had some type of caring responsibilities, with only three reporting none.

Six participants were recruited through an online survey they had previously completed for a different research project and in which they had indicated their willingness to be followed up for interview. The remaining six were recruited through professional networks.

Learning across the lifespan

Learning emerged as an important feature of the stories of the women in the English study. All needed qualifications for entry into employment. Louise explained how, during the last two years of her compulsory education, her parents had sent her to night school to study shorthand and typing so that she could become a secretary, which she hated:

> I went to a private college for two years, so I started work at 15, a fully trained shorthand typist ... then I went on to be a secretary. But I still hated the actual sitting and taking shorthand, typing it back and sitting at a typewriter all day long, hated it!

Alice left school at 16 and took temporary work in an office, until she reached the age (18 years) at which she could start nurse training. She described the formal training she had needed before qualifying as a nurse, as well as the additional specialist courses she undertook, because of her personal interests. All of Alice's training had been funded by her employer:

> I then went on to do my student nurse training, which led to registration as a nurse. I worked as a nurse for probably about three years before I went on to do midwifery training. And during that period of working as a nurse I did two courses. I did a course in (city), just concentrating on gynaecology, because that was where I was really interested in developing a career and I did a family-planning course. Well, the first one wasn't job related, because it was done more for ... more because I wanted to do it, rather than anything else.

Formal learning continued for some participants throughout their employment, sometimes at considerable expense to themselves. Sue explained how she had undertaken a Masters' qualification in management, with no support from her employer. In fact her salary was reduced to compensate for the half day she attended the course:

> In the last four years of my working history, there were very few learning opportunities available ... the company did have very structured programme

of training, particularly for practitioners, but not for managers. My MBA was most satisfying and I actually had to pay for that. Actually, a big bone of contention personally, because I had a reduced salary. That's how enlightened my employer was. So, I took a half a day's less.

Informal learning also played an important role in the lives of the women. Louise explained that this was a strong expectation related to the voluntary work she undertook: 'We have appraisals all the time ... to make sure that you're keeping up to date with legislation and so forth. There's lots of training, and we have to do it.'

Reflecting upon learning, passion and commitment shone through the women's stories. For example, Laura described the positive impact that learning had on her: 'I remember feeling vibrant and, you know, I was like a sponge, soaking up my colleagues in the lecture theatres, and exploring things, and discussing things and writing and studying. I loved it.'

Transitions

Significant transitions and their lasting, sometimes profound impact, on the lives of the participants were evident in the women's stories. Alice focused on child birth:

> Obviously one of the biggest transitions that you go through, I think, is having children, and I would say that's probably the biggest learning curve that you'll ever have in your life, and I think that continues, you know, as you feel that your children are grown and don't need you anymore. You find that actually they do, but in a very different way.

The responses of the women to personal transitions were often both vivid and poignant. Laura recalled:

> I had attempted to leave my husband. I was told to go back and be a good Catholic wife, but it just became intolerable and, I can't remember ... something must have happened, some sort of catalyst must have occurred, but then I said, 'That's it, it's over. I'm not going back!'

Ways of coping with job transitions were also described. For example, Paula explained how she had literally talked herself into one job change:

> Yes, I thought I really just don't want to do that. It was just sort of, it's almost sort of self-talking, you know: well if I was looking for a job and I found that one, would I go for it? Well, no I wouldn't; so why are you worrying about it? Just don't go for it and get on and do something else.

Intrapersonal influences

A range of intrapersonal influences was identified by the English women. Three have been selected here for discussion: self-confidence, values and age. Having enough self-confidence was important for career progression, because this enabled the women to take on things that seemed ambitious; as Isabel explained:

> I'm quite good at saying, 'Well, I'll take responsibility for doing that'. So even though, in those early stages, the jobs were reasonably prescribed, I've never felt bounded by that. I've always felt that I could make it up as I went along, if you like. So that's been really helpful.

Equally, not having sufficient self-confidence was identified as an impediment by Laura:

> I would love to do a doctorate, but there's no way ... I'm trying to sort my dissertation out at the moment and of course, that is hard, hard, hard, and to take it up a level, I don't know if I could do it ... I don't know if I could apply myself. You have to have enormous self-discipline, at any age, and I keep thinking, you know, I'm twice the age of most of the other students, and it's not easy.

Personal values influenced lifestyle and career decisions. Jennie talked about the importance of the voluntary work she undertook: 'I like the voluntary work because it's not sullied by earning any money. I quite like the thought you're giving time, you know, I quite enjoy doing that.' Stella explained how a strong motivation throughout her life had been a driving personal ambition to do better: 'But, being me of course, I wanted to do it the best I could, so a lot of preparation and trying it out really.' Alice highlighted the crucial importance of close relationships: 'I think the most important thing to me, personally, is sort of my family and my relationship with my husband.'

Age was a recurrent issue in the stories of the women. Reflections on the gender constraints operating on job choices 40 years ago were recalled, with missed opportunities regretted. Louise reflected that:

> I think probably all women of my age were just carried along with what you were supposed to do ... I've always been interested in food, and I wanted to do something with cooking ... I think that I should have done that path (college) from the very beginning, but where I came from, you didn't do that.

Sue was slightly nonplussed by a suggestion from a neighbour that age was a factor in her difficulty in finding employment after redundancy:

> I had a conversation with a neighbour this morning who I haven't spoken to for ages and she knew that I'd been made redundant. She said, 'Well, do you think it's about your age, why you're not getting a job?' My God! I wouldn't have even thought of it was anything to do with my age!

In contrast, the positive influence of age was emphasised by Laura:

> In the classroom, or in the lecture theatre at university, I know that I, in so many ways, have an edge on my colleagues, simply through all experience and, you know, the places that I've been and stuff like that, because these young people, they just don't have that, and I think, for me it's been a positive thing.

Work influences

It has been argued that most women get promoted to a level below their competence and operate below the level they could easily manage (Sculler 2012). A vivid example is provided by Sue who, already in a management position, applied unsuccessfully for promotion:

> I felt then very much a victim, like a piece of flotsam and jetsam ... I applied for the role and didn't get it. The person brought in was an ex-(occupation) male, another male, who had no clue! It was a horrible time of my life ... I felt so wretched about the whole situation and it just seemed so, dare I say, unfair.

Experiences of work influenced career progression in a number of ways. Louise talked about how she felt trapped in her job as a secretary, with apparently no escape:

> I worked for 14 years in an office as a shorthand typist. Jobs were easy to come by. I had lots of jobs, shorthand typing and so on ... Yeah, about 12 or so ... I didn't get pleasure out of going to work, and doing the typing and shorthand ... I hated it ... But, it was just what had to be done. I used to worry about not being able to read my shorthand back. I used to dread going to work on the Monday. All those things, but I just did it, because that's what you did, yes, people just got on and did it, didn't they?

The notion that frequent job changing has become a feature of working lives in the twenty-first century is challenged by Debbie's experiences of no fewer than 26 job changes during the 1960s, 1970s and 1980s:

> I did work at 26 jobs since I graduated ... a lot have been very short-term and bits and pieces that were done in parallel with each other. So there's been a lot of employers, mainly in the public service.

Some talked about the satisfaction they had gained from their work. Jennie, self-employed in one of the alternative therapies, explained:

> What I've liked about that (the job) is the privilege actually of that intimate contact and the way that people do kind of trust you and, you know, open up

to you, also the fact that what you do, you can see whether you've actually helped somebody or not, you know, so that's in a much more direct way than it ever was in social work. So you see whether you're a success or a failure from that.

For women, age discrimination is compounded by other forms of discrimination including sex, gender, ethnic origin, disability, levels of poverty, sexual orientation, gender identity, migrant status, family status and literacy (Advisory Committee on Equal Opportunities for Women and Men 2012). Job dissatisfaction, caused by experiences of discrimination, triggered radical change in career direction. Sam, who had worked as an engineer for a large manufacturing company for over two decades, spoke about the discrimination that prevented her promotion: 'Between 86 and 92 I felt as though I didn't really get that far, and I was a bit frustrated by, what I would say was a bit of a glass ceiling in the organisation, frankly'. In response, Sam moved from one part of the company to another. When things still did not improve, she eventually left the company to work in a completely different occupational sector:

> But as it turned out, I think that the political, and frankly, testosterone-fuelled environment that was (that part of the) business, was quite objectionable to me ... I wanted to move out of (that side of the) business, and then when I found out the (other side of the) business was horrible, I wanted to move out completely.

Other examples of sex discrimination are evident in some of the stories of the English women. One relates to Debbie, who had been formally selected for a job. However, just before she was due to start the job:

> I discovered I was pregnant, and I made the stupid mistake of actually telling the people ... and really, I shouldn't have told them, because they said: 'Well, we won't be able to start you, then, unless you give us a letter in advance, post-dated, saying you're going to resign, as soon as you start.' So I only worked for them for about four months in (place) and left a couple of months before (name of daughter) was born. It was dirty.

Financial influences

The financial consequences of low wages for future retirement prospects have become an important social issue. Despite more women working for longer, millions have been let down by the pension system and are consequently approaching retirement with inadequate savings (Whiting 2013). Debbie's husband was worried by her suggestion that she reduced her hours to part time when she reached 60, because of the consequences for their retirement income:

We've got to make sure we've got enough money and all the rest of it, so there's a bit … and, you know, kind of, that's not greed, I think that's a more primeval thing there, you know, in terms of the changing world collapsing … all that stuff, yeah. So I think he's a little bit unsettled about me down-incoming and, you know, losing a little bit of money … and I'm not quite sure how best to talk about that anymore.

Financial influences were important factors in many of the lives of the women. Sue recognised that the financial support from her family has provided a cushion of privilege:

I didn't have to think about, oh, God, I've got no money, how are we going to manage, I've got supportive family … So, I don't have that pressure that other people would have I haven't got the financial pressure. And that must be huge for some people.

Mary explained how only her careful financial planning had averted financial difficulties when she lost her job unexpectedly and money became tight:

If I hadn't been able to find work … I'd be having to spend capital … But my financial planning would've got me through till I was 60. I wouldn't have been able to keep the house all the way through, I would have had to downsize.

Social influences

Social networks provided support for many of the women. Close family, for example, provided critical support at stages of transition. This was the case for Rosalie, who reflected: 'It was only my mum and a very good friend who kept me going.' Wider community networks similarly proved to be highly influential. For Debbie, stranded in a strange city, pregnant and without job prospects because of her pregnancy, a network of new friends carried her through: 'it all went into oblivion very, very quickly, because of nice, supportive people I met … who were very, very sort of happy, supportive, and made a new community for me'. For Sam, her husband provided the support she needed when she contemplated leaving employment: 'My current husband … was very supportive, and understanding of how big a deal it was for me, you know, moving house, moving jobs, and taking on stepchildren, and those sorts of things.'

The influence of gendered social roles is illustrated by Louise, who described the dominance of the role of homemaker for women at the time she had a family: 'to make sure that everything at home was running smoothly. My family and the girls and (husband) were more important than anything really. If anything went wrong, it was my job to put it right'.

Relocation

The career pathways of the women participants were characterised by relocations to different places, for different reasons. The husband's need to be geographically mobile for his career emerged as the trigger for much physical relocation. Debbie, who had had 26 jobs, provides one example: 'So I worked for four (type) organisations, but moved around following my husband's path in that time. That's why it chopped and changed quite quickly, every two years at a different place, type of thing.'

Advice to others

None of the twelve English participants had accessed careers support. When asked what advice they would give to others, preparation and planning was a common theme. For example, Stella's view was:

> Well, I think based on my experience, I think I would encourage them to ask a lot more questions about what was involved, to be very clear about what they were going into ... so that would be the preparation.

Similarly, Alice suggested: 'that having a good idea of what you're getting into is perhaps the, you know, a good piece of advice, perhaps researching ... I think if you can prepare for those opportunities, I think that that really helps'. Louise, however, was an advocate of simply being open to opportunities:

> I think you need to do lots of things, just learn as much as you can, and take in as much as you can, and get out in the world ... we've all had life experiences, even from bad ones, you learn.

Future planning

Finally, the women participants talked about future plans. Rosalie talked about wanting to change jobs:

> I want to change my job role – something more stimulating ... it's not well paid – no careers structure. I don't think I have a career ... I want to broaden out my job role to make it more interesting for me.

Alice talked about continuing in stimulating employment and the long-term planning in which she was engaged so that she could achieve this ambition:

> I've actually been doing two things in recent years. I've actually been doing some work related studies, like, because I've been doing a catering course at a local college, which I've really, really enjoyed, and I'm going to do another course next year. I really enjoy that because it's a very different sort of education,

and that's sort of looking perhaps towards when I retire, because I'd actually like to set up a business of my own.

The one participant who had already retired (Louise) but who was busy with voluntary work, spoke about her dread at having to give this work up altogether:

> I enjoy the home visits, yeah. Yeah, I dread the thought of being 70 and not being able to do it … You have to retire at 70. Unless things change. If you're over 70, then really you shouldn't be going.

Reflections

The position of women in the UK labour market has been well researched over recent decades. There is no shortage of quantitative data that provide detailed and statistically reliable insights into the nature, level and persistence of deep-rooted gender inequality. Yet the stories of these English women provide a particular poignant understanding of the perceptions of career progression over four to five decades, through an exploration of the individual in context. Data from this qualitative research study undoubtedly extend and deepen our understanding of statistical trends, which reveal the enduring characteristics of women's employment experiences in the UK labour market across economic cycles of boom and bust. These include a disproportionate share of part-time work, a gender pay gap, both vertical and horizontal occupational segregation, as well as experiences of workplace discrimination and sexual harassment. During the economic crisis triggered by global factors in 2008, something of a paradox arose in relation to women's position in the labour market in England. Whilst they did not suffer the same levels of unemployment as men, this was because they were more prepared to take part-time, low paid work. Moreover, women's career promotion to middle and senior management positions stalled because they had been most successful at securing promotion in the public sector, which proved to be the most vulnerable to the austerity measures introduced by government.

In an ageing society, like the UK, there is an already heightened awareness about, and increased sensitivity to, the combined impacts of different dimensions of social inequity, like gender and age. The women in the sample were all in the age group 45 to 65 years and provided views from a range of different socio-economic backgrounds, educational and training pathways, occupational sectors and family circumstances. The levels of their highest educational qualifications varied from a technical diploma to a doctorate, with their current occupations ranging from 'retired', to self-employment, to senior management in organisations, freelance consultancy and religious ministry. The occupational sectors in which the women were employed were sectors traditionally regarded in the UK labour market as 'female', like health care, administrative and secretarial and teaching. Only one participant originally entered engineering, a traditionally male domain, and after struggling in that environment for over two decades, she changed to a sector that is traditionally female (health care) to escape a toxic employment environment. Stories of discrimination emerged, with the responses of the women often reflecting acceptance and resignation of 'the way it was'. None of the women had formal support or help navigating their way through the labour market and most wished that they had had this available.

The findings from this study are confirmatory, revelatory and challenging. On the one hand, they tell us what is already known. On the other hand, they are powerfully illustrative of individual journeys, revealing strategies for overcoming impediments to progression. In order to construct a better future, we need better to understand the past. This study provides a micro understanding of the pathways of older women in England required to help construct that better future.

References

Advisory Committee on Equal Opportunities for Women and Men (2012) 'Opinion on the gender dimension of active ageing and Solidarity between generations'. Available at: http://ec.europa.eu/justice/gender-equality/files/opinion_active_ageing_en.pdf (accessed 27 June 2013).

Centre for Women and Democracy (2013) 'Sex and power 2013. Who runs Britain?', Counting Women In Coalition, the Electoral Reform Society, the Fawcett Society, the Hansard Society and Unlock Democracy. Funded by the Joseph Rowntree Charitable Trust. Available at: www.countingwomenin.org/wp-content/uploads/2013/02/Sex-and-Power-2013-FINALv2.-pdf.pdf (accessed 22 June 2013).

Dolan, P., Layard, R. and Metcalfe, R. (2011) *Measuring Subjective Well-being for Public Policy*, South Wales: Office for National Statistics. Available at: http://eprints.lse.ac.uk/35420/1/measuring-subjective-wellbeing-for-public-policy.pdf (accessed 25 June 2013).

Equality and Human Rights Commission (2010) 'How fair is Britain? Equality, human rights and good relations in 2010. The first triennial review', Equality and Human Rights Commission. Available at: www.equalityhumanrights.com/sites/default/files/documents/triennial_review/how_fair_is_britain_-_complete_report.pdf (accessed 9 September 2014)

Fawcett Society (2013) 'Women and work'. Available at: www.fawcettsociety.org.uk/women-and-work/ (accessed 25 June 2013).

Low Pay Commission (2013) *Low Pay Commission National Minimum Wage Report 2013*. Cm 8565, London: The Stationery Office Limited. Available at: www.lowpay.gov.uk/lowpay/report/pdf/9305-BIS-Low_Pay-Accessible6.pdf (accessed 27 June 2013).

Office for National Statistics (2012a) 'Census, population and household estimates for England and Wales'. Available at: www.ons.gov.uk/ons/rel/census/2011-census/population-and-household-estimates-for-england-and-wales/index.html (accessed 27 June 2013).

Office for National Statistics (2012b) '2011 Census, population and household estimates for the United Kingdom'. Available at: www.ons.gov.uk/ons/rel/census/2011-census/population-and-household-estimates-for-the-united-kingdom/index.html (accessed 27 June 2013).

Office for National Statistics (2012c) '2011 Census: population estimates for the United Kingdom, 27 March'. Available at: www.ons.gov.uk/ons/dcp171778_292378.pdf (accessed 27 June 2013).

Robertson, P. J. (2013) 'The well-being outcomes of career guidance', *British Journal of Guidance & Counselling*, 41: 254-66. Available at: www.tandfonline.com/doi/pdf/10.1080/03069885.2013.773959 (accessed 20 June 2013).

Sculler, P. (2012) 'The Paula Principle: Most women work below their level of competence'. Available at: www.paulaprinciple.com/category/paula-at-work/ (accessed 23 June 2013).

Spence, A. (2011) *Labour Market. Social Trends 41*. South Wales, Cardiff: Office for National Statistics. Available at: www.ons.gov.uk/ons/rel/social-trends-rd/social-trends/social-trends-41/social-trends-41—labour-market.pdf (accessed 27 June 2013).

Trade Union Congress (2012) 'Women's pay and employment update: A public/private sector comparison. Report for Women's Conference 2012'. Available at: www.tuc.org.uk/tucfiles/251.pdf (accessed 17 June 2013).

Trade Union Congress (2013a) 'Gender pay gap twice as large for women in their 50s'. Available at: www.tuc.org.uk/equality/tuc-21942-f0.cfm (accessed 27 June 2013).

Trade Union Congress (2013b) 'Age immaterial campaign. Briefing note: Women over 50: work and pay'. Available at: www.tuc.org.uk/tucfiles/542/AgeImmaterialBriefing1.pdf (accessed 17 June 2013).

Whiting, R. (2013) 'Gender pay gap for over 50s: TUC analysis', Trade Union Congress. Available at: www.tuc.org.uk/equality/tuc-21942-f0.cfm (accessed 27 June 2013).

13 Voices of older women from Germany

Simone R. Haasler

As in most other countries, female labour force participation in Germany has grown significantly in the last forty years. This increase from 47 per cent in 1971 to 71 per cent in 2011 (Bundesagentur für Arbeit 2012) can be considered as one major reason for the significant restructuring of the German labour market during this period. Two characteristic features contribute towards upholding Germany's distinctive labour market segmentation by gender: first, the specific connection between skills formation and labour market resulting from the German dual system of vocational education and training; and second, the prevalence of the male breadwinner model that makes it likely for women to remain the secondary wage earner (BMFSFJ 2011). These two factors, in combination with conservative family policies, perpetuate female labour market discrimination in Germany despite many favourable developments during recent decades that have allowed women to play a prominent role in today's labour market.

Over centuries, the German labour market developed a close connection between skills formation and occupational labour markets (Rubery and Grimshaw 2003). In this context, the socialising function of vocational education and training played, and still plays, a central role in directing individuals' learning and career orientations (Kirpal 2011) which, as a result, tend to be anchored in the occupational domain for which they trained. Combined with standardised and stratified educational and occupational routes, this limits employees' job flexibility and mobility in Germany more than in many other countries, where making transitions between different jobs is not only easier, but also more strongly institutionally facilitated and supported.

Work-based socialisation and vocational training not only provide individuals with a particular set of vocational skills, qualifications and orientations, but also function as a means of social integration both at the level of the company and the level of the labour market in general. Thus, individuals are assigned a social status based on the division of labour derived from vocational profiles with specific career progression routes. Skilled workers (Facharbeiter) with institutionalised patterns of career progression benefit from high levels of skills protection and social security compared to, for example, unskilled workers (Baethge and Baethge-Kinsky 1998). The Facharbeiter career is furthermore associated with full-time, continuous and protected employment and collective workers' participation rights, parameters which in Germany constitute the basis of the social security system. This affects female workers insofar as much of the female labour participation rise since the 1990s has been in part-time and marginal employment (Bundesagentur für Arbeit 2012). Today, a high proportion of female workers are in non-standard and, to a large extent, precarious employment, which implies that they are disadvantaged in terms of their entitlement to social security and retirement benefits.

Through the central role of the dual system of education and training for the German economy, the relative position of the vocational track, compared to the academic route, has traditionally been strong, much stronger than in other countries. The dual model combines subject-oriented and general education in vocational schools and company-based training, whereby companies also hold employment contracts with apprentices. Despite the erosion of the dual system since the 1990s, coupled with decreasing numbers of apprentices (Baethge 2008; BMBF 2005), the vocational route is still followed by almost 60 per cent of school leavers (BMBF 2012) and tends to ensure a fairly smooth school-to-work transition (OECD 2008), at least for the majority of male employees. Furthermore, the three-pillar school system after completion of primary school results in an early stratification between vocational and academic tracks, which significantly restricts future educational and career choices (Allmendinger 1989). For some women, this early stratification could be identified as a major obstacle to realising possible career development opportunities.

Gendered professions and career development pathways are another result of the German system of vocational training. Historically, the craft-based apprenticeship model was introduced for skills formation in industry and was complemented by vocational schools between 1890 and 1920, mainly to supply the newly emerging factories with standardised skills and to pacify the growing numbers of proletarian youth by enrolling them in formalised in-company training (Greinert 1997). Almost at the same time, full-time vocational schools were established in areas which did not form part of the crafts or industrial training system of skilled labour. These schools were targeted to provide a decent vocational education for young women to prepare them for roles as housewives, governesses or other jobs in personal services (Kleinau and Mayer 1996). From this tradition there developed a school-based vocational training system that mainly covered skills formation for the social, educational and medical professions such as childcare, nursing, elder care, speech therapy, physiotherapy, and so on. Today, this track covers more than 100 professional domains, which to date remain female-dominated.

While the school-based vocational routes also cover theoretical and practical (work-based) training, they differ from the approximately 350 dual apprenticeship schemes in that they are not equally standardised and nationally regulated by the Vocational Training Act (Berufsbildungsgesetz) (Füssel and Leschinsky 2008). Regulated at the federal level, school-based vocational routes: display non-standardised and heterogeneous curricula and training providers; are anchored predominantly in personal services; provide for restricted career development pathways and lower salaries (as compared to the male-dominated professions of the dual system); and display 70 per cent female representation against 41 per cent in the dual system (Hall 2012).

Finally, women increasingly contribute to the household income, but nevertheless continue to carry most of the household and family responsibilities (BMFSFJ 2011). In Germany, this is supported by family policies that make it difficult for women with children to pursue a continued career over their life course, with insufficient infrastructure for childcare facilities being one of the main hurdles (Keck and Saraceno 2013). Furthermore, taxation policy favours a stratified income structure among married couples (Mühling and Schwarze 2011; Vollmer 1998). These factors combine with a particularly marked gender wage gap, which is higher in Germany than in most other European countries (Mischke and Wingerter 2012).

As a consequence, women remain the secondary wage earner in many German households (BMFSFJ 2011), in contrast to countries where more diversified wage earner models prevail (Lewis and Giullari 2005). As secondary wage earners women predominantly work part-time or hold other forms of non-standard or marginal employment, mainly to be able to combine their work and family commitments flexibly. More than 80 per cent of the female workforce works in the service sector, which is characterised by lower average wages and a high proportion of non-standard employment as compared to employment in the industry sector. Thus, women are disadvantaged in terms of employment security, wages, occupational status, social benefits and professional development and career progression opportunities.

Listening to the women

In this section, the findings from interviews with twelve German women aged between 45 and 57 years are presented. The methodological approach followed the jointly developed research methodology which is described in Chapter 7. Based on theoretical sampling, the women represented diverse work and family situations, as detailed in Table 13.1.

Learning across the lifespan

The sample reflects German labour market specificities in various ways. From their educational background, all but one woman started their working lives with either dual or school-based vocational training. Four had trained in craft-based professions (restoration carpenter, seamstress, gardener, florist), three in a commercial area (industrial and bank clerk), one in a technical profession as a radio technician and three as nursery teachers. One woman had obtained a degree in social pedagogy from a Higher Education College. However, when the interviews were conducted, only two women were still working in their original profession, whereas ten had redirected their career more or less radically to either move into a related occupational field or to do something else professionally. With the German vocational and academic tracks being distinctly stratified, a career change typically requires another formal qualification and thus major learning effort. Consequently, the women had to undergo major retraining programmes to change their career, with six of them having completed adult education programmes to obtain a university entry qualification and a Masters degree later on.

Table 13.1 German sample

Pseudonym	Age	Marital status	Employment status	Income per annum (in €)	Dependents	Highest qualification	Current employment
Petra	47	Married	Part-time (33 hrs)	30,000–40,000	2	Degree (masters)	Architect
Karin	47	Single mother	Unemployed	10,000–15,000	1	'Abitur', skilled worker	Unemployed
Andrea	48	Single mother	Full-time	40,000–50,000	1	Degree (masters)	Primary school teacher
Lisa	52	With partner	Full time	30,000–40,000	1	BSc engineer	Computer engineer
Anke	47	With partner	Self-employed (full-time)	15,000–20,000	2	'Meister' (master of crafts)	Seamstress/trainer
Silke	46	With partner	Full-time	40,000–50,000	1	Degree (masters)	Service manager
Inge	57	Married	Part-time (32 hrs)	20,000–30,000	1	Diploma	Special needs teacher
Martina	45	Married	Self-employed (part-time)	10,000–15,000	1	Degree (masters)	Historian
Sabine	45	Married	Part-time (20 hrs)	20,000–30,000	2	Degree (masters)	Family therapist
Ina	47	Single mother	Partly self-employed	15,000–20,000	2	Diploma	Speech therapist
Claudia	48	Married	Full-time	30,000–40,000	0	'Abitur', skilled worker	Industrial business assistant
Ruth	52	Single	Full-time	20,000–30,000	0	Diploma	Nursery teacher

Major career changes were represented by: Petra, who trained as a restoration carpenter and later became an architect; Karin the gardener, who studied languages and culture and who in the context of longer periods of unemployment developed a 'learner career' in that successive (mostly formal) training became a central part of her life, substituting for regular employment; Andrea, who initially trained and worked as an industrial clerk before becoming a primary school teacher; Silke, who had worked at a bank for twenty-two years, then studied German language and journalism and who worked as a service manager with a large international logistics association; Inge, who initially opted to train as a gymnastics teacher in the low-entry qualification route, but who then went through a series of further training programmes to become a special needs teacher; and Martina, who trained and worked as a florist for several years before studying history to become a freelance historian.

These trajectories reveal that for women of this generation, lifelong learning has a real practical meaning and that both formal and informal learning, often in combination with considerable training on the job, have been instrumental in redirecting their careers. Professional ambitions other than those suggested to them when they were young resulted in half of the women pursuing a university degree later in life. The reasons why these women started their working life with vocational training ranged from: (1) parental suggestions or financial pressure; (2) job security; (3) not knowing what they wanted to do professionally; and (4) not finding a job or training opportunity in the field in which they were interested. Parental expectations thereby combined with traditional role models that directed the women towards pursuing a lower qualification and a less ambitious career path after school – the expectation was for them to get married and stay home after having worked for some years.

Transitions

Analysing career adaptability was crucial when investigating how the women were making adjustments to manage career transitions. Career adaptability makes reference to attitudes, competencies and behaviours that individuals use to fit themselves to work that suits them (Savickas 2005). In addition to exerting considerable learning effort, the women had to deal with societal and institutional obstacles when seeking to redirect their professional lives. They experienced overcoming such obstacles as difficult and painful and, in many cases, as stretching personal and family resources, but also as rewarding, giving them new motivation, strength and self-confidence. Gaining control over their own working lives and shaping them as routes towards self-realisation were, therefore, key motivators for initiating a career change. Silke explained:

> I decided ... normally if you work in banking you study at least business, or economics, or law, but I said to myself 'I'm going to take a break for these years. I'm going to do this for myself, and I don't know what will come afterwards.'

And afterwards I won't concentrate on business studies, because I was a bit fed up with the subject. Instead, I wanted to do something towards self-fulfilment, and since I always wanted to study German language and literature studies, I did that.

Inge also realised that changing her attitude to work paved the way to explore new career options in the direction of working more independently:

> Well, like I said, the whole thing has been more of a gradual process. Looking back, I've often taken stock of the whole situation and seen that my attitude about my work has changed a lot. The last kick in the rear was suddenly being able to believe that I can do this work freelance too, that I can find a new and different way of doing the work I've been doing, that was an impulse for me ...

Intrapersonal influences

Striving for self-realisation was one example where the notion of self came out strongly when the women made adjustments to shape their own career paths. Making compromises was another facet of women sticking to their own values and aspirations, while at the same time seeking to comply with role expectations and accepting limited educational and career opportunities. Thus, women made compromises in terms of their educational pathways, jobs and employment status to align their work trajectories with their family lives.

For example, appropriate vocational training for women in the 1970s or 1980s meant moving into an occupational domain that either guaranteed job stability and a decent income, such as working in a bank or moving into a female profession such as child care, social work or floristry. However, there were a number of participants who started an apprenticeship as expected by their parents but who, at the same time, refrained from complying with dominant female career pathways, for example by opting for a male profession such as carpentry or radio technology. This constituted a compromise in that they accepted early school-leaving to make the transition into employment on the one hand but, on the other hand, rejected moving into a profession that was not in line with their own sense of self and career interests. Petra's case demonstrates the difficulties in realising an untraditional career pathway:

> After school ... I pretty much knew what I wanted to do, um, and I could do it, but I just didn't get an apprenticeship, because I wanted to learn a manual trade and I simply didn't get an apprenticeship because I was a woman. I bridged this gap by doing au-pair work, writing massive amounts of applications, and then finally did an apprenticeship, an apprenticeship as a carpenter.

Work influences

Petra's quote further illustrates the influence of the workplace and experiences at work on the women's work trajectories. Both negative and positive experiences had a strong impact. Discrimination at work stood out as a negative experience and was articulated in particular by women who had worked in male-dominated professions. Examples included: Petra, who was not considered for an apprenticeship; Lisa, who trained as a radio technician working on container ships for several years where she experienced harassment and isolation in a 'men's world of military leadership'; and Silke, who had to overcome major obstacles to make a career in the bank (such as completing a number of formal training courses that were not required by her male colleagues). Silke reflected that:

> Back in the 1980s, young women new in banking were encouraged to decide if they wanted to become assistants, yeah, this just means secretaries to some manager, or if they wanted to go into bookkeeping. I was not happy about it, because I had already figured out during my training that I wanted to go into lending above all. And women did not go into lending at that time, it was a man's world, and if you did then it was as secretarial help.

While Silke experienced the organisational structure and working culture at the bank as a hindrance to career progression, she also emphasised that she was highly supported by her supervisor when visiting the adult education programme to obtain a university entry qualification. Ultimately, she could only attend the evening classes and continue with her studies because she continued working at the bank, on a flexible hours, part-time basis, to secure financial backup.

Another sub-theme of work influences evolved around women striving for work–life balance and how they experienced tensions between different roles. Seeking to balance work demands and their own career aspirations with their family commitments and/or private life was relevant for all women, despite their different family and living situations. However, working women with caring responsibilities felt particularly stretched between their different commitments. In this situation, initiating a career change that required additional learning and training was perceived as difficult and challenging, sometimes putting great pressure on personal and family resources over several years. For example Anke, the self-employed seamstress, undertook the two-year German 'Meister' qualification when her children were young, sacrificing a considerable amount of her family time to training. Other women gave up a chosen career or training route altogether, because it was not compatible with their family situation. Among other cases, this was exemplified by Karin who, as a single mother, gave up working and subsequently became dependent on social benefits. Another example was Lisa, who stopped working on container ships when starting a family. As a computer engineer she expressed interest in 'moving up' in her position, but had given up when she discovered that the flexibility and mobility demands required from her would be incompatible with her family situation:

> ... it's not so easy to find your way in the business world when you also have a child ... Because in our company you can only take on leadership tasks, and that would mean even more work for me, you know? Not just full-time work, but also endless unpaid overtime and lots of travelling. And I don't feel up to it anymore. I simply don't have the strength anymore.

However, there were also examples where women, in addition to working and caring for their children, assumed a range of other responsibilities like caring for an elderly relative or voluntary work. Interestingly, women without children experienced similar pressures and stress to those with caring responsibilities. Here it seemed that work intensification, high expectations on work performance, and demands on their availability from employers gave them less time for other (social) activities. These women displayed a high degree of work centrality, which could compensate for missing social or family ties. Ruth, for example, had always lived alone and had been working in her dream job as nursery teacher for twenty-eight years. She, together with Claudia, an industrial business management assistant, were the only two women with a continuous and linear career, having always worked full-time. This linearity might be based on the lack of career flexibility demands due to family responsibilities.

Financial influences

The extent to which the women were able to mobilise resources to overcome formal and financial obstacles to career advancement and to improve their educational level as well as their work and income situation, was striking. Major efforts also were undertaken to leave an unsatisfying job, improve the quality of work performance or turn a situation of instability or conflict into a positive learning experience. Financial constraints were a major reason why the women made compromises in terms of their working life. They related financial constraints to limited resources due to their current family commitments, lack of support from their parents to pursue a desired career pathway when they were young and to their employers who, for example, would not financially support training.

A dominant theme emerged around parents' – and more often the father's – influence on determining their daughters' educational attainments and on guiding them into subsequent employment and specific professional areas. Thereby, financial aspects significantly limited the women's career options when they were young. In six of the cases the parents did not financially support their daughters' further schooling, but insisted on early school-leaving and following a vocational training path instead. Thus, financial limitations in their early careers were identified as a main reason for later career disruptions and redirections.

Social influences

Social networks were referred to as the most valuable resource to initiate and/or support a career change. For women in stable partnerships, their partners played a key role – as did friends – in providing emotional and also practical support. The women emphasised that at their age, they could benefit from their established stable social networks and family relations. As Inge put it, in a situation of change and instability she could 'save' resources at the social end and was able to 'harvest' and benefit from emotional support instead of needing to invest in establishing social ties. Friends and partners also provided opportunities for intensive reflection and communication, to talk things over besides providing practical support in the household or in terms of sharing caring responsibilities. Through friends and social networks, the women were also inspired, developed new ideas and gained access to other resources and support structures.

Silke, however, portrayed a different picture. When she decided to leave the bank after twenty-two years in order to redirect her career, her friends and colleagues proved to be the greatest hindrance. Rather than providing support, they emphasised that the security, benefit structure and good working conditions at the bank should not be something one should give up. As a response, Silke sought support from professional networks and career guidance programmes, which were encouraging and which provided practical advice. Overall, lack of support structures could be a major hindrance to career development, for example financial constraints, lack of information about possible career progression or training routes, lack of child care facilities, or friends and parents not being supportive.

Relocation

Relocation or geographical mobility did not emerge as major influences on these women's career development. In fact, eight women had never relocated, while three had gone to another town to pursue a particular qualification or study, or they had used travel periods, like spending a year abroad or doing au-pair work, to bridge learning and employment periods. Ina, for example, spent several years abroad which, she reflected, were a combination of travelling, learning and working. These relocations only randomly intersected with the women's career development pathways because they usually took place before they had entered regular employment or had a family. Only in the case of Lisa was relocation interconnected with her career changes, starting with when she was working on container ships as a radio technician. In the following years she relocated several times together with her partner, setting up their own business abroad, which they gave up after two years to return to Germany. Lisa reflected that reorganising her working and family life due to relocation was challenging and required compromises.

Advice to others

Advice to others reflected coping strategies that the women had developed in the past in order to manage career transitions. The participants emphasised that women should be open to new developments and creatively explore alternative and unconventional routes towards realising their own career ambitions, which may differ from familiar, institutionalised pathways. Furthermore, women should take initiative, develop their own sense of self and pay attention to positive and also negative former learning experiences, in particular to gain self-confidence to manage new and unexpected situations. This may also mean endurance, sometimes to cope with a difficult conflict or unsatisfying situation, and demonstrating persistence to overcome institutional barriers. Using social and professional networks as support structures, including professional coaching and exchanging ideas with colleagues and friends, was identified as an important resource. Identifying a female role model was mentioned by Andrea as having been central for her career development. Ultimately, a job should provide scope for self-realisation and women should seek to align their working lives with their identity.

Future planning

Future planning was related to ideas and wishes, often connected to unfulfilled professional dreams, as well as to concrete changes anticipated in the near future. Six women stated that they would like to engage with some kind of learning to obtain or broaden either general (e.g. languages) or job-specific skills. Realistically, however, the women stressed that they would have neither the energy nor the time for significant learning activities. Petra and Andrea tentatively raised the idea of becoming self-employed as a possible future career option. In contrast to these rather vague ideas, three dominant themes emerged around future career plans. First, none of the women really anticipated another major career change. Rather, they felt that they had reached the end of their careers despite the majority of them being in their late forties. Second, in getting closer to retirement age, the women identified pressures to continue working full-time or even working extra hours or taking on extra jobs to accrue a better level of financial backup when they retired. This was even the case for Claudia and Ruth, who had been working full-time continuously throughout their lives but in low paid jobs. Third, there was a notion of striving or wishing for work–life balance. Karin and Andrea, who were not working, were hoping to get back into employment, while those who worked full-time (Lisa, Anke, Silke, Claudia and Ruth) would have liked to work fewer hours, but considered this to be unrealistic either due to financial pressures and/or the working culture at their workplace, which required high levels of commitment and, in the case of Claudia, working unpaid extra hours.

Reflections

Except for two cases, the older female workers' career paths were non-linear, displaying a high level of complexity as women sought to fulfil the demands of traditional role models in combination with realising their own working lives. Their trajectories thereby intersected with institutional barriers framed around the gendered German education and training system, which pre-structures subsequent career development pathways and income levels. Societal expectations, combined with institutional barriers, made all the women pursue a compromise strategy when shaping their individual careers over the life course. This was reflected in patterns of constrained careers in that these women could not, or could only partly, realise their own career aspirations. Gender discrimination at the workplace, parental influence, role expectations and financial constraints made the women opt for a non-academic, lower qualification route and a less ambitious career path when they were young. While more than half of the women were able to redirect their careers later in life, significantly broadening their career opportunities by having obtained an academic education, women with caring responsibilities were predominantly working part-time to balance their work and family commitments. Thus they accepted limited subsequent career development opportunities. Women also had disrupted careers as they moved in and out of work in connection with taking maternity leave, which for the sample ranged from one to up to ten years.

Experiencing multiple constraints, for these women learning and social networks played a key role in facilitating career adjustments and labour market transitions. All women had engaged in both formal and informal learning to varying degrees, which had been of critical importance to how their working life developed. In some cases this implied that they completed two, three or even four different qualification programmes. However, these training programmes also provided an important space for reflecting and re-evaluating their life direction. Social and professional networks were emphasised as playing a key role for facilitating career changes, but also for creating continuities across career transitions. Furthermore, the women were also aware of intrapersonal influences, such as their own values, interests and personality traits, which influenced their work choices and work satisfaction, but which they generally did not prioritise in the context of their families. This contrasted with women experiencing workplace discrimination and harassment, which, in some cases, had a strong influence on their careers too.

Whilst the present study focused on a female cohort that might have been disadvantaged due to traditional role models and career expectations, the gendered segmentation of the German labour market remains remarkably distinct to date. Despite young girls and women having outperformed men in terms of their qualifications over the last decade (BMFSFJ 2011), they remain discriminated against at the level of pay, workforce participation rates and career development opportunities. As a result, new research has emerged and efforts are being made to explain why the high level of female investment in education and human capital do not pay off in terms of labour market returns. A key explanation in this context is that, while role models have changed considerably since the 1970s, the institutional reproduction of gender inequality in the labour market obviously has not, keeping women disadvantaged in the labour market in many respects.

References

Allmendinger, J. (1989) 'Educational systems and labour market outcomes', *European Sociology Review*, 5: 232–50.

Baethge, M. (2008) 'Das berufliche Bildungswesen in Deutschland am Beginn des 21. Jahrhunderts', in K. S. Cortina, J. Baumert, A. Leschinsky, K. U. Mayer and L. Trommer (eds) *Das Bildungswesen in der Bundesrepublik Deutschland. Strukturen und Entwicklungen im Überblick*, Reinbeck bei Hamburg: Rowohlt, (2nd ed.), pp. 541–98.

Baethge, M. and Baethge-Kinsky, V. (1998) 'Jenseits von Beruf und Beruflichkeit? – Neue Formen von Arbeitsorganisation und Beschäftigung und ihre Bedeutung für eine zentrale Kategorie gesellschaftlicher Integration', *Mitteilungen aus Arbeitsmarkt- und Berufsforschung*, 31(3): 461–72.

BMBF (2005) *Berufsbildungsbericht 2005*, Bonn and Berlin: Bundesministerium für Bildung und Forschung.

BMBF (2012) *Berufsbildungsbericht 2012*, Bonn and Berlin: Bundesministerium für Bildung und Forschung.

BMFSFJ (2011) *Erster Gleichstellungsbericht – Neue Wege-Gleiche Chancen – Gleichstellung von Frauen und Männern im Lebensverlauf*, Bonn and Berlin: Bundesministerium für Familie, Senioren, Frauen und Jugend.

Bundesagentur für Arbeit (2012) *Arbeitsmarktberichterstattung. Der Arbeitsmarkt in Deutschland. Frauen und Männer am Arbeitsmarkt im Jahr 2011*, Nürnberg: BfA.

Füssel, H.-P. and Leschinsky, A. (2008) 'Der institutionelle Rahmen des Bildungswesens', in K. S. Cortina, J. Baumert, A. Leschinsky, K. U. Mayer and L. Trommer (eds) *Das Bildungswesen in der Bundesrepublik Deutschland. Strukturen und Entwicklungen im Überblick*, Reinbeck bei Hamburg: Rowohlt, (2nd ed.), pp. 131–203.

Greinert, W.-D. (1997) *Das duale System der Berufsausbildung in der Bundesrepublik Deutschland*, Stuttgart: Holland+Josenhans.

Hall, A. (2012) 'Lohnen sich schulische und duale Ausbildung gleichermaßen?', in Becker, R. and Solga, H. (eds) *Soziologische Bildungsforschung*, Wiesbaden, Springer, pp. 281–301.

Keck, W. and Saraceno, Ch. (2013) 'The impact of different social-policy frameworks on social inequalities among women in the European Union: The labour-market participation of mothers', *Social Politics*, 1–32.

Kirpal, S. (2011) *Labour Market Flexibility and Individual Careers – A Comparative Study*, Dordrecht: Springer.

Kleinau, E. and Mayer, Ch. (1996) (eds) *Erziehung und Bildung des weiblichen Geschlechts. Eine kommentierte Quellensammlung zur Bildungs- und Berufsbildungsgeschichte von Mädchen und Frauen*, Weinheim: Deutscher Studien Verlag.

Lewis, J. and Giullari, S. (2005) 'The adult worker model family, gender equality and care: The search for new policy principles and the possibilities and problems of a capabilities approach', *Economy and Society*, 34: 76–104.

Mischke, J. and Wingerter, Ch. (2012) *Frauen und Männer auf dem Arbeitsmarkt – Deutschland und Europa*, Wiesbaden: Statistisches Bundesamt.

Mühling, T. and Schwarze J. (eds) (2011) *Lebensbedingungen von Familien in Deutschland, Schweden und Frankreich – Ein familienpolitischer Vergleich*, Opladen and Farmington Hills, MI: Budrich.

OECD (2008) *Education at a Glance. OECD Indicators*, Paris: OECD.

Rubery, J. and Grimshaw, D. (2003) *The Organization of Employment. An International Perspective*, Basingstoke, Hampshire and New York: Palgrave Macmillan.

Savickas, M. L. (2005) 'The theory and practice of career construction', in S. D. Brown and R. W. Lent (eds) *Career Development and Counselling*, Hoboken, NJ: Wiley.

Vollmer, F. (1998) *Das Ehegattensplitting: eine verfassungsrechtliche Untersuchung der Besteuerung von Eheleuten*, Baden-Baden: Nomos.

14 Voices of older women from Italy

Massimo Tomassini

For various reasons, deeply rooted in cultural and economic structures, patterns of female employment in Italy are historically weak and distinct from those of male employment. For example, according to the National Bureau of Census (Instituto Centrale di Statistica (Italian Bureau of Census) 2011), when the Italian economy was still largely agricultural in 1951, the employment rate for men was 80.8 per cent, compared with the employment rate for women of 26.0 per cent. Since then, women's participation has steadily increased. Ten years later, with an economic recovery that brought a more industry-based economic structure, these figures were respectively 72.9 per cent and 23.2 per cent. By 1971, when Italy's gross national product (GNP) was comparable to those of most industrialised countries, the ratio had shifted again in favour of women to 71.5 per cent vs. 25.1 per cent. At around the same time, the importance of the pivotal role played by a type of worker defined as male, middle-aged, low–middle skilled in the labour market was being emphasised (Paci 1973). Subsequent decades saw female employment rates continue to increase steadily. By 1981, male and female employment rates were respectively 68.0 per cent compared with 32.9 per cent; in 1991, 64.9 per cent compared with 35.0 per cent; and in 2001, 60.5 per cent compared with 37.6 per cent.

More recently (Statistical Office of the European Commission 2012) such ratios have further risen in favour of women: 75.5 per cent vs. 49.6 per cent in 2006 and 72.6 per cent vs. 49.5 per cent in 2011. These statistical trends indicate that Italy is at present well below the European average female employment rate (calculated in relation to the population between 16 and 64 years old), representing − 12.6 in comparison with the EU-27 (the conventional definition of the European Union when it comprised 27 States), which places the country just before Greece (− 13.5) and Malta (− 18.7). Such a gender gap is part of a wider gap regarding the overall employment structure. Intrinsically weak, Italy's consolidated employment rate in 2011 (61.0 per cent) compares unfavourably with that of other countries, such as France (69.3 per cent), the UK (74.2 per cent), Germany (76.7 per cent) and Sweden (79.4 per cent).

These statistics, however, require closer scrutiny in order to gain a more accurate understanding of the position of women in the Italian labour market. First, the marked regional variations in women's employment patterns between the so-called two Italies (along the North–South axis) must be taken into account. In the southern regions (representing about 30 per cent of the total population of Italy), the female employment rate is below the national average. Compared with the national female employment rate of 49.5 per cent (2011), the rate for Northern Italy is 56.1 per cent (Sabbadini 2012), which is similar to France (59.7 per cent) and to Belgium (56.7 per cent). Additionally, most of the new additional jobs created in the period 1993–2008 have been taken by women: by 2008 there were 1,649,000 more women in employment than in 1993 (again, with most of this increase in female employment in Northern Italy: 1,471,000) (ibid.). However, with the economic crisis of 2008, the rate of male employment in Italy fell from 75.4 per cent in 2008 to 71.6 per cent in 2012 compared with the EU-27 decline in employment in the 27 members of the European Union from 77.8 per cent to 74.6 per cent. The decline was much higher than that for women in Italy, from 50.6 per cent in 2008 to 50.5 per cent in 2012 and in the EU-27, from 62.8 per cent to 62.4 per cent.

These labour market statistics indicate that women's employment rates have steadily increased and are now higher than men's. This is partly a real phenomenon, partly illusory. Recently, this has been due to the effects of greater permanence of women in employment, resulting from changes in social security legislation, especially the increase of the retirement age from 60 to 65. Moreover, the statistics hide the realities of significant inequalities regarding the quality of work available for women. First of all, some features of female employment are hidden in national and international statistics, in particular those relating to irregular employment (i.e. the so-called black or sunk work). According to some estimates (e.g. Confederazione Generale Italiana Artigianato 2012), this involves about three million workers employed within generically under-paid, fiscally fraudulent or illegal activities. These workers produce a quantity of additional, hidden gross national product (GNP), which is calculated as 6.5 per cent of the official rate. Most of this hidden army is located in Southern Italy and is largely composed of women (especially immigrants). Second, the official statistics reveal that the rise in the number of women employed in unskilled and lower paid jobs (plus 218,000 between 2008 and 2010) is counterbalanced by an equivalent reduction in the availability of more qualified jobs (minus 270,000 in the same period) (Sabbadini 2012). More women than men are compelled to accept unskilled and lower paid jobs, which includes short-term jobs involving a range of activities and duties similar to colleagues holding long-term contracts, as well as various forms of casual jobs, regulated by a plethora of different types of employment contracts (Instituto per lo Sviluppo della Formazione dei Lavoratori (Italian Institute for the Development of Employees' Education and Training) 2012).

Women also occupy lower status jobs than men within organisations (35.2 per cent accept more precarious jobs, while this percentage for men is 27.6 per cent). More female graduates (52.0 per cent) work in jobs requiring lower levels of education compared with men (41.7 per cent; Sabbadini 2012), despite Italian women's educational attainment being greater than men's, thus following a generalised trend in advanced countries. The percentage of women holding an upper education level is 58.8 per cent, while the same figure for men is 55.7 (the EU-27 average is 74.2 per cent). The ratio is much more in favour of women (23.6 per cent vs. 17.2 per cent) as far as tertiary education is concerned (the EU-27 average is 35.8 per cent).

Motherhood, however, is the most important factor contributing to gender inequality in Italy where there is a strange co-existence between modernisation processes, unbalanced cultural heritages and deficiencies in social–civil development (especially as far as social services are concerned). One woman out of four has to leave her job after the birth of her first child, and the employment rate decreases in an inverse ratio with the birth of other children: 63 per cent of women without offspring are employed, while 58 per cent of women with one child are employed, 54 per cent of those with two children, and 41.7 per cent of those with three children (Sabbadini 2012).

The apparent stability of the low employment rate of women therefore appears to be a paradox within a difficult labour market. Keeping a professional job and a social life tends to exclude the possibility of a family life, and vice versa, with being a mother and spouse hindering opportunities for a professional life. This is considered as one of the main causes of the very low fertility rates of the Italian population: Italy is ranked 202 in a global ranking of 220 countries (CIA 2012). The difficulties in combining work and family are well known, but are particularly evident in Italy, due to the lack of adequate services for children as well as for the elderly, whose care is largely the responsibility of women. The inactivity rate (i.e. people 'that are not actively in search of a job although they might be ready to immediately accept a job offer', Instituto Centrale di Statistica (Italian Bureau of Census) 2011: 102) of women represents another serious issue. While in Europe in 2012, the inactivity rate was around 20 per cent, it peaked at 35.4 per cent in Italy, compared with Malta (46.3 per cent) and Turkey (64.8 per cent) (Statistical Office of the European Commission 2012). The inactivity rate of Italian women is four times higher than in the rest of Europe (16.6 per cent vs. 4.4 per cent). It is difficult for women to find jobs, but when female care of family members is integral to family balance, it is often impossible for women to even think about employment as a real possibility.

Such conditions particularly affect older women. The female employment rate for the older age cohort (age 55–64) is strikingly low, below 30 per cent for Italy, which is similar to Malta, Slovenia, Greece and Poland (European Commission 2012). This reflects the conditions of older women and especially of grandmothers in a society where social services are severely lacking and cultural stereotypes about older women's duties are still strong. Thus the diffusion of the sandwich grandmothers' phenomenon has been identified as a contemporary feature of society (Sabbadini 2012), where some older women are employed, at the same time very often looking after their grandchildren, whilst also helping their even more disadvantaged young daughters and daughters-in-law. Alternatively, they still have to take care of their grown-up children, even those aged around 30, who are still at home as difficulties in finding employment force them to delay economic independence. Other older women carry the heavy burden of their very old parents (in many cases sick and alone).

Employment dynamics are strictly intertwined with wider social phenomena and work–life relationships for Italian women are complex. It is therefore not surprising that the Gender Gap Index in 2012 placed Italy eightieth in the ranking of 135 countries, from Iceland to Yemen (World Economic Forum 2012). This is a poor score for a country which is eighth in the world GNP ranking and twenty-eighth in terms of GNP per capita (CIA 2012). It is against this background that we listen to the voices of older Italian women.

Listening to the women

Women who told their stories for the research study have made their way through three decades of the historical processes described earlier. They have witnessed the expansion of female employment and participated in the cultural evolutionary process that changed women's social image and brought about new levels of awareness about civil and human rights. The storytellers (please see Table 14.1) have been involved in the many contradictions of a society characterised by economic ups and downs and by significant deficiencies in civil development as well. Their stories have been analysed within the methodological research tenets that are detailed in Chapter 7, with the research themes structuring the discussion, the first of which focuses on learning across the lifespan. The context in which the women have lived their lives is acknowledged, with particular attention paid to their social and labour market structures.

Learning across the lifespan

Learning across the lifespan, in terms of both formal and non-formal learning, is a crucial issue in all the older women's stories. For the women who were self-employed in different occupational areas (including some who can be typically considered as knowledge workers), learning was intrinsic in their life projects and ways of working. Some of the group had excellent educational backgrounds and had accumulated various work experiences that allowed significant experiential learning for them. Teodora, for instance, educated as a psychologist and at present consulting as a registered psychotherapist, had other kinds of professional engagement in previous phases of her life, which were important sources of learning:

> The business experience was crucial for me: I learnt how to persevere, how to get support from all those that offered their support. All that matters is to be able to recognise this and to learn step by step from what happens in reality.

On the formal learning side, a good example is provided by Iris, a highly qualified nurse seeking career development as a teacher/trainer in her hospital. Some years ago she enrolled in a Faculty of Education Science and discovered a totally unknown world. She was passionate about her learning path:

> I would say that trainer behaviour is an intrinsic trait of nursing work. For instance, as nurses, we always had to assist newcomers (novices) in our profession. On-the-job training is also crucial. So nurses must have training in our professional DNA! And I'm interested in continuously evolving such intrinsic elements.

Table 14.1 Italian sample

Pseudonym	Age	Marital status	Employment status	Income (data not collected)	Dependents	Highest qualification	Current employment
Amanda	50	Married	Full-time		17-year-old son	Studies in modern literature (did not complete)	Retail management (bio-food)
Teodora	56	Single (stable relationship)	Full-time		None	Degree – psychology	Psychotherapist
Paola	52	Divorced	Unemployed			Degree – literature, then european languages (did not complete)	Unemployed
Carmela	55	Single (long-term relationship – recently died)	Full-time		None	Degree – sociology	Real estate agent
Iris	50	Married	Full-time		18-year-old son	Nurse training and masters degree	Nurse
Maria	48	Single	Part-time, temporary		None	Studies in sociology (did not complete)	Domestic help/baby sitter
Maura	47	Divorced	Part-time, temporary		Partly daughter aged 30 and her son aged 5	Compulsory school +2	Cleaning and attending course for unemployed
Rossella	58	Widow	Full-time		Sons aged 25 and 22	Degree – architecture	Consultant
Monica	54	Divorced	Part time, temporary		None	Degree – political science	Call center operator
Rita	49	Divorced	Full-time		11	Degree – economy	Owner/manager advertising company
Umberta	53	Divorced	Part-time, temporary		None	Sociology degree – did not complete	Call center operator and market research interviewer
Carla	56	Married	Full-time		Sons aged 24, 22, 17 and 15	Degree – economics	Delicatessen shop manager

Stories of other women reported very different realities: some, for instance, dropped out of the educational system; some, having a regular – or even very good – educational background, found themselves in situations which hindered them from learning anything significant from their work activities (e.g. working in certain kinds of outbound call centres). Formal training seemed to represent an opportunity or at least hope, as in the case of Rosa who attended a European Social Funded (ESF) remedial training course for unemployed people. She had a very poor educational background and made her living from occasional cleaning work. She was in many ways a person whose choices had always been determined – even reactively – by the nature of her relationship with her parents, husband, daughter, etc. At the time of the interview, her life project seemed unfortunately inclined towards an unclear ending. Concerning her ESF learning opportunity she tended to manifest resigned, and just apparent, hope:

> The course is not bad. They help us in creating our CV according to the European format. They encourage us a lot to feel engaged and to do our best for succeeding. We, the participants, need a lot (of) this kind of encouragement as we are all in critical positions, due to age, family conditions, in some cases disabilities. Many of us have lost hope and feel really discouraged. The help of the course is important first of all on this human side. It's a support for regaining trust in ourselves even if we are definitively outside of the stable jobs area. And in the very end, who at present is still in this area? Very few people. Stable jobs do not exist anymore.

Transitions

Transitions are very good tests for understanding the ways in which a woman takes care of basic wishes for personal realisation, develops specific micro-politics in her life and work environments and finds her modus vivendi, in which personal and social identity are plausibly aligned. Carla is an example of a woman making successful transitions between different work experiences. At the time of the interview she was a partner in holding and managing a delicatessen shop (also offering trendy meals), but in the past she had been an economist and had work experiences in different companies. She was also the mother of four sons (aged between 14 and 24). In her very active life, she tried to interpret every transition in terms of valorisation of her previously accumulated competencies and capabilities:

> I can look at this activity (the delicatessen shop) also through the frames of marketing and financial promotion. The cycle starts with an idea (e.g. a cheese to sell, a dish to serve) and then, passing through other phases (choice, presentation, explanation), it is possible to verify the extent to which that idea is accepted by the clients. In this business, success has very concrete proxies: not only the economic result as such, but also the satisfaction of specific human desires. Thinking about my previous activity I can say that financial products

are rather abstract: their value can be manifested only in the future. Food products, on the contrary, are very tangible; they are to be consumed immediately and they are immediately satisfying, or they aren't. It's interesting to work on something that begins (the desire for a piece of food) and ends (when the food is bought or eaten) within a short period of time.

Such cognitive competence, allowing a proactive use of acquired interpretation frames about work realities and life opportunities, is completely absent in most of the other participants' stories. A sad example is offered by Monica. After a normal beginning to her adult life, which included obtaining a degree, finding a rewarding job in a company and getting married, she then became disheartened by the world of work for a variety of reasons, both at the objective (firm crises) and subjective (desire for a different life) level. Soon she became involved in a spiral of depression, cancer and the deaths of close friends. At the time of the interview she worked part-time and was severely underpaid in a call-centre. She seemed incapable of redesigning her life project and looking on her past experiences as having any kind of value.

> Of course it can sound strange that a woman aged 54, with past experiences in highly qualified areas, is now a worker in a call centre. Moreover it can sound strange that such a woman can make her living because of the help of a dear friend (I live with her in her house, sharing our cats and dogs) and of her old parents. But now this is my life. I think nowadays the call centres represent one of the very few opportunities – maybe the only one – for women of different ages, even for young women.

Intrapersonal influences

The balance between aspirations and the realism needed for a life project is of course not easy to achieve. Giovanna illustrates well a modern knowledge worker still very much linked (and conditioned) to her family needs and values. After her graduation in architecture and some initial experiences in architectural design, she renounced her career desires in order to support her family budget and her husband's academic career. At that time she was very fond of her discipline and interested in her own professional development. But she let the sense of family prevail in the traditional manner and she had to choose less skilled employment:

> I married him just right after my degree. He was a man much older than me. A university teacher, a pure and exalted designer. With a strong influence on the ways I behaved in the world of architecture. For instance, I was interested in keeping a place in the academia and trying to find a position in it, but he didn't help me at all, assuming that this wouldn't have been ethical. And in private business it was more or less the same. So, considering that we attended

the same environments and that from time to time I introduced myself as his assistant, I couldn't find any space for myself.

At the opposite extreme, one can situate the most recent developments of Paola's story. After many years spent managing an agri-tourism business and after a painful divorce, she left her adolescent sons and moved from the country to a big city, trying to satisfy her artistic bent and her desire for an authentic life. Her last transition was radical, probably more an escape than a conscious choice of her project reshaping:

> I know that there have been periods in my life in which I really wanted stable employment, when many people of the same age wanted uncertainty. At the same time I know that all my life I've been ready to compromise to survive (in the family situation). But now it is different. I'm living days now as they are. I just want to do what I can do ... I understand that most of us, as I did for a long time, live in a physical and mental condition in which death is avoided, but life is not lived to the full. Now, acting as an artist, I want to question these topics. I want to see life in a non-conventional perspective.

Work influences

In the stories of more autonomous women, the positive influence of stimulating workplaces can ensure remarkable growth in competencies, capabilities and recognised knowledge. Carmela, a real estate agent, is a good example in this regard:

> You have to know very specifically what you are doing and which product is selling ... This is typical of my present job: you have to be concretely open-minded. In general, this is only possible in working environments that are conducive. Working in a pleasant environment, with pleasant people, offering pleasant products: this is very important. And being well-paid is also very important. These are the pre-requisites for me in order to perform at my best.

For less-equipped individuals, work environments can be the source of painful surprises. Maria, for instance, dropped out of her university studies, had different low-level work experiences and then arrived in a law firm, where she became a very effective and appreciated secretary. After some disagreements with the firm's chief, she experienced severe forms of bullying that deeply affected her physical and mental health:

> I always had to just silently obey and to stand to be treated like a zero ... Sometimes I was unable to get up in the morning because I started to suffer

from several painful symptoms, from simple headaches to real difficulties in keeping together my thoughts.

Afterwards she was fired and had to seek psychiatric treatment, where she found the means for self-defence and started re-thinking her life project (she wanted to manage a small Bed & Breakfast).

Financial influences

Their financial situation was obviously a major issue for all the storytellers, not only in and of itself, but also as a factor that shapes attitudes towards opportunities for improvement. Being financially independent is a fundamental structural issue, directly co-related with agentic dispositions. Two cases seem particularly relevant for explaining such dynamics. Rita, a communication consultant, recalled her financially healthy situation when reflecting on the bad time she and her colleagues had in a previous work situation. Financial independence keeps open the possibility not only of surviving but of thinking about a different future:

> I personally was stabbed in my back, but the worst thing was witnessing situations in which other people, even people playing important roles in the company, were put off in three minutes without any chance for explanations. I know very well that in our capitalistic system enterprises must be free of hiring and firing but the way things were conducted there was really unjustifiable … It was a deep human and professional delusion for me. Luckily I've some degrees of economic independence (I own the house where I live, I have no mortgage to pay, I'm not in terrible situations such as those I saw in that case). And I think I have certain levels of resilience.

On the contrary, Monica – as described before – could not see any future ahead of her, although her basic starting-point and cultural background were not very different from those of Rita. The difficulties Monica encountered at a certain point of her career trajectory triggered negative changes including the loss of her financial autonomy. Her meagre salary and needy condition were now in many ways the impassable limits of her world.

Social influences

Usually the social influences which are considered more relevant in women's life projects and practices are those linked to family and to the double role of worker and mother. Several examples are present in this Italian sample. Here it seems useful to also quote the influences from the original family and from other factors that can be considered as 'social'. Umberta led a tiring life doing two casual jobs with a market research company (interviews) and with a call centre (inbound and outbound calls). She had other plans when she was younger. She enrolled in the Faculty of Statistics and passed a number of exams. At a certain point she was asked to help her family after an earthquake in her village in Southern Italy:

> My father used to own a small farm. After the quake he decided to profit from the State incentives allocated to local economic re-start. He wanted to create a much bigger farm. He also invested all his own private resources (selling some apartments he had there) in such a project. But it was a failure. He lost everything, mostly because a very important tranche of the public financial support never arrived. So I stayed with my family for about three years, I participated in that catastrophe. I further understood that I definitively don't like the place of my origins, and I got back to Rome. But I was unable to begin a student life again. I left the university. I tried several part-time jobs.

Relocation

Relocation is a powerful trigger for changes in which life circumstances and desired transformations are closely entangled. In some of the analysed cases relocation was consciously chosen as a means for self-development and self-promotion. Teodora, for instance – the previously described psychotherapist – moved to different geographical settings (all within national borders) before finding her present setting. Most of her relocations were linked to changes in work and in life perspectives.

In other cases relocation had more radical causes and circumstances, such as for Amanda, who worked in a bio-food shop. She was born and grew up in Germany but had lived in Italy for a long time and still had problems with adaptation:

> I love Italy and its lifestyle. This is why I didn't leave this country after the divorce from my husband, ten years ago. It wouldn't have been so difficult for me to get back to Germany and to find a way for living there but I preferred to stay here. First of all, of course, in order to maintain a relationship with my son – who lives with his father but needs very much my support – but also because I feel engaged in living and working here, despite the indisputable difficulties I still have with this country.

For some of the participants, relocation was an open adventure, like for Paola – the previously mentioned artist. Maybe she would go back home to the Tuscan village. Maybe she would stay in the big city. She did not want to think too much about the future, but some worrying questions were always crossing her mind: 'What can I do? How can I earn my living? How will I survive when my present modest money reserve is depleted?'

Advice to others

Carla, a partner in a delicatessen shop after several different experiences in different companies and also the mother of four young boys, helps in understanding the non-superficial sense that can be regarded as advice to others:

> In my original family I learnt the spirit of community: one is fine if all the others are fine. This is highly relevant for me. I integrated this kind of principle in my family and in my working life as well. What really counts, I think, is listening and understanding others' needs. One can understand if one is able to listen and to silently observe the thoughts and behaviours of the others. What (do) they really want? What do they think? Which way (do) they want to be perceived? As I said, I experienced this kind of attitude as valid either for a son of mine or for a young man in the sales-force or for a client in my present work.

Future planning

The more autonomous women in the sample seemed to not have particular problems for their future planning, except the already quoted real estate agent, Carmela, who was facing a difficult crisis in the real estate sector. She seemed, however, to have personal resources in terms of acquired professional and social competencies for muddling through.

For others, the future was increasingly tough because of the decline of available public support and the shrinking labour market opportunities for all, especially for older women outside stable work conditions. The following are sad examples of such a situation: (1) the course for unemployed people that Rosa was attending had no specific occupational outlet; (2) the public psychiatric help used by Maria was going to be closed for budget reasons; (3) Monica could count only on the solidarity of her friend; and (4) Umberta was losing hope, as she knew that older women were increasingly excluded from market research and call centre activities, where the age limit increasingly tends to be established at 35. In response to the question 'how can you define your prospects about the future' Umberta's answer was that she did not want to think about the future because she was too fearful to do so.

Reflections

These glimpses of older Italian working women's stories concerning issues such as learning across the lifespan and transitions are clues to the complexity of individual careers that take place within the broader scope of social and labour market structures, but stem from a wide variety of causes and conditions. The women's stories reported here reflect very particular individual realities, captured by the qualitative analysis. The latter has dealt with specific concerns, projects and practices of the storytellers, within a theoretical perspective that rejects any hydraulic deterministic model of human life and mobility (Archer 2007).

From this research, aspects of both career guidance and counselling practices that might be sensitive to women's needs, and of theoretical models supporting such practices, include the following. First of all, practices and theories in this field should carefully take into account differences not only between genders, but also at the intra-gender level. The overall gender gap is a macro-phenomenon that co-exists with a myriad of other phenomena at the meso and micro levels in which women's lives are embedded. In this regard it seems important to further refine the analytical categories concerning both the labour market position and individual reflexivity.

Regarding the latter, the landscape of available approaches is vast and intriguing. Career guidance and counselling, as well as other activities like those of skills auditing, should be considered as exploratory, possibly open to solutions (even partial solutions) involving not only the work dimension but also other life dimensions, such as solidarity, friendship, and networking, in order to discover new meanings and opportunities which might maximise survival opportunities. Skills and competencies should be assumed within a broader framework in which the technical–professional and the cognitive, social and emotional dimensions are all fundamental.

Stimulating resilience is of course a key issue. Problems that trigger the demand for career guidance and counselling services should be, as much as possible, tackled in terms of the development of resilient attitudes towards the personal conditions that generate and accompany such problems. In the multidimensional perspective called into play by the overall scheme of this research study, resilience development should not be assumed only in the traditional sense of resistance to changes and adversities. The fundamental correlate of resilience seems to be identified in terms of self-transformation, based on the acceptance of reality and driven by the awareness of personal agency factors involved in making choices and taking actions, especially in relation to the self-promotion of learning and the increase of individual autonomy (Bimrose et al. 2011). In parallel, the same sense of acceptance and transformation should reflexively involve career guidance and counselling practitioners, whose work is severely limited by the overall socioeconomic–political conditions described by statistical macro-data.

References

Archer M. S. (2007) *Making Our Way through the World: Human Reflexivity and Social Mobility*, New York: Cambridge University Press.

Bimrose J., Brown A., Barnes S.-A. and Hughes D. (2011) *The role of career adaptability in skills supply. Evidence report 35 (Main Report)*, Wath-upon-Dearne, UK: Commission for Employment and Skills. Available at: www.ukces.org.uk/publications/er35-role-of-career-adaptability (accessed 16 October 2013).

CIA (2012) 'World factbook', Available at: www.cia.gov/library/publications/the-world-factbook/ (accessed 16 October 2013).

Confederazione Generale Italiana Artigianato (2012) 'Lavoro nero: 3 milioni di addetti "producono" 42,7 mld di Evasione'. Available at: www.cgiamestre.com/?s=lavoro+nero (accessed 16 October 2013).

European Commission (2012) 'Report on progress on equality between women and men in 2010'. Available at: www.european+commission+report+on+progress+on+equality+between+women+and+men+in+2010 (accessed 16 October 2013).

Istat (2011) *L'Italia in 150 anni. Sommario di statistiche storiche 1861-2010*, Roma: edizioni Istat. Available at: www3.istat.it/dati/catalogo/20120118_00/cap_10.pdf (accessed 15 September 2014).

Paci, M. (1973) *Mercato del lavoro e classi sociali in Italia*, Bologna: Il Mulino

Sabbadini L. L. (2012) 'Il lavoro femminile in tempi di crisi', *Paper for CNEL*, unpublished paper.

Statistical Office of the European Commission (2012) 'Labour force survey'. Available at: http://epp.eurostat.ec.europa.eu/portal/page/portal/microdata/lfs (accessed 16 October 2013).

World Economic Forum. (2012) 'Gender gap index'. Available at: www3.weforum.org/docs/WEF_GenderGap_Report_2012.pdf (accessed 16 October 2013).

15 Voices of older women from Portugal[1]

Filomena Parada, Carolina Correia and Isabel P. Gomes

Personal experiences and lives are shaped and co-constructed in relation to the multiple historical and social contexts in which individuals participate (Richardson 2012). Emphasising the relationship between self and work or other interrelated social contexts (e.g. family) allows for a more holistic understanding of how people experience their careers, that is, of their 'hopes and dreams, goals and projects, and associated life trajectories' (Richardson 2009: 78). Thus, to understand the career pathways of Portuguese women aged 45–65, we must not only listen to their stories but also consider the country's recent history and highlight the crucial general background in which these women's lives, especially their work and learning-related experiences, took place. A particular emphasis will be given to gender and to the Portuguese labour market of the last 40 years.

During the last century, Portugal experienced intense political and economic instability. In the 1930s, the country was governed by a non-democratic regime known as Estado Novo. Estado Novo was the result of a 'methodical, systematic, and balanced' (Oliveira 1996: 414) construction of a personalised and authoritarian regime, grounded in a corporatist, nationalist and anti-parliamentary political system highly embedded with Catholic principles. Family was the regime's prime organic core constituting the basis of social stability (Pimentel 2000).

Men and women were seen by the regime as family members with specific, hierarchically different and unequal roles and responsibilities. A subordinate status was assigned to women. Married women were the heart of the family and men, understood as the head of the family, were the providers. In the labour market, striking wage differences prevailed between both genders (Monteiro 2010). Also, there were certain careers (e.g. diplomats, magistrates) and specialised occupational categories (e.g. in toxic or underground industries) that were not allowed for women, who were mostly limited to unskilled, poorly paid tasks in the auxiliary or apprentice occupational categories of trades like shoemaking, textiles, or ceramics (Pimentel 2000). Women in these positions usually earned 30–50 per cent less than men and faced many restrictions to their career progression (e.g. often they did not have access to the highest positions in the occupational hierarchy).

During Estado Novo, Portugal experienced profound changes in its economic and social structure and shifted from a rural, agriculture-based economy to an urban, industrialised economy (Amaral 2010). Unions were 'completely controlled by the

State and destitute of power' (Dias 2005: 382), thus allowing for the maintenance of low wages. Although an unemployment subsidy was created, it was not universal. Estado Novo was also responsible for Portugal's first consistent and successful fight against illiteracy. From the 1960s, schooling the Portuguese population was set in motion and, for the first time, became a reality for children (Candeias and Simões 1999).

In April 1974, as a result of a peaceful, military-led revolution, democracy was reinstituted. The revolution introduced and triggered many significant changes in Portuguese society, specifically concerning the employment conditions of its workforce. A 'rather protective view' (Centeno 2013: 39) of employment was institutionalised. Portugal became viewed as a country with rigid labour market legislation, even though from 1976 onwards, many measures were 'progressively liberalized' (Amaral 2010: 31). As a result, a dichotomy exists between workers benefiting from long-term or permanent contracts who are 'very much protected' (ibid.: 71) against unemployment, and workers hired on a contract basis who are vulnerable to precarious work conditions.

In January 1986, Portugal formally completed its full integration as a European Union (then the European Economic Community) member state. By then, the country's new democratic regime had consolidated and, until the year 2000, Portugal 'lived a long period of optimism' (ibid.: 11) due to what was believed to be a well-performing economy. However, over time, long-term deficiencies in the country's economic structure, the quality of its institutions and the political economy became evident (Lairns 2005). Since 2002, after having joined the European economic and monetary union in 2001, a 'very negative' (Amaral 2010: 43) trend was once more exhibited by the Portuguese economy. This scenario was aggravated by the 2007 recession and, in April 2011, Portugal was forced to ask for international financial aid for the third time in 40 years.

Unemployment rates have grown by more than 10 per cent since 2001, with the national unemployment rate over 17 per cent in the first trimester of 2013. In 2012, more than 50 per cent of unemployed people held that status for over 12 months. Older workers were amongst the most affected, with the duration of their unemployment 'more severe' (Centeno 2013: 76). Further, the number of private sector employees over 45 years of age working in the same position in the labour market for 20 or more years has decreased by more than 10 per cent in the last ten years. In 2008, 20 per cent of private sector employees held a job for two or less years (Centeno 2013).

Available data concerning female unemployment do not differ significantly from those of the general population, and, as they grow older, women's activity rates decrease. This is particularly obvious for women aged between 45 and 64 years (Instituto Nacional de Estatística 2012). Most women not in the workforce are homemakers. Nonetheless, Portugal presents one of the highest female activity rates within the European Union, and Portuguese women tend to hold full-time positions in the labour market (Torres et al. 2005). In 2011, women's employment rate was 48 per cent, and the national female activity rate was 55.2 per cent (Instituto Nacional de Estatística 2012).

According to Statistics Portugal, the activity rate concerns the proportion of the active population in the total population. The economically active population includes all individuals, employed or unemployed, belonging to the workforce; that is, all individuals available to supply labour for the production of goods and services during a specified time-reference period (Instituto Nacional de Estatística 2013). Portugal's high female activity rates were achieved rapidly (Torres et al. 2005), mostly between the 1970s and the 1980s.

However, strong asymmetries prevail as a result of a persistently traditional social environment (e.g. Ferreira 2010; Monteiro 2010). These asymmetries help to explain some of the ongoing paradoxes characterising the lives of Portuguese women, especially in terms of their labour market integration. Portuguese women are the primary homemakers and caretakers, thus taking almost exclusive responsibility for performing unpaid work tasks and activities, regardless of being in paid work. Including paid and unpaid work, Portuguese women tend to work almost two hours a day more than men (Torres et al. 2005). Furthermore, women almost exclusively require leave of absence from work for maternity reasons or the need to provide assistance to family members.

Additional asymmetries exist concerning women's distribution across occupational categories and areas of economic activity. Although women are employed in many non-traditional female occupations (e.g. medicine, journalism, judiciary), they are also largely concentrated in highly feminised occupations (e.g. education, commerce, health care services), mostly in the tertiary sector of economic activity (Ferreira 2010). An equally high number of women are concentrated in work and occupational categories characterised by precariousness and low wages (e.g. domestic services, certain traditionally low-skilled positions in the textile or shoe industries).

The coexistence of women at two opposite ends of a spectrum (i.e. a high concentration of women in jobs requiring high qualifications and specialisation or in jobs that are precarious, unskilled, and poorly paid) largely mirrors the 'significant change' (Alves et al. 2010: 10) in the country's qualification structure. From 1986 onwards, with the implementation of nine years of compulsory schooling (which, in 2008, became 12 years), the distribution of the population's education level significantly changed and for some time now, women have been the majority of those attending and acquiring secondary and higher education diplomas. Their presence is particularly relevant in areas such as the social sciences, commerce, law, health and social protection and education (Instituto Nacional de Estatística 2012). Nonetheless, jobs in these fields are not necessarily paid the highest wages.

The difference between men's and women's wages is not high, due to the weight of the public sector in the overall employment distribution of the population and, in particular, in women's employment (Ferreira 2010). However, women find it harder to access higher supervisory or administrative positions, both in the public and the private sector. The highest paying positions within public administration are male dominated, although the civil service is highly feminised (ibid.). The same applies to the private sector, where differences in wages and in rank are even more striking than in the public sector, especially disadvantaging women with higher qualifications and schooling levels (ibid.). A potential explanation lies in the fact that, in Portugal, collective negotiations are centralised, and unions operate as highly politicised, fragmented structures, often conservative and gender-biased, that tend to focus most of their influence on the negotiation of wage increases (Dias 2005).

Wages play a crucial role in the segmentation and segregation of the Portuguese workforce, affecting individuals as a result of gender, their position in the employment structure hierarchy, qualification level (there is a high return from investing in education) or benefits they are entitled to (Centeno 2013). In Portugal, wages are low, falling in the lower end of wage distribution in the euro area (ibid.). Portugal is also the third most unequal country within the European Union (Amaral 2010), and striking wage differences prevail between workers with a fixed-term or a permanent contract, even if performing the same tasks, a difference that is accentuated by the worker's age (Alves *et al.* 2010). This is the general background against which Portuguese older women's stories were heard.

Listening to the older women

Our 12 interviewees, detailed in Table 15.1, were selected because we believed their stories would give us access to work and learning pathways both diverse and typical for Portuguese women aged 45–65 years. However, ours is not intended to be a representative sample. All interviewees were born before April 1974, and part of their learning and/or work lives unfolded during Estado Novo. They all resided in the Porto area, and exhibited diverse qualifications. Some were studying at the time of the interview. Three participants attended 'Novas Oportunidades', a government programme allowing adults with low qualifications to acquire additional certification, namely by seeing their prior learning recognised and validated (RVCC, Reconhecimento, Validação e Certificação de Competências).

Given Portugal's current economic situation we believed it important to include unemployed women in our sample and to listen to their voices too. They constitute a significant portion of the national workforce.

Details on the research methodology are presented in Chapter 7. The present results will be structured around the nine major themes emerging from the study. All participant names are pseudonyms.

Learning across the lifespan

Participants' learning pathways followed two main patterns: those who left school early – typically after completing elementary school – and had engaged in little to no formal learning since then; and those who continued to engage in formal learning. For the former, since leaving school, most of their learning had been informal, either in their work contexts or as a result of their life experiences (e.g. travel). Nonetheless, learning through experience, working under a more experienced worker or as a result of the need to adapt to new or changed work circumstances, was mentioned by several interviewees.

Table 15.1 Portuguese sample

Pseudonym	Age	Marital status	Employment status	Income per month	Dependents	Highest qualification	Current employment
Alexandra	62	Divorced	Retired (with disability pension)	Up to 585 euros	1	Grade 9 (RVCC)	N/A – used to work as a factory worker
Bárbara	45	Married	Unemployed (laid-off)	Up to 585 euros	3	High school (grade 12)	N/A – used to work as a sales assistant in a butchery
Carla	50	Married	Full-time	From 585 to 1,200 euros	2	High school (grade 12)	Coordinator of the administrative services at a local government institution
Diana	53	Married	Full-time	From 585 to 1,200 euros	1	High school (grade 11)	Entrepreneur – owns small ironing business
Eva	54	Separated	Unemployed (rescinded contract)	Up to 585 euros	3	High school (grade 12)/dropped out of masters in psychology	N/A – used to work as a clinical analysis lab technician
Fátima	51	Married	Full-time/student	From 1,200 to 3,000 euros	2	Degree (licentiateship in biology)/current studies: PhD in geology	High school teacher (biology and geology)
Gabriela	64	Single	Retired (with disability pension)	Up to 585 euros	Nil	Grade 6 (RVCC)	N/A – used to manage the family small textile company

(Continued)

Table 15.1 Portuguese sample (Continued)

Pseudonym	Age	Marital status	Employment status	Income per month	Dependents	Highest qualification	Current employment
Helena	58	Married	Unemployed (rescinded contract)	From 1,200 to 3,000 euros	Nil	High school (grade 11)	Administrative assistant
Ilda	61	Divorced	Retired/student (part-time)	From 1,200 to 3,000 euros	1	Degree (equivalent to licentiateship in nursing)/current studies: MA in psychology	N/A – used to work as a nurse
Joana	55	Single	Unemployed (laid-off)/student	From 585 to 1,200 euros	Nil	Degree (licentiateship in history)/current studies: graduate certificate program in gerontology	N/A – used to work as an editor
Luísa	52	Common law	Full-time	From 585 to 1,200 euros	1	Grade 9 (RVCC)	Main store operator at a large Portuguese supermarket chain
Marta	53	Married	Homemaker (since the return of the family to Portugal, 8 years ago)	Nil (husband: from 585 to 1,200 euros	2	Grade 4	N/A – used to work in tourism-related services in Switzerland

Regardless of when they stopped studying, some participants continued learning formally either through their own initiative, as a requirement of their workplaces, or both. Some had progressed their studies while working, with their investment in education being strategic; Joana 'knew beforehand that the more qualified people are ... the higher the likelihood of being given more responsibilities and of progressing in the hierarchy'.

Overall, interviewees made it clear how much they valued learning and the opportunities to do so. However, for those participants combining work and study, it was not always easy to reconcile both activities for reasons such as working hours, overlapping work and course schedules, and self-funding courses. Training did not always correspond to interviewees' expectations. Sometimes learning was too theoretical, and at other times participants considered that there simply wasn't enough time to learn everything.

Geographic barriers and social norms were two other constraints identified by interviewees. As noted by Marta, 'at that time women didn't study (beyond four years of school) ... in the 1960s everything was very closed'. Bárbara talked about the distance she had to travel between home and the school she attended in order to complete grade 9:

> I was born in a small village ... the resources were very few. I had tremendous difficulties to study ... I had to travel 52 kilometres (laughter), of which 12 were made on foot. So, I had to leave home at six in the morning and returned only at nine in the evening.

Transitions

Most unanticipated events mentioned by participants had to do with unexpected family or life circumstances (e.g. the death of one or both parents, an unplanned pregnancy, personal illness or illness of a family member). Examples of work-related unforeseen events concerned being laid-off (Bárbara and Diana) or, for Helena, being replaced in the supervision tasks she was performing by a younger person who had recently joined the company.

Interviewees tended to describe their initial response to chance events as a 'tremendous shock' (Luísa), saying that 'It was hard, very hard' (Marta). They expressed similar sentiments to Luísa when she declared that 'I had to adjust because life doesn't stop. Life must move forward.' Acceptance followed, and for some it meant 'making the best out of the situation' (Ilda) or 'to always look at things from a positive perspective' (Carla). That was precisely what was done by Diana, who created her own business, by Fátima who decided to enroll in a Master's programme (which soon became a PhD) and by Helena, who chose to face 'things the best way ... one has to be realistic'.

Another common response to unexpected events had to do with participants mobilising their social networks. For example, Bárbara explained 'we use the resources we have ... and say: look, I'm unemployed, so if there is something that you know of ... you let me know'. Children played a key role in how interviewees handled chance events in their lives. As Eva said:

> my salvation are my children, otherwise I would have already made some twenty depressions or more. Only I can't, I can't, because if they see a depressed mother they get to be really sad, right? So, I can't. And that is where I go and get my reserves.

Different strategies could be identified in the participants' narratives regarding how they adjusted to changing circumstances. Some, like Bárbara, when questioned whether changes in her life had been planned, answered 'No, of course not, absolutely, not all, no.' For others it was the opposite. For example, Marta carefully planned going to Switzerland as an emigrant and also her return to Portugal. Carla described the changes she had experienced as being 'all foreseen, changes were foreseen with time ... I decided, I invested'. Other participants, like Ilda, in spite of anticipating change, preferred not to plan for it. She said, 'we will see. I think about it ... maybe, perhaps because I didn't prepare anything. Things just ran'.

Intrapersonal influences

Interviewees valued tolerance and openness to differences, together with the opportunity to establish and maintain positive, respectful interpersonal relationships, economic security and the possibility of living with some material comfort, personal fulfilment or the opportunity to learn, to be independent and to help others. The importance of feeling useful was highlighted, among others, by Bárbara, as well as 'being serious in what we do, and honest and authentic'. Variety, challenges and the opportunity of dealing with new situations were also important to several participants.

However, what interviewees valued most was their role as mothers. For almost all participants, motherhood was what they ranked highest in terms of their priorities in life. Diana's words sum it up:

> What was most important, really, was being a mother. To me it is the most important ... I think all women have the dream of becoming mothers. My generation, a lot more than perhaps now. In my children's generation you don't see that so much ... and to me my children are before anything else ... They are my priority.

This does not mean that having a job was not important to them, only that motherhood and the responsibilities that come with it superseded everything else. Again, as Diana said, 'to have a job, to me, it was also very important because ... I would have my independence'.

An equally high consensus prevailed around participants' past (life, role) satisfaction. Usually, they appreciated their previous opportunities and experiences. This does not mean they did not have any regrets or unfulfilled expectations. For the most part, participants' regrets concerned not having been able to pursue their studies, either in general or in a specific area, and the impact this had on their work lives. Fátima was the most adamant in expressing her regret about having moved to the city where she lived for the past 20 years:

> Today, I wouldn't have come and lived in [name of the city] ... I left the exact place I enjoyed ... I was very much dragged by my husband, you know? He thought about it, he compared prices, and he made the decision. Today I don't think it would happen to me ... Perhaps because ... I had a childhood and a youth maybe, maybe very much directed by my parents, I just signed the papers, you know? ... I was the youngest daughter of an extremely conservative family. My father was the authority, right? ... We were very much directed, were very much formatted to be whatever our parents wanted us to be.

Others were somewhat or extremely dissatisfied with their current circumstances. For example, Diana felt the lack of institutional support and personal fulfilment on account of Portugal's current economic crisis. Marta, who never really adjusted to her new life in Portugal, did not enjoy the city in which she was living and missed her work and connections in Switzerland. Bárbara, who 'would like to be working, to feel fulfilled', also complained about the lack of acknowledgment for all the work she did for her family as a homemaker and a caretaker:

> We have a lot to do, no one appreciates us ... every day I am more tired than when I used to work. And it is a work that is recognised little to nothing because I do the same thing every single day.

Ilda felt strongly about her retirement, saying:

> I can't say I'm not angry ... I was forced to stand still. Me and other colleagues like me ... I was an expensive nurse ... I think I still had the ability to do many things. To contribute more.

Age was mentioned by several interviewees as being significant in their current lives. Eva and Ilda talked about their concerns about going to college at their age. They mentioned, at first, not being sure if they would be accepted or feel integrated by their colleagues and professors. Specifically concerning (an absence of) employment opportunities, Diana was the most eloquent:

> I worked as a sales assistant, and at 47 years no one is going to call me, right? ... because it isn't easy, anyone, a woman or a man, to be unemployed with 47 years ... You may have a lot of experience but it's not worth it, because young people are more qualified than I am, so it's normal ... No one would give me a job ... even if I applied I was over 45 ... and it's not easy to find a job and with my age it is even worse. And, for now, I'm not entitled to a pension or anything of the sort.

Work influences

Irrespective of their current employment status, all interviewees had long pathways in the labour market. Alexandra and Gabriela started working at an early age. Alexandra was 11 years old when she was hired by the tyre factory where she stayed until she retired, at the age of 55 for health reasons: 'I was swallowing gasoline and stuff. I was bleeding.' Like Alexandra, most participants experienced little to no employment changes. Some kept their first job or position for more than 20 years. Others progressed either by performing different activities or by moving upwards in the organisational hierarchy.

Eva and Joana were the exceptions. Eva changed jobs every 8–10 years and, since rescinding her contract, had several different odd-jobs: 'I was always on the move … I changed every time an opportunity for better wages came up.' Joana's job turnover mostly resulted from being laid-off and then being hired in a similar post in another company. Twice she worked as a researcher with a scholarship, however she abandoned it because 'there was no money in it. Because I needed to survive'.

Participants emphasised different features of their workplace dynamics. Some provided rather vivid, highly positive accounts believing to be 'privileged … having gone to that company, where we were a family' (Luísa), or stressing that 'I always worked with people that respected me a lot, and that even today are my friends' (Helena). Company gatherings (e.g. picnics, Christmas parties for employees and their families) were among the activities interviewees valued the most. However, competition amongst co-workers, 'sometimes in rather unequal circumstances' (Joana), was frequently mentioned. The same applied to conflicts with management, which was the reason why Eva rescinded her contract.

Additional features of workplace dynamics mentioned by participants concern highly centralised organisational management and, at times, lack of knowledge about their respective areas of activity from those in charge of decisions (e.g. administration, the Ministry of Education). Often, according to interviewees, these circumstances explained management's poor performance as well as decisions leading to their dismissal: 'all of us at Porto … we were a little marginalised … information doesn't always reach us … we were the first to go' (Joana).

Low wages, precarious employment, lack of acknowledgement and gender biased management practices were also mentioned by participants. According to Diana: 'in our country, if there is a woman and a man to fire, you fire the woman and the man stays. And that's what happened… the men stayed and I had to leave'. Luísa went even further and, while talking about a possible promotion to middle management, said:

> I already had that possibility. And I didn't take it … That would imply things that, for us as women, sometimes … we are penalised … We had to lie down to move up. And that didn't work for me. It never did. Maybe that's why I'm still at the position I am today.

Balance between the demands of their paid work and family lives was usually accomplished at the expense of their own interests, plans or ambitions. Interviewees either chose to abandon their earlier dreams or to postpone them to when either work or family demands made it easier for them to find the time. Carla explained that it is 'very hard to manage ... daily household chores, with a job and studying ... when I have only my husband and I'm more independent, maybe I'll decide to go back to school'. According to Diana:

> My husband worked and was politically active, and often he wasn't at home. Many times, at night and ... that's why I came in later. That's why I say that often women give up their places ... because one of us had to. If he liked politics as he does, and I like it too, but, in any way, one of us had to yield, and it's on these things that I believe women yield a lot more than men ... I stepped down from a position in the City's Assembly because of that, because the both of us couldn't go (they had small children).

Financial influences

References to past financial circumstances mostly concerned the economic hardships faced by their families and how this led them to drop out of school:

> My parents didn't have much money ... many years ago, it wasn't easy to study. Only those with a little bit of money ... My parents wanted to, but it was really hard... there was no money to take the bus to study ... to have a snack ... I had a meal, I ate, I wasn't hungry ... it really made me go and work.

Behind participants' references to their present financial circumstances was, without exception, Portugal's economic crisis, as Marta explained: 'Only it's really hard ... and we keep on going like this, but it's getting hard.' The need to plan more carefully their families' budgets and, often, to make cuts in their expenses were particularly evident: 'Everything is very complicated ... financially ... To go from nearly 2000 euros a month to 400 ... Suddenly we have to cut back in everything and then, even after cutting back in everything, it's not enough' (Eva). No references concerning participants' future financial situations were identified.

Social influences

References to support networks almost always concerned interviewees' families, regardless of their positive or negative influence:

> Up to 4 years ago, she (mother) would do everything for me ... I'd arrive home and it was impeccable, I just had to sit down and eat dinner ... It was a time we had a lot, a lot of work ... now I'm more than obliged to give her back all that, and give her all the affection I can.

After having children, Ilda began:

> not seeing eye to eye (with her ex-husband) ... I thought I was a good mother, a good wife ... when we got married he began imposing his views ... A woman must stay at home, she is not supposed to work ... because children come from mothers and they need to spend a lot of time at home.

Occasionally, references were made to positive support provided by work colleagues or employers.

Negative influences on participants' career development refer to 'the bureaucracy of it all. Every little thing a person wants gets them in trouble because we are a country of papers ... one is required to fill in a bunch of papers, a bunch of budgets' (Diana). Additional (negative) administrative influences concerned a lack of transparency in how the system operates and an absence of employment opportunities or incentives for people in their situation (e.g. while as a mother of three children, trying to build and maintain a small business).

For example, Joana mentioned having applied for positions in the local administration and realising that, 'it was already directed to the person getting the job. All that (the call) was only a formality'. Eva said:

> once, someone at the employment agency told me ... 'They will never call you (for a job) because there is no room for you anywhere. You are overqualified for the majority (of positions offered) ... They cannot ever call a person to something that is lower than what they used to do.' And, so it will be very difficult.

Relocation

Few references to relocation experiences were made by interviewees. Most concerned their coming from their (small) hometowns to the Porto area, either to study or in search of better employment prospects. Marta was the exception. As a child, she emigrated with her family to Latin America. Soon after she returned to her hometown and, as an adult, emigrated to Switzerland. About eight years prior to the interview, she returned to Portugal with her family.

Advice to others

Advice participants gave to others resembled how they adapted to unexpected events in their lives, for example, to 'always have goals in life ... and strategies' (Joana), allowing them 'to move forward, accept, and then make an analysis ... if it was worth it or not' (Luísa). Bárbara advised women to persist and to believe in themselves, so 'they don't give up ... we only lose when we stop fighting' and Helena said to accept and remain optimistic because '(people) must accept (change) the best they can ... always looking for what good might come out of it'.

Participants also believed in being 'down to earth, and making things with wisdom, and enjoy all opportunities, without wasting a single one ... work, work, work, work' (Fátima). For Eva they must do it 'without ever losing the ability to dream ... While we are able to dream we dare enough to overcome certain obstacles ... and we must have someone to fight for ... that's another thing giving us some strength'.

Future planning

Participants' future planning always involved some sort of work activity, paid or unpaid, allowing them either to bring some continuity to current work or study commitments, or to materialise some earlier dreams or ambitions (e.g. to resume their studies; to invest in a small business, etc.). Their plans were usually set against Portugal's severe economic crisis: 'At this point, it is best to see it day-by-day and not go on thinking a lot about the future' (Marta). Eva was 'really afraid because I don't see many alternatives ... as things are, and thinking about the country's situation, I don't see much (opportunities)'.

Reflections

One of Portugal's most distinctive features has been its persistent and continuous distancing from other Western European nations. Specifically, in major structural dimensions affecting the country's economic (e.g. the prevalence, well into the twentieth century, of an agricultural-based economy marked by low salary rates and a lack of investment in technology) and human (e.g. the population's average education levels, and its birth and mortality rates) development (Lairns 2005). The last four decades have been marked by a 'disappointing' even 'mediocre' (Amaral 2010: 13) performance of the Portuguese economy that further distanced the country from most of its richer counterparts. At the time of writing, Portugal was experiencing another historical crossroad in its development. In the last few years the country faced several tough choices and strict austerity measures and there is not an easy solution (Amaral 2010).

Stories told by our interviewees reflect the country's past and present circumstances concerning its economic and human development, as well as the highly traditionalist and bureaucratic functioning of its structures. All through the participants' narratives, the profound political changes the country went through, as well as the significance of economic constraints and factors, influenced how their careers progressed and are expected to progress. The generalised absence of references to future financial circumstances and the constraints self-imposed by interviewees on their future planning makes us question the degree of volition they are able to exert in their career choices and development. It is almost as if they are divided between two of the 'three human needs working optimally can fulfil: the need for survival and power ... and the need for self-determination' (Blustein 2011: 4).

Also pervasive in their stories is the conflict they experience between tradition, that imposes a number of 'established and scripted patterns of behavior'

(Richardson 2012: 193), particularly concerning women's role in society, and the demands of contemporary life, namely in the market work domain. Gender and age significantly affect how participants make and experience work-based decisions and transitions. They constrain career opportunities for the older women, thus limiting the power they are able to exert over their lives. In fact, a sense of embedded powerlessness, never explicitly acknowledged by interviewees, underlies not only their ability to be resilient and to progress, but also to accept whatever comes their way. Paradoxically, this is also where their strength comes from.

Portuguese older women's stories clearly illustrate the uniqueness of female perspectives and experiences and the conflicts underlying their attempts to reconcile the 'discourse of career development and work and family that has become everyday parlance' (ibid.: 196) with the demands of contemporary life. Their stories also allow us to argue for the need for more holistic, inclusive career development theories providing us with a more accurate understanding of how (older) women work and how their learning pathways are influenced and shaped by the proximal and distal contexts individuals participate in.

Note

1 The study was partially funded through a partnership with the Vila Nova de Gaia Delegation of the Portuguese Red Cross.

References

Alves, N., Centeno, M. and Novo, A. (2010) 'O investimento em educação em Portugal: Retornos e heterogeneidade', *Banco de Portugal: Boletim Económico*, 16(1): 9–39. Available at: www.bportugal.pt/pt-PT/EstudosEconomicos/Publicacoes/BoletimEconomico/BEAnteriores/Documents/bol_primavera10_p.pdf > (accessed 23 March 2013).

Amaral, L. (2010) *Economia Portuguesa: As Últimas Décadas*, Lisbon: Fundação Francisco Manuel dos Santos.

Blustein, D. L. (2011) 'A relational theory of working', *Journal of Vocational Behavior*, 79: 1–17.

Candeias, A. and Simões, E. (1999) 'Alfabetização e escola em Portugal no século XX: Censos nacionais e estudos de caso', *Análise Psicológica*, 1: 163–94.

Centeno, M. (2013) *O Trabalho: Uma Visão de Mercado*, Lisbon: Fundação Francisco Manuel dos Santos.

Dias, J. (2005) 'A organização do trabalho', in P. Lairns and A. F. Silva (orgs) *História Económica de Portugal: 1700-2000*, Lisbon: Imprensa de Ciências Sociais, pp. 373–95.

Ferreira, V. (2010) 'A evolução das desigualdades entre salários masculinos e femininos: Um percurso irregular', in V. Ferreira (ed.) *Igualdade de Mulheres e Homens no Trabalho e no Emprego em Portugal: Políticas e Circunstâncias*, Lisbon: CITE, Comissão para a Igualdade no Trabalho e no Emprego, pp. 139–90.

Instituto Nacional de Estatística (2012) *Estatísticas no Feminino: Ser Mulher em Portugal, 2001–2011*, Lisboa: INE, IP. Available at: www.ine.pt/xportal/

xmain?xpid=INE&xpgid=ine_publicacoes&PUBLICACOESpub_boui=136501356&PUBLICACOESmodo=2 (accessed 23 March 2013).
Instituto Nacional de Estatística (2013) *Estatísticas do Emprego 2013*, Lisboa: INE, IP. Available at: www.ine.pt/xportal/xmain?xpid=INE&xpgid=ine_publicacoes&PUBLICACOESpub_boui=153369091&PUBLICACOESmodo=2 (accessed 10 September 2013).
Lairns, P. (2005) 'Introdução', in P. Lairns and A. F. Silva (eds) *História Económica de Portugal: 1700–2000*, Lisbon: Imprensa de Ciências Sociais, pp. 25–36.
Monteiro, R. (2010) 'Genealogia da lei da igualdade no trabalho e no emprego desde finais do Estado Novo', in V. Ferreira (ed.) *Igualde de Mulheres e Homens no Trabalho e no Emprego*, Lisbon: Comissão para a Igualdade no Trabalho e no Emprego, pp. 31–56.
Oliveira, C. (1996) 'Da ditadura militar à implantação do salazarismo', in A. Reis (ed.) *Portugal Contemporâneo - Volume 2*, Lisbon: Publicações Alfa, pp. 397–416.
Pimentel, I. F. (2000) *História das Organizações Femininas no Estado Novo*, Lisbon: Círculo de Leitores.
Richardson, M. S. (2009) 'Another way to think about the work we do: Counseling for work and relationship', *International Journal for Educational and Vocational Guidance*, 9: 75–84.
Richardson, M. S. (2012) 'Counseling for Work and Relationships', *The Counseling Psychologist*, 40: 190–242.
Torres, A., Silva, F.V., Monteiro, T. L. and Cabrita, M. (2005) *Homens e Mulheres entre Família e Trabalho*, Lisbon: CITE, Comissão para a Igualdade no Trabalho e no Emprego.

16 Voices of older women from South Africa

Mark Watson

There is a need to consider the macrosystemic contexts within which women's careers develop. McMahon *et al.* (2010: 67) encourage career practitioners 'to consider the sociopolitical factors that may have influenced the lives of older women and to listen carefully to their personal career stories'. Some of those stories can be heard later in this chapter, but it seems apposite to begin by considering the influence of the broader South African context, both positive and negative, in which Black South African women have constructed their career development.

Women have been at the forefront of sociopolitical development in South Africa for well over a century, from resistance to discriminatory laws implemented during the apartheid era to the present times where the challenge of ensuring gender equity requires constant monitoring. A striking example of South African women's sociopolitical influence was their resistance to discriminatory laws that racially defined areas of residence and that consequently restricted the geographic movement of Black South Africans. This resistance culminated in an historic march in the mid-1950s by over 20,000 women of all races. During this march a freedom song was sung ('Wathint' abafazi, wathint' imbokodo') which translates to 'when you strike the women, you strike a rock'. This phrase symbolises in South Africa the resilience, courage and adaptability of women. That Black South African women have needed to be resilient and adaptable is evident in the more traditional social and patriarchal structure of African society for much of the last century, which has reinforced males as the dominant role players in most aspects of African life including the work environment.

The advent of a post-apartheid, democratic South Africa has provided both opportunities and obstacles for Black women in the workplace. There is a general acceptance that South Africa's democratic laws are progressive. Thus there has been international praise for legislation aimed at ensuring gender equity in the workplace, resulting in some improved statistics for women in senior management positions. Yet, there is also a widespread recognition in South Africa that women, and in particular Black women, remain with a few prominent exceptions largely ignored at executive and leadership levels (Geldenhuys 2011; Ndungu 2010).

Statistical analyses of the role of women in the South African labour market continue to make for depressing reading. For instance, the lowest paid employees in South Africa at present are Black women working in private households (i.e. in domestic service), who do not belong to a union, and who are between the ages of 15 and 24 years (Statistics South Africa 2013). While there is an emerging middle-class Black population (Johnson 2006), the median age of White earners remains four times higher than that of Black earners in general and skilled workers earn six times as much as unskilled workers (Statistics South Africa 2013).

Unemployment in South Africa is recognised as a particular issue for women who have consistently represented higher unemployment rates throughout South Africa's sociopolitical history (Statistics South Africa 2012). Thus, while the unemployment rate for women was 27.1 per cent in 2012, it was 6.6 per cent lower for men. Further, women were 1.2 times more likely to be unemployed than men in 2012 and their unemployment rate for that year had moved downwards by only 3.6 per cent since 2004. The labour statistics for the last quarter of 2012 provide a detailed description of the limitations that women face in the employment market. Over half (53.7 per cent) of women were employed in either trade or in community and social services (traditionally a lower paid occupational field than other industries); conversely, only 11.5 per cent of employed women were in managerial and professional positions, with 41.3 per cent of women in semi-and unskilled employment. Only 2.3 per cent of all employed women were employers and of those who were employees, 21.0 per cent had verbal rather than written contracts. The working conditions of women demonstrate the difficulties they face in their workplace: 24.5 per cent of women worked longer than 45 hours a week and 53.4 per cent were not eligible for a pension or retirement fund. In terms of not qualifying for a variety of leave conditions, 38.5 per cent of women were not entitled to paid leave, 33.6 per cent were not entitled to sick leave, and 46.1 per cent were not entitled to maternity leave (ibid.).

There have been several recent analyses of labour statistics for South African women. Geldenhuys (2011), for instance, points to the significant increase in women working in the informal sector in occupations that require lower skill levels and hypothesises that women may seek more flexible working conditions in order to meet family and carer role responsibilities. Complicating an understanding of women's employment are geographic factors. Statistics suggest that up to a third of all working age women live in traditional rural areas that are largely impoverished.

A consideration of labour statistics for South African women raises the question as to how far we have come since our much lauded democratisation process. The answer must be a qualified 'not far enough'. Women in South Africa, and particularly Black women, remain between a rock and a hard place. Geldenhuys (2011) points out, for instance, that increasing diversity in the workplace does not translate to all occupational levels, with women remaining firmly entrenched in lower skilled and lower paid occupations. Geldenhuys attributes this in part to the process of industrialisation in South Africa, which has led to an increase in jobs, but of lower pay, lower stability, and poorer working conditions in general. Thus the consequences of democratisation and development have not always been positive for women in the workforce. Addressing gender equality at the macrosystemic level with new legislation does not easily translate to the realities on the ground. De Braine (2011) makes this point in describing the aftermath of the apartheid years, particularly for older women, who are economically limited through inadequate training and underdevelopment of relevant skills.

There is also the historic culture of male dominance in the workplace for women to contend with. While this is not unique to South Africa, Black South African women's experience of male-dominated work environments can be further exacerbated by their cultural upbringing. De Braine (2011: 54) describes the 'more masculine management style' of South African work organisations, with their promotion of patriarchal values. Similarly, tertiary academic environments have been identified as representative of a masculine culture (MacGregor 2007). There is a need for successful Black women to act as role models to counter this prevailing gender climate but, given South Africa's sociopolitical history, there is a scarcity of such women, particularly in the older age bracket. Even the legislation that promotes gender equality in the workplace may have a downside to it. Grundling and Bosch (2011) make the valid point that, while unintentional, such legislation can reinforce gender stereotypes of women being unable to make it on their own. Thus legislation can redress gender inequality issues at the macrosystemic level but it cannot address gender equality at the meso and micro levels of work environments and worker attitudes, where the reality of change needs to take place. It is against this national context that the voices of the South African women are heard.

Listening to the women

The research methodology is detailed in Chapter 7. The purposive sample consists of Black South African women working or studying in a tertiary educational institution. As such, the sample represents a minority group within the employment statistics of Black South African women. Women have become the majority gender at South African institutions since 1995, although they are clustered in certain more traditional study fields such as the humanities and social sciences (MacGregor 2008), with a minority in vocational fields such as science and technology (South African history online 2013). Their position in relation to higher qualifications and management levels is limited at present, with under-representation at higher qualification levels and higher faculty ranks. For instance, by the second half of the last decade only one in four senior university positions was held by women (MacGregor 2007). The inequalities in employment in South African tertiary institutions has improved, but Black South Africans (38 per cent) and women (42 per cent) still represent a minority component of academic staffing (MacGregor 2008).

There were several reasons for focusing on this more homogenous, but less representative, sample. The women were all employed or studying at a tertiary level in South Africa and thus represented a particular subgroup of Black women who have increasingly become the focus of attention in more recent years. Statistics provided earlier indicate that Black women represent substantial numbers in South African tertiary institutions at administrative, staff and student levels. Given the age bracket of the international research project, the focus here was on the career narratives of older women who were presently employed and who indeed had managed to progress within the education system from beyond the primary and secondary level of education of most South African Black women (UNESCO 2008). The age bracket of these older women is useful too when one considers South Africa's sociopolitical history. The women participating in this research were born at a time when the system of apartheid was firmly entrenched and indeed would have been of working age when labour legislation severely prohibited their work opportunities. At the time of this research the women would have been working or studying in a post-apartheid South Africa for over a decade-and-a-half. Table 16.1 provides a description of the demographics of the sample.

The home language for 11 of the women was Xhosa, which is the major language in the South African province where the research was conducted (although they were all fluent in English). The remaining woman spoke English as her first language. Given the university workplace setting from which the older women were drawn, their profile for educational qualification level is atypical of the general Black South African population. Participants in the sample were voluntary, with women responding to a general invitation to participate in the research. This chapter reports on prominent themes that emerged from coding the interview transcripts of the 12 South African women. All names of women used in this chapter are pseudonyms.

Learning across the lifespan

The women told stories that involved formal and informal learning. Most of the women had completed several tertiary qualification levels or were in the process of commencing such studies. Nosisi spoke of a typical commitment to formal learning:

> Since school I have been doing short courses some with a correspondence college on labour relations … there was a little bit of a break between 2003 and 2004 because of my work schedule … but I started my labour relations honours in 2009.

There was a consistent theme of informal learning as well, with this even identified as part of the work experience. Thus Lindiwe identified her employer as providing opportunities for learning: 'Sometimes he had invested a lot in me in that area, took me for short courses, conferences … I attended a lot of things that I never thought I would find myself in.'

Transitions

All the South African women could identify transitions and their responses to them, as well as provide evidence through reflection of how they had learned from these transitions. The career narratives of all the South African women illustrated considerable transition over the decades of their career development. These transitions were unexpected as well as planned and there was evidence of the women's adaptability in responding to systemic factors that impacted on them. Most women were

Table 16.1 South African sample

Pseudonym	Age	Marital status	Employment status	Income	Dependents	Highest qualification	Current employment
Andisiwe	52	Married	Full-time	R 280–300,000	1	PhD	Academic management
Babalwa	45	Married	Full-time	R 120–150,000	5	Degree (honours)	Faculty administration
Celiwe	62	Single	Full-time	R 130–140,000	5	PhD	Academic lecturer
Domboza	45	Single	Full-time	R 204–300,000	1	Degree (honours)	Academic support/admin
Esona	45	Married	Full-time	R 180–200,000	8	Degree (masters)	Student counsellor
Faniswa	45	Single (long-term)	Full-time	R 196–245,000	3	Degree (masters)	Academic lecturer
Khanyiswa	60	Married	Full-time	R 180–200,000	2	PhD	Academic lecturer
Lindiwe	46	Married	Full-time	R 130–150,000	5	Degree (honours)	Faculty officer
Ndileka	45	Married	Student (full-time)	Nil	1	Grade 12 degree (current study)	Student
Nombulelo	45	Married	Student (full-time)	Nil	5	Grade 12 degree (current study)	Student
Nosisi	45	Single/widow	Full-time	R 180–190,000	3	Degree (technical)	Academic administration
Sanele	45	Single	Full-time	R 100–148,000	5	Degree (public admin)	Academic support/admin

able to reflect on their responses to transitions. Two examples demonstrate transitions the women faced and their ability to reflect on this.

Domboza was concerned about her transition from one working environment to another. She realised that the physical relocation to another form of employment did not in itself represent a new beginning and that negative experiences in one work setting should not be regarded as the expected norm: 'For any new environment ... you may have your baggage from elsewhere ... because you have had bad experiences in your past ... that shouldn't be your life's script.'

Andisiwe, on the other hand, could see a pattern to her career transitions, which seemed to take place at regular decade intervals. Andisiwe's response demonstrates her ability to informally learn and understand her career transitions in relation to her lifespan development. There is also the suggestion here of Andisiwe understanding intrapersonal influences such as over-commitment of self to work and, over the longer term, the lack of work role satisfaction:

> As we are talking I am realising that maybe the nine year cycles are self-protection cycles as well because I do tend to get into a job, give it my all and then I think that sometimes I have to rebalance myself.

Intrapersonal influences

An understanding of self in relation to career as well as reflection on role satisfaction in an individual's past and present work and life transitions formed a major theme in the career transitions (or the lack of them) for several Black South African women. For instance, some women were able to identify aspects of themselves that impacted on work transitions, calling for them to adapt and respond to unexpected chance events. There was a theme of resilience and self-responsibility in some of the women's perceptions of their responses to transitions. Domboza, for example, believed that coping with career and learning transitions called for inner strength and an inner locus of control: 'I am my own driver in life.'

While all women in the South African sample had experienced career and learning transitions, for some this had stabilised as a result of role satisfaction either in their past or in their present work role. An example of such role satisfaction was Celiwe, who had spent a major part of her career in one profession. Her transition to a second career in academia represented an extension of her first career into the lecturing field. Here she had thrived and she felt confident about her level of role satisfaction in her present career, viewing future transitions as taking place within her chosen work environment:

> I don't even think about leaving academia because I think that is where I belong. I think that is what I have been looking for in my life ... I need to actually expand my horizons within the frame of this institution.

Work influences

A major theme to emerge from the stories of the South African women was the negative work dynamic that they experienced throughout much of their working lives. Most women were able to provide examples of both discrimination and harassment in the work place. This theme is hardly surprising given the contextual introduction to this chapter. Several authors have pointed, for instance, to the male-dominated work environment that most South African women work in. This was reflected in the career narratives of the South African women. Esona faced opposition within her career in education, particularly when she was promoted into middle management positions. This affected her self-confidence, an example of how the themes of work influences and intrapersonal influences can recursively interrelate. Esona demonstrated her ability to learn from the discrimination she experienced in her work environment by reflecting on her own personality traits and values (i.e. intrapersonal influences): 'Maybe I can start with myself, gaining some confidence and how I deal with situations as an African woman. Sometimes you feel that you have to listen and succumb to other men like whether they impose things or what.'

There are other more subtle forms of discrimination that fail to acknowledge the cultural and indeed language background of women employees. The medium of English is a dominant language in the South African work setting, leading those in management to presume that its idiosyncrasies have been mastered by second language speakers. Celiwe was able to reflect with self-deprecating humour her struggles as a second language speaker in a tertiary institution. Although fluent in the English language, she struggled to comprehend the instruction given in her first week of employment that, 'You need to empty your pigeon-hole everyday.'

She couldn't understand how pigeons would be part of her job description. It is a simple example but Celiwe felt depowered by the instruction and she was reluctant to ask for an explanation at such an early stage of her employment.

Financial influences

None of the sample of older Black South African women had experienced a privileged, middle-class start to life. Financial struggle was part of their own upbringing and remained, albeit to a lesser degree, part of their lives as parents, partners, and community members. Listening to the women's financial struggles, it became evident that financial considerations had a relational influence on the transitions in work and learning that they experienced. Some women related the financial burdens that they faced as part of their career development to intrapersonal influences that empowered them to cope. Thus Celiwe stated that there was a need to be strong as an individual, to show personality traits of resilience and courage in the face of financial pressure:

> You know, to be honest, when you are a sole breadwinner at home with so many people that are looking upon you for assistance, especially financially, you

sometimes keep up that face so that they do not see that you are also struggling, because if you are struggling financially and they can see it, it is going to affect them.

Some career transitions relate directly to financial need. Babalwa describes how the need to earn in order to maintain a better lifestyle may prescribe the career choices available:

> I was hoping that my life would be much better. I wanted big things. I was hoping that I would get this big job. The job was not very big when I started here but I had to take the job because my husband was moved and then with the children I wanted better schools for them.

Babalwa's narrative also demonstrates the recursive interrelationship of several influences on a woman's career transitions. The transition was unexpected (transitions and responses), the employment was less than ideal (work influences), there was resultant role dissatisfaction (intrapersonal influences), there were social influences in terms of whose career was more important, and there was also the move necessitated by her husband's transfer (relocation).

Social influences

The predominant theme to emerge from the South African women's career narratives was that of the social influences that had impacted on their career and learning transitions over their lifespan. All 12 women could provide examples of such influence and most of these focused on their support systems, the role models in their lives, and their life roles in general. The influence of individuals in their support networks, as well as those living in their wider community, impacted on their career development in a variety of ways. Older people such as parents have traditionally been powerful role models in younger Black women's lives and several of the women, in reflecting on their earlier frustrated career ambitions, could relate this to such influence. Thus Babalwa knew that she wanted to be an interior decorator, but she faced the dominant opinions of her mother and the broader community who were opposed to this career on the grounds of practicality and probably a lack of knowledge and exposure to the career:

> When I was younger I thought I would have been an interior designer but unfortunately my mum, since she is from the rural areas, she wouldn't allow me to do such stuff ... I wanted to do something like that but I know people used to say that in our culture it doesn't pay well.

Cultural perceptions are entrenched within the societies within which one lives. Black South African women live and work in an environment which remains largely patriarchal. This male dominance can be reflected in societal definitions of roles and their appropriateness for women, for instance. Resisting prescriptive role definitions can come at a personal cost and the following example demonstrates this, as well as how intrapersonal influences and self-belief systems can empower a woman to resist such gender stereotyping. Faniswa wanted to establish herself in a career and she met resistance from significant others around her as to the appropriateness of such a role definition:

> Because where I come from being a mother, a parent, is the most important thing … for me that was not going to be the case … it was not about being selfish, it was also about looking after myself and doing what felt good for me at the time.

Social influences can also be evident in relationships where gender stereotypical perceptions of a partner, for instance, can impede a woman's career development. Esona provides a typical example of several women's narratives, in which she struggled to establish herself in a career because of the gender stereotypical upbringing of her husband and his difficulty in seeing her in this life role:

> It is the sense that African men are supposed to remain as head of the household and that can affect relationships and also their status within the family … That is why I spent thirteen years (before making a career transition) because I was contemplating doing things and I was checking how it was going to affect our relationship, the status there.

Not all social influences are negative in terms of women's career transitions. Social support systems can be vital for successfully transitioning between life roles such as home and work. Support systems were identified by most women within their immediate or extended family. Domboza, for instance, returned to tertiary education as a single mother. She credits her parental support system as making it possible for her to make this transition:

> My parents were so helpful. Remember my daughter was very young at that time … I would pick up her bag and take her to my mum's crèche and she would look after her. My father would help with the transport.

Andisiwe credited her husband as a source of support and she reflected on the importance he had in empowering her intrapersonally to adapt and cope with the demands of a career and those of a mother:

> I always say that my husband is my truest reflector in that he will give me credit where credit is due and he will give me all the support in career goals of whatever I pursue … he is your best friend but is also the person that kicks you the hardest when you need to be kicked and for me that is important.

Some women saw social influences as a substitute for the lack of career services available to them at the time they were making decisions about career transitions. Thus Esona pointed out that, even where career services were available, cultural tradition could lead women to seek advice 'closer to home': 'People would like to get support and share their problems with people they know, with people closer to their families ... there are support structures that were in place but people would go to their extended family.'

Relocation

Relocation as an influence on career development was identified by most women, although some experienced this as a more positive experience than others. Andisiwe perceived relocation as enhancing her career: 'Then we relocated here to ... really for my husband's work and not for mine. That has been the irony that my career has taken off here in ... more than his'. Similarly, Babalwa experienced relocation as positively enhancing her career and lifestyle: 'At least my dreams came true when I had to move to ... and it's friendly, it became a nice city.'

Advice to others

All women were able to offer advice for others, most of which seemed to focus on the need to plan and goal set. Nosisi stated that, 'Firstly, to sit and analyse what you are aiming for, what you to want to achieve at the end of the day.' Much of the advice offered was inspirational and motivational in tone and called for women to internalise the locus of control for their own career development. Babalwa urged women to trust and follow their ideals: 'I would advise them to go for it. I think what is more important in life is to listen to your inner voice.' This was echoed by Faniswa, who felt that women should take the initiative for the career exploration process, 'For me it is about knowing what you want and the strategy is around, look around yourself.' Similarly, Domboza advised women to 'go back and do some introspection and come back and learn from experiences'.

Future planning

Finally, most women were able to reflect on the need for future planning. Several of the women were developing perspectives about impending retirement and the choices this would present. Andisiwe wondered about future opportunities that could arise if work commitments could be lessened, 'For in the future like thinking about retirement I would really want to not have to work till sixty-five if my pension allows for that and really think about reducing.'

Few women saw a future without some form of work. Their stories seemed to emphasise the need to change direction and possibly to limit formalised work. Babalwa's perspective of a future in which there is sufficient time to balance lifestyle with a more flexible working environment is typical of most women in the present sample:

> When I heard about this retirement thingy (sic) I thought, ja, this isn't the right thing to do because you can easily grow old and just stay at home so if

> I can be able to work flexible hours and have more time to myself when my children are older because I spent most of my time looking after them. I would love that.

Reflections

The Ovambo people of Namibia have a saying that a woman is a basket, i.e. that a woman never walks around without carrying a basket. This proverb highlights the fact that women are resilient, resourceful and adaptable to the changing (and sometimes unchanging) environments that they live and work in. The proverb also implies that women constantly have to engage with their environment as they load and unload a variety of ongoing influences that affect their lives.

Gender inequality in the South African workplace, for instance, is one such influence that will require consistent monitoring over the ensuing decades. Twelve years after employment equity and affirmative action measures were implemented, Ndungu (2010: 1) concluded that gender equity remained more a policy than a reality in many work environments, and that 'race, class and gender have intersected powerfully to deny many women a foothold in the labour market'. South Africa faces critical social, health, economic, and educational issues that will need to be prioritised if the country is to move forward and realise its developmental potential. There have been great expectations from the majority, disadvantaged population since democratisation for a better life and some commentators believe that gender equality may be relegated to secondary importance as other urgent social and economic needs become increasingly prioritised. Thus, Shackleton (in MacGregor 2007: 1) states:

> South Africa has favourable legislation and policies, supportive of gender initiatives, and we are all saying the right things. But somehow this has not made a sizeable difference. I believe there are deep cultural issues at play that make it difficult to achieve greater gender equity.

The patriarchal nature of work in South Africa requires redress at a macrosystemic and microsystemic level. Most women in the present sample had struggled with discrimination and harassment that was based on their gender. Grundling and Bosch (2011) point out in this regard that we need to move beyond gender as a woman's issue to the viewpoint that it is a social issue and, as such, it needs to be addressed by both genders. The latter point would bring us to the microlevel where there is a need to educate males in general and male managers in particular about gender diversity in the workplace.

Finally, a consistent theme underlying these stories of career transitions is that they provide evidence of the remarkable resilience and adaptability of these older women whose careers have progressed steadily and against considerable odds through times of major sociopolitical and economic change in South Africa.

References

De Braine, R. (2011) 'The South African woman's work identity', in A. Bosch (ed.) *The South African Board for People Practices (SABPP) Women's Report*, Parktown, South Africa: SABPP, pp. 51–7.

Geldenhuys, M. (2011) 'Demographics of women in the workplace', in A. Bosch (ed.) *The South African Board for People Practices (SABPP) Women's Report*, Parktown, South Africa: SABPP, pp. 13–22.

Grundling, J. and Bosch, A. (2011) 'Reflections on the women's report', in A. Bosch (ed.) *The South African Board for People Practices (SABPP) Women's Report*, Parktown, South Africa: SABPP, pp. 77–86.

Johnson, M. (2006) 'Rise of the Black diamonds', *Campaign (UK)*, 35: 24–5.

MacGregor, K. (2007) 'South Africa: A staffing pyramid with men at the top', *University World News*, p. 6. Available at: www.universityworldnews.com/article.php?story=20071115141448408 (accessed 10 June 2013).

MacGregor, K. (2008) 'South Africa: Challenges of equity, ageing, expansion', *University World News*, p. 57. Available at: www.universityworldnews.com/article.php?story=20081214092139847 (accessed 10 June 2013).

McMahon, M., Bimrose, J. and Watson, M. (2010) 'Older women's career development and social inclusion', *Australian Journal of Career Development*, 19(1): 63–70.

Ndungu, K. (2010) 'South Africa: Women shut out of the labour market', *Pambazuka*, 480, pp. 1–2. Available www.pambazuka.org/en/category/wgender/64256 (accessed 10 June 2013).

South African history online (2013) 'Women's struggle, 1900-1994'. Available at: www.sahistory.org.za/womens-struggle-1900-1994/work-and-education (accessed 10 June 2013).

Statistics South Africa (2012) *Quarterly Labour Force Survey: Quarter 4, 2012*, Pretoria, South Africa: Statistics South Africa.

Statistics South Africa (2013) *Men, Women And Children: Findings of the Living Conditions Survey 2008/2009*, Pretoria, South Africa: Statistics South Africa.

UNESCO (2008) 'South African national report on the development and state of the art of adult learning and education' Available at: www.unesco.org/fileadmin/MULTIMEDIA/INSTITUTES/UILconfintea/pdf/National_Reports/Africa/Africa/South_Africa.pdf (accessed 10 June 2013).

17 Life stories

A synthesis of the voices of women

Maria Eduarda Duarte

When the editors wrote to me presenting the book's layout, they wrote:

> The concept for the book originated from international research that we've been undertaking since 2009, across nine countries into the career trajectories of older women, focusing on their learning and employment pathways and the careers support to which they have access. Findings have emphasised the need for a more nuanced understanding of women's labour market experiences to be gathered from the voices of older women about their experiences across their working lives. In turn, hearing their voices could stimulate the development of theory, policy, research and practice that is more responsive to their needs.
>
> (Editorial proposal 2012)

Afterwards, the lead editor assigned me the following task: "Your chapter would comprise a synthesis of the nine chapters in Part II."

It appears to me that such a synthesis could essentially revolve around two main axes: the first, stemming from the reading of the first parts of all of the chapters, in which the authors look to present statistical data while at the same time contextualising political, cultural and social realities in an effort to give "human" meaning to quantitative statements. The second axis, which is perhaps the most impressive, is that which stems from real testimonies that have both life and feeling. They are stories of women who draw attention to the need to consider not only statistics, official reports and quantitative data, but to reflect on the radically human sense of life, which also includes working life. Although it is sometimes not written in stone, those same women also draw attention to the stories of other women; women who do not have a voice, perhaps because of political, economic, ethnic or religious reasons.

Statistics and contexts

Tomassini (Chapter 14) rubs salt into the wound by reinforcing the necessity for a human analysis of statistics: "Some features of female employment are hidden in national and international statistics, in particular those relating to irregular employment."

From Australia, as well as from England and Germany, comes the reality of the feminisation of the workforce; however there still remains a profound imbalance compared with salaries received by men, type of work and conditions for career progression: for example, the gender pay gap and the identifiable disadvantage for women in Australia, women in professional employment comprise 51.2 per cent of the total workforce, the gender pay gap for weekly earnings are 21.1 per cent for full-time workers and 12 per cent for part-time workers (Mary McMahon, Chapter 9 this volume); and in England, the measured gender pay gap increased in 2011 from 8.3 per cent to 9.6 per cent (Jenny Bimrose, Chapter 12 this volume); in both cases in favour of males! In Australia, only a third of all Members of Parliament are female and there is a notable underrepresentation of women in the most senior corporate positions, as well as in the Australian public service (Mary McMahon, Chapter 9 this volume); From the Centre for Women and Democracy, Bimrose (Chapter 12 this volume) takes a phrase that is profoundly explanatory with regards to the inequality between the sexes: "And at the current rate of progress, a child born today will be drawing her pension before she has any chance of being equally represented in the Parliament of her country". In Germany:

> more than 80 per cent of the female workforce is in the service sector, which is characterised by lower average wages and a high proportion of non-standard employment as compared to employment in the industry sector (male prevalence). Thus, women are disadvantaged in terms of employment security, wages, occupational status, social benefits, professional development and career progression opportunities.
> (Simone Haasler, Chapter 13 this volume).

From Argentina as well as Portugal comes evidence of the importance of the socio-political history of a people and how it is reflected in the life stories of each individual. For example, the strength of dictatorial regimes particularly affected those women who are today aged between 45 and 65 years old. The "terrorist phase of the Argentinian history" (Pamela Suzanne, Chapter 8 this volume) coincided with the university life of women, impinging on their studies. In Portugal, up until the installation of a democratic regime in 1974, women were impeded from choosing careers such as diplomats or magistrates (Filomena Parada *et al.*, Chapter 15 this volume). In both countries, an increase in the female workforce is identifiable, although certain inequalities still persist. In Argentina, while it is the case that more women finish their university studies than men, there is still a prevalence of male university professors (Pamela Suzanne, Chapter 8 this volume). The same happens in Italy, where "more female graduates (52.0 per cent) work in jobs requiring lower levels of education compared with men (41.7 per cent) (…) despite Italian women's educational attainment being greater than men's" (Massimo Tomassini, Chapter 14 this volume). While Portugal presents one of the highest female activity rates within the European Union, women find it harder to access higher supervisory or administrative positions within the public administration, which remains male dominant (Filomena Parada *et al.*, Chapter 15 this volume). The bottom line is that the same thing happens in Australia, Germany, Canada, Italy and England, which are countries which have not lived under the pressure of a dictatorship in recent times.

On another continent, Africa, the women of South Africa, in particularly black women, are an example of resistance against discrimination. As Watson (Chapter 16 this volume) affirms:

> In an historic march in the mid-1950s by over 20,000 women of all races, a freedom song was sung … "when you strike the women, you strike a rock". Today, women in South Africa, and in particular black women, remain between a rock and a hard place.

As in China (Ying Kuang, Chapter 11 this volume), relative to layoffs, rates are between 70 to 80 per cent to the detriment of women in some provinces. In South Africa, discrimination does not only affect women, but is also reflective of their skin colour, as explained in the example given by Watson (Chapter 16 this volume) in which the most underpaid jobs in South Africa are held by black women in private households, while white earners earn four times as much. Another example of discrimination that is one of the more explicative for a book such as this is that referred to by Kuang (Chapter 11 this volume), which affirms that the existence of the gender gap in Chinese society cannot be underestimated, affirming that "neither women's labour nor their reproductive capacity has been valued, remaining largely ignored both by society and by history".

Arthur (Chapter 10 this volume) develops her chapter around migrant women as part of the context of emigration. One of the issues which should be highlighted relates to an immigration policy that incorporates categories through which individuals may apply for immigration. The economic category includes policy directives to assess the viability of immigrants to be successful in the labour market and includes highly educated and/or skilled labour. Despite this policy, the employment market is still more punitive to women than to men: "In general, immigrant women have lower employment rates than immigrant men, when comparing length of time living in Canada" (Nancy Arthur, Chapter 10 this volume). What these immigrant women bring is a sense of hope, of a will to overcome barriers and a commitment to integrate into the employment market.

From Germany comes more relevant evidence of structural inequalities evident in the relationship between the education system (a dual system separated into vocational education and training) and a distinctive labour market segmentation by gender. As Haasler (Chapter 13 this volume) points out: "Today, a high proportion of female workers are in a non-standard and, to a large extent, also in precarious employment which implies that they are disadvantaged in terms of their entitlement to social security and retirement benefits".

In the first part of their chapters, all of the authors of Part II of the book look to situate and make the reader aware of a number of aspects that may be summarised in the following way: the problems that affect the careers of women and which are different from men can be conceptualised in terms of barriers and enablers, both of which are to be considered on different levels: those that arise from the conditions of contexts – the situational variables – and those which are intrinsic to human development itself and which are conditioned by socialisation – the personal variables. However, and this is what permeates throughout all of the chapters, namely when giving voice to women, the distinction between barriers and enablers is not rigid, in the sense that barriers can become enablers from the moment that the element which acts as a barrier is altered.

As Arthur (Chapter 10 this volume) affirms: "The importance of cultural identities for career development rests not only with the salient aspects identified by women but also with the social perceptions and actions shown towards women across their life contexts." In short, what is being addressed are people: each person needs affinities that are culturally embedded and determined by context. What this means is that culture, manifested through affinities, gestures, behaviour or rituals stemming from tradition, inherited from previous generations and transmitted to the following generation, is one of the determining factors in the identity of each individual (Duarte 2003) (see Nancy Arthur, Chapter 10 this volume). That is why it is often the case that a collective, whenever it moves to settle in another territory and in a different cultural context, takes with it all, or at least those elements which are identified in that moment as being the most significant to the group's identity. The Greeks did this when creating the Hellenic world; the Romans did it when defining Romania – with all of the cultural baggage of discrimination between men and women.

The voices of women

Older women give us real examples, in that they act as testimonies of that same discrimination. A total of 109 older women made themselves heard and, while we do not know if they were representing 2,000 or 1,000,000 women, that is not important here. What is important, what is really very important, is that their voice was given to those who symbolise effort, tenacity and a will to win and to occupy a place as a worker in society without taking anybody else's place – not in the least those of men.

In that respect, the second axis of this synthesis revolves around what McMahon (Chapter 9 this volume) wrote by way of summary at the end of her chapter:

> Unlike the quantifiable data, the stories provide a more nuanced understanding of women's lived experience in the labour market. The stories revealed the individual nature of women's careers and the recursive relationship between their objective experiences and their subjective experiences. Moreover, the stories reveal the intersectionality of a range of influences (e.g. age and gender) which recursively weave through the women's lives.

From Argentina, Australia, Canada, China, England, Germany, Italy, Portugal, and South Africa come the echoes of the contours of career identity (Duarte, 2003) as the traces of cultural history, seen as part of the heritage of inheritance and as a project for the future: a career, for the majority of the women who were interviewed, no longer means adequateness for a particular role, such as the "Cinderella Syndrome – to be submissive, dependent, invisible and passive" (Hansen 1984: 225). Nor is it reflective of dominant ideologies that try to package the plural dimensions and contexts that build up the story of a people, of a group of people and of the individual into one single discourse.

We can hear the history of Leticia (Pamela Suzanne, Chapter 8 this volume) who, during the time of the military dictatorship in Argentina, was able to overcome all of the barriers and risks associated with attending university classes or classes at the home of a professor banned from university by the dictatorial regime. This is the meaning of learning across the lifespan. From Canada (Nancy Arthur, Chapter 10 this volume) come tales of tenacity to learn, learn, learn; to comprehend a new cultural context to gain entry into work. Such is the story of Vivian, who brings us tenacity and a will to win: "…I feel like overwhelmed and almost like stressed out or depression…But fortunately I overcome – and still survive and I hope – I'm doing better than before" (Nancy Arthur, Chapter 10 this volume). The transitions and responses in search of a future that, without knowing what it will be, is full of answers and of a willingness to deal with change.

Two examples of successful women? Or two examples of a lot of effort and hard work? Should we place this question into the field of psychological analysis (Betz and Fitzgerald 1987) or the study of gender differences (Cook 1993), or indeed into models or theories that study women in their work contexts (Fassinger 2005), we find the main concern of the women interviewed is of being citizens, working women or mothers; the majority of them, or almost all, look to interlink working life with the needs of supporting the family. For example, Rong, in China (Ying Kuang, Chapter 11 this volume), changes from her job of planting vegetables to carrying wood in order to earn more money to help a family of eight people. This is a typical example that happens in the lives of many women: transitions and responses are understood more as a moral value, an ethical imperative or the search for personal satisfaction. Or the voice of Amanda, born in Germany, but who lived for a long time in Italy, who tells us of her reasons for not wanting to go back to the country from where she originated:

> I love Italy and its lifestyle. This is why I didn't leave this country after the divorce from my husband ten years ago. It wouldn't have been so difficult for me to get back to Germany and to find a way for living there but I preferred to stay here. First of all, of course, in order to maintain a strict relationship with my son – who lives with his father but needs very much my support – but also because I feel engaged in living and working here, despite the indisputable difficulties I still have with this country.

Amanda assumes, therefore, control of her own life and integrates it with reconciliation in her life perspectives.

But we have to speak the truth, even when knowing that truth is always provisional and that certainty is always probabilistic: in the second decade of the twenty-first century, male dominance continues to exist. We can read the affirmation made by Haasler

(Chapter 13 this volume): "Despite young girls and women having outperformed men in terms of their qualifications over the last decade ... they remain discriminated against in the level of pay, work force participation rates and career development opportunities." What life stories bring us is not only about differences between genders, but about the asymmetry between the two genders. Those stories reinforce the significance of the concept of gender (Bimrose 2006), which since the 1950s has been utilised to distinguish the social from the biological: if sex distinguishes between the different biology of male and female, gender designates the classification of masculine and feminine (Héritier 1996). However this classification is hierarchical, in that gender contains the three elements of the social system of sex (Delphy 1991). First, the different social and arbitrary contexts in which the sexes are located. The story brought to us by Diana is indicative of such work influences: "In our country (Portugal), if there is a woman and a man to fire, you fire the woman and the man stays. And that's what happened... the men stayed and I had to leave" (Filomena Parada et al. Chapter 15 this volume). The second element of the social system of sex refers to gender and the genders as part of the principle of partition. Tomassini (Chapter 14 this volume) noted that work environments can act as a source of painful surprises; and gives voice to Maria, from Italy, who tells us a part of her life story with work influences acting as a relentless source of bullying:

> I always had to just silently obey and to stand to be treated like a zero ... Sometimes I was unable to get up in the morning because I started to suffer from several painful symptoms, from simple headaches to real difficulties in keeping together my thoughts.
>
> (ibid.)

The third element of the social system of sex is the actual hierarchical notion that considers the relationships between the two parts, in particular when addressing work influences. An example is narrated in the story of Sue from England, who shows us the hierarchy in favour of the male sex:

> I felt then very much a victim, like a piece of flotsam and jetsam ... I applied for the role and I didn't get it. The person brought in was an ex-(occupation) male, another male, who had no clue! It was a horrible time of my life ... I felt so wretched about the whole situation and it just seemed so, dare I say, unfair.

And what better example than the testimony given by Giovanna (Massimo Tomassini, Chapter 14 this volume) to illustrate the difference between the genders?

> I married him just right after my degree. He was a man much older than me. A university teacher, a pure and exalted designer. With a strong influence on the ways I behaved in the world of architecture. For instance, I was interested in keeping a place in the academy and trying to find a position in it, but he didn't help me at all, assuming that this wouldn't have been ethical. And in private business it was more or less the same. So, considering that we attend the same

environments and that from time to time I introduced myself as his assistant, I couldn't find any space for myself.

In short, the world in which we live is not a world of ideas or of logical arguments. If the notion of gender is formed in the realm of ideas, the work of François Poulain de La Barre (1984), published in 1673 under the title of *De l'egalité des deux sexes*, would certainly be in the *top ten* best-selling books. The author bases his argument on the idea of the Cartesian notion of the body/mind and argues that women are only different to men in the body and not in the mind (Watson, Chapter 16 this volume). Nothing, other than cultural inheritance, precludes that women should be educated as men are and that they should be by nature equal to men. The voice of Esona, from South Africa, reinforces this perspective, particularly in the realm of social influences that impede the natural development of careers:

> It is the sense that African men are supposed to remain as head of the household that can affect relationships and also their status within the family…That is why I spent thirteen years (before making a career transition) because I was contemplating doing things and I was checking how it was going to affect our relationship, the status here.

All of the chapters emphasise the uniformity that is only apparent in the world of work and look to interpret the multiplicity of the situations and transformations in the world of work that have taken place over the last decades. However, in the success stories of such women, the reference is not what happens to other women, meaning that such stories are not told, but built – comprising what happens to those women and what makes them successful. The specific situation of a woman's success is, normally, told from a masculine reference point (Fitzgerald and Harmon 2001), acting as a sub-group of the general masculine model, which only sometimes, upon reflection, comes out in favour of women! The voice of Andisiwe, coming from South Africa, reinforces this perspective: "Then, we relocated here… really for my husband's work and not for mine. That has been the irony that my career has taken off here…more than his" (Study participant Chapter 16 this volume).

The set of new social movements which began in the 1980s, designated as ecological, anti-nuclear and other movements, together with post-modernist thought (Savickas 1993), have brought the contours of identity into the public eye. The ideas that advocate the end of absolute truths, in a way that aims to open new pathways to the plurality of thought through a negation of logical positivism and the assumption of epistemological eclecticism – for example, interpretivism (Duarte 2012) allow us to start contextualising identity. Expressed differently, this means to establish the contours of individual identity.

The collection of ideas brought by the voices of these women permeates the idea that career identity is ceasing to be prescriptive and is instead transforming into an exemplary concept and a construction. It adds the dimension of modernity that expresses processes of social, political, economic and cultural change, as well as a search for a process that implements values of liberty that are fundamental and informed, therefore assuming the contours of identity of a career. An example is provided by Silke (Germany) in telling us the story of working in a bank:

> Back in the 1980s, young women new in banking were encouraged to decide if they wanted to become assistants, yeah, this just means secretaries to some manager, or if they wanted to go into bookkeeping. I was not happy about it, because I had already figured out during my training that I wanted to go into lending. At that time, it was a man's world and if you did then it was as secretarial help.

It is important to highlight that these aspects also relate to the bigger questions connected to the contexts: learning about and interpreting realities and considering what "fabrics" (rather, contexts) are made of is what humanity demands, it is what reason dictates, and it is what politics should not shy away from (Duarte, in press). The voices of the women transform the ideas into realities: the construction or the designing of a working life is always compromised by the context.

As much as it may sound controversial, in truth, identity has a sex. Being a male or a female is to possess a number of characteristics that are common to other men and women. However, it could be argued to avoid over-generalising: a woman, Caucasian, of European origin, middle-aged and of a professional intellect, has, without doubt, more things in common with a man of her generation, rank and culture than of a woman who lives in an Amazonian tribe, no matter how inconvenient that may seem. Realistically, what some of these stories show us is that working life is an achievement and, more solidly, that the framework for career construction is not the same for both sexes. It is because of this that men and women are different, or better: that they end up *becoming* different.

Careers for women and the construction of their identity can be seen as a social construction process and, like any kind of construction, different materials are needed: people are needed, then those people need recognition and after that they need other people through which they can identify the construction of human groupings. The comments provided by Laura, from Argentina, about her plans for the future reveal that same idea: "If I can turn into an Academic Consultant or a Consultant with academic credentials, it'll be a very interesting source of work and of development for the next 20–30 years" (Study participant Chapter 8 this volume). The fight for recognition is also present in the story from China told by Rong:

> In 2001, I had an idea. Opening my own restaurant … I am proud that I have supported my two daughters through university, through self-employment. If I had chosen to work in a factory, my daughters would not have had enough money to complete their studies.

The truth is that identity begins in the cradle and that sex is a fundamental element in our own identity. Investigations developed in the Western world – Europe and the United States – provide evidence about the differences in the behaviour of adults determined by the sex of a child: when presented with a film sequence of a baby, with it being previously affirmed that it is a boy or a girl, the adults interpret the baby's behaviour in a different way: if it is a girl the behaviour is described as fear (Cole and Cole 1993); if it is a boy the behaviour is described as anger/rage and, "c'est la vie!". The older women were comfortable with this kind of stereotype; transposing these findings for intrapersonal influences, the voice of Louise, from England, shows the burden of that stereotype that comes right from the cradle:

> I think probably all women of my age were just carried along with what you were supposed to do … I've always been interested in food, and I wanted to do something with cooking … I think that I should have followed that path [college] from the very beginning, but where I came from, you didn't do that.

We continue to speak about the career, or better, career identity, and the need for recognition. People need objects, self-concepts and meaning that they see as belonging to themselves, which includes the family, customs and physical and psychological characteristics (we have the *gens* of the Romans, the clans or tribes, and the clubs). Moreover, a career is also related to customs, habits and satisfaction with a set of needs. More specifically, the masculine and feminine categories of recognition do not describe men and women as if they were two natural groups, but rather define the characteristics of each in the function of the position that they occupy within the social and sexual division of work (see the example of Germany) and in function of their socio-historical context (Blustein 2006). As far as we are aware, such division in work has always existed, but the conceptions of the place of women in the employment market has varied in time and space. However, such a division continues to be led by the guiding phrase of "for men, production, for women, reproduction", in doing so burdening women with the purest of all discrimination, giving men the power over the concept of creation and silencing women, as if reducing division exclusively to a thought process, thereby promoting the discrediting of women as creators of life and at the same time as creators of art. Does the threat of sharing power with women, potentially as powerful as men, justify such discrimination? The voices of women suggest not. The voice of Andisiwe speaks well here, in talking about sharing and not "taking power" (Watson, Chapter 16 this volume):

> I always say that my husband is my truest reflector in that he will give me credit where it is due and he will give me all the support in the career goals of whatever I pursue … he is your best friend but is also the person that kicks you the hardest when you need to be kicked and for me that is important.

In summary, social factors, stereotypes and negative attitudes towards female competition in the workplace easily create barriers to the development of careers similar to those of men. This is evident in the voices of the 109 women interviewed. A voice has been given to those women, but what about those whose voices were never allowed to be heard? Who knows of the composer Fanny

Hensel (1805–74), the sister of Felix Mendelssohn? The painter Constance-Marie Charpentier (1828–1915) to whom the painter David owes so much? Or even the composer Cécile Chaminade (1857–1944), who composed more than 400 works that were only opened up to the wider audience in 1988? (Beltrando-Patier, 2002). Maybe we have heard of Clara Shumann, who in 1839 wrote: "I once believed that I possessed creative talent, but I have given up this idea." (Litzmann, 1913: 202). Or who knows of Alma Mahler (1879–1967), banned from composing by her husband Gustav Mahler? (Boffi, 1999). Or why did the writer Amantine-Lucile-Aurore Dupin (1804–76) adopt the masculine name of George Sand? What a punishing nineteenth and start of a twentieth century for women! But women, in one way or another, are successful in the end, even if that success simply be through the study of their work following their deaths by people from a specific area, or by those studying the paths traced by those women.

Anybody who likes music thinks about *Carmen*, *Aïda*, *Norma*, *Butterfly*, *Isolda*, and many other works – all of which are about humiliated, persecuted, buried, suicidal women who are, in the end, all victims. However, at the same time, they are women who embody the spirit of resistance against marginalisation and who imposed themselves through their difference.

In the end, where are those 109 women who filled the chapters of this book? In work, hard at work doing jobs that are the human effort to tackle reality, because work is a risky experiment that does not leave anybody indifferent. Success implies commitment and delivery and all of the women who were interviewed were, to some extent, in their uniqueness as women committed to society and the family, embracing the idea of shared citizenship.

Through a psychological analysis of work (Blustein 2006) it is possible to find descriptions of work that include, for example, experiences of an emotional nature (Bimrose 2008) that, through identity, belong to the female sex. Here we find the voice of Helena, from Portugal, when she refers to her affection for her mother in times of hard work:

> Up to 4 years ago, she (mother) would do me everything ... I'd arrive home and it was impeccable, I just had to sit down and eat dinner ... It was at a time that we had a lot of work, a lot of work ...now I'm more than obliged to give her back all of that and I give her all the affection I can.

Or, from the same analysis, we can find narrative paradigms for the universal commonality of success (Savickas 2008). To this end, we can speak about success in another way, such as the way that is provided as *advice to others* through the voice of Kay, from Australia:

> Identify your network ... you've got to do a lot of it on your own. Have confidence to do it on your own, knowing that you're not always going to be supported. Don't close your eyes to the full range of opportunities. Don't be too narrow in what you think you might want to do...There could be all

sorts of interesting things that you could do. I think building on the skills you have is good.

To speak about success is to speak about peace, development and absence of discrimination. It is, in that light, to also talk about anonymous success that may never become known, as reflected in the words of the seventh Secretary-General of the United Nations and Nobel Peace Prize Laureate, Kofi Annan, speaking at the holding of the International Women's Health Coalition Third Annual Gala in 2004, and which still have the same now, as then, political economic, social impacts that clearly confirm why books such as this must continue to exist:

> Study after study have taught us that there is no tool for development more effective than the education of girls and the empowerment of women. No other policy is as likely to raise economic productivity, lower infant and maternal mortality, or improve nutrition and promote health, including the prevention of HIV/AIDS. When women are fully involved, the benefits can be seen immediately: families are healthier; they are better fed; their income, savings, and reinvestment go up. And what is true of families is true of communities and, eventually, whole countries.
>
> (Annan 2004)

The English poet John Donne (1572–1631), referring to an older woman, wrote: "No Spring nor summer beauty hath such grace / As I have seen in one autumnal face" (Donne 1977); I am not disputing the literal quality of the poem, but rather observing the psychological meaning of the words. The autumnal face, meaning older, is a reflection of life that includes working life. Listening to the voices of women aged between 45 and 65 years of age, ages during which the past is re-evaluated and during which the future still stretches out ahead, is a challenge that helps to better understand the meaning of learning across the lifespan, of transitions and responses, of intrapersonal influences, of work influences, of financial influences, of social influences, of relocation, of advice to others and of future planning; codes which have emerged from the thematic analysis undertaken (see Chapter 7 this volume) and which permit for the contextualisation, on the one hand, of life stories and of changes in inter/intrapersonal relationships shared in their significance and motivation (and which invariably escape any quantitative approach) and, on the other hand, allow for the identification of regularities characterised by a great plasticity of psychological, social and political conditions. For example, in the realm of intrapersonal influence, many references relate to children, but also to parents and their aging. However, in some voices we can hear the echo of the search for the meaning of life and of the development of interiority (Jung 1933). In the realm of work influences, the reality of the voices of these 109 women is that: some are the reflection of discrimination that has impeded career progress, others prepare or face retirement, be that planned or imposed, and others start new careers or return to study.

The life stories told in the first person help to give shape to evidence: young women continue to this day to be the heirs of the contributions of previous generations that led social change, in a way that is least recognised in females (Peterson and Klohen 1995). Throughout the nine chapters of this part of the book, not only is the importance of social science for the study of career identity affirmed, but also the interlinkage of the multiple aspects that interfere in the construction (Savickas, *et al.* 2009) of the careers of women; better, that interfere in the construction of life projects that also include working life. The experience transmitted through the voices of these women is an internal experience that corresponds to an analysis of the past and a perspective for the future, formed in a present that is still discriminatory but no longer silently so. If the realm in which the authors of the nine chapters work is social scientific, then the analysis here may only be considered as political.

References

Annan, Kofi (2004) "Meeting global challenges: Healthy women, healthy world". Keynote address at the International Women's Health Coalition Third Annual Gala, USA. Available at: www.iwhc.org/index.php (accessed 22 November 2013).

Beltando-Patier, M.-C. (2002) *Histoire de la musique* [The history of music], Paris: Larousse.

Betz, N. E. and Fitzgerald, L. F. (1987) *The Career Psychology of Women*, Orlando, FL: Academic Press.

Bimrose, J. (2006) "Gender", in C. Feltham and I. Horton (eds) *Handbook of Counselling and Psychotherapy*, London: Sage, (2nd ed.), pp. 24–8.

Bimrose, J. (2008) "Guidance for girls and women", in J. Athanasou and R. Van Esbroeck (eds) *International Handbook of Career Guidance*, New York and Heidelberg: Springer Science, pp. 375 and 404.

Blustein, D. (2006) *The Psychology of Working*, Mahwah, NJ: Lawrence Erlbaum.

Boffi, G. (1999) *Tutto Musica – Storia Della Musica Clássica*.[All Music – the History Of the Classical Music], Novara: Instituti Gregoriano De Agostini.

Cole, M. and Cole, S. (1993) *The Development of Children*, New York: Scientific American Books (2nd ed.).

Cook, E. P. (1993) "The gendered context of life: Implications for women's and men's career-life plans", *The Career Development Quarterly*, 41: 227–37.

Delphy, C. (1991) "Penser le genre" ["Thinking the gender"], in M.-C. Hurtig, M. Kail and H. Rouch (eds) *Sexe et genre. De la hiérarchie entre les sexes*, Paris: Ed CNRS, pp. 89–107.

Donne, J. (1977) *John Donne, The Complete English Poems*, UK: Penguin, Classics.

Duarte, M. E. (2003) "Das identidades e contextos no espaço luso-brasileiro: Uma abordagem psicológica" ["About identities and contexts in the Portuguese – Brazilian spaces: A psychological approach"], *Convergência Lusíada*, 20: 132–46.

Duarte, M. E. (2012) "Reflections on the training of career counsellors", *Cypriot Journal of Educational Sciences*, 7(4): 265–75.

Duarte, M. E. (in press) "A vida da orientação na vida do século XXI: Constrangimentos e desafios" ["The life of counselling in twenty-first century life: Constraints and challenges"], *Revista Brasileira de Orientação Profissional*.

Fassinger, R. (2005) "Theoretical issues in the study of women's career development: Building bridges in a brave new world", in W. B. Walsh and M. L. Savickas (eds) *Handbook of Vocational Psychology*, Mahwah, NJ: Lawrence Erlbaum, pp. 85–124.

Fitzgerald, L. E. and Harmon, L. W. (2001) "Women's career development: A postmodern update", in F. T. Leong and A. Barack (eds) *Contemporary Models In Vocational Psychology. A Volume in Honor of Samuel Osipow*, Mahwah, NJ: Lawrence Erlbaum, pp. 207–30.

Hansen, L. S. (1984) "Interrelationship of gender and career", in N. Gysbers and Associates (eds) *Designing Careers*, San Francisco, CA: Jossey-Bass, pp. 216–479.

Héritier, F. (1996) *Masculin / féminin. La pensée de la différence* [*Masculin / Feminin. The Thought of Difference*], Paris: Odile Jacob.

Jung, C. (1933) *Modern Man in Search of a Soul*, NY: Harcourt Press.

Litzmann, B. (1913) *Clara Shumann*, Berlin: G. Grote.

Peterson, B. and Klohnen, E. (1995) "Realization of generativity in two samples of women at midlife", *Psychology and Aging*, 10(1): 20–9.

Poulain de la Barre, F. (1984) *De l'égalité des deux sexes. Discours physique et moral où l'on voit l'importance de se défaire des préjugés* [*About Equity of the Two Sexes. A Physical and Moral Speech or an Important Way to Get Out Prejudices*]. Paris: Fayard (Original work published in 1673).

Savickas, M. (1993) "Career counseling in the postmodern era", *Journal of Cognitive Psychoterapy*, 7: 205–15.

Savickas, M. (2008) "Helping people choose jobs: A history of the guidance profession", in J. Athanasou and R. Van Esbroeck (eds) *International Handbook of Career Guidance*, New York and Heidelberg: Springer Science, pp. 97–114.

Savickas, M., Nota, L., Rossier, J., Dauwalder, J.-P., Duarte, M. E., Guichard, J., Soresi, S., Van Esbroeck, R. and Van Vianen, A. (2009) "Life designing: A paradigm for career construction in the 21st century", *Journal of Vocational Behavior*, 75(3): 239–50.

Part III
Looking to the future

18 Implications for career theory

David L. Blustein

Women's issues have been discussed and debated in career theory and practice for nearly 50 years. Indeed, one can argue that the contemporary revolution in career theory and practice, as reflected by the psychology-of-working framework (Blustein 2006, 2013a) Systems Theory Framework of career development (Patton and McMahon 2014), and other new perspectives (e.g. Richardson 2012), has been inspired to a great extent by the broad and systemic critiques offered by feminism and the social and intellectual movements that it has spawned. This current book, which has been so thoughtfully constructed and edited by Bimrose, McMahon, and Watson, offers a valuable opportunity for the next phase of a needed feminist infusion of critical thought into the discourse on work and career. Indeed, this book, which creatively combines qualitative research with reviews of international research, provides grist for the mill that forces a serious reckoning of the fundamental assumptions of existing and emerging theoretical ideas.

Examining the chapters collectively reveals several pernicious and pervasive barriers that women face, which I argue are becoming the norm for nearly everyone who works and who wants to work. Indeed I propose that the vast majority of working people faced these barriers, even during the mid to late twentieth century when many career theorists based their work on an insular view of white, middle-class men as the normative group. In my view, the focus on the figure of white, middle-class men served as the foundation for most of the existing theories, which contrasted sharply with the ground of women, people of colour, the poor and working classes – the vast majority of people around the globe. I argue in this chapter that women's experiences in developing and adjusting to their work lives ought to be the normative view in contemporary theory development. The challenges that women have faced and continue to face in balancing competing roles, dealing with oppressive social forces, and confronting a labour market with constricting options is the modal experience for most working people around the globe. As reflected in many of the chapters in this book, even privileged and well-educated workers are struggling with their work lives as the recent global fiscal crisis has ravaged job security, wages, and stability (cf. Sharone 2014; Zickar 2013). So, the question that this book poses is how adequate are existing theories in confronting a world where the oppression and marginalisation experienced by most women in the workforce are the norm for the majority of working people around the globe?

The early history of career theory (c. early-to-mid-twentieth century) harkens back to an era when the Industrial Revolution created a burgeoning occupational context that was characterised by a rapidly growing number of jobs and an increased demand for people to make informed decisions about education and training (Blustein 2006). The evolution of the person-environment fit (PE-Fit) perspective, as exemplified in Parsons' (1909) work and Holland's (1997) creative synthesis, provided the foundation for many theoretical initiatives that have sought to explain how people negotiate various work-based tasks across the lifespan. As a counterpoint to the prevailing PE-fit theories, Super's (1957, 1980) intellectual curiosity culminated in a lifespan, life-space view of career choice and development, which still had at its core the fundamental assumptions of PE-fit in which people seek out environments that are good matches for their interests, values, and abilities. The post-World War II theories, for the most part, were based on the proposition that market work (that is, paid employment) was the most salient role for people and offered the opportunity to manifest one's self-concept in a way that could optimally lead to life satisfaction and well-being.

By the 1970s, the feminist revolution began to shape career theory and practice, challenging the core assumptions of the field in research, theory development, and practice. One of the best exemplars of this infusion was Super's (1957) revision of his life-stage theory to a more contextual theory (Super 1980) that used the life-career rainbow as the iconic vision of a life in which people seek to manage their diverse roles and responsibilities, which includes caregiving as well as other familial and citizenship responsibilities. During the last two decades of the twentieth century, feminist psychologists and social scientists have critiqued many of the taken-for-granted assumptions of career theory, yielding the framework for emerging theories that will be reviewed later in the chapter. For example, feminist scholars highlighted the degree to which prevailing theories cast women as inherently non-normative in their often more circuitous pathway to market work (e.g. Betz and Fitzgerald 1987). In addition, feminist theorists and practitioners identified the many external barriers that exist in education, work, family contexts, and the broader social milieu, which functioned to inhibit the full expression of women's capacity in the world of work (Harmon and Farmer 1983; Heppner 2013). Furthermore, the sexist practices of unequal pay for equal work and the pervasiveness of sexual harassment were clearly identified in career development scholarship, public policy, and in the counselling literature as major barriers and sources of social injustice (Betz and Fitzgerald 1987; Richardson 1993).

Women and work: a contemporary review

This expansive volume offers scholars and practitioners an opportunity to once again be shaped by research on women and work and by women's voices about work and life. Several themes that cut across many of the chapters serve as contemporary critiques of existing career choice and development discourse, which, for the most part, still emphasises market work and self-concept implementation. Perhaps the most obvious point that emerges in a collective analysis of the chapters is the important role of context. Contextual factors are illustrated by diverse cultural assumptions about women's roles, the varied nature of market-place work across nations and cultures, and the complicated ways in which women strive to balance market work and caregiving work. Furthermore, the diverse ways that aging is experienced and treated within different cultures is a noteworthy issue when considering a collective analysis of the chapters. In addition, vast differences exist across the labour markets of the countries represented in these chapters. For example, the differences noted by Kuang (Chapter 11 this volume) in China between the planned economy and the more recent market-based economy are striking, underscoring how broader economic and social forces can profoundly shape people's lives. In addition, vast distinctions between the various countries included in the narrative analyses revealed that women's working lives are powerfully shaped by legal initiatives, cultural norms, political movements, and economic conditions.

Another salient theme in the chapters is that equal opportunity is the exception rather than the norm. As Duarte noted in her thoughtful synthesis, 'there still remains a profound imbalance compared with salaries received by men, type of work and conditions for career progression' (Duarte, Chapter 17 this volume). A similar conclusion was reached by Haasler in her observations about the experiences of working women in Germany: 'While role models have changed considerably since the 1970s, the institutional reproduction of gender inequality in the labour market obviously has not, keeping women disadvantaged in the labour market in many aspects' (Haasler, Chapter 13 this volume). The chapters, when considered collectively, tell the story of some modest progress in reducing sexist barriers to work for women in some locales while, at the same time, narrating the painful reality of unequal wages, inadequate relational support, and harsh working conditions. In addition, the unique challenges that women face in light of their aging underscores another social identity that evokes further marginalisation for many of the women interviewed in the qualitative chapters. Furthermore, the intersection of ethnicity, social class, race, and age with gender was a striking theme in the chapters. Taken together, these observations attest to the difficulty that theories have in creating conceptual structures that clearly include the role of context as a central factor in women's work lives.

Another issue that was evident in many of the chapters is the association between poverty and gender. As many of the chapter authors noted, women often have much lower labour participation rates than men as well as lower wages, even for the same level of work. In addition, the fact that women live longer than men on average often leaves women as the sole means of support for themselves and their families in their later years. This picture of the gendered nature of poverty is pervasive throughout the career development literature (Heppner 2013; Kantamneni 2013) as well as in broader studies of poverty (Kristof and WuDunn 2009; Sachs 2005). The prevalence of sexist practices, which are both institutionalised as well as more covertly embedded in many cultures, often leaves women in positions of powerlessness, with few advocates within communities and within the political leadership.

A feminist critique of existing and emerging theories

Building on a noble tradition that goes back nearly 50 years, this section is devoted to a feminist critique of traditional and emerging theories, as informed by the material presented in this book. To organise the major career choice and development theories, I use Swanson's (2013) taxonomy wherein she categorised theories as traditional or emerging. According to Swanson, the traditional perspectives include PE-fit theories (Dawis 2005; Holland 1997), developmental theories (Gottfredson 2005; Super *et al.* 1996), and social cognitive career theory (Lent *et al.* 2002). (As reflected below, I consider social cognitive career theory to be a transitional theory, linking some of the traditional attributes of career choice and development theory with newer, more context-based perspectives). According to Swanson, the emerging theories include career construction and life design theories (Savickas 2013; Savickas *et al.* 2009), counselling for work and relationships (Richardson 2012), the psychology of working (Blustein 2006, 2013b), and the relational theory of working (Blustein 2011). I add a few notable non-US based theories to Swanson's taxonomy of emerging theories to provide a broader and more international perspective, which is consistent with the theme and mission of this book.

Traditional and transitional theories

One of the characteristics of the traditional theories is their focus on career choice and development, with a particular emphasis on delineating the factors that promote decisions that will optimise one's well-being at work. An implicit assumption of the traditional theories is that people have some degree of choice in their lives; in this context, the focus of the traditional theories is on developing a knowledge base that will enhance the quality of people's choices, thereby fostering a future of job satisfaction, congruence between one's attributes and the occupational context, and the capacity to determine one's own life course. These are all very admirable attributes; indeed, as I have argued elsewhere (Blustein 2006, 2013b), vocational psychologists ought to advocate that these sorts of choices be part of our inherent human rights. As noted in earlier feminist critiques (e.g. Betz and Fitzgerald 1987; Richardson 1993), the traditional theories often failed to attend sufficiently to the complexities of sexism, the multiple demands placed upon women who generally had to devote more time to caregiving than their male peers, and the constraining impact of gender-based socialisation and sexist labour market practices.

Another implicit assumption of the traditional theories is the privileging of market-place work. According to Richardson (2012), market-place work reflects the effort that we put forth in preparing for work in the paid labour market and the effort that we expend to earn money. While Super's (1980) lifespan, life-space revisions sought to reduce the hegemony of market work, the career discourse throughout most of the twentieth century tended to reify the work that people did to earn money. The consequence of this biased view was the relative neglect of personal care work, which Richardson defines as the effort that we expend in caring for ourselves and for others within our families and communities.

As Swanson (2013) noted, the traditional theories function well for clients and students who face career choice and development challenges that involve some degree of decisional volition. Applying the traditional theories to the material presented in this book raises some of the same critiques that have characterised the feminist position within vocational psychology as well as raising some additional concerns. For example, most of the women across the various settings reported having to juggle multiple life roles, often in ways that reduced their flexibility and negatively influenced their overall sense of self-determination. In addition, many of the women in the interviews reported explicit or implicit sexism, which created a major negative impact on their work lives and their overall level of well-being. However, some additional themes emerged that raised further questions about the utility of the traditional theories outside of the insular world of relatively privileged people. First, the impact of aging coupled with a growing lifespan certainly expands the horizon beyond the traditional purview of pre-implementation vocational behaviour in late adolescence and young adulthood, which has characterised many of the traditional theories. The sorts of problems that the women reported often transcended concerns about finding an optimal outlet for one's interests and values, which characterises traditional theories. Second, the often devastating effect of the Great Recession that began in 2008 was palpable in many of the narratives, underscoring the notion of career choice privilege, which is implicit in the traditional theories and becoming increasingly more difficult to attain and sustain.

By the early 1990s, the feminist revolution had been effective in challenging the prevailing discourse in vocational psychology, which clearly shaped the development of social cognitive career theory (SCCT; Lent 2013; Lent et al. 2002). Emerging initially from a social cognitive analysis of the role of self-efficacy in occupational aspirations (Betz and Hackett 1981), SCCT reflected a full infusion of Bandura's (1997) social cognitive theory to the world of work and career, and soon blossomed into a full-fledged theory that has sought to explain the development of interests, choice behaviour, performance, and more recently, career management skills (Lent and Brown 2013). SCCT has thoughtfully incorporated contextual factors in its models and also has generated a number of promising practice applications. In relation to the material presented in this book, SCCT offers some useful ways of understanding the women's narratives and the research data presented in the earlier chapters. The focus on understanding how people construct meaning about themselves and their context links well to the newer perspectives that have emerged in the past decade or so. In addition, the important role of positive self-efficacy and outcome expectations was evident in some of the participants' narratives.

Emerging theories

Swanson (2013) described a paradigm shift that has yielded theories that offer greater attention to the context, less rigidity, attention to both market work and care work, and an explicit inclusion of people who may not have access to the relatively volitional choices that make up the *grand career narrative*. Another attribute of the newer perspectives is a reliance on a more diverse epistemology, encompassing post-modern, systems-based frameworks, relational, and social constructionist perspectives. The expanded epistemology is perhaps the most notable cohering attribute of the new perspectives. Rather than relying upon a strict adherence to logical positivism (i.e. the use of the empirical scientific method as the prevailing way to derive knowledge and to prove inferences), the newer perspectives embrace post-modern and social constructionist thought, which assumes that knowledge is created in relationships and via culture (McMahon 2014). Social constructionist and post-modern perspectives, for the most part, view knowledge as relativistic as opposed to universal (Gergen 2009; Stead 2013). The relational theme of the emerging perspectives posits that people make meaning about life (and work) via relationships; indeed, relationships are viewed as an inherently human experience that provides the means for people to understand themselves, others, and many of their life tasks (see Stead 2013, for an overview of social constructionist thought and work and Blustein 2011, for an overview of relational theories.).

Another theme of the emerging theories, as detailed in McMahon's (2014) recent synthesis of new theoretical innovations, is the focus on the infusion of a systems-based framework into our understanding of work and careers. The contributions of Patton and McMahon (2014) from Australia have significant relevance to the understanding of the material presented in this volume. The Systems Theory Framework (STF) of career development provides a meta-theoretical analysis of work-based behaviours and tasks that illuminates numerous themes in the narratives and in the research reported herein. For example, the recursiveness theme of STF was evident throughout many chapters in this volume, particularly in the complex ways that the women described the ways that their individual aspirations and values interacted with broader systemic issues.

The Chaos Theory of Careers (Pryor and Bright 2011), which reflects another important theoretical contribution from Australia, is also a useful lens with which to understand much of the material in this book. Applying chaos theory from the physical sciences to the world of career development, Pryor and Bright (2011; Bright and Pryor 2005) have developed a means of understanding how chance events impact the work lives of people. The chapters in this volume that describe events that are far out of reach of volitional and planful behaviour underscore the need to infuse thoughtful means of accounting for chance and chaos in our understanding of work and careers.

The material presented in this book provides much fuel for thought for the emerging perspectives. The international comparison underscores the difficulty in deriving universal theories that would be applicable across contexts. Each of the cohorts of participants told stories about their lives that were rooted in their cultures and historical periods. For example, Suzanne (Chapter 8 this volume) noted in her analysis of the narratives from Argentinian women that the historical and political context of the military dictatorship during the 1970s played a substantial role in their lives, creating barriers that often impacted on their work trajectories for decades. Taken together, the work lives of the women interviewed in the qualitative study portion of this book, coupled with the empirical data in the initial chapters, underscores how pervasive the role of the context is in the nature and expression of women's work lives. In contrast to the traditional theories, the emerging theories have appropriately placed environmental factors and the relativistic world that we inhabit at the forefront of theoretical considerations. While the emerging theories lack the precision of the traditional theories, they seem to more accurately describe the contemporary nature of working in people's lives. One might argue that the precision that has existed in the traditional theories and in SCCT may be very compelling, particularly in an era when statistical tools exist to assess the level of precision of theories. However, the reality of work, as reflected in many of these chapters, is perhaps best understood from a more fluid perspective, wherein one might need to sacrifice precise linear models for the complex, murky nature of a working life that exists amidst family commitments, shifting political factors, radically transforming economic structures, and complex and nuanced cultures.

A number of themes emerged in the chapters that provide an in-depth view of some of the more complex attributes of the emerging theories. One notable theme is the importance of story and narrative in the qualitative studies. The women who participated in the interviews clearly had a story to tell, one that is not easily conveyed via large-scale quantitative studies or macro-level public policy analyses. The stories also provided a vivid example about how work and non-work life experiences weave in and out of each other in a seamless way, evoking complex causal pathways that are hard to capture in theoretical statements. The use of stories underscores many of the newer theoretical positions. The work of Guichard (2009), in particular, was exemplified in the narratives as the women sought to construct meaning about themselves and their contexts in ways that would provide coherence and stability.

In addition, the importance of political and economic factors emerged in vivid clarity in this volume. While the psychology-of-working framework (Blustein 2006, 2013b) is perhaps the most politically-oriented of the new perspectives, Richardson's (2012) counselling for work and relationships and the relational theory of working (Blustein 2011) also include specific references to the impact of political and economic affordances in the work lives of women and men. One of the advantages of this international comparison is the unique opportunity to examine the degree to which universal assumptions and inferences can be proposed and tested. A key aspect of the social constructionist critique is the notion that the social sciences cannot unequivocally support many universal theories given the profoundly important ways that people's lives emerge within a cultural and relational matrix (Gergen 2009). A wide-angle view of the chapters of this book does not provide easy answers to this question. Even assumptions about people seeking out work that is a good fit for their values, interests, and abilities may need to be revisited as some of the women reported making decisions about their work lives based on the needs of their families and communities. For example, Tomassini's chapter on Italian women conveyed the multitude of decisional factors that went into the choices that the women had to make, including family factors, health issues, shrinking economic opportunities and the like (Tomassini, Chapter 14 this volume).

The material presented in this book offers both challenges and opportunities for the existing, transitional, and emerging theories. As reflected in the narrative chapters in the second section of the book, the lived experiences of the women interviewed in these studies underscores the relativistic nature of working. Interestingly, the striving for a good fit in the world of work seems pervasive across the contexts and cultures. The motivation for a good working life seemed to reflect a striving for self-determination (Blustein 2006; Deci and Ryan 2000) as well as a clear need for survival (Blustein, 2006). At the same time, many of the decisions that people made were embedded in a relational context, underscoring Richardson's (2012) essential points about relationships and work as well as Blustein's (2011) relational theory of working. A challenge, however, for all of the theories noted in this discussion is that they are inherently psychological theories, focusing on individual experience. The upheavals described by many of the authors reflected huge changes in the social and economic contexts of the women's lives – for example, the women in South Africa (Watson, Chapter 16 this volume) had to deal with the crushing blows of apartheid followed by a rocky road to democratisation; the women in Portugal (Parada, Correia and Gomes, Chapter 15 this volume) had to cope with a devastating economic recession that has ripped apart much of the social and economic safety net.

Despite the gallant attempts to contextualise career theories, the core focus of much of the discourse in our field is on individual choice and behaviour. The opportunity offered by these chapters is embedded in the multidisciplinary nature of the material. Following this pluralistic lead, I suggest that the next generation of theory development in our field will need to occur within a context of a broader and more inclusive intellectual framework. While many options exist in a broad social scientific examination of work and careers, I believe that the ideas emerging from human development economics, most notably Sen (1999) and Nussbaum (2011), are particularly informative in articulating the complex ways that individuals and societies can create progress in the empowerment of women. As I suggest here, I believe that these theoretical initiatives help to provide the intellectual foundation for public policies, educational efforts, and counselling interventions that can help to fully empower women to challenge a status quo that has kept the glass ceiling in place across so many diverse cultural contexts.

Human development economics theory

Perhaps the best known human development economist is Amartya Sen (e.g. 1999), whose work has resulted in the Nobel Prize for economics. Sen's (1999) work has numerous trajectories and themes that have created a theoretical framework for many anti-poverty programmess around the globe. Nussbaum (2011) has expanded on the human development theme in constructing a theory of social justice that seeks to delineate the conditions that foster individual growth and agency as well as the development of more equitable and supportive societies. While detailed analyses of these perspectives is beyond the scope of this chapter, a number of core elements, which are described next, may form the basis for integrative theory development efforts that will have particular relevance for the career development of women.

The human development approach (which is also known as the human development and capability approach) reflects both a political position as well as a theoretical statement. (As I have argued elsewhere (Blustein 2006, 2013b), I believe that values are inherent in the work of social scientists; as such, the explicit political ideology of the human development approach strikes me as a welcome respite from the myth of scientific neutrality.) In the human development paradigm, individual experience and behaviour is inextricably related to economic and social conditions. Following this assumption, Sen and his colleagues have argued that human agency is essential for people to create lives of meaning, dignity, and self-determination. Agency refers to 'the ability to define one's goals in an autonomous fashion and act on them' (Pick and Sirkin 2010: 68). A core assumption of the human development approach is that people do best when they have agency. In order for people to develop and sustain agency, they need access to the following five core human freedoms: political freedoms; economic facilities; social opportunities; transparency guarantees; and protective security. Sen is clear in implicating the social and economic contexts as essential in creating the conditions for agency and self-determination.

Nussbaum has expanded on Sen's views by emphasising the importance of capabilities, which are defined as the answer to the question: 'What is each person able to do and to be?' (Nussbaum, 2011: 18). Nussbaum further proposes that capabilities are:

> *focused on choice or freedom* (italics in original), holding that the crucial good societies should be promoting for their people is a set of opportunities, or substantial freedoms, which people then may or may not exercise in action; the choice is theirs ... Finally, the approach *is concerned with entrenched social injustice and inequality* (italics in original), especially capability failures that are the result of discrimination or marginalisation. It ascribes an urgent task to government and public policy—namely to improve the quality of life for all people, as defined by their capabilities.[1]
>
> (2011: 18–19)

Given the complexity of the women's lives described in this volume and the extensive array of theories in vocational psychology, occupational sociology, career management, and related fields, one might wonder why we need a new perspective that places agency in the context of human affordances and barriers. Many readers will recognise some of the concepts of human development economics in social cognitive career theory, developmental systems theories, and Richardson's (2012) perspective on counselling for work and relationships, among others. My view is that human development economics theory has the distinct advantage of having been used extensively and effectively in developing programmes that have demonstrated clear evidence of reducing poverty (e.g. Nussbaum 2011; Pick and Sirkin 2010; Sachs 2005). Moreover, in articulating the five core human freedoms, human development theory is clear about the necessary conditions required to foster agency and empowerment. In addition, human development economics theory has focused extensively on the struggles that women face in attaining and sustaining dignified working lives (Nussbaum 2011; Pick and Sirkin 2010).

In a sense, the infusion of human development economics theory provides a conceptual analogue to the complexity that is inherent in many of the chapters of this volume. A broad examination of the women's work lives, especially from the vantage point of middle-age and beyond, reveals a rich tapestry of agency that is, at times, nurtured by others and the broader social world, as well as constricted by the absence of human freedoms. In my view, the next generation of theories of women's career development will necessarily include the political and context-rich vantage point of macro-level analyses of human behaviour. In this way, we will avoid generating obvious conclusions that simply implicate social forces and/or the context as major factors in career development. With the input of human development economics, we can create more precise understandings of *how* access to freedom across the full range of human experience functions to provide people with the capacity to determine the course of their own lives.

Conclusion

Career development, as a profession and as a scholarly field, has benefitted considerably from the consideration of women's issues and challenges. As reflected in this theoretical analysis, our field owes a considerable debt to feminist scholars and to the brave women who have (and continue to) fight against the hegemony of male-dominated models and discourses. I view this volume as the next step in this courageous struggle to place women's voices at the forefront of our intention to create a world that offers opportunities for meaning and dignity for all at work.

Note

1 Reprinted by permission of the publisher from CREATING CAPABILITIES: THE HUMAN DEVELOPMENT APPROACH by Martha C. Nussbaum, pp. 18-19, Cambridge, MA: The Belknap Press of Harvard University Press, Copyright © 2011 by Martha C. Nussbaum.

References

Bandura, A. (1997) *Self-efficacy: The Exercise of Control*, New York: Freeman.
Betz, N. E. and Hackett, G. (1981) 'The relationship of career-related self-efficacy expectations to perceived career options in college women and men', *Journal of Counseling Psychology*, 28: 399–410.
Blustein, D. L. (2006) *The Psychology of Working: A New Perspective for Counseling, Career Development, and Public Policy*, Mahwah, NJ: Lawrence Erlbaum Associates.
Blustein, D. L. (2011) 'A relational theory of working', *Journal of Vocational Behavior*, 79: 1–17.
Blustein, D. L. (ed.) (2013a) *The Oxford Handbook of the Psychology of Working*, New York: Oxford University Press.
Blustein, D. L. (2013b) 'The psychology of working: A new perspective for a new era', in D. L. Blustein (ed.) *The Oxford Handbook of the Psychology of Working*, New York: Oxford University Press.

Bright, J. E. H. and Pryor, R. G. L. (2005) 'The chaos theory of careers: A user's guide', *Career Development Quarterly*, 53: 291–305.
Dawis, R. (2005) 'The Minnesota theory of work adjustment', in S. D. Brown and R. W. Lent (eds) *Career Development and Counseling: Putting Theory and Research to Work*, Hoboken, NJ: John Wiley & Sons.
Deci, E. L. and Ryan, R. M. (2000) 'The "what" and "why" of goal pursuits: Human needs and self-determination of behavior', *Psychological Inquiry*, 11: 227–68.
Gergen, K. J. (2009) *Relational Being: Beyond Self and Community*, New York: Oxford University Press.
Gottfredson, L. S. (2005) 'Applying Gottfredson's theory of circumscription and compromise in career guidance and counseling', in S. D. Brown and R. W. Lent (eds) *Career Choice and Development: Putting Theory and Research to Work*, Hoboken, NJ: John Wiley & Sons (1st ed.).
Guichard, J. (2009) 'Self-constructing', *Journal of Vocational Behavior*, 75: 251–8.
Harmon, L. W. and Farmer, H. S. (1983) 'Current theoretical issues in vocational psychology', in W. B. Walsh and S. H. Osipow (eds) *Handbook of Vocational Psychology* (Vol. 1), Hillsdale, NJ: Erlbaum.
Heppner, M. J. (2013) 'Women, men, and work: The long journey to gender equity', in S. D. Brown and R. W. Lent (eds) *Career Development and Counseling: Putting Theory and research to work*, Hoboken, NJ: John Wiley & Sons (2nd ed.).
Holland, J. L. (1997) *Making Vocational Choices: A Theory of Vocational Personalities and Work Environments*, Odessa, FL: Psychological Associates Research (3rd ed.).
Kantamneni, N. (2013) 'Gender and the psychology of working', in D. L. Blustein (ed.) *The Oxford Handbook of the Psychology of Working*, New York: Oxford University Press.
Kristof, N. D. and WuDunn, S. (2009) *Half the Sky*, New York: Random House.
Lent, R. W. (2013) 'Social cognitive career theory', in S. D. Brown and R. W. Lent (eds) *Career Development and Counseling: Putting Theory and Research to Work*, Hoboken, NJ: John Wiley & Sons (2nd ed.).
Lent, R. W. and Brown, S. D. (2013) 'Social cognitive model of career self-management: Toward a unifying view of adaptive career behavior across the life span', *Journal of Counseling Psychology*, Advance online publication, doi: 10.1037/a0033446.
Lent, R. W., Brown, S. D. and Hackett, G. (2002) 'Social cognitive career theory', in D. Brown (ed.) *Career Choice and Development*, San Francisco, CA: Jossey-Bass.
McMahon, M. (2014) 'New trends in theory development in career psychology', in G. Arulmani, A. Bakshi, F. Leong and T. Watts (eds) *Handbook of Career Development: International Perspectives*, New York: Springer.
Nussbaum, M. C. (2011) *Creating Capabilities: The Human Development Approach*, Cambridge, MA: Harvard University Press.
Parsons, F. (1909) *Choosing a Vocation*, Boston, MA: Houghton-Mifflin.
Patton, W. and McMahon, M. (2014) *Career Development and Systems Theory: Connecting Theory and Practice*, Rotterdam, The Netherlands: Sense Publishers.
Pick, S. and Sirkin, J. (2010) *Breaking the Poverty Cycle: The Human Basis for Sustainable Development*, New York: Oxford University Press.
Pryor, R. G. L. and Bright, J. E. H. (2011) *The Chaos Theory of Careers: A New Perspective on Working in the 21st Century*, New York: Routledge.
Richardson, M. S. (1993) 'Work in people's lives: A location for counseling psychologists', *Journal of Counseling Psychology*, 40: 425–33.
Richardson, M. S. (2012) 'Counseling for work and relationships', *The Counseling Psychologist*, 40: 190–242.

Sachs, J. D. (2005) *The End of Poverty*, New York: Penguin Press.
Savickas, M. L. (2013) 'Career construction theory and practice', in S. D. Brown and R. W. Lent (eds) *Career Development and Counseling: Putting Theory and Research to Work* New York: Wiley (2nd ed.).
Savickas, M. L., Nota, L., Rossier, J., Dauwalder, J. P., Duarte, M. E., Guichard, J., Soresi, S., Van Esbroeck, R. and van Vianen, A. E. M. (2009) 'Life designing: A paradigm for career construction in the 21st century', *Journal of Vocational Behavior*, 75: 239–50.
Sen, A. (1999) *Development as Freedom*, New York: Knopf.
Sharone, O. (2014) *Flawed System/Flawed Self: Job Searching and Unemployment Experiences*, Chicago, IL: University of Chicago Press.
Stead, G. (2013) 'Social constructionist thought and working' in D. L. Blustein (ed.) *The Oxford Handbook of the Psychology of Working*, New York: Oxford University Press.
Swanson, J. L. (2013) 'Traditional and emerging career development theory and the psychology of working', in D. L. Blustein (ed.) *The Oxford Handbook of the Psychology of Working*, New York: Oxford University Press.
Super, D. E. (1957) *The Psychology of Careers*, New York: Harper.
Super, D. E. (1980) 'A life-span, life-space approach to career development', *Journal of Vocational Behavior*, 16: 282–98.
Super, D. E., Savickas, M. L. and Super, C. M. (1996) 'The life-span, life-space approach to careers', in D. Brown and L. Brown (eds) *Career Choice and Development*, San Francisco, CA: Jossey-Bass (3rd ed.).
Zickar, M. J. (2013) 'A more inclusive industrial-organizational psychology', in D. L. Blustein (ed.) *The Oxford Handbook of the Psychology of Working*, New York: Oxford University Press.

19 Implications for career research

Mary Sue Richardson, Kristin Elizabeth Black and Yoko Iwaki

It is an honour to be asked to address the implications for research of this ambitious international exploration of women's career development across the lifespan. This exploration actually comprises two different areas of focus, an interdisciplinary research dimension followed by a collaborative qualitative research project across nine countries. In this chapter, we address a number of major implications for research based on these two areas of focus. Both areas of focus support a shift in discourse from speaking about women's career development to speaking about women's (and men's) working lives (Patton 2013; Richardson and Schaeffer 2013a, 2013b), a discourse that we use throughout the chapter. In this new discourse, women's (and men's) working lives refer to both market work (work that is paid) and unpaid care work (work to care for self, others, and community that is not paid). We then consider implications of the new discourse for research.

The interdisciplinary research dimension

Drawing from psychology, sociology, economics, geography, and business, the interdisciplinary chapters in the first section of this volume provide a fascinating examination of the contexts that shape women's working lives. The authors, who represent a range of countries and diverse disciplinary commitments, tackle very general issues such as class, privilege, and geography, but also more specific aspects of contemporary market work including organisational/human resource policies and the employment patterns in two industries expected to be growth areas for women across diverse economies.

The chapter by Vindhya (Chapter 3 this volume) from India makes a powerful case that most psychological research in India has focused on more educated and privileged women and has ignored women with lower levels of skills and education, many of whom work in the growing unregulated and casualised paid care industries or who are restricted to unpaid care work in the home. In so doing, this body of research has contributed to the devaluing and invisibility of much of women's work. While this is a valid critique across national contexts in that, in general, little attention has been paid to less privileged women in the career development literature, in India these issues are further intertwined with caste and religion. This example is illustrative of how a critical issue that is relevant across national borders takes on a particular shape and form in different national contexts and cultures. Reading about an issue relevant to one's own country written by someone from a different cultural vantage point encourages the reader to see the issue through new eyes. It is an enriching experience. Vindya's chapter enabled us to have a deeper appreciation for the ways in which traditional career discourse has rendered women's work invisible and for the ways in which both paid and unpaid care work are affected by a devaluing gender bias.

Vindhya's (Chapter 3 this volume) research also highlights how women's employment in both the regularised and casualised labour markets relates to their empowerment and disempowerment, a needed corrective to most psychological and vocational research that tends to neglect issues of power (Blustein 2006, 2013; Blustein et al. 2005; Prilleltensky and Stead 2013). That how we frame the research we do is both highly personal and highly political is a critical perspective for vocational fields. Such a perspective requires a definition of work and working broad enough to encompass all facets of women's work and all women who work. This is a major implication for future research in the field that we return to later in this chapter.

Green's (Chapter 2 this volume) chapter on geographical perspectives on women's careers pays this attention to both highly skilled and less skilled women in the labour market as well as the way that women's unpaid care work interfaces with their market work. Green makes a convincing argument that, due to their unpaid care work, women, in general, are more likely to be tied to market work closer to home, a constraint that affects poor and less skilled women more than their privileged and educated counterparts. Privileged women have both more options for employment and greater resources to enable them to travel further to locations of market work. The concept of gendered localisation is a major contribution to the literature on women's working lives and introduces a significant aspect of context to be considered in future research.

Eikhof and Warhurst (Chapter 5 this volume) review the ways in which the creative and retail industries, both considered employment sectors favourable for women, may, in fact, curtail women's employment prospects, each in different ways. In their critique of these industries they underline how market forces are changing the nature of the workplace in ways that may significantly shape older women's market work paths. Their description of the culture clash between the creative industry and unpaid care work is particularly illuminating and suggests that we are only just beginning to discover the complex interactions between women's unpaid care work and employment opportunities in the global economy.

Similarly, the research on organisational structures and policies – and the mismatch between these structures and policies and women's needs – are especially relevant for this volume of research on the working lives of older women. Earl, Taylor, Williams, and Brooke (Chapter 4 this volume) offer rich insights about the implications of the absence of workplace policies for older women as well as an understanding of why mid-age and older workers of both genders are an increasingly important focus of research. Parker and Roan (Chapter 6 this volume) examine policies affecting advancement in organisations and, in particular, the disconnect between organisational policies and women's needs with respect to their unpaid care work. Both chapters underscore that women working in organisations with outmoded male-centric policies regarding advancement will clearly encounter a different set of opportunities and constraints than women working in organisations with policies more carefully tailored to the realities of their lives.

By placing the study of women's working lives in context, these chapters begin to build an interdisciplinary dimension to research that is essential for two reasons. The first reason is theoretical. Informed by a social constructionist lens, contextualism locates the mechanism of change in the interactions between individuals and their social contexts, not primarily in the individual (Pepper 1942; Richardson 2012a, 2012b). While there is general agreement in the vocational literature that the nature of market work in the contemporary world requires agentic actors, people who can purposively navigate this constantly changing world, contextualism decentres this narrative and shifts the focus to the individual-in-context. These interdisciplinary chapters help to push research on women's working lives into this space between the individual and the social worlds they inhabit, a space mostly unlanguaged and undertheorised, referred to by Guichard (n.d.; Richardson in press) as "go between" space.

The second reason is political. Without the strong presence of context in research on women's working lives, any discussion of agency or individual agentic action immediately triggers a concern about neoliberal discourses that place the onus for managing market work paths on the individual, thereby masking systemic disempowerment (Irving 2010, 2012). While this is always a concern, the inclusion of these interdisciplinary chapters in this volume on women's working lives with the set of qualitative research chapters provides an example of how to establish a strong presence of context in research on individuals. In other words, these chapters do not merely provide background. They, in part, constitute a strongly contextualised component to the study of women's working lives. While not exhaustive, this set of chapters points the way towards developing the interdisciplinary context of knowledge about women's working lives.

The collaborative qualitative research project: the internationalisation of vocational guidance and vocational psychology

Without a doubt this project has made a major contribution to advancing the internationalisation of the discipline that we refer to as both vocational guidance and vocational psychology. By internationalisation, we refer to the effort to develop an inclusive understanding of basic processes in the study of working lives that moves far beyond the classic etic (universal) and emic (culture-specific) approaches and the oft-cited distinction between individualism and collectivism (Brouwers *et al.* 2004; Markus and Kitayama 1991) to encompass culture as context for any study of working lives. Although we have long known that it is crucial to move beyond Western and Anglo-oriented models of theory and practice, actually doing so is a major undertaking and this project has taken us some way down this road.

What is particularly valuable is the focus on specific countries as the primary context for each research sample and the efforts of the researchers from each country to provide the historical, sociological, and political background that shapes the working lives of the women from each of their respective countries. The background component in each of the qualitative research chapters highlights major historical events and features of the employment context that are essential for understanding the experience of the research participants in that country. For example, knowledge about the long history of Portugal's repressive Estado Novo regime, the persistent asymmetry of traditional gender roles, and its current financial crisis following the Great Recession of 2008 is crucial for understanding the kind of hopelessness and lack of future orientation that was identified in some of the research interviews from Portugal (Chapter 15 this volume). Similarly, although no particular historical crisis was identified in the chapter by Tomassini (Chapter 14 this volume) from Italy, the description of Italy's weak employment system suggests that some significant structural factors are contributing to the kind of hopelessness that was identified among some women in the Italian sample.

In a different vein, the level of employment motivation, what might be called vocational agency, and the willingness to pursue lifelong learning opportunities in the German sample is fascinating in the face of Germany's highly structured and potentially disempowering system that tightly links education and employment (Chapter 13 this volume). Although this could easily be attributed to the strength of the German labour market, might it also be possible that this result is due to the effects of early scaffolding of productive market work experience along with the accessibility of opportunities for lifelong learning?

What is most important here is to underline the importance of this background information regarding national context as a significant part of any strongly contextualised research on women's or men's working lives. Although gender and age were the parameters of the research samples in this project, what we know about the working lives of people in any specific country needs to be interpreted in the light of the national context in which they live. It is hoped that the background component of each of the research chapters will provide a guide for the continued development of our understanding of the impact of history, the social system, and national politics on working lives.

Additionally, the background component of each research chapter provides exemplars of how issues of gender equity are understood in each national context. Clearly, there are multiple ways of looking at gender equity including standardised international measures such as the Global Gender Gap Index, the Women's Economic Opportunity Index, and data provided by the Organisation for Economic Co-operation and Development as well as more local measures idiosyncratic to specific countries. Issues addressed include wage gaps, hours worked outside the home, discrepancies between educational and professional attainment, differences in unemployment rates, horizontal and vertical occupational segregation by gender, rates of part-time employment by gender, and disproportionate effects of local or national constraints by gender. Hopefully, this collection of research chapters will enable us to not only learn from one another, but to develop increasingly sophisticated ways of assessing gender equity that are sensitive both to differences as well as to similarities across national contexts. To the extent that gender equity is a goal of researchers and policy makers with respect to women's employment, the ongoing evolution of an internationally relevant gender equity template is necessary both for interpreting what we are finding out about women's working lives and for assessing the results of efforts to improve equity. Additionally, the lens of gender equity needs to be extended to encompass the unpaid care work of both men and women.

A collaborative approach to research across national contexts

Although the basic qualitative study design for this collaborative research project was initially conceptualised and developed by three investigators from three different national contexts, the project expanded to include researchers from six other countries, each responsible for testing the relevance of the study design and implementing it in their respective countries. This strategy is to be commended for its contribution to building an international research community of scholars of vocational guidance and vocational psychology who speak the same research language. As such, it might be conceived of as a project to scaffold research expertise within diverse international professional and research communities with the goal of promoting a collaborative community of scholars (Van de Vijver 2013). This approach can be contrasted to one in which "experts" from one national research community are exported into a different country to do research based on their expertise. The experts then leave doing little to build research capacity among researchers in the host country. Clearly, in our minds, the development of an international community of scholars who speak a similar research language and who are committed to developing an internationalised or globalised understanding of women's working lives is an important goal that complements and enriches the goal to study women's working lives.

At the same time, building the research capacities of collaborating communities of scholars is important. With this in mind, it is worth noting that Kuang (Chapter 11 this volume) from China appears to have extended the basic grounded theory design used across all research samples to identify two distinct orientations toward market work among this sample, a survival orientation in which women's employment transitions were tightly constrained and determined primarily by geographical location and financial needs, and a developmental orientation in which the women demonstrated greater agency in exploring and pursuing careers that might meet their own needs and desires. This is a finding that may be more broadly applicable to less privileged women in other national settings. It also is a finding that demonstrates the explanatory potential of grounded theory.

Further collaborative efforts across multiple national contexts might profitably build on this effort by establishing elements of a set of research questions and a basic study design that would be similar across national contexts along with encouraging each national research team to elaborate on or otherwise supplement this design

The salience of women's unpaid care work

The major finding in this set of qualitative research studies was the extensiveness and complexity of the ways in which women's unpaid work complicated and informed their market work experience. In the first place, the ways in which family roles and caretaking responsibilities impinged on and constrained market work paths in all countries was striking. For example, Suzanne (Chapter 8 this volume) from Argentina states that:

> All women in the study experienced at some point tension between their work and other life domains, especially taking care of young children. Many of them left jobs they enjoyed as a consequence ... others changed to part-time jobs to be able to enjoy their children more.

Tomassino (Chapter 14 this volume) from Italy describes Giovanna:

> after her graduation in architecture and some initial experiences in architectural design, she renounced her career desires in order to support her family budget and her husband's academic career ... she let her sense of family prevail in the traditional manner and she had to choose less skilled employment.

Parado, Correia, and Gomez (Chapter 15 this volume) from Portugal note about their research participants that, "balance between the demands of their paid work and family lives was usually accomplished at the expense of their own interests, plans, or ambitions", and Haasler (Chapter 13 this volume) from Germany describes how "working women with caring responsibilities felt particularly stretched between their different commitments". Most interestingly, this constraint was apparent both for mothers of young children and for grandmothers tasked with the care of grandchildren and of adult children not yet able to live independent lives.

At the same time, another facet of the relationship between market work and unpaid care work is revealed by Suzanne (Chapter 8 this volume) from Argentina who notes that "in many cases mothers provided assistance that allowed women [their daughters] to keep working", and by Kuang (Chapter 11 this volume) from China who reports that for one research participant:

> Working in the kindergarten also gave me a chance to learn a lot of professional preschool education knowledge and it made me suddenly realise the duty of parents. I thought it gave me great help in how to educate and take care of children after my marriage.

In other words, the worlds of work and family can be mutually enhancing and supportive.

The ways in which women went to great lengths to provide for their families through their market work is described by Kuang (Chapter 11 this volume) who concludes that older Chinese women who experienced the radical social transformation of China in the past 50 years were forced to tolerate hard work and perseverance. Despite the low status and grim working conditions of many of the jobs they occupied, the women took on any kind of employment for the benefit of the family. In this case, while there may have been conflicts between competing sets of responsibilities, under severe economic deprivation, caring for their families is what drove women's market work.

Finally, the meaning of unpaid care work and of the relationships that are nurtured by this care is well illustrated by McMahon (Chapter 9 this volume) from Australia, who states that:

> Of the women, 10 had children. Some described parenting as their most valued role. Janice believed that "I'm really pleased that we did have two children It would have been a very selfish life without them ... parenting has been very satisfying." Similarly, Clare values most "Being a mother. That's my most important role in my life above all else."

Clearly unpaid care work is part and parcel of the most meaningful relationships in women's lives.

While these stories and research chapters are saturated with the complexly intertwined paths of market work and unpaid care work, referred to by a number of terms such as caregiving, caring responsibilities, family commitments, family and carer role responsibilities, carer roles, and unpaid work tasks, the realities of unpaid care work in these women's lives continues to be rendered somewhat opaque, though far from invisible. For example, the tables in each chapter, for the most part, only describe the market work, the educational status, and the number of dependents of each participant. They do not fully describe their unpaid care work responsibilities. Although the quotes provided highlight care work responsibilities for children by mothers and grandmothers, there is less attention to other caretaking demands such as the care of disabled adults or the care of elderly parents and relatives. Thus, the specific contours of women's unpaid care work commitments remain somewhat unspecified and tend to be buried in a more generalised sense of women's family responsibilities.

Given the traditional discourse of career development, the lack of detail about women's unpaid care work is inevitable. After all, career development discourse does not label unpaid care in home and family settings as work. Yet, in these research studies, the voices of the research participants across nine countries say loud and clear that providing care is central to their lives. While the nature of the relationship between the market work and the unpaid care work of the research participants is inextricably and powerfully shaped by the social history and social context of gender discrimination and bias in each country, it would be a mistake to read the commitment of these women to providing care as simply the voices of internalised oppression. Rather, their commitment can also be read as a commitment to care values and to the people they care about that provides a needed counterweight to the market values that dominate capitalistic economies and culture. It is for this reason that we promote the adoption of a discourse that renders visible both unpaid care work and market work as two important strands of women's working lives.

Qualitative versus/and quantitative research methods

We applaud the use of qualitative methods in this study as more exploratory, experience-near and theory-building rather than the more typical theory-driven approach to research and we encourage future research designs that sample from the wide array of qualitative methods. Without giving in to methodolotary or the worship of methodological advancements, the increasing sophistication of qualitative approaches has made the issue of "listening to women's voices" or experience-near methods a far more complicated endeavour. For example, a number of special journal issues on qualitative methodology begin to map out the growing terrain of qualitative methods (Carter 2007a, 2007b; Haverkamp et al. 2005). The literature on these methods continues to advance.

Just as in research using quantitative methods where assessment and statistical issues may sometimes seem to trump substantive understandings of a research question, it is also true in qualitative research that how one listens, or the method that is used, has much to do with what is heard. Moving forward, we hope that the project to build an international community of research scholars in vocational guidance and vocational psychology will focus on developing expertise across both qualitative and quantitative methods, with the method of choice dictated by what we need to know rather than by ideological commitments. In this endeavour to build an international collaborative community of scholars, we adhere to a postmodern approach to knowledge in which knowledge is not something that simply needs to be accrued, but rather is always a part of a reflexive process of knowledge generation (Richardson et al. 2005). In order for this process to be more fully internationalised in our increasingly globalised world, the collaborative approach followed in this research project provides a model for nurturing this process.

The meaning of purposive sampling

A major implication of the dual focus of this exploration of women's working lives is its support for an enhanced understanding of the significance of purposive sampling. In order to pursue research that is strongly contextualised, sample selection, whether for qualitative or quantitative research, must pay careful attention to the social contexts in which research participants are embedded. Clearly the need to expand the lens of inquiry to study women who are poor as well as privileged, in mid-life as well as at other points in their working lives, is one major implication of this research. In selecting research participants, researchers also need to consider carefully where their participants are located with respect to their market work and unpaid work paths, taking into account participants' employment status such as employed, underemployed, or unemployed, whether they are employed in part-time work by choice or not, the kinds of industries and organisations in which they are employed, and the kinds and levels of their unpaid care work responsibilities (Corrigan 2013). Researchers also need to take into account gendered localisation and consider carefully where their research participants live. Such an enhanced attention to the parameters of the research samples enables a fuller interpretation of the results with respect to the social contexts of research participants. It enables researchers to draw on the kinds of context-driven research represented in the first section of this volume to more fully understand their findings.

From career development to working lives

Both the interdisciplinary research dimension and the collaborative qualitative research project provide strong support for the centrality of unpaid care work in women's lives and for a shift in discourse that fully acknowledges that market work and unpaid care work are two components of women's working lives. Unpaid care work, in and of itself, constitutes a significant dimension of women's working lives. Women across the world are committed to, and struggle with, the work they do for pay and the care work they do in their personal and private lives. To fully acknowledge that women have two major work paths in their lives lifts unpaid care work out of the background of women's working lives and into more central focus. This shift in what we mean by women's work, in turn, has significant implications for research.

In light of this consideration of unpaid care work as one of two significant work paths for most women, a first and major research task is descriptive. What are we really talking about when we talk about unpaid care work? We need to develop ways to describe the unpaid care work that people do. Implicit in this discussion is the need to have a broad lens for defining unpaid care work. Clearly such a definition needs to encompass a range of care responsibilities that extends beyond care for children and that is relevant across the lifespan. Other guides for this definitional endeavour are an international cadre of care theorists, who differ somewhat in their definitions of care and care work (Daly and Standing 2001; Folbre 2012; Harrington *et al.* 2000; Kittay with Jennings and Wasunna 2005; Sevenhuijsen 2003; Standing 2001; Tronto 1993, 2006). Among these, the distinctions made by Folbre between interactive, support, and supervisory care work may be particularly useful.

Another approach pioneered by Corrigan (2013) is to simply assess the level of care work demand experienced by women, to use this variable as a measure in research using quantitative analyses, and to then provide additional descriptive data to detail the kinds and complexities of the unpaid care work that research participants report. This approach has merit in that it enables research to focus on the subjective experience of the demands of providing care without getting lost in the complexities of these demands. For example, many of the research participants in Corrigan's research in the United States were immigrants living in very different kinds of family systems with transnational as well as local family responsibilities.

This descriptive and definitional task will also be enhanced by qualitative studies that address how women themselves think about and experience their unpaid care work. Needless to say, this is a research question relevant to women both privileged and poor, and across the lifespan. Older women are of particular interest. Although we tend to think of the elderly as requiring care, some research has indicated that older people across gender categories are highly involved in providing care to others (Midlarsky *et al.* in press).

Research questions beyond the descriptive and definitional abound. What is the relationship between market work paths and unpaid care work paths over time and for women in different social locations? How are these paths and the relationship between them affected by the social policy ecology of the national state in which they live, by the policies of the organisations in which they work, and by other critically important contextual factors? How do considerations of unpaid care work affect market work decisions of women, such as the kinds of employment to pursue, where to pursue employment, and the level of engagement in their market work and in their aspirations for market work in their futures? How do unpaid care work responsibilities affect women's ability to cope or not to cope with the discontinuities of market work in today's world? To be able to address these research questions with the kind of contextualised interdisciplinary and international research lens exemplified in this volume of research will be invaluable.

Conclusion

Finally, this volume on women's working lives has major implications for research on men's working lives. The same kind of interdisciplinary and international lens needs to be applied to research on men's experience of working across the world, including their market work and their unpaid care work. In fact, we foresee a world where the focus of research attention will be on working lives, encompassing market work and unpaid care work, with gender only one of many relevant contextual variables.

References

Blustein, D. L. (2006) *The Psychology of Working*, Mahwah, NJ: Lawrence Erlbaum.
Blustein, D. L. (2013) *The Oxford Handbook of the Psychology of Working*, New York: Oxford University Press.
Blustein, D. L., McWhirter, E. H. and Perry, J. (2005) "An emancipatory communitarian approach to vocational development theory, research, and practice", *The Counseling Psychologist*, 33: 141–79.
Brouwers, S. A., van Hemert, D. A., Breugelmans, S. M. and van de Vijver, F. J. R. (2004) "A historical analysis of empirical studies published in the *Journal of Cross-Cultural Psychology* 1970–2004", *Journal of Cross-Cultural Psychology*, 35: 251–62.
Carter, E. (ed) (2007a) "Qualitative issues and analyses in counseling psychology: Part III", *The Counseling Psychologist*, 35(2).
Carter, E. (ed) (2007b) "Qualitative issues and analyses in counseling psychology: Part IV", *The Counseling Psychologist*, 35(3).

Corrigan, E. (2013) "Work-family conflict among non-professional, low-wage, direct-care workers in the field of developmental disabilities" (Unpublished doctoral dissertation), New York University, New York.

Daly, M. and Standing, G. (2001) "Introduction", in M. Daly (ed.) *Care Work: The Quest for Security*, Geneva, Switzerland: International Labour Office.

Folbre, N. (ed.) (2012) *For Love and Money: Care provision in the United States*, New York: Russell Sage Foundation.

Guichard, J. (n.d.) "Helping people face their career and life issues in liquid modernity: Processes of identity construction and counseling intervention".

Harrington Meyer, M., Herd, P. and Michel, S. (2000) "Introduction: The right – or not – to care", in M. Harrington Meyer (ed.) *Care Work: Gender, Labor, and the Welfare State*, London: Routledge.

Haverkamp, B. E., Morrow, S. L. and Ponterotto, J. G. (2005) "Knowledge as context: Qualitative methods in counseling psychology research" [Special Issue], *Journal of Counseling Psychology*, 52.

Irving, B. A. (2010) "(Re)constructing career education as a socially just practice: An antipodean reflection", *International Journal of Educational and Vocational Guidance*, 10: 49–63.

Irving, B. A. (2012) "Access, opportunity, and career: Supporting the aspirations of dis/abled students with high-end needs in New Zealand", *International Journal of Inclusive Education*, 16: 1–13.

Kittay E. F. with Jennings, B. and Wasunna, A. A. (2005) "Dependency, difference and the global ethic of long term care", *The Journal of Political Philosophy*, 13: 443–69.

Markus, H. R. and Kitayama, S. (1991) "Culture and the self: Implications for cognition, emotion, and motivation", *Psychological Review*, 98: 224–53.

Midlarsky, E., Kahana, E. and Belser, A. (in press) "Prosocial behavior in later life", in D. A. Schroder and W. Graziano (eds) *Oxford Handbook of Prosocial Behavior*, Oxford: Oxford University Press.

Patton, W. (2013) "Understanding women's working lives", in W. Patton (ed.) *Conceptualising Women's Working Lives: Moving the Boundaries of Discourse*, Rotterdam: Sense Publishers.

Pepper, S. C. (1942) *World Hypotheses*, Berkeley, CA: University of California Press.

Prilleltensky, I. and Stead, G. B. (2013) "Critical psychology, well-being, and work", in D. Blustein (ed.) *The Oxford Handbook of the Psychology of Working*, New York: Oxford University Press.

Richardson, M. S. (2012a) "Counseling for work and relationship", *The Counseling Psychologist*, 40: 190–242.

Richardson, M. S. (2012b) "The ongoing social construction of the counseling for work and relationship perspective", *The Counseling Psychologist*, 40: 279–90.

Richardson, M. S. (in press) "A conversation with Jean Guichard: Reflexivity in action", in A. DiFabio and J.-L. Bernaud (eds) *Psychological Construction of Identity in the 21st Century: A New Intervention Theory for Self-developing in Turbulent Times*, Hauppauge, NY: Nova Science Publishers.

Richardson, M. S. and Schaeffer, C. (2013a) "From work and family to a dual model of working", in D. L. Blustein (ed.) *Handbook of the Psychology of Working*, New York: Oxford University Press.

Richardson, M. S. and Schaeffer, C. (2013b) "Expanding the discourse: A dual model of working for women (and men's) lives", in W. Patton (ed.) *Women's Working Lives: Moving the Boundaries of Our Discourse*, Rotterdam: Sense Publishers.

Richardson, M. S., Constantine, K. and Washburn, M. (2005) "New directions for theory development in vocational psychology", in W. B. Walsh and M. L. Savickas (eds) *Handbook of Vocational Psychology* Mahwah, NJ: Lawrence Erlbaum (3rd ed.).

Sevenhuijsen, S. (2003) "The place of care: The relevance of the feminist ethic of care for social policy", *Feminist Theory*, 4: 179–97.

Standing, G. (2001) "Care work: Overcoming insecurity and neglect", in M. Daly (ed.) *Care Work: The Quest for Security*, Geneva, Switzerland: International Labour Office.

Tronto, J. C. (1993) *Moral Boundaries: A Political Argument for an Ethic of Care*, New York: Routledge.

Tronto, J. C. (2006) "Vicious circles of unequal care", in M. Harrington (ed.) *Socializing Care*, Lanham, MD: Rowman & Littlefield.

van de Vijver, F. J. R. (2013) "Contributions of internationalization of psychology: Toward a global and inclusive discipline", *American Psychologist*, 68: 761–70.

20 Implications for career policy

Ken Roberts

Implications for career policy leap vividly from previous chapters. The authors from all the countries implicitly make the case for career information, advice and guidance, and related education and training that address the successive life-stage and gender-specific circumstances of women from the perspective of those aged 45/50 and above. The life course perspective offers a privileged view of the policy options. The aim of the present chapter is to make the policy implications explicit, and to set these implications within the broader employment and economic contexts.

We proceed by acknowledging that career policies were originally developed for, and explain their continuing pre-occupation with, children and young people. We then review the past careers and current situations of the over-45s: how women's earlier working lives have typically been affected by their own changing life situations and simultaneously by macro-economic and employment trends. The chapter concludes with some complications posed by these wider contexts.

Career policies for the young

Career information, advice and guidance services, as well as mainstream education and training, were originally introduced primarily for children and young people who have remained the priority targets and recipients. This is despite the now long-standing acknowledgement that jobs for life have become scarcer, and that the pace of economic and technological change requires more and more people to restart, retrain, top-up and upgrade qualifications and skills recurrently. Even so, education, training and career services have become more front-loaded than ever before. This situation is easily explained:

- In most countries beginning workers are at above-average risk of unemployment which can leave long-term career scars and huge costs for the individuals, their families and their wider societies.
- Most parents want their children at least to equal and if possible to exceed their own educational attainments.

- This pressure to expand education is amplified by young people themselves, who appreciate the importance of starting their working lives as well-qualified as possible. Many gain personal insights into the decline in the quantity and quality of employment open to poorly-qualified early-leavers.
- The student status and lifestyle have intrinsic, immediate attractions.
- Young people are attractive to employers seeking to train novices because the young are flexible and cheap – prepared to accept internships, minimum pay and even lower training allowances.

In Chapter 4, Catherine Earl and her colleagues note that employment policies that address women's gender-specific interests are nearly always aimed at young women who can benefit from maternity leave, the right to return, family-friendly employment regimes and the right to request flexible hours. The interests of older women do not receive equal or even any consideration. These gender sensitive policies have tended to amplify rather than redress the focus on the young.

Non-linear careers

The work histories of most women whose voices are heard in the previous chapters had been non-linear, meaning that the women had taken career pauses, and/or had moved sideways into new occupations, and sometimes backwards, on one or more occasions. This applied even in Germany, where labour markets are regulated and occupationalised, and in the normal course of events people have been expected to base long-term careers on their initial education and vocational training. Simone Haasler (Chapter 13 this volume) argues that this German regime makes it more difficult to sidestep than, for example, in the UK and the USA, where labour market regulation is relatively weak and employers are able to hire and train whoever and however they wish. Yet the German system provides opportunities for formal retraining that are relatively rare in the UK and USA.

Women's family careers often disrupt their employment careers. There are many examples in previous chapters of women being unable to resume earlier careers, having taken breaks while caring for young children. Some women's careers had been unhinged by needing to relocate because their husbands' jobs required this. However, non-linearity has not been peculiar to women's twentieth-century work histories. In the UK, most of the young males who may have thought that they were being trained and becoming skilled for life after they left school in the 1960s were in entirely different occupations when they reached the age range of the women whose voices are in this book, and often long before then (see Goodwin and O'Connor 2007; Vickerstaff 2003).

All the countries featured in previous chapters had experienced major changes in their economies and occupational structures during the women's working lives. In China the women had been born when 80 per cent of the population lived in rural villages. By the time of the interviews, 50 per cent of China's population was urban, and before all the women interviewees die the country may well have become 80 per cent urban. The women whose careers are reported by Ying Kuang

(Chapter 11 this volume) had lived through China's Cultural Revolution in the late-1960s and early-1970s, followed by waves of market reform from 1978 onwards. These changes had undermined many careers. In South Africa (see Mark Watson's account in Chapter 16 this volume), the women had been born and educated under apartheid and had celebrated the subsequent arrival of new freedoms and opportunities, but most Black South Africans were still awaiting personal career benefits when Nelson Mandela died in 2013. In Portugal, Filomena Parada and colleagues (Chapter 15 this volume) describe how the women who were interviewed had grown up under Salazar's version of fascism, experienced the birth of democracy in 1974, accession to European Union (its current name) in 1986, the subsequent economic boom, then the implosion that followed the 2008 international banking crisis and the ensuing Eurozone crisis. Pamela Suzanne (Chapter 8 this volume) describes Argentina's comparable recent turbulent history: a period of military dictatorship from 1976 to 1983, followed by a return to democracy and a succession of economic crises including the hyper-inflation of 1988–90, and the frozen bank accounts and default on international debts in 2001, then slow recovery. Men's and women's careers alike were liable to have been disrupted during all the above turbulent national histories.

It is therefore surprising that some women in some of the countries (mainly Portugal) had experienced linear careers. This is a reminder that just as there never really was an era when most people occupied 'jobs for life', there are still some such jobs, mainly in public services such as education and health care. Also, in contrast to the experiences of the urban women in China, in Ying Kuang's account (Chapter 11 this volume), at the time of her fieldwork, around a half of the country's population still lived in rural villages. In India, where the booming cities and their new middle classes receive most international attention, Undurti Vindhya (Chapter 3 this volume) tells us that around 85 per cent of all women workers are still engaged informally in agriculture. In the south of Italy Massimo Tomassini (Chapter 14 this volume) explains that there are still women whose adult lives are wholly domestic and family-oriented. Globally, and within countries, there have been and continue to be huge differences in people's experiences of working life, and even in Europe there are places where men and women continue to spend their lives in traditional occupations. However, throughout the world young people are leaving these traditional locations and migrating to cities in search of modern occupations and lifestyles (see Hansen 2008).

All the economically advanced countries featured in this book had completed the transition from industrialism into post-industrialism during the careers of the women who were interviewed. Employment had shifted from manufacturing into service sectors. By the beginning of the twenty-first century, services accounted for over 80 per cent of all employment in some of these countries. During this change, manual jobs had been lost and employment in management and professional occupations had grown. Industry-based working classes had become minorities rather than the mass of the labour forces. In the early- and mid-twentieth century, employment in lower-level office jobs expanded, and absorbed huge numbers of women workers. Subsequently, with the introduction of information and communication technologies, these occupations have contracted. The net result has been hour-glass-shaped, hollowed-out occupational structures. Middling skilled manual jobs in manufacturing and lower-level non-manual jobs have been lost (see Kalleberg 2011).

Sometimes, as in the account by Doris Eikhof and Chris Warhurst in Chapter 5, the outcome is described as more good jobs and more lousy jobs. Women who were formerly employed in middling occupations, and those who would formerly have entered such jobs on leaving education, have often needed either to move up or risk demotion. However, Eikhof and Warhurst's main argument is that some former good jobs have gone bad, while some former bad jobs have become even worse. The explanation lies in globalisation: freer movement between countries of goods, services and (most importantly) capital. This has heightened competition and facilitated the financialisation of capitalism (see Lapvitsas 2011). This latter development, with the owners of capital moving funds between firms and countries in search of the best returns, has been facilitated and accelerated by the use of information and communication technologies, and has contributed to the demise of the organisational career as discussed by Polly Parker and Amanda Roan in Chapter 6. Large enterprises have ceased to be reliable, solid fixtures in local economies. Most kinds of work have become easier to relocate to places with lower labour costs and/or lower taxes on corporate earnings. Senior managers cannot guarantee anyone's jobs, even their own, because at any time their firms can be taken-over or merged, and everyone's jobs might then be eliminated. Hence the all-round erosion of job security.

The good jobs that have 'gone bad' include Silicon Valley-type occupations and other jobs in creative industries whose main asset is intellectual property rights. These jobs include the production of software and other content for old and new media. There are now surpluses of qualified labour seeking all these jobs. Employment is increasingly tied to projects rather than permanent. Employees must expect to spend periods between projects during which they must keep their skills updated and maintain their professional contacts (see Benner 2002; Hesmondhalgh and Baker 2010; McKinlay and Smith 2009; Siebert and Wilson 2013). Meanwhile, many poor jobs have become worse. More are paid at or close to countries' minimum rates. More of the jobs are part-time. Some employees have zero-hours contracts. This means that no hours are guaranteed but employees are expected to be on-call, available if and when the employer requires them. Temporary work has become more common. Guy Standing (2011) has charted the spread across Europe of this new 'precariat', which he describes as a 'dangerous class'. The overarching context, which makes all these developments possible, is huge global surpluses of labour with all levels of qualifications (see Brown *et al.* 2011). If labour does not migrate to the jobs, then the jobs can be migrated.

Men's and women's careers have been vulnerable in the face of these changes. Employment is increasingly regulated by global markets rather than by national governments. These governments have become mere conduits for global market signals. We shall return below to how this has reduced governments' ability to implement efficacious employment and career policies.

Agency and opportunity from the viewpoints of older workers

The career stories in previous chapters illustrate the variety of career situations that have been faced by older women workers, over the period of their working lives. In the later years of their career trajectories, it is apparent that some of the women were 'hanging on' to what had been long-term linear careers. Others had become dislodged. Some had made several restarts during their working lives. Others were trying to get back in. A few had effectively withdrawn from the labour market. The same spectrum of career situations would be found among a male sample in the same age group, albeit with a different distribution across the different career situations.

The career stories challenge the view that older workers are inflexible. Many of the women had been flexible throughout their working lives. Women, probably more so than men, need to be adaptable. When interviewed, many were studying, adding to their qualifications. This applied among the Canadian immigrant women, all of whom had been, and still were, under-employed relative to their qualifications (Chapter 10 this volume). Nancy Arthur explains that none had given up. They were determined to continue to struggle. The case studies also show that older women workers are willing, if necessary, to 'step down' into inferior jobs to those they held in the past. They accept that it is unlikely that their existing skills and experience will transfer directly and wholesale into new occupations. Older workers are realists. They have all seen what happened to workers older than themselves. Financial pressures required many of the women in this book to continue working for as long as they were able to do so. They needed to remain in employment to meet their current households' living costs and also, if possible, to save towards retirement.

Massimo Tomassini (Chapter 14 this volume) describes women in the late-career stage as a sandwiched group. Some among his Italian sample were still caring for grown-up children who remained at home, while also assisting with the care of grandchildren and sometimes taking on responsibility for the care of older relatives. Amid all this, they were trying to retain employment and usually needed to do so for financial reasons, among others. It would have been easy for them to quit, but the evidence in this book indicates that older women strongly prefer remaining in employment and coping with their sandwiched situations rather than being squeezed out of the labour market.

There appears to be just one way in which older women (and probably older men also) are less flexible than the young: the former are less able and willing to relocate. They are rarely able to countenance moving their entire households and have no intention of becoming separated from their families. Anne Green (Chapter 2 this volume) reminds us that there are huge geographical differences within all countries in levels of employment and unemployment, and in the total number and variety of jobs that are available. People who live in large metropolitan areas find it relatively easy to change jobs without moving address. Those in smaller towns have narrower options. This, of course, applies to both women and men, and men aged 50-plus will experience many of the same pressures as women. They will want to remain in employment and, as 'main family breadwinners', will feel that they must do so for financial reasons.

The gender dimension

The contributors from all the countries in this book report increases over time in the proportions of women in employment. However, we should not be misled into thinking that the working woman is a historical novelty. In pre-industrial times it was normal for women and girls to work in their homes and in the fields. It was during the early industrial era, when paid work was relocated from homes into mines, factories, and offices that men normally became family providers and women's main roles became domestic – reproductive rather than productive. This lasted until contraception, lower birth rates, and the expansion of service sector jobs, which were considered more suitable for women than heavy extractive and industrial occupations, led to a progressive rise in the proportion of women holding paid jobs outside their homes. In the economically advanced countries, this trend began before, then continued throughout, the working lives of the women whose voices are in the earlier chapters of this book. Labour market participation within this female cohort had not necessarily risen as the women grew older. It was rather a case of these women overall having higher lifetime employment rates than their mothers, and the women's daughters having still higher rates.

Globally women have been closing gaps:

- Their employment rates have risen towards male levels.
- Their educational attainments now exceed those of males in many countries, and in employment they have closed the gaps with men's skill and occupational levels.
- The overall gaps between men's and women's earnings have been closing.

However, there is still no country in which parity has been achieved. There is still horizontal and vertical occupational segmentation everywhere, meaning that some jobs are still performed mainly by men and other jobs are performed mainly by women. This division of labour is always to women's overall disadvantage: they still tend to be lower paid, in more junior posts, and in jobs that are more precarious than those occupied by men.

That said, as noted above, occupational structures have been polarising into hourglass profiles. Many women today are in higher-paid management and professional jobs. Highly educated women are over-represented among the voices in most of this book's chapters. In England (see Chapter 12 this volume, by Jenny Bimrose) four of the women were earning £50,000 a year or more. This meant that they were within the top 10 per cent of all income tax payers. Maybe these women could be described as disadvantaged compared with men with equal qualifications, but the women were hugely advantaged vis-à-vis most female and most male employees. Well-qualified women who build careers in management and the professions will seek parity with male peers, but at the bottom of polarised labour forces this kind of parity will be less appealing. Women's main complaint is more likely to be about the quantity and quality of the jobs to which both they and any male partners have access.

What do (older) women want? There is plenty of evidence in this book that women do not speak with a single voice. There are differences between and within countries. Women do not all seek to build the same kinds of lives. In many countries today an expanding proportion of women aim for continuous full-time occupational careers, like most men. They take maternity leave rather than exiting employment. However, these women are still a minority. Other women, a declining proportion in most countries, are content to be full-time housewives and do not seek paid employment following child-bearing until their children have grown up. Some argue that in most post-industrial countries the largest group of women seek 'balanced' lives, in which their commitment to the labour market is weaker than is normal among men, meaning that the women seek to work and actually work fewer hours and/or less continuously (see Hakim 1999). Overall gender parity remains elusive, but it is quite likely that the minority of women who currently work like men are already equalling men's career achievements. If so, the problems of women at successive career stages (those which are not general labour market problems, on which more will follow) will owe more to age than gender.

Agency, opportunity, and later life career transitions

Workers do not need special career services geared to age-specific needs. Their requirements are no different across their lifespan (than those of other age groups). Older workers may benefit from (though they will not necessarily need) employment exchange services, plus professional career information, advice, and guidance. Young people are more likely to need and benefit from a professional career services. Rather than using public or commercial employment exchanges, older workers are more likely to use their own professional and personal social networks. The same applies to seeking information and advice. Personal and professional networks are more likely to offer customised assistance than public career services for all-comers. None of the women's voices in previous chapters called for enhanced career services.

Nowadays the age-specific career problems and opportunities of the 50-plus age group are most likely to arise from the recent de-institutionalisation of the life course (see Kohli *et al*. 1992). This is a trend that has affected post-industrial and late-developing societies alike. Older chronological milestones have been broken. At one time there was a retirement age. Until they reached this age, people were expected and could confidently expect to remain in employment. Some looked forward optimistically to this great event and the advent of their 'golden years', while others feared the step into the unknown. Deniers preferred not to think about what was to happen. Nowadays it is different. People retire at a variety of ages, often via a series of steps rather than one huge leap (see Vickerstaff and Cox 2005). This applies in Europe, North America, Australia and also in India, China, Africa, and Latin America. During this transitional life stage, people are exposed to different and often contradictory pressures and expectations. They are likely to feel too young to be fully retired, but too old to make further career progress and, if dislodged from their main lifetime careers, too old to obtain further jobs that are commensurate with their experience (see Young and Schuller 1991). Plans that individuals make are liable to be blown off course by changes in their employers' human resource requirements and policies, and sometimes by changes in health (Vickerstaff and Cox 2005).

Formerly, older employees knew that they had to continue to work even if their careers had stalled. They had to continue working, doing time, until their release (retirement) dates. The difference today is that it has become possible for more people to retire earlier. Indeed, they may come under pressure to quit their main career jobs. Even if they want to do so, there is no longer an imperative to carry on. Firms that need to downsize invite applications for redundancy. Employees with many years of service can be offered generous packages: offers that look too good to refuse. We must note that it is mainly male employees who can be offered the generous packages. Women's interrupted careers, and episodes working part-time, leave them with inferior pension entitlements. Pension enhancement, permitting exit on a full pension, may be an additional inducement. For women, the enhancement will usually be inferior and from a smaller base pension. Even so, they may be encouraged and tempted to take 'the package'. Older workers who accept these packages may feel confident that, with their skills and experience, they will regain employment. They will be congratulated on their heroic sacrifice if they create space for youth by terminating their main careers. Those next in line can be promoted. At the bottom of the chain there will be a vacancy for a new starter. Older employees suspect, probably know, that their employers and junior employees hope that they will 'take the package'. From 1979 until 1987, the UK government operated a Job Release Scheme which offered financial inducements when older employees quit and enabled a job to be offered to an unemployed young person.

However, there are contradictory pressures and expectations today. People are living longer. Governments and private pension fund managers need to balance income and spending. So employees are being encouraged to increase the amounts that they invest in 'pension pots'. Governments and private pension schemes are currently raising the ages at which full pensions can be drawn. So older employees are expected to work longer. Due to the pension gap (males' entitlements generally exceed those of females), women may feel the greater need to carry on. Employers are aware that older workers have much to offer. They are often in excellent health, have much relevant experience, and have track records that prove their reliability. They will not become entitled to maternity or paternity leave. They will not expect 40-year careers. The problem for older employees is the expectation that they will restart their working lives on junior salaries, drop down career chains and expect zero prospects of promotion. Professional employees may become self-employed 'consultants'. Skilled workers may set up new businesses. The success stories are counter-balanced by those who struggle to stay afloat. It can be demeaning. Job-hunting is frustrating: streams of ignored and rejected applications. Work is normally good for personal well-being (see Haworth 1997), but if older people have finances and interests that enable them to build lives outside paid work, this can do more for their well-being than endless job-hunting, then accepting occupational demotion (Jackson and Taylor 1994).

De-institutionalisation of the life course does not just permit but requires workers to make more choices. There are options, but often none of the options look attractive. Doris Eikhof and Chris Warhurst (Chapter 5 this volume) write about how good jobs have gone bad and bad jobs have become even worse. In later career stages the dilemma faced by increasing numbers of women and men is that what could be a win-win has become a lose-lose choice. Staying in a main career has become a struggle. Quitting means risking status, and also risking a long retirement on an inadequate income and becoming a dependent on, rather than a supporter of, state welfare and family.

Conclusion

Demand for career services looks certain to grow. This is not because career information, advice and guidance will deliver the ideal outcomes that the age group seeks. It is because none of their first resort personal and professional networks will deliver. So clients will seek independent authoritative advice with which to be agentic, setting themselves realisable goals.

We are in an era in which employment policies have become subordinate to economic policies, which are currently regulated by global markets. Finance ministries are in charge of economic policies that include interest rates and money supply, though these matters are likely to have been delegated to central banks, which are supposed to be more sensitive to global economic indicators than elected politicians. Finance ministries are also responsible for taxation and levels of public spending. In today's global economy, currency exchange rates are set by markets. Employment ministries are responsible for employment law, employment services, and manage in-work and out-of-work welfare benefits for the economically active population. Levels of employment and unemployment are set by markets.

During the 30 years that followed the Second World War, employment policies took precedence. Full employment was the priority and economic policy was subservient. National governments took charge of their nations' economies. Neo-liberal globalisation has subsequently placed markets in overall charge. This has occurred alongside a huge expansion in the global workforce as labour has been drawn from traditional sectors into the emerging market economies' cities and modern business sectors. Population growth and rising rates of female labour market participation have also contributed. Labour supply has outstripped demand, and in this context the proportion of global GDP accounted for by wages and salaries has fallen. Unemployment rates have risen in the Western and former Communist countries, where full employment was maintained from the 1940s up to the 1970s. Levels of joblessness are checked only by depressing wages to subsistence levels, and increasing the proportion of jobs that are part-time, temporary, or otherwise precarious, which leads to welfare regimes that maintain beneficiaries in rather than lifting them clear of poverty. Young people spend extended periods in transition between education and adult employment. Older workers try to avoid or alternatively cope with tattered conclusions to their working lives. Needless to say, the avoiders tend to be in the top segments of hour-glass-shaped occupational structures.

Career policy cannot change this situation. Nor do clients expect this. Responsibility for outcomes is privatised, and likewise the rewards for winning and the penalties for losing. In this situation, career information, advice, and guidance can ensure that individuals feel that they have explored all possible options and are not culpable through failing to choose wisely. Maybe the best advice for careers services to echo to all age groups is that recommended by the voices of the older women in this book. They are unanimous in urging younger women to choose occupations that they really like, to do something that makes them feel good, then to persist and to be resilient. I doubt if anyone will resent receiving and following this advice. Careers advisers themselves can learn by listening to the voices of older clients.

References

Benner, C. (2002) *Work in the New Economy: Flexible Labor Markets in Silicon Valley*, Oxford: Blackwell.
Brown, P., Lauder, H. and Ashton, D. (2011) *The Global Auction: The Broken Promises of Education, Jobs and Incomes*, Oxford: Oxford University Press.
Goodwin, J. and O'Connor, H. (2007) 'Continuity and change in the experience of transition from school to work', *International Journal of Lifelong Education*, 26: 555–72.
Hakim, C. (1999) 'Models of the family, women's roles and social policy', *European Societies*, 1: 33–58.
Hansen, K.T. (2008) 'Introduction: Youth and the city', in K.T. Hansen with A. L. Dalsgaard (eds) *Youth and the City in the Global South*, Bloomington, IN: Indiana University Press, pp. 3–23.
Haworth, J.T. (1997) *Work, Leisure and Well-Being*, London: Routledge.
Hesmondhalgh, D. and Baker, S. (2010) *Creative Labour: Media Work in Three Cultural Industries*, Routledge, London.
Jackson, P. R. and Taylor, P. E. (1994) 'Factors associated with employment status in later working life', *Work, Employment and Society*, 8: 553–67.
Kalleberg, A. (2011) *Good Jobs, Bad Jobs: The Rise of Polarized and Precarious Employment Systems in the United States, 1970s–2000s*, New York: Russell Sage Foundation.
Kohli, M., Rein, M., Guillemard, A.-M. and Gunsteren, H. van (1992) *Time for Retirement*, Cambridge: Cambridge University Press.
Lapavitsas, C. (2011) 'Theorising financialisation', *Work, Employment and Society*, 25: 611–26.
McKinlay, A. and Smith, C. (eds) (2009) *Creative Labour: Working in the Creative Industries*, Basingstoke: Palgrave Macmillan.
Siebert, B. and Wilson, F. (2013) 'All work and no pay: Consequences of unpaid work in the creative industries', *Work, Employment and Society*, 27: 711–21.
Standing, G. (2011) *The Precariat: The New Dangerous Class*, London: Sage.
Vickerstaff, S. A. (2003) 'Apprenticeships in the "golden age": Were youth transitions really smooth and unproblematic back then?", *Work, Employment and Society*, 17: 269–87.
Vickerstaff, S. and Cox, J. (2005) 'Retirement and risk: The individualisation of retirement experiences', *Sociological Review*, 53: 77–95.
Young, M. and Schuller, T. (1991) *Life After Work*, London: Harper Collins.

21 Implications for career practice

Mary McMahon, Mark Watson and Jenny Bimrose

In beginning this chapter on implications for career practice, it is sobering, in view of our passion for career guidance, to reflect on its limited use by the women during the course of their careers and its absence from their advice to others. While the absence of, or limited reference to, career guidance and counselling by the women in the nine participating countries may be explained where career guidance has not traditionally held a place in society (e.g. China, South Africa), in other countries where it has been available to citizens for many years and where lifelong guidance is advocated (e.g. England, Canada, Australia), it is less easy to explain. Paradoxically, the women's stories also illustrate instances of career decision making and career transition where career guidance may have been beneficial.

The women's stories clearly explicate the recursive intertwining of their paid employment with other facets of their lives (e.g. parenting) and with the cultural and contextual locations of their stories. Simply stated, 'careers are always careers in context' (Mayrhofer *et al.* 2007: 215). The inseparability of person, culture, and context (at multiple levels) portrayed in the women's stories delivers a clear message to a field that has been criticised for oversimplifying practice by neglecting context and suggests that emergent holistic models and approaches are likely to better accommodate the complexity of women's career trajectories.

Related to the contextual location of the women's stories, another sobering message with implications for practice that resonates throughout these stories regards the long-term, deeply entrenched systemic disadvantages that women have experienced and continue to experience in the labour market. The causes of such disadvantages are multileveled and range from policy-level decisions, to cultural traditions, to workplace culture and include the intersection of such factors.

It is timely therefore, in the context of this chapter and of this book, to learn and to reflect on the possible implications for career practice of the women's stories. The chapter concludes by considering possible futures for career practice.

Learning from the women's stories

Listening to the stories of the women provided a powerful insight into 'women's working lives' (Patton 2013: 3). In essence, the women told rich stories that testify to their capacity to manage their lives in ways that accommodated both market work (paid employment) and care work (unpaid care work in families and communities; Richardson et al. Chapter 19 this volume) which, across time, demanded varying degrees of attention and a range of responses. In so doing, the women displayed a range of career management skills and personal qualities that are consistent with recent theoretical accounts of career development (e.g. see Patton 2013) and competency frameworks that inform career practice such as the Canadian Blueprint for Life/Work Designs (Haché et al. 2006) and the Australian Blueprint for Career Development (Ministerial Council for Education, Early Childhood Development and Youth Affairs 2010). For example, the women referred to personal qualities such as adaptability, responsiveness, resilience, and the ability to prioritise as essential to managing their lives. In the career field, such qualities (e.g. adaptability and resilience) have gained some prominence and have come to be regarded more as psychological traits that can be measured (see Porfeli and Savickas 2012). By contrast, the women's stories provided nuanced and individual manifestations of such qualities that suggest their complexity may not be easily quantified as well as the importance of qualitative understanding.

Recent theory and practice has emphasised the importance of personal agency in constructing careers as reflected in the question: 'How may individuals best design their own lives in the human society in which they live?' (Savickas et al. 2009: 4). Agency, as it is conceptualised in career development and in career counselling, primarily concerns determining a course of action about learning and/or market work (Richardson et al. Chapter 19; Richardson and Schaeffer 2013) that advantages individuals and has potential for satisfaction, success, and meaningful careers. Agency is seldom, if at all, discussed in relation to decisions about care work, which supports contentions that the career field has paid little attention to a broad understanding of work in all its forms (Blustein 2006; 2011; Richardson et al. Chapter 19 this volume).

The women's stories illustrated their personal agency in designing their lives through their decisions and actions, with Domboza from South Africa claiming 'I am my own driver in life' (Watson, Chapter 16 this volume). However, the women's stories also contextually located such agency in relation to their personal needs and the preferences and needs of others. Although the women could be regarded as agentic, in many cases their decisions and actions were predicated on the needs of others and therefore agency was qualified by their values (e.g. valuing care for children over paid employment) and cultural traditions. Thus, many of the decisions made by the women were to the detriment of their own paid employment or learning, but concerned their commitment to their families. For example, Lorraine from Australia told a story similar to those of other women about being the primary carer of her children when she explained how her job was 'second place' and that she was 'just supplementing the income and so if I never really attained what I really wanted it was not that detrimental ... you just worked for the family' (McMahon, Chapter 9 this volume). Similarly an immigrant woman from Canada told stories of how 'I left a good position ... a good life to come to ... to Canada' (Arthur, Chapter 10 this volume) and Umberta from Italy told how she had left her university study to assist her family after an earthquake and subsequently 'was unable to begin a student life again' and 'left the university' (Tomassini, Chapter 14 this volume). In the Chinese context, Rong explained how she met her filial responsibilities by doing the dangerous and tiring work of carrying wood for more than a year 'to help my parents to keep our big family' (Kuang, Chapter 11 this volume). This more nuanced and contextualised understanding of agency in relation to both market work and care work raises questions about the present usage of contemporary career constructs in relation to women's careers and their relevance in all contexts. Moreover, it suggests a recursive relationship between agency and the notion of subjective careers which may be simply and usefully defined as 'the individual's own interpretation of his or her own career situation at any given time' (Khapova *et al.* 2006: 2). As reflected in the stories, many of the women engaged in holistic interpretations of their market work and care work, and made agentic decisions on the basis of their values, culture, or the needs of others rather than the visible trappings of market work such as promotion or income.

The women's stories clearly highlighted the importance of the subjective career, which throughout the history of the career field has been afforded less importance and attention than objective careers by theorists, researchers, and practitioners. Objective careers are more concerned with observable and measureable markers and positions and visible activities, behaviours, and events. By contrast, subjective careers are more concerned with a personal sense of career and of being and becoming. The elements of subjective careers include less tangible and less visible perceptions, attitudes, and orientations. There has been awareness for over 80 years of the importance of subjective careers with Hughes (1937: 410) explaining that 'subjectively, a career is the moving perspective in which the person sees his (sic) life as a whole and interprets the meaning', and how 'in the course of a career the person finds his (sic) place ... carries on his (sic) active life with reference to other people, and interprets the meaning of the one life he (sic) has to live' (Hughes, 1937: 413). This whole of life conceptualisation by Hughes suggests that paid employment as well as other forms of work could be accommodated in understandings of the subjective career.

A more recent account of the subjective career explains that it 'emerges from thought or mental activity that constructs a story about one's working life' and that it imposes 'meaning and direction on vocational behavior' (Savickas 2013: 150); this suggests a less holistic conceptualisation, with more of a focus on market work. The dominance in the career field of a focus on market work and the objective career focus has resulted in the silencing of longstanding calls for greater emphasis on subjective careers (e.g. Collin 1986; Khapova *et al.* 2006) including emotion (e.g. Kidd 2004). Such dominance is multifaceted as reflected by the statistical presentation of labour market information (e.g. occupational segregation; pay gap; employment contracts), and career assessment, which has emphasised the measurement of personal traits, linear and rational models of career decision making, and quantitative research methods. By contrast, the career trajectories of the women were frequently determined by their values (e.g. family values) rather than congruence with personal traits, and their stories offered insight into the personal impact of systemic labour market disadvantage that is not reflected in statistics. Thus the notion of subjective career seems particular apposite to many of the stories told by the women and has implications for career guidance practice.

The systemic nature of labour market disadvantage and discrimination illustrated in many of the stories invites us to consider the ethical position of career practitioners providing career services for women. For example, labour shortages in science, technology, engineering, and mathematics fields have seen young women being encouraged to enter these fields, many of which are male dominated. The stories of Sue, Sam, and Debbie from England contextualise the potential ethical dilemmas for career guidance practitioners preparing and supporting women, especially young women, to enter such fields (Bimrose 2004), as the discrimination that could occur in such industries can be profoundly damaging personally and professionally. So how do career practitioners navigate the potential ethical dilemmas of supporting young women to enter such fields, or indeed any young person as discrimination is not limited only to these fields or to young women? How do career practitioners prepare young women for the labour market and financial disadvantage of combining market work and care work? In this regard, Bimrose (ibid.: 115) asks whether career practitioners should 'confine themselves to working with individual clients or should they work also with the structures in which clients make and implement their career decisions'. Such a question is challenging for a field that is steeped in the psychological traditions of working with individuals rather than on changing or influencing the systemic structures in which clients are located. Indeed, Bimrose contends that not to address such issues may constitute 'unethical guidance practice' (ibid.: 119).

In a field with a long history of commitment to social justice (e.g. Parsons 1909), it is curious that the training of career practitioners generally does not include the skills and knowledge related to advocacy or systemic interventions. However the women's stories provide examples of where systemic interventions may have been useful. For instance, the example of immigrant workers' qualifications not being recognised by governments, employers, and professional bodies suggests that advocacy from the career profession as a whole may be warranted. Other stories suggest that systemic advocacy by individual career practitioners may be useful. For example, a career practitioner may be able to advocate with employers for clients like Carmen from Canada, who explained that despite anti-discrimination laws, 'it's still the employer's choice who they'll hire.' Preparing career practitioners for advocacy and systemic interventions has been advocated (e.g. Arthur and McMahon 2005; Bimrose and McNair 2011; McMahon et al. 2010) with some authors suggesting that systemic interventions may foster better work environments and access to role models and mentors (e.g. August 2011; Cook et al. 2002a).

Systemic interventions indicate the need to take holistic views of individuals and their careers as reflected in theoretical propositions based on ecological (e.g. Cook et al. 2002b) and systems theory (e.g. Patton and McMahon 2014). Consistent with the women's stories, such theoretical frameworks emphasise the importance of considering the cultural and contextual location of career guidance, reminding us that career guidance is a deeply cultural exchange. For example, Argentina has a long tradition of people accessing therapists for assistance with life decisions

(Suzanne, Chapter 8 this volume) whereas in the South African context, Esona explained how cultural tradition would influence people to seek advice and support from 'closer to home' through their extended families even if services were available (Watson, Chapter 16 this volume). Indeed, Arulmani (2014: 81) reminds us that 'career itself is a culture-bound concept with specific historical and economic connotations'. Similarly, the foundation of the career field in psychological science is also 'a by-product of the Western tradition, fashioned by particular cultural and historical conditions' (Gergen et al. 1996: 496). Thus the internationalisation of the career profession warrants careful attention and sensitivity to ensure contextual and cultural resonance (McMahon et al. 2014).

As career guidance has gained greater international prominence, developing countries such as South Africa, India, and China have begun to focus some attention on the development and provision of career services. Kumar (2013) however, reminds us of the dearth of an appropriately trained workforce in developing countries that can deliver culturally resonant career services. This has resulted in the import of Western theories and models, predominantly from the United States, into countries and cultures where they may lack cultural resonance in several important ways, such as a lack of understanding of the social and political value structures, labour market contexts, and institutional infrastructures that were outlined in a resource book for policy makers considering career services in lower and middle-income countries (Hansen 2006). Social and political value structures, such as cultural values, the position of work in society, attitudes towards change and mobility, the role of family and community, the hierarchy of occupational status, the influence of socio-economic status, reward structures, and the communication of values and information are central to considering differences between developed and developing countries (ibid.). Further, the characteristics of the labour market, such as the prevalence of unemployment, underemployment, and poverty, the sectoral structure, the dominance of an informal economic structure, demographic factors, the impact of globalisation, migration and urbanisation (ibid.), have profound implications for career practice. Moreover, the limitations of institutional infrastructure in low- and middle-income countries, such as inadequate resources (e.g. career information) and equipment (e.g. access to information technology facilities), and personnel with little or no background in the career field fundamentally challenge its introduction to such countries.

While Hansen (2006) emphasises these factors in the context of low- and middle-income countries, the uniqueness of such factors in all countries reminds us that adopting practices from one setting into another risks their cultural and contextual relevance (Watson 2013). Thus, the tendency for some international (predominantly Western) training organisations to see developing countries as potential markets for their training products needs to be tempered with restraint and caution. Just as the extant theories and practices were nurtured in particular contexts, so too must other contexts seeking to develop career guidance services have the opportunity to do so in ways that best meet their needs. However, in a field dominated by Western traditions and English language literature, there are few voices to be heard from such contexts, leaving Hou and Zhang (2007: 47) to express concern about the 'voicelessness' of authors who are less proficient in English.

Possible futures for career guidance practice

In this regard, it is timely to reflect on three questions posed about the future of career guidance couched in terms of vocational psychology: 'Where should new knowledge for vocational psychology come from? How do career theories and research find their way into practice? What is the nature of career development and vocational choice in a global economy?' (Reardon et al. 2011: 241). In considering possible responses to such questions it is apposite to turn to voices from non-Western as well as Western contexts. At a fundamental level, the women's stories are reflective of concerns about the field's emphasis on personal variables rather than contextual and cultural variables; self-actualisation and job-satisfaction as goals of career choice; and high levels of free choice and opportunities to make several decisions over time (Leung and Yuen 2012).

Placing greater emphasis on culture and context in career guidance may go some way to addressing such concerns. Indeed, a number of authors (e.g. Arthur 2008; Arulmani 2010, 2011, 2014; Collins and Arthur 2010a, 2010b; Leong 2007; Watson 2010a, 2010b; Watson et al. 2011; Watson and Fouche 2007) have emphasised the centrality of culture in career guidance, with Stead and Perry (2012: 59) advocating that career guidance should be viewed as a 'cultural enterprise'. In relation to indigenous populations, Mkhize (2012) emphasises the importance of worldviews in relation to balance and harmony, interconnectedness, communal consciousness, the moral and ethical nature of being, balancing multiple identities, the dialogic conception of personhood, conceptions of time, and alternative approaches to decision making. A broad definition of culture is advocated. Collins and Arthur (2010a, 2010b) propose that career practitioners become aware of their own personal cultural identity and that, in a culturally sensitive working alliance, they develop cultural awareness of their client by understanding their worldview.

Consideration of the future of career guidance practice needs to be understood in the context of the theory base from which it is informed. In particular, for over half a century, the capacity of career theory to provide an adequate account of women's careers has been questioned (Bimrose 2008; Gilligan 1979; Patton 1997) and attempts to provide more appropriate accounts have been proffered (e.g. Astin 1984; August 2011; Psathas 1968; Super 1957) most recently by Richardson (e.g. Richardson and Schaeffer 2013; Richardson et al. Chapter 19 this volume), who has advocated a dual model of working lives that values both market work (paid employment) and care work (unpaid care work in home, families, and communities) that may be applied to women and to men. It has become increasingly apparent that career theory does not adequately account for the majority of the world's people (Blustein 2006, 2011, Chapter 18 this volume). Indeed Blustein (Chapter 18 this volume) contends that 'women's experiences in developing and adjusting to their work lives ought to be the normative view in contemporary theory development'. Central to the critique of career theory have been its traditional emphasis on stages of career development, the assessment of traits, and its decontextualised nature. Thus caution is needed about developing practices and resources that are culture-based and cannot easily be transported to other contexts (Leung and Yuen 2012).

Consistent with recent trends in practice towards narrative approaches grounded in ecological and systemic models, career guidance that places value on relationships (e.g. Cook *et al.* 2002a) and stories (e.g. Blustein, Chapter 18 this volume; McMahon *et al.* 2013), and that provides safe spaces to tell stories may be most appropriate. However, a sense that career guidance practice may be headed in the right direction should not lead to complacency. While it is possible to identify several transition points in the career trajectories of the women when career guidance may have been useful to them that would suggest support for the concept of lifelong career guidance (see McMahon *et al.* 2013), it was also evident that the women negotiated these transitions, successfully in most cases, without career guidance. Only Silke from Germany had received support from guidance programmess and coaching and had found it encouraging and practical. Bárbara from Portugal profoundly sums up the women's approach to their career decision making and transitions: 'we use the resources we have' (Parada *et al.*, Chapter 15 this volume). For most of the women, such resources largely referred to their social networks, particularly their families. Despite the widespread use of social networks by the participants, Kay from Australia pointed out that 'you've got to do a lot of it on your own'. The stories of the women presented in this book reveal a much more fundamental issue for career guidance than which approach could best serve women; the stories raise questions about whether career guidance does have a place in women's lives.

Conclusion

The implications for career practice identified in the women's stories are considerable. Three sobering questions must be asked: (1) Does career guidance practice have a place in the careers of women and if so, what is that place? (2) Given the entrenched systemic disadvantages experienced by women from all countries in the study, what responsibility, if any, do career practitioners have in the promotion of social justice and social change? (3) Given diverse cultural contexts and the limited history of career guidance in non-Western and developing countries, how can career guidance be introduced in such a way to avoid the pitfalls of imposing Western models and practices? The reflections contained in this chapter not only have implications for practice but also profound implications concerning the training of career practitioners. No longer can career guidance practitioners be trained through a narrow and ethnocentric perspective (Arthur 2008); rather they must be prepared with a 'global mindset and an international outlook' (Leung and Yuen 2012: 86) that is aware and respectful of culture and context and systemic in its analysis of client issues. Moreover, career guidance practitioners must be trained in the skills that enable such a mindset and outlook to be implemented in practice.

While the learnings in this chapter have been derived from the career stories of older women, the implications have wider relevance for all client groups. The importance of critical engagement in practice to ensure its cultural and contextual sensitivity for every client is critical. In reflecting on these questions, a challenge for career practitioners is how to raise the profile of career practice so that it is not only visible, credible, and sought after, but also ethical and culturally and contextually resonant.

References

Astin, H. S. (1984) 'The meaning of work in women's lives: A sociosychological model of career choice and work behavior', *The Counseling Psychologist*, 12: 117–26.

Arthur, N. (2008) 'Qualification standards for career practitioners', in J. A. Athanasou and R. Van Esbroeck (eds) *International Handbook of Career Guidance*, London: Springer.

Arthur, N. and McMahon, M. (2005) 'Multicultural career counseling: Theoretical applications of the Systems Theory Framework', *The Career Development Quarterly*, 53: 208–22.

Arulmani, G. (2010) 'The internationalization of career counselling: Bridging cultural processes and labour market demands in India', *Asian Journal of Counselling*, 16: 149–70.

Arulmani, G. (2011) 'Striking the right note: The cultural preparedness approach to developing resonant career guidance programmes', *International Journal for Educational and Vocational Guidance*, 11: 79–93.

Arulmani, G. (2014) 'The cultural preparation process model and career development', in G. Arulmani, A. Bakshi, F. Leong and T. Watts (eds) *Handbook of Career Development*, New York: Springer.

August, R. A. (2011) 'Women's later life career development: Looking through the lens of the kaleidoscope career model', *Journal of Career Development*, 38: 208–36.

Bimrose, J. (2004) 'Sexual harassment in the workplace: An ethical dilemma for career guidance?', *British Journal of Guidance and Counselling*, 32(1): 109–23.

Bimrose, J. (2008) 'Guidance for Girls and Women', in J.A. Athanasou and Van Esbroeck, R. (eds) *International Handbook of Career Guidance*, London: Dordrecht Springer (1st ed.).

Bimrose, J. and McNair, S. (2011) 'Career support for migrants: Transformation or Adaptation?', *Journal of Vocational Behavior*, 78(3): 321–92.

Blustein, D. L. (2006) *The Psychology of Working: A New Perspective for Counseling, Career Development, and Public Policy*, Mahwah, NJ: Lawrence Erlbaum Associates.

Blustein, D. L. (2011) 'A relational theory of working', *Journal of Vocational Behavior*, 79: 1–17.

Collin, A. (1986) 'Career development: The significance of the subjective career', *Personnel Review*, 15: 22–8.

Collins, S. and Arthur, N. (2010a) 'Culture-infused counselling: A fresh look at a classic framework of multicultural counselling competence', *Counselling Psychology Quarterly*, 23: 203–16.

Collins, S. and Arthur, N. (2010b) 'Culture-infused counselling: A model for developing multicultural competence', *Counselling Psychology Quarterly*, 23: 217–33.

Cook, E. P., Heppner, M. J. and O'Brien, K. M. (2002a) 'Career development of women of colour and white women: Assumptions, conceptualization, and interventions from an ecological perspective', *The Career Development Quarterly*, 50: 291–305.

Cook, E. P., Heppner, M. J. and O'Brien, K. M. (2002b) 'Feminism and women's career development: An ecological perspective', in S. G. Niles (ed.) *Adult Career Development: Concepts, Issues and Practices*. Alexandria, VA: National Career Development Association (3rd ed.).

Gergen, K. J., Gulerce, A., Lock, A. and Misra, G. (1996) 'Psychological science in context', *American Psychologist*, 51: 496–503.

Gilligan, C. (1979) 'Woman's place in man's life cycle', *Harvard Educational Review*, 47: 481–517.

Haché, L., Redekopp, D. E. and Jarvis, P. S. (2006) 'Blueprint for life/work designs'. Available at: http://206.191.51.163/blueprint/components.cfm (accessed 13 June 2014).

Hansen, E. (2006) *Career Guidance: A Resource Book for Lower and Middle Income Countries*, Geneva, Switzerland: International Labour Organization.

Hou, Z. and Zhang, N. (2007) 'Counseling psychology in China', *Applied Psychology: An International Review*, 56(1): 33–50.

Hughes, E. C. (1937) 'Institutional office and the person', *American Journal of Sociology*, 43: 404–13.

Khapova, S. N., Arthur, M. B. and Wilderom, C. P. M. (2006) 'The subjective career in the knowledge economy', in H. Gunz and M. Peiperl (eds) *Handbook of Career Studies*, Thousand Oaks, CA: Sage.

Kidd, J. M. (2004) 'Emotion in career contexts: Challenges for theory and research', *Journal of Vocational Behavior*, 64: 441–55.

Kumar, S. (2013) 'Resources, strategies, and structures for establishing career services in developing countries: Illustrations from India', *Indian Journal of Career and Livelihood Planning*, 2(1): 15–32.

Leong, F. T. L. (2007) 'Cultural accommodation as method and metaphor', *American Psychologist*, 62: 916–27.

Leung, S. M. A. and Yuen, M. (2012) 'The globalization of en ethnocentric career theory and practice', in M. Watson and M. McMahon (eds) *Career Development: Global Issues and Challenges*, New York: Nova Science.

McMahon, M., Bimrose, J. and Watson, M. (2010) 'Older women's career development and social inclusion', *Australian Journal of Career Development*, 19(1): 63–70.

McMahon, M., Watson, M. and Bimrose, J. (2013) 'Older women's careers: Systemic perspectives', in W. Patton (ed.) *Conceptualising Women's Working Lives: Moving the Boundaries of Our Discourse*, Rotterdam, The Netherlands: Sense.

McMahon, M., Watson, M. and Patton, W. (2014) 'Context-resonant systems perspectives in career theory', in G. Arulmani, A. Bakshi, F. Leong and T. Watts (eds) *Handbook of Career Development*, New York: Springer.

Mayrhofer, W., Meyer, M. and Steyrer, J. (2007) 'Contextual issues in the study of careers', in H. Gunz and M. Peiperl (eds) *Handbook of Career Studies*, Thousand Oaks, CA: Sage.

Ministerial Council for Education, Early Childhood Development and Youth Affairs (2010) *Australian Blueprint for Career Development*. Canberra, Australia: Commonwealth of Australia. Available at: www.blueprint.edu.au/Portals/0/resources/Blueprint_v1.2_.pdf (accessed 13 June 2014).

Mkhize, N. (2012) 'Career counselling and indigenous populations', in M. Watson and M. McMahon (eds) *Career Development: Global Issues and Challenges*, New York: Nova Science.

Parsons, F. (1909) *Choosing a Vocation*, Boston, MA: Houghton-Mifflin.

Patton, W. (1997) 'Women's career development', in W. Patton and M. McMahon (eds) *Career Development in Practice: A Systems Theory Perspective*, North Sydney, Australia: New Hobsons Press.

Patton, W. (ed.) (2013) *Conceptualising Women's Working Lives: Moving the Boundaries of Our Discourse*, Rotterdam, The Netherlands: Sense.

Patton, W. and McMahon, M. (2014) *Career Development and Systems Theory: Connecting Theory and Practice*, Rotterdam, The Netherlands: Sense.

Porfeli, E. J. and Savickas, M. L. (2012) 'Career adapt-abilities scale: Construction reliability and measurement equivalence across 13 countries', *Journal of Vocational Behavior*, 661–73.

Psathas, G. (1968) 'Towards a theory of occupational choice for women', *Sociology and Social Research*: 253–68.

Reardon, R. C., Lenz, J. G., Sampson, Jr J. P. and Peterson, G. W. (2011) 'Big questions facing vocational psychology: A Cognitive Information Processing perspective', *Journal of Career Assessment*, 19: 240–50.

Richardson, M. S. and Schaeffer, C. (2013) 'Expanding the discourse: A dual model of working for women's (and men's) careers', in W. Patton (ed.) *Conceptualising Women's Working Lives: Moving the boundaries of Our Discourse*, Rotterdam, The Netherlands: Sense.

Richardson, M. S., Black, K. E. and Iwacki, Y. (2014) 'Implications for research' (this volume), in J. Bimrose, M. McMahon, and M. Watson (eds) *Women's Career Development Throughout the Lifespan: An International Exploration*, London: Routledge.

Savickas, M. L. (2013) 'Career construction theory and practice', in S. D. Brown and R. W. Lent (eds) *Career Development and Counseling: Putting Theory and Research to Work*, New York: Wiley (2nd ed.).

Savickas, M. L., Nota, L., Rossier, J., Dauwalder, J., Duarte, M. E., Guichard, J., Soresi, S., Van Esbroeck, R. and Van Vianen, A. E. M. (2009) 'Life designing: A paradigm for career construction in the 21st century' *Journal of Vocational Behavior*, 75: 239–50.

Stead, G. B. and Perry, J. C. (2012) 'Practice Trends, Social Justice and Ethics', in M. Watson and M. McMahon (eds) *Career Development: Global Issues and Challenges*, New York: Nova Science.

Super, D. E. (1957) *The Psychology of Careers*, New York: Harper and Row.

Tomassini, M. (2014) 'Voices of older women from Italy' (this volume), in J. Bimrose, M. McMahon and M. Watson (eds) *Women's Career Development Throughout the Lifespan: An International Exploration*, London: Routledge.

Watson, M. (2010a) 'Career psychology in South Africa: Addressing and redressing social justice', *Australian Journal of Career Development*, 19(1): 24–9.

Watson, M. (2010b) 'Transitioning contexts of career psychology in South Africa', *Asian Journal of Counselling*, 16(2): 133–48.

Watson, M. (2013) 'Deconstruction, reconstruction, co-construction: Career construction theory in a developing world context', *Indian Journal of Career and Livelihood Planning*, 2(1): 15–32.

Watson, M. B. and Fouche, P. (2007) 'Transforming a past into a future: Counselling psychology in South Africa', *Applied Psychology: International Review*, 56(1): 152–64.

Watson, M., McMahon, M., Mkhize, N., Schweitzer, R. and Mpofu, E. (2011) 'Career counselling people of African Ancestry', in E. Mpofu and L. Blokland (eds) *Counselling People of African Ancestry*, Cambridge: Cambridge University Press.

22 Epilogue

Jenny Bimrose, Mary McMahon and Mark Watson

It can be argued that the career field has now come of age, at least in many Western societies. Careers services have gained broad recognition and acceptance with the general public. Politicians also increasingly acknowledge their potential value in supporting the labour market transitions of vulnerable populations (for example, migrant populations and young people). This is not to deny, nor to underplay, its critics, with questions frequently raised about its efficacy, positive impact and value for money (where services are funded from the public purse). In the face of such criticisms, and in response to the growing demands for proof of its usefulness and effectiveness, a substantial and robust evidence base has been developed which continues to expand.

Professional associations have been established and become embedded in countries around the world, with some operating globally, supporting continuing professional development and providing leadership in the career field in crucial issues like codes of ethical practice, core competencies and standards for practice. A theoretical base for practice draws on a range of academic disciplines that provide frameworks to guide practice, though American models still dominate. Research agendas that attempt both to push back the frontiers of knowledge in the field and improve practice are probably more vibrant than ever before, with scholarship and collaboration an encouraging feature of an emerging research community.

While the origins of the career field can be traced largely to Western, capitalist societies, an increasing level of interest is being shown by developing countries seeking to espouse best practice, with a key motivating factor often being the aspiration to increase economic competitiveness. How career theory, research, policy and practice effectively accommodate fundamental cultural and contextual difference amongst potential clients and consumers of careers services in both developed and developing countries represents quite a challenge for the profession. Even though multicultural awareness of value systems that represent dramatic contrasts to the theoretical and practice approaches that have emerged from Western economies is undoubtedly growing amongst the career profession, this has not yet become a primary focus.

The primary target group for this book, women, currently occupy a marginal position in the career theory and practice across the world. Although data were collected from participants aged 45 to 65 in the nine country studies, it quickly became apparent that the retrospective and prospective reflections across their life courses illuminate the career trajectories of women of all ages, not just issues related to older women. The book therefore contributes to the knowledge base by challenging the profession to pay greater regard to the particular needs of marginalised groups, typically those occupying social positions of lower status and privilege than those sharing the demographic profile of the founding fathers of the careers profession.

A number of agendas have been addressed by this book. Chapters presented in Part I provide broad frameworks within which the position of women in contrasting social systems and contexts can be reviewed and evaluated. Multidisciplinary in approach, these chapters together provide frameworks for evaluating gender inequality drawn from a range of disciplines, including economics, sociology, geography, organisational and management studies. Critical analyses presented in each of these chapters are sensitive to the societal and/or organisational contexts from which they derive, yet there is the potential to transfer learning and insights gained across cultural and contextual boundaries. Part II presents research studies from the nine participating countries. These provide deep and rich insights into the ways in which women have navigated their career trajectories through contrasting social systems and across different historical periods. The qualitative methodology adopted across all country contexts adds to the broad understanding of cross-cultural research methodologies. It also provides vivid examples of the universal constraints operating on women's participation in labour markets across societies, spanning decades. Chapters in Part III ponder the implications of the research studies for career theory, research, policy and practice. Each contribution identifies challenges into how the career field could, and should, develop in the future in ways that better serve those for whom it exists. Moreover, these chapters suggest that through collective conversation and action, theorists, researchers, policy makers and practitioners could make a difference.

Unlike other books which "talk about" women, this book has provided a space for women from many countries to speak about their careers across their lifespans and to be heard. Their voices provide insight into a way forward for career theory, research, practice and policy and attest to the value of including women in discussions and debates about charting a way forward. Constructing a future for women that is not beset by the inequalities that have been so pervasive throughout history remains a challenge, but the graphic experiences depicted in this book through the stories of the women may serve as a motivation and for that, we thank them.

Index

Figures and tables are given in italics

Abercrombie and Fitch 58
adolescent girls 27
aesthetic labour 58–60
aestheticisation 58
age discrimination 2–4, 42, 56, 59, 95, 144–6, 190
agency 249–51, 254
Ainsworth, S. 59
Alexandra (case study) 186
Alice (case study) 142, 144, 148–9
Amanda (case study) 173, 208
Ana (case study) 92–3
Andisiwe (case study) 197, 200, 212
Andrea (case study) 156, 161
Anke (case study) 158, 161
Annan, Kofi 214
apartheid era 192–3, 195, 226, 245
apprentices 153
Argentina 88–90, 92–9, 205, 208, 236, 245, 256–7
Arthur, Nancy 206–7, 247, 258
Australia: Blueprint for Career Development 254; intersection of age and female gender 42–4, 49; lack of progression from entry level 68; and methodological considerations 85; voices of older women 101–3, *104*, 105–11; women in professional employment 205–6
Australian Human Rights Commission (AHRC) 103
Austria 13–14

Babalwa (case study) 199, 201–2
Bangladesh 12, 116
bankruptcy 128, 131, 133
Bárbara (case study) 183–4, 188, 259

Belgium 12, 14–15, 165
Belisle, D. 60
Bilimoria, D. 71, 80
Bimrose, Jenny 192, 205, 219, 256
Blake-Beard, S. 72–3
Blueprint for Career Development (Australia) 254
Blueprint for Life/Work Designs (Canada) 254
Blustein, D. 80, 258
Bonnett, H. R. 85
Bosch, A. 194, 202
Boserup, E. 31
Broadbridge, A. 57–8
Brooke, Elizabeth 232
Bruegel, I. 15
Buenos Aires 88, 90, 97

Canada: Blueprint for Life/Work Designs 254; and methodological considerations 85; public administration remains male dominant 206; voices of older women 113–16, *117*, 118–24, 208, 247
capitalism 246
care work 222–3, 231–3, 235–40, 254–6, 258
careers: boundaryless 69–70; development 228, 258; guidance practice implications 253–9; identity 212; policy 243–52; protean 70–1; services 263; theory and practice 219–20
Carla (case study Italy) 169–70, 174
Carla (case study Portugal) 183–4, 187
Carmela (case study Australia) 95
Carmela (case study Italy) 171, 174
Carmen (case study) 116, 119–21, 123, 256
case studies: Argentina 88–99; Australia 101–11; Canada 113–24; China 127–37; England 139–50; Germany 152–62;

Italy 164–75; learning from 253–7; Portugal 177–90; South Africa 192–202; *see also* under individual names
caste ideology 33
Celiwe (case study) 197–9
Centre for Women and Democracy 205
Chaminade, Cécile 213
Chaos Theory of Careers (Pryor/Bright) 224
Charpentier, Constance-Marie 213
China: gender gap 206; immigrants from 101; labour markets of 221; urban population of 244–5; voices of older women in 116, 127–9, *130*, 131–7, *135*, 237; working in the kindergarten 236
Cinderella Syndrome 208
Clare (case study) 105–6, 108
Claudia (case study) 159, 161
Collins, S. 258
Commission on Older Women 3, 5
commuting 16–19, 22
Connell, C. 58–9
contextual factors 221, 224–5
Correia, Carolina 236
Corrigan, E. 239
Crang, P. 58
creative industries introduction 52–3; jobs in 53–7
credentialisation 22
Cristina (case study) 94, 97
critical mass approach 68
crowdsourcing 22–3
cultural identity 123–4, 258
Cultural Revolution (China) 137, 245
Cutcher, L. 59

data analysis/coding 82–5, *85*; Phase 1(data familiarisation) 83; Phase 2 (independent analysis) 83; Phase 3 (emergence of master codes) 83; Phase 4 (initial validation of master codes) 83; Phase 5 (trustworthiness of codes) 83; Phase 6 (defining and applying the master codes) 83; Phase 7 (refinement of the master codes) 84; Phase 8 (verification by an independent coder) 84; Phase 9 (saturation of codes) 84; Phase 10 (application of codes) 84
data collection 81–2
De Braine, R. 193–4
De l'egalité des deux sexes (Poulain de La Barre) 210
Debbie (case study) 145–7, 256
Denise (case study) 107–8, 110–11

Denmark 15, 97
Descartes, René 210
Development of Women and Children in Rural Areas (DWCRA) 34
developmental theories 222
DeVoy, J. 80
DeWine, D. 80
Diana (case study) 183–5, 187–8
Discrimination: age 2–4, 56, 59, 95, 144–6, 190; in Argentina 89; in Canada 114–15, 120; in China 134; gendered labour market 3, 20, 146; sex 146; in South Africa 206
Diversity Council Australia (DCA) 103
Domboza (case study) 197, 200, 254
domestic work: gendered allocation of 2, 15; geographical/temporal constraints 21; in India 27, 32–3; unpaid labour 67
Donne, John 214
dual career households 17–20
dual system model (Germany) 152–4
Duarte, Maria Eduarda 4, 221
Dupin, Amantine Lucille Aurore *see* Sand, George

Earl, Catherine 232, 244
Educated Youth to the Countryside Policy (China) 133, 137
education 152–3, 157
Eikhof, Doris Ruth 232, 246, 251
Ellen (case study) 116, 118, 121, 123
email 80, 83, 129
emerging theories 223–6
Emily (case study) 106–7, 109
Employers Network for Equality and Inclusion (ENEI) 49
Employment Distribution Policy (China) 133
employment practices 20, 55–6, 61, 234
empowerment 31–4
England 139–40, *141*, 142–50, 205–6, 256; *see also* United Kingdom
English language 123, 139, 195, 198
equal opportunity 68, 101, 111, 221
Equal Opportunity for Women in the Workplace Act 1999 *see* Workplace Gender Equality Act 2012 (WGE)
escalator effects 19
Esona (case study) 197–8, 200–1, 210, 257
Estado Novo (Portugal) 177–8, 234
ethnic groups 21
etic/emic approaches 233
European Social Fund (ESF) 169
European Union *13–14*, 178, 205, 245
Eve (case study) 184, 186–7, 189

Facharbeiter (skilled workers) 152–3
Fang (case study) 132
Faniswa (case study) 199
fascism 245
Fátima (case study) 183–4, 189
feminism 219–20, 223
Feng (case study) 132–3
Finland 12, 14–15
Fleur (case study) 107, 109
Florida, Richard 53, 56–7
Folbre, N. 239
France 69, 165
Fulop, L. 76
future planning 161, 174

Gabriela (case study) 186
Geldenhuys, M. 193
Gender: ageism 42, 144; asymmetry of traditional roles 234; concept of 209; creative work 53–4; dimension 248–9; discrimination 237; discrimination in Germany 162; discrimination in India 33–4, 36; discrimination in Portugal 190; dispersion of regional employment rates 15–16; equality a basic human right 1; equality localisation 15–17; gaps 12, 175; labour market discrimination 3, 20, 146; localisation 232; pay gaps 72, 102, 140, 154, 177–8, 180, 205; and poverty 221; relations in China 128; and socialisation 222; ways of assessing equity 235; working in retirement 72
Gender Gap Index (2012) 166
Germany: experiences of working women in 221; female workforce and the service sector 205–6; geographical perspectives 13–15; highly structured system of 234; and methodological considerations 85; and non-linear careers 244; voice of Amanda 208; voices of older women 152–4, *155*, *156–62*; working women with caring responsibilities 236
Giovanna (case study) 170–1, 209–10, 236
GIS (geographical information systems) 21
Glasgow 57–9
glass ceiling 68, 129, 146
Global Gender Gap Index 1, 234
globalisation 26, 251, 258
Gomes, Isabel P. 236
Goos, M. 52
grand career narrative 224
Great Recession (2008) 223, 234
Greece 13, 164, 207

Green, Anne 232, 247
grounded theory 79–80, 82, 85, 235
Grundling, J. 194, 202
Guichard, J. 225, 233

Haasler, Simone R. 206, 208–9, 221, 236, 244
Hansen, E. 257
Helena (case study) 183, 186, 188, 213
Henry, C. 54
Hensel, Fanny 212–13
Holland, J. L. 220
Hopkins, M. M. 80
Hort, L. 76
Hou, Z. 257
hourglass economy 17, 52, 60, 62
Hua (case study) 131–2, 134
Hughes, E. C. 254
human development approach 226–8
Hungary 15

Ilda (case study) 183–4, 188
illiteracy 178
immigration 114–16, 118, 120–4, 206, 256
Ina (case study) 160
India: conclusions about women's work 37; emigration to Australia from 101; empowerment/employment/identity 31–3; introduction 4; women's agency 33–5, *33*; women's work research 28–31; women's work scenario in 26–8, *28*; work/gender/generation 35–7
Industrial Revolution 220
industrialism/post-industrialism 245
information and communications technologies (ICT) 22–3
Inge (case study) 156–7, 160
Ingols, C. 72–3
International Labour Organisation 22
international perspectives introduction 12; local 15–17; regional dispersion in employment rates *16*; sub-national 12–15, *13–14*, 22
International Women's Health Coalition Gala (2004) 214
internationalisation 233, 257
interpretivism 210
intersectionality: across class/caste/region/ethnicity 27; description of 2, 21
Iraq 116
Iris (case study) 167
Isabel (case study) 144
Italy 13, 164–7, *168*, 169–75, 205–6, 208, 247

Janice (case study) 103, 106–10
Jennie (case study) 144–6
Joana (case study) 183, 186, 188
job flexibility/mobility 152
Job Release Scheme (UK) 250
Jordan 116

kaleidoscope 17, 68, 71
kaleidoscope career theory (Manierio/Sullivan) 71
Kanter, R. M. 67–8
Karin (case study) 156, 158, 161
Kate (case study) 107, 109–10
Katie (case study) 121–3
Kay (case study) 105, 107–8, 110–11, 213–14, 259
Kenna, A. 80
Kuang, Ying 206, 221, 236–7, 244–5
Kumar, S. 257

labour markets 20, 22, *28*
labour participation rates (LPR) 28, *28*
labyrinth 68
Laura (case study Argentina) 93–4, 96–8, 211
Laura (case study England) 143–5
Leticia (case study) 92, 95, 98, 208
Liliana (case study) 94
Lindiwe (case study) 195
Ling (case study) 132–3
Lisa (case study) 158–61
Liu (case study) 133, 136
locker room culture 67–8
London 18–19
Lorena (case study) 90, 96–8
Lorraine (case study) 105–8, 254
Louise (case study) 142–3, 145, 147–9, 212
low wages 137, 146, 178–9, 186
Luísa (case study) 183, 186, 188

McMahon, Mary 192, 207, 219, 224, 237
Madhuri (case study) 118–19, 121, 123
Mahler, Alma 213
Mahler, Gustav 213
Mainiero, L. A. 71
Mala (case study) 118–19, 123
Malaysia 101, 116
Malta 164, 166
Mandela, Nelson 245
Manning, A. 52
Mantel, Hillary 54–5
Marcela (case study) 90, 92–5, 98
Maria (case study Canada) 120–3
Maria (case study Italy) 171–2
Marta (case study) 183–4, 187–9

Martin, R. L. 58
Martina (case study) 156
Mary (case study) 147
maternity/paternity leave 43–5, 48, 56, 162, 179, 193, 244, 249, 250
Mayer, Marissa 54–5
Mead, Margaret 71
Megan (case study) 103, 108, 110
'Meister' qualification (Germany) 158
Mimidek (case study) 119, 121, 123
Mkhize, N. 258
Mobility: geographical 19, *19*; social 17, 22; spatial 17–20, 22
Monica (case study) 170, 172
motherhood 166
Munka, L. M. 85
Murphy, K. 80

Namibia 202
National Rural Employment Guarantee Scheme (NREGS) 34–5
Ndungu, K. 202
neo-liberalism 26, 36, 251
Netherlands 12
New Zealand 101
Nobel Prize for economics 226
non-governmental organisations (NGOs) 95
Norway 12, 69
Nosisi (case study) 195, 201
Novas Oportunidades 180
Nussbaum, M. C. 226–7

occupational strategies 17
older women: absence of workplace policies 232; agency/opportunity 247–8; in Argentina 88–90, *91*, 92–9; in Australia 101–3, *104*, 105–11; in Canada 113–16, *117*, 118–24; in China 127–9, *130*, 131–7, *135*, 237; conclusions 49, 259, 264; defining for sampling purposes 81; desires of 249–52; employer policymaking 41–4; in England 139–40, *141*, 142–50; with fewer domestic responsibilities 36–7; in Germany 152–4, *155*, *156–62*; good practice 48–9; involved in providing care to others 240; in Italy 164–7, *168*, 169–75; and the national studies 4; needs of 44–8; not likely to start working later in life 26; in Portugal 177–80, *181–2*, 183–90, 190n.1; in retail 59; in South Africa 192–5, *196*, 197–202; specific issues confronting 30; voices of 207–15

Index   269

One-child Policy (China) 134
O'Neil, D. A. 71, 80
Organisation for Economic Co-operation and Development (OECD) 41, 234
Ovambo people 202

Pakistan 116
Pako (case study) 119, 121
Paola (case study) 171, 173
Parada, Filomena 236, 245
paradigmatic "decommodified" workers 59
Parker, Polly 232–3, 246
Parsons, F. 220
part-time work 20
Part-time Workers Directive (EU) 57
Patricia (case study) 107–8
Patton, W. 224
Paula (case study) 142
PE-fit theories 222
pensions 49, 250
Perry, J. C. 85, 258
Petra (case study) 156–8, 161
Philippines 101, 116, 120
Ping (case study) 131–2, 136
Portugal 177–80, *181–2*, 183–90, 190n.1, 205, 226, 234, 236
'post-menopausal zest' (Mead) 71
post-modernism 210, 224
Poulain de La Barre, François 210
'precariat' 246
public transport 20
purposive sampling 238–9

QQ 129
QSR NVivo 9 (software package) 84
qualitative research 79–80, 238
quantitative research 238

racism *see* discrimination
relocation 148, 160, 173
retail industry: introduction 52–3; jobs in 57–60
retirement 129
Richardson, M. S. 222–3, 225–7, 258
Rita (case study) 172
Roan, Amanda 232–3, 246
Romania 14–15, 116, 207
Rong (case study) 131–5, 208, 211, 254
Rosa (case study Australia) 92–3
Rosa (case study Italy) 168, 174
Rosalie (case study) 147–8
Royal Flying Doctor Service 109
Russell, C. 42

Russia 116
Ruth (case study) 159, 161

Salazar, António de Oliveira 245
Sally (case study) 118–20, 123
Sam (case study) 146
Sammy (case study) 121, 123, 256
sampling 80–1, 154, 238–9
Sand, George 213
Sandberg, Sheryl 54–5
Sandra (case study) 105–6, 109–10
Savage, M. 17
segregation *see* discrimination
self-help groups (SHGs) 36
Sen, A. 226–7
sex 209, 211
sexism 42, 146, 222–3
Shackleton, Lesley 202
Shacklock, K. 76
Shapiro, M. 72–3
Shareen (case study) 119, 121–3
Shiban, A. P. 87
short-term assignments 18–19
Shumann, Clara 213
Silicon Valley occupations 246
Silke (case study) 156–7, 160–1, 211, 259
Skill equilibrium theory 59–60
Skillset 54–5, 62n.1
Skype 83
Slovakia 14–15
social cognitive career theory (SCCT) 222–3, 225
social constructionism 224
social networks 20, 160
Sophia (case study) 103, 105, 109
South Africa: and cultural tradition 257; and methodological considerations 85; and new freedoms and opportunities 245; voices of older women from 192–5, *196*, 197–202; women and resistance against discrimination 206, 226
Spain 13–15
Standing, Guy 246
state-run enterprises 128
Statistics Portugal 179
Status of Women Canada (2013) 115
Stead, G. B. 85, 258
Stella (case study) 144, 148
Sue (case study) 142–5, 147, 209, 256
Sullivan, S. E. 71
Sun (case study) 131, 134, 136
Super, D. E. 220, 222
Suzanne, Pamela 224, 236, 245

Swanson, J. L. 222–4
Sweden 12, 69
Switzerland 13
Systems Theory Framework (STF) 224

taxation policy 154
Taylor, Philip 232
Teodora (case study) 167
therapists (in Argentina) 97
three-pillar school system (germany) 152–3
Time-Space Geography 21
Togo 116
Tomassini, Massimo 204, 209, 225, 234, 236, 245, 247
Tomlinson, J. 58, 60
traditional theories 222
travel-to-work patterns 15
Turkey 166

Umberta (case study) 172–3, 254–5
unemployment, in China 128
unions 177–8, 180, 193
United Kingdom 13, 15, 68–9, 85, 101, 244; *see also* England
United States 239, 244, 257
Universal Declaration of Human Rights (UDHR) 1

Valeria (case study) 90, 96, 98–9
Vera (case study) 103, 105
Vietnam 101
Vindhya, U. 231–2
Vivian (case study) 118–19, 208

vocational agency 234
vocational training 152–3, 157
Vocational Training Act-Germany (Berufsbildungsgesetz) 153
VUCA environment 69

Warhurst, Chris 232, 246, 251
Wathint' abafazi, wathint' imbokodo (South African song) 192
Watson, M. 192, 206, 219
Whyte, W. H. 66
Williams, C. 58–60
Williams, Ruth 232
Women: fisher 30; municipality sweeper 30; older *see* older women; urban slum 30
Women's Economic Opportunity Index 12, 234
women's stories *see* case studies
working hours 179
workplace discrimination 134
Workplace Gender Equality Act 2012 (WGE) 101, 111
Workplace Gender Equality Agency (WGEA) 101

Xhosa language 195

Ying (case study) 131–4, 136

zero hours contracts 20
Zhang, N. 257